THE ANGLO-IRISH AGREEMENT

The First Three Years

To

Chirsto Kritzinger

with many happy memories
of many a fine meal

Druel.

THE ANGLO-IRISH
AGREEMENT

The First Three Years

ARWEL ELLIS OWEN

UNIVERSITY OF WALES PRESS
CARDIFF
1994

British Library Cataloguing-in-Publication Data.
A catalogue record for this book is available from the British Library.

ISBN 0-7083-1274-8

Cover design by Design Principle, Cardiff
Typeset by Action Typesetting Limited, Gloucester
Printed in Great Britain by Cromwell Press, Melksham, Wiltshire

For Margaret,
Rhodri, Rebecca, Catrin and Sara

Contents

Preface   ix

Introduction   1

1 Hillsborough and after   12

2 The mini-election, the strike and the RUC   45

3 Unionist disunity, terrorism and the first anniversary 83

4 Protests, feuds and elections   109

5 Talks, extradition and Enniskillen   146

6 Fraud, justice and the Gibraltar shootings   172

7 Talks, the media and terror   204

8 Languishing in a dispirited state?   230

Index   255

Preface

In May 1985 I flew from Cardiff to Belfast to start my new job as Head of Programmes with the BBC in Northern Ireland. The car that was to collect me from Aldergrove airport was half an hour late arriving, which gave me time to buy the local newspapers and observe the security presence. It was then, over a cup of tea, that I promised myself I would keep a regular record of events as I observed them unfold during my time in the province.

This book draws heavily on those notes, written contemporaneously, during the years that followed the signing at Hillsborough of the Anglo-Irish Agreement. Three and a half years later, when I left Belfast for a BBC sabbatical year as the first Guardian Research Fellow at Nuffield College, Oxford, I was able to look back on those notes and set them alongside the published comments of fellow journalists and broadcasters on which this book also draws extensively.

It is not a book of answers, nor of explicit analysis. Instead, I have tried to show the complex daily interaction of factors that condition the life of Northern Ireland: the politics of its own communities, the pressures and tensions in Dublin and in London, and beyond in Europe and the United States.

The origins of the IRA ceasefire of 31 August 1994 can be traced to the first three years of the Hillsborough accord. This permanent, international agreement put the double squeeze on the Republican movement. Ostracization from political dialogue and infiltration of the military wing by the security services, north and south of the border, led to a fundamental realignment of power within Sinn Fein/IRA and a subsequent cessation of military operations.

The first three years of the Anglo-Irish Agreement cover the period of the Stalker inquiry, the Gibraltar shootings, the Andersonstown and Milltown cemetery killings and the introduction of the broadcasting ban on Sinn Fein. These were all matters that received a great deal of attention in Britain; they were also episodes in which those of us who worked in the media were players and not merely observers. But while I naturally draw on my own experience, this is not a book of personal anecdote. I have resisted the temptation to privilege those episodes which received wide publicity or in which I was directly involved, over the other daily happenings. If there is a pattern here and an interpretation, it is in the counterpointing of complex events. Readers will draw their own conclusions, and will, I hope, be better equipped to do so.

Those who wish to plunge into the subject with the run-up to the Hillsborough agreement should move directly to Chapter 2. But one can never take even a schematic knowledge of Irish history for granted outside Ireland, so the book's first chapter aims to supply that minimum of historical background. It is written from secondary sources and owes a particular debt to Jonathan Bardon's *History of Ulster* (Belfast, 1992).

This is the place to acknowledge my indebtedness to Janet Davies who has helped me rewrite this book from what was originally a University of Wales thesis. The first chapter is entirely hers.

I must also thank the Scott Trust and the Regional Directorate of the BBC who, between them, made possible my sabbatical year at Nuffield College.

Finally, I am particularly grateful for the friendship and support of my colleagues in BBC Northern Ireland, and in a broader sense, to the people of the province. In spite of everything, I have always viewed the future of Northern Ireland with the kind of optimism so well expressed by the Ulster poet John Hewitt:

> Slave to and victim of this mirror hate,
> Surely there must be somewhere we could reach
> A solid track across this quagmire state,
> And on a neutral sod, renew the old debate
> Which all may join without intemperate speech.

Introduction

Ulster, the most northerly of the four provinces of Ireland, lies behind a natural barricade, a line of drumlins – huge mounds of boulder clay – which T. Estyn Evans called 'a necklace of beads some thirty miles wide suspended between Donegal Bay and Strangford Lough'. It was a centre of the Gaelic civilization celebrated in the sagas of the Ulster Cycle. It played an important part in the spread of Christianity in the island; much of the work of both Patrick and Columba is associated with Ulster. Neither the Vikings nor the Normans succeeded in establishing a firm footing in the province; it came to be regarded as the most Gaelic part of Ireland, a 'province beyond the Pale'. It was finally conquered, after long and bitter resistance, in the reign of Elizabeth I.

Ulster, under-populated and undeveloped, attracted colonizers. In 1610 the 'Printed Book', a list of conditions for successful applicants for land in the province, was issued in London. The largest group of colonizers or planters, called undertakers, contracted to remove the native Irish completely from their land. Twenty-four Protestant English or 'inland' Scots, drawn from at least ten families, were to be settled on every 1,000 acres. The plantation of Coleraine was financed by the London City companies and it was renamed County Londonderry. The reaction of the dispossessed Irish came in 1641, when there was a savage revolt which was with difficulty put down. Cromwell's period of power brought further bloodshed and repression and more planters. By 1688 less than 4 per cent of the counties of the province of Ulster, with the exception of Antrim, was owned by Catholics.

A period of peace followed the Restoration of Charles II and the economy of Ulster, particularly Belfast, benefited from it. The situation changed with the accession of James II and the consequent threat to Protestant supremacy. James, forced to flee from England, landed in Ireland with an army in 1689. In Derry, the last walled city to be built in western Europe, the army of the Catholic earl of Antrim was denied

entry by the action of thirteen apprentice boys who raised the draw-
bridge and closed the gates. The siege lasted for 105 days before the
Protestant garrison was relieved. James was defeated at the battles of
the Boyne (1 July 1690) and Aughrim (12 July 1691).

Under the new dispensation Catholics were subject to the Penal
Laws, which among other things forbade them to own land. Meanwhile
Presbyterian Scots, fleeing from a famine in Scotland, were coming to
Ulster in great numbers; Presbyterian congregations doubled between
1660 and 1715. Attempts were made by the Church of Ireland to check
the spread of Protestant dissent, but after 1719 Presbyterians experienced no serious discrimination. Many nevertheless left for America in
the early eighteenth century, a time of bad harvests and rising rents, but
from about 1740 onwards Ulster became markedly more prosperous as
a result of the growth of linen-making, a long-established domestic
industry which was now booming because of technological advances.

The middle of the eighteenth century was a time of general prosperity
in Ulster. The expansion of the linen industry led to a growth in
population, which in turn stimulated farming. Towns and roads were
improved and canals built. Ulster was the most prosperous part of
Ireland. After 1770, however, a succession of bad harvests led to a rise
in the price of bread. There was a slump in the linen industry, rents
were raised and the consequent evictions led to riots and repression.
New ideas followed in the wake of the revolutions in France and
America, and radical ideas were particularly prevalent among the
companies of Volunteers raised and subsequently armed by the government to guard against French invasion.

In most of Ireland, Protestants were a small minority; in Ulster,
however, Protestants and Catholics were roughly equal in numbers
west of the Bann, while in the counties of Antrim and Down Protestants
were an overwhelming majority. As Presbyterians, they were no friends
of the Established Church. They had, moreover, been influenced by the
ideas of the Enlightenment. In 1784 the 1st Belfast Volunteer Company
invited Catholics – who were still subject to the restrictions of the Penal
Laws – to enlist in their ranks, thus striking a blow at the exclusiveness
of the Protestant Ascendancy. In 1791 the Society of United Irishmen
was founded in Belfast; it aimed at 'a cordial union among all the
peoples of Ireland' and a reform of the Irish parliament to 'include
Irishmen of every religious persuasion'. Pitt's government, fearing an
alliance between Presbyterian radicals and Catholics, gave Catholics
the right to vote and to enter the legal profession, but stopped short of
full emancipation.

The ideas of the United Irishmen, who were crushed following
abortive revolts in 1797 and 1798, were not shared by the majority of
the population. The formation of the Protestant Peep o' Day Boys and

the Catholic Defenders ushered in a decade of sectarian warfare. The Orange Order was founded in 1797 after a victory by the Peep o' Day Boys at Loughall in Armagh and threats from the new order led large numbers of Catholics to flee the county.

The Act of Union was passed in 1801 and the Irish parliament ceased to exist. It was expected that Catholics would be granted full civil rights in the wake of the Union, and when this did not occur they turned against it. Protestants, on the other hand, had on the whole been un-enthusiastic about the Union, but came to regard it as the guarantee and bulwark of their privileged position. Catholic Emancipation did not reach the Statute Book until 1829 and Daniel O'Connell, visiting Ulster to speak in favour of the repeal of the Union in 1841, received a hostile reception.

After 1800 evangelical Protestantism spread in Ulster, displacing the liberal Presbyterianism that had taken root in Belfast at the end of the eighteenth century. The liberals, who believed that a range of beliefs could be tolerated within Presbyterianism, were isolated and the great majority united in 1840 to form the General Assembly of the Presbyterian Church in Ireland. There was a resurgence of Puritanism and a growing intolerance of political dissent.

Belfast, meanwhile, was becoming established as an economic and commercial centre. Eastern Ulster, where the introduction of power-spinning gave the linen industry a new lease of life, was the only part of Ireland where the Industrial Revolution made significant progress in the nineteenth century. The situation in the rest of the province was less promising. The countryside was over-populated, the subdivision of land had been carried to extremes and the poorer classes lived very close to subsistence level. In 1845 the potato crop failed and Ulster, like the rest of Ireland, suffered the ravages of the Famine; between 1841 and 1851 Ulster's population fell by 15.7 per cent (374,000).

A period of prosperity followed the Famine in rural Ulster. Tenant farmers, Catholic and Protestant, banded together in an attempt to break the stranglehold of the great landlords and supported the activities of the Land League. The condition of the landless poor, how-ever, had changed little, and they were attracted in increasing numbers by the prosperity of Belfast.

By 1891 Belfast was the largest city in Ireland. It was a great commercial centre, growing fast. Banks, newspapers, theatres and all the usual civic appurtenances flourished and multiplied. The linen industry was still a major employer, but it had been joined by engineer-ing and shipbuilding firms. Harland and Wolff was established at Queen's Island in the early 1850s and was by 1900 the most important single employer of labour in Ulster. By 1914 it was responsible for almost 8 per cent of world output. The *Oceanic*, the first modern liner, was built for the White Star line in Belfast. It was natural that such a city should attract the landless poor of the countryside, and they came in such numbers that they changed the religious composition of Belfast. By 1871 there were more Catholics living there than were to be found in County Fermanagh, where they formed the majority. The newcomers, from all sects, imposed on Belfast the sectarian divisions which were to be found in rural Ulster, and in 1864, 1872 and 1886 there was savage rioting.

Belfast's experiences and problems were mirrored in Derry. By 1911 it was the fourth largest town in Ireland, its major industry being shirt-making. Large numbers moved in from the countryside in search of employment; by 1891 there were 4,500 more Catholics than there were Protestants in Derry and there was sectarian rioting, particularly between 1868 and 1870 and in 1899.

By the mid 1880s the situation had polarized in the countryside too. In the election of 1885, Ulster returned sixteen Conservatives (all Protestants) and seventeen Nationalists (all Catholics). The Liberals, who had benefited from cross-sectarian co-operation, failed to win a seat. Home Rule had replaced Land Reform as the major preoccupation of the Irish Parliamentary Party, and in Ulster the lines of future conflict had been drawn up, with the Union as the issue at stake. Following Gladstone's conversion to Home Rule in 1886, there was a close alliance between the Conservatives and the Orange Order, and Lord Randolph Churchill made his famous pronouncement: 'Ulster will fight, and Ulster will be right.' The rejection of the Home Rule Bill led to fierce rioting in Belfast.

The fall of Parnell in 1890 split the Irish Parliamentary Party. Gladstone's second attempt to pass a Home Rule Bill was defeated in the House of Lords in 1892 and circumstances did not favour another attempt until 1910. The opposition of Ulster Protestants to the idea of Home Rule did not lessen during those years. Although in only a small majority in Ulster (865,856 to 833,560) they dominated the world of commerce; only 3 per cent of the Belfast Chamber of Commerce was Catholic. Most landowners, owners of businesses, local government officials and skilled artisans were Protestants, and they feared becoming subject to a Dublin government which they felt would have little sympathy with or understanding of Belfast and its concerns. This fear was intensifed by the increasing clericalism in Nationalist circles after the fall of Parnell, while the Gaelic Revival, though it had its origins in Ulster, put forward the ideal of an anti-industrial Ireland which was essentially antipathetic to the bustling commercial city of Belfast.

By 1910 the Liberal government of Asquith was once more dependent on Irish support and a Home Rule Bill was introduced in the House of Commons in April 1912. The passing of the Parliament Act in 1911 ensured that the House of Lords could do no more than delay the passage of any bill approved by the Commons. On 19 September 1912 Sir Edward Carson made public the Ulster Solemn League and Covenant, which was signed all over the province on Ulster Day, 28 September. The original Ulster Volunteer Force was instituted to defend Protestant Ulster and preserve the Union, and the Ulster Unionist Council – formed in 1904 to co-ordinate the activities of local Unionist associations – held itself in readiness to act as a provisional government. In November 1913 the Irish Volunteers were formed to fight for Home Rule for a united Ireland; nearly a third of them were enrolled in Ulster. Ireland was on the brink of civil war when the First World War began in August 1914. The Home Rule Bill became law on 18 September 1914, but its implementation was postponed until the end of the war. Asquith promised that amending legislation would be passed later to make special provision for Ulster.

In December 1918 the first general election for eight years was held. Four years of world war, the Easter Rising in Dublin and a Reform Act which more than doubled the Irish electorate had their effect. The Irish Parliamentary Party retained only six of the sixty-eight seats they had held previously, four of them in Ulster. The Ulster Unionists, at twenty-three, had gained five seats. Elsewhere, Sinn Fein swept the board; it was obvious that the mild measure of devolution proposed before the war would no longer suffice. Home Rulers had virtually disappeared, leaving the field to Republican separatists and Ulster Loyalists.

In February 1920 the Government of Ireland Bill was introduced in the House of Commons. It proposed two separate parliaments, one for the six north-eastern counties of Ireland and one for the other twenty-six counties. Both parts of Ireland were to continue to send representatives to Westminster and a Council of Ireland, with twenty representatives from each side, was also to be created. The province of Ulster was divided, losing the counties of Donegal, Cavan and Monaghan. It was considered that the remaining six counties, Antrim, Down, Armagh, Londonderry, Tyrone and Fermanagh, represented the largest area in which the Protestants were sure of a viable majority. The Ulster Unionists were in a strong position while the Bill was being debated at Westminster, since the Irish Parliamentary Party had been reduced to a rump at the general election, while Sinn Fein members refused to take their seats. The Bill, which was due to come into force in May 1921, was rejected out of hand by Sinn Fein.

Meanwhile violence was escalating throughout Ireland. Sir Edward Carson urged Unionists to organize in order to resist Sinn Fein attacks. The Ulster Volunteer Force (UVF) was revived by the Ulster Unionist Council in June 1920 and the following October the Ulster Special

Constabulary was formed. This force, which consisted of full-time (A Specials) and part-time (B Specials) police, attracted whole units of the UVF, whose commanders were also given senior positions in the new force. There was violence in Belfast. Catholic property was attacked and Catholic and socialist workers driven out of Harland and Wolff and a number of mills and factories.

In the general election of May 1921, held immediately after the Government of Ireland Bill became law, Northern Ireland returned (by the single transferable vote system) forty Unionists, six Nationalists and six members of Sinn Fein. In the South, Sinn Fein won 124 of the 128 seats. Fighting between British government troops and the Irish Republican Army (IRA) intensified, but a truce was eventually declared in July 1921. In December 1921 a treaty was signed, giving the Irish Free State dominion status, similar to that of Canada.

The July truce had no effect on violence in the North. Raids, kidnappings, shootings and house-burnings continued. Sixty-one people died in one week in March 1922 and Belfast was virtually in a state of war. The Royal Ulster Constabulary (RUC) was formed in April 1922, bringing the number of regular and part-time police to 50,000. Also in April the Civil Authorities (Special Powers) Bill gave the minister of home affairs the right to detain suspects and to set up courts of summary justice.

The situation changed with the outbreak of war in the Free State between those who supported the treaty with the British government and those who opposed it. IRA units were drawn into the conflict in the South and by 1923 Northern Ireland was relatively peaceful. Five hundred and fifty-seven people had died there between July 1920 and July 1922.

The newly created Northern Ireland had an established industrial base, representative institutions and a substantial and prosperous middle class. It also had a minority, comprising one-third of its inhabitants, opposed to its separate existence. Little attempt was made to conciliate or attract that minority. The vast majority of civil servants were, and remained, Protestants, the B Specials were exclusively Protestant and the number of Catholics in the RUC declined steadily. Proportional representation in local government elections, which had resulted in Nationalist-Sinn Fein majorities in twenty-one local authorities, was revoked and boundaries were redrawn in such a way as to create in-built Unionist majorities, this process being aided by a Nationalist–Sinn Fein boycott of the boundary commission. There was discrimination in educational provision, Protestant schools being fully funded and Catholic schools only partly so. Proportional representation in parliamentary elections was abolished in 1929, and there was again some redrawing of boundaries. The Orange/Green divide was perpetuated and Labour, which had won some seats in the election of 1924, lost ground.

The Northern Ireland government, whose seat at Stormont, in east Belfast, was officially opened in 1932, had little real power. Control of the army and navy, trade agreements, the currency, the making of war and peace, most taxation, the postal service and the supreme court was retained by Westminster. The new government's position was made no easier by the depression of the post-war years, which had a disastrous effect on its three main industries, linen-making, shipbuilding and agriculture. Unemployment averaged 19 per cent between 1923 and 1930, climbed to 28 per cent in 1932 and reached a high point of 29.5 per cent in February 1938. Distress gave rise to the only example of cross-sectarian co-operation in those years, the riots in Belfast in 1932 in support of an ultimately successful demand for an increase in outdoor relief for the unemployed. On the whole, the depression aggravated sectarian tensions; there were fierce riots in Belfast in 1935 when Protestants celebrated the jubilee of George V.

The dominion status of the Irish Free State was brought to an end by the External Relations Act of 1937; it now had only tenuous links with the Commonwealth. At the same time a new constitution was proposed and approved in a referendum. Article 2 of the new constitution claimed jurisdiction over the whole of Ireland for the Irish nation. Article 3 accepted that the laws of the Irish state had force only in the twenty-six counties, 'pending reintegration'. There were also clauses emphasizing the special position of the Roman Catholic Church. The new constitution seemed intent on creating a Catholic state for a Catholic people, a mirror image of the situation in the North, and equally opposed to cultural diversity. The divergence between North and South became greater.

The gap widened still further after the Second World War. Most of the Labour government's welfare legislation was applied to Northern Ireland and the government in London, grateful for Stormont's support during the war and mindful of Northern Ireland's continuing strategic importance, underwrote the cost. The housing stock, which had been badly depleted by bombing, was increased, the education system overhauled and a health service introduced. In the South, which became the Republic of Eire in 1948, the Church objected to the introduction of similar measures, regarding increased state intervention as an approach to totalitarianism.

In June 1949 the Attlee government's Ireland Act gave a formal guarantee that Northern Ireland 'would not cease to be part of his Majesty's dominions and of the United Kingdom without the consent of the parliament of Northern Ireland'. The efforts of the Anti-Partition League, formed in 1945 to mobilize opinion in favour of a united

Ireland, achieved little and the League was disbanded in 1951. Another threat to the status quo in Northern Ireland was removed in 1962 when the IRA, which had been vigorously suppressed north and south of the border, called off its military campaign.

Northern Catholics had, in any case, given little support to the activities of the IRA, preferring to pursue a constitutional course. The Unionist government, however, did nothing to integrate them into the institutions of the state. Any overture by an individual minister in that direction was sharply checked by the Unionist rank and file. Discrimination against the Catholic minority, in particular in electoral practice and in the allocation of council houses, was one of the topics taken up by the Northern Ireland Labour Party, which won four seats in the election of 1958 with cross-community support.

In 1963 Lord Brookeborough resigned as prime minister and was replaced by Captain Terence O'Neill, who unlike his predecessors had not been personally concerned in the establishment of Northern Ireland. O'Neill declared that he had two aims, to strengthen the economy and to build bridges between the two communities in the province.

A plan for regional economic development was proposed – a new departure, since Brookeborough had considered planning a socialist expedient – and O'Neill secured union support by persuading a reluctant cabinet to recognize the Northern Committee of the Irish Congress of Trade Unions. New industries were attracted to the province, though this was offset by the fact that Northern Ireland's traditional industries, shipbuilding, linen manufacture and farming, were experiencing difficulties. The new approach was also marred by insensitivity to the interests of the minority; all the proposed regional development centres except Derry were in the Protestant heartlands.

O'Neill was also anxious to establish warmer relations with the South. It was a propitious moment; the republic was reversing its policy of economic self-sufficiency and tariff protection, and the taoiseach (the prime minister of the Republic), Sean Lemass, wished for a *rapprochement* with the North, believing that the way to unite Ireland was to close the economic gap between North and South. In January 1965 Lemass visited O'Neill at Stormont and despite criticism of the move from, among others, Revd Ian Paisley, O'Neill increased his support in the election of November 1965.

Paisley had been active as a member of the National Union of Protestants, a body which opposed mixed marriages, the allocation of council houses to Catholics and the appointment of Catholic teachers in state schools. He had come to prominence through his criticism of the ecumenical movement. In the general election of 1964 Paisley had called on the RUC to remove a tricolour from the Republican headquarters in Belfast; the ensuing rioting was the worst since 1935. In 1966 he organized counter-demonstrations to those marking the fiftieth anniversary of the Easter Rising. There were violent incidents and a group of Loyalist militants revived the Ulster Volunteer Force to bring about the fall of O'Neill and to fight the IRA.

Despite O'Neill's stated willingness to bridge the gap between Northern Ireland's two communities, there was little evidence of more than superficial change. The civil service still contained only a small number of Catholics. Protestants still stood a much better chance of being allocated a council house. Boundaries were still arranged so as to create an in-built Unionist majority and the franchise was confined to ratepayers, which meant that the many Catholics who were obliged by the housing shortage to share accommodation were deprived of a vote. The situation was particularly acute in Derry, where the Unionists controlled Londonderry Corporation although the adult population contained almost twice as many Catholics as Protestants.

In January 1967 the Northern Ireland Civil Rights Association was founded, with cross-community support, to bring about change. In October 1968 members of the association marched to Derry, and television cameras recorded pictures of unarmed demonstrators being baton-charged by the RUC. O'Neill announced a five-point programme of reform: Londonderry Corporation would be replaced by a development commission, a fair points system for council-house allocation adopted, sections of the Special Powers Act repealed, grievances investigated by an ombudsman and universal suffrage in local elections considered.

The leaders of the Civil Rights Association agreed to call a halt to demonstrations in order to allow the reforms to be implemented, but the more radical People's Democracy group determined to continue their protest by marching from Belfast to Derry. They met with Loyalist attacks on the way, the conduct of the police was partisan and Loyalist protesters were in many cases identified as B Specials. In Derry itself police discipline gave way and there was an attack on the Catholic Bogside. Once again, the events were recorded on television and O'Neill's attempts to play down what had happened were at variance with the visual evidence. The RUC's credibility among the Catholic minority collapsed, sectarian passions were inflamed and moderates left the civil rights movement, which came under the control of militants and Republicans. O'Neill conceded the principle of universal suffrage in local elections, and it was accepted by the parliamentary Unionist Party by twenty-eight votes to twenty-four, but his support was slipping away and in April 1969 he resigned.

Violence continued throughout the summer of 1969, and in August the annual Apprentice Boys parade in Derry developed into the Battle of the Bogside. The police were unable to contain the situation and the Stormont minister of home affairs announced to the Commons that the army had been sent in. The rioting in Derry sparked off further riots in Belfast and between 12 and 16 August some 900 people were injured and 1,820 families (1,505 of them Catholic) fled their homes. The army was sent in to Belfast also, and barricades were erected in the streets.

The army presence on the streets of Northern Ireland, which was initially welcomed by many, was not intended to be permanent. Attempts were made to reassure those on both sides of the sectarian divide; the continuance of the Union was again confirmed, the Cameron Report on discrimination was published – as a result public housing came under the control of the Northern Ireland Housing Executive and little power was left in the hands of local councils – and so were Lord Hunt's recommendations that the Ulster Special Constabulary should be disbanded, the RUC disarmed and a new part-time force under the control of the general officer commanding the British army (GOC) established.

The new situation gave rise to new initiatives. The IRA, under the leadership of Cathal Goulding, had for some time been moving towards political activity and away from violence. A coup split the movement in 1969, when those supporting the use of violence set up the Provisional IRA, with Seán MacStiofáin as chief of staff and Ruairí Ó Brádaigh as president of the new group's political counterpart, Provisional Sinn Fein. By the summer of 1970 the Provisionals were in a position to undertake a bombing campaign in Belfast.

In April 1970 those Unionists opposed to violence and in favour of reform and reconciliation left the Unionist Party and launched the Alliance Party. In August the Social and Democratic Labour Party (SDLP) was formed and became, despite a few Protestant members, the voice of the Catholic minority. In 1971 Ian Paisley launched the Democratic Unionist Party (DUP) to represent those Protestants who were dissatisfied with what they regarded as a weak and conciliatory Unionist government. Also in 1971, a Loyalist paramilitary organization was set up in Protestant working-class districts: the Ulster Defence Association (UDA).

In August 1971, in an attempt to contain the continuing violence and mollify its critics, the Stormont government introduced internment. It was essentially a one-sided measure – all those interned were anti-partitionists – and it gave rise to violence on an appalling scale. The situation became progressively worse, culminating in January 1972 with the events of Bloody Sunday, when the army got out of control and killed thirteen men during a civil rights demonstration in Derry. On 2 February a crowd of thirty thousand marched to the British Embassy in Dublin and burned it down.

In March, Prime Minister Brian Faulkner and his colleagues in the

Northern Ireland cabinet were informed that Westminster was taking control of security in the province. They resigned, Stormont was prorogued for a year and William Whitelaw was appointed secretary of state for Northern Ireland. This was the beginning of a period of direct rule that was expected to last for twelve months.

The imposition of direct rule did not bring an end to the violence in Northern Ireland. During 1972, its first year, 103 soldiers, 41 police and Ulster Defence Regiment (UDR) and 323 civilians were killed. In March 1973 a referendum was held to decide whether or not Northern Ireland should remain as part of the United Kingdom. It was boycotted by nearly all Catholics and returned a decisive verdict in favour of maintaining the Union. Later the same month a White Paper was published giving details of the proposed form of self-government for the province; an assembly was to be elected by proportional representation and the executive would have the power to legislate on transferred matters. There would be a Council of Ireland to facilitate discussion between Belfast, Dublin and London on matters of common interest. In October agreement was reached in principle on the formation of a power-sharing executive and a month later the membership of the government-designate was announced; it contained six Unionist ministers, four from the SDLP and one Alliance minister. In December the ministers went to Sunningdale, in Berkshire, to take part in tripartite discussions with the British and Irish governments.

In January 1974 the Ulster Unionist Council voted to reject the proposed all-Ireland Council and Faulkner was forced to resign as party leader. The alliance of Unionists opposed to the Sunningdale agreement won eleven of the twelve Westminster seats in the election of February 1974 and in May the Ulster Workers' Council Strike, organized by a group of Protestant workers with the assistance of Ian Paisley and other anti-agreement Unionists and of the paramilitary UDA, made Northern Ireland effectively ungovernable. Faulkner resigned as prime minister and Loyalists were left to conclude that they could wreck any political initiative proposed by the British government which did not meet with their approval. It was a conclusion full of significance for the future.

1

Hillsborough and after

In December 1980 Margaret Thatcher, the British prime minister, met Charles Haughey, the Irish taoiseach, at Dublin Castle. At this historic meeting the two leaders agreed to commission a series of joint studies on such issues as security, economic co-operation, citizenship rights and measures to encourage mutual understanding, 'in order to assist them in their special consideration of the totality of relationships within the islands'.[1] What brought them together was the prospect of developing a lasting solution to the Northern Ireland question.

In June 1981 Haughey's Fianna Fáil government was replaced by a coalition of Fine Gael and Labour under the leadership of Garret FitzGerald. The minority position of his party in the Dáil did not prevent FitzGerald from launching his 'constitutional crusade' to lead the Republic out from the shadow of de Valera's constitution with its 'confessional state' and claim to sovereignty over the whole of the island of Ireland. FitzGerald wanted a united Ireland, but by consent. Unionists in the North would have to be persuaded, not coerced, into a 32-county Ireland. According to his biographer, FitzGerald had gone into politics 'to make his contribution to try and solve the Northern Ireland problem. It had become a *raison d'être* that had dominated and inspired the launching' of his constitutional crusade.[2]

At a meeting in Downing Street on 6 November 1981, FitzGerald built on the foundations laid by Haughey eleven months previously. Thatcher and the new taoiseach established an Anglo-Irish Inter-governmental Council, which involved regular meetings between the two governments at ministerial and official levels to discuss matters of common concern. The official communiqué stated the known stand-points of both partners:

---

[1] Joint Communiqué, Dublin Summit, December 1980.
[2] Raymond Smith, *Garret the Enigma* (Aberlow, 1985), 445.

The Taoiseach affirmed that it was the wish of the Irish Government and, he believed, of the great majority of the people of the island of Ireland, to secure the unity of Ireland by agreement and in peace. The Prime Minister affirmed, and the Taoiseach agreed, that any change in the constitutional status of Northern Ireland would require the consent of a majority of the people of Northern Ireland. The Prime Minister said that, if that consent were to be expressed as a result of a poll conducted in accordance with the Northern Ireland Constitutional Act 1973, the British Government would of course accept their decision and would support legislation in the British Parliament to give effect to it.[3]

The Irish saw this as an opportunity to create the necessary consent for a united Ireland. The four-year period between the Downing Street summit of 1981 and the Hillsborough summit of 1985 was one of exceptional political development and activity within Ireland. At the head of this national campaign was the taoiseach.

The British prime minister had other issues – an economic recession, the Falklands War and the Miners' Strike – on her political agenda. Her interest in and commitment to Irish affairs depended on the ebb and flow of events, mostly dictated by the IRA. The Downing Street summit represented the third British attempt within a little less than two years to find a solution to the Northern Ireland problem. Their 1979 general election manifesto had committed the Conservatives to 'seek to establish one or more elected regional councils with a wide range of powers over local services'. This was the brainchild of Airey Neave, an advocate of the full integration of Northern Ireland into the United Kingdom and widely expected to be the secretary of state for Northern Ireland in the next Conservative government. His assassination by the Irish National Liberation Army (INLA) on the day that Prime Minister James Callaghan called a general election, together with the killing later in the year of Earl Mountbatten and members of his family in County Sligo, and of eighteen soldiers at Warrenpoint, County Armagh, panicked the new Conservative administration into launching a badly prepared Northern Ireland initiative. The new secretary of state, Humphrey Atkins, announced a conference of all political parties to find a devolutionary solution. The initiative achieved little, except to split the SDLP; Gerry Fitt was replaced as leader by John Hume and the party took up a more nationalist stance.

Hunger strikes in the Maze prison in 1980–1 led to Atkins being replaced by Jim Prior, who introduced the concept of 'rolling devolution'; a new assembly would be elected, with an advisory and consultative role, and executive power would be transferred only if the

---

[3] Joint Communiqué, Downing Street Summit, November 1981.

development received cross-community support. Rolling devolution was conceivably the last possible variant of a devolutionist strategy.

Meanwhile the IRA had involved itself in 'elective politics in the guise of Sinn Fein, and the combination of the armalite and the ballot paper was begun'.[4] In the 1983 general election, Gerry Adams was returned as Sinn Fein MP for West Belfast, defeating the sitting SDLP member, Gerry Fitt. The Republicans polled 13.4 per cent of the total vote in Northern Ireland, the SDLP claimed 17.9 per cent, the DUP 20 per cent and the Official Unionist Party (OUP) 34 per cent. John Hume's party looked vulnerable to a Republican take-over. His reply was to arrange the New Ireland Forum – a meeting of all the Irish democratic parties. Sinn Fein was not invited to attend the deliberations, which started on Monday 30 May 1983. The chairman was the president of University College, Galway, and its twenty-seven members included the leaders of Fine Gael, Fianna Fáil, the Labour Party and the SDLP. They took a year to agree on a framework within which a new Ireland could emerge. They offered three options: a unitary state, a federal/confederal system, and joint authority shared by London and Dublin. The Forum's report set the pace for political developments in the Republic, Northern Ireland and Britain. It served as a catalyst, provided an agenda and helped to prepare the ground for a phase in Anglo-Irish relations when the 'Irish dimension' was again regarded as an essential part of any new political initiative by the British.

Whitehall had made various attempts to solve the problem of Northern Ireland. Sir Frank Cooper, a former permanent secretary at the Northern Ireland Office, summed up the civil service view of the province: 'Northern Ireland is a quagmire for anyone however long they may or may not have been involved. And I think it was probably very unlikely that some relative newcomer could come and throw some brand new light on the whole situation.'[5] Such pessimism was not shared by Thatcher. The audacious and frightening IRA attack on the Grand Hotel in Brighton during the Conservative Party Conference in the autumn of 1984 led to a major reappraisal of British policy on Northern Ireland. Although the Forum Report's three options were rejected in a very public way by Prime Minister Thatcher after the second Intergovernmental Council Summit in November 1984, cabinet committees were already discussing ways in which the joint authority idea of the Forum could be developed. FitzGerald, the Irish taoiseach, knew of these detailed discussions and understood better than most observers that Thatcher's 'Out, out, out' press conference comments – when she rejected all three of the Forum's options – were prompted by

---

[4] John Cole, *The Thatcher Years* (BBC, 1987), 187.
[5] Hennessey, Morris and Townsend, *Strathclyde Paper on Government and Politics*, No. 31.

her style of government. FitzGerald knew that Thatcher would have to negotiate with him if her plans to defeat the IRA had any chance of succeeding. His position was strengthened by his successful promotion of the Forum's recommendations in the United States and in Europe. FitzGerald created an expectation that a historic breakthrough in Anglo-Irish affairs was now possible. It took twelve months to negotiate the details of the Hillsborough agreement.

In Northern Ireland, the Unionist parties reacted to the New Ireland Forum Report by producing their own blueprints for the future of the province. The OUP's *The Way Ahead*, and the DUP's *Ulster – The Future Assured* concentrated on the need for an internal settlement within the province before any elements of an 'Irish dimension' were considered. The Alliance Party favoured increased co-operation with the Republic, but was opposed to any institutional role for the Republic in the political affairs of Northern Ireland. The most detailed response to the New Ireland Forum and to the Unionist Party documents came from the Kilbrandon Committee, an unofficial group set up at the request of the British-Irish Association. It proposed 'co-operative devolution', arguing that Dublin could be offered a role in the North if real power was returned to locally elected politicians in the province.

The Kilbrandon Report was rejected by representatives of all three participating parties in the Northern Ireland Assembly. Four days later came the meeting between Thatcher and FitzGerald at Chequers and Thatcher's rejection of the New Ireland Forum proposals at the 'Out, out, out' press conference. It was felt in Ireland that the taoiseach had been humiliated, but FitzGerald reported to the Dáil that the discussions in London had reached a 'crucial and critical stage'. The Unionists failed to notice this upbeat message from Dublin; they interpreted the prime minister's press conference statement as fact: 'I have made it quite clear – and so did Mr Prior when he was Secretary of State for Northern Ireland – that a unified Ireland was one solution that is out. A second solution was confederation of two states. That is out. A third solution was joint authority. That is out. That is a derogation from sovereignty. We made that quite clear when the Report was published.'[6]

The taoiseach noted the prime minister's reference to 'derogation from sovereignty'. If 'joint authority' could be developed in a way that did not affect British sovereignty, there was scope for negotiation. The official communiqué at the end of the Chequers summit included the crucial commitment, agreed by FitzGerald and Thatcher, that 'the identities of both the majority and minority communities in Northern

---

[6] *Times*, 20 November 1984.

Ireland should be recognised and respected, and reflected in the structures and processes of Northern Ireland in ways acceptable to both communities'.[7] This clause evolved from informal negotiations started in the spring of 1984. After the Chequers summit, Mrs Thatcher visited the United States and was told by Ronald Reagan of his interest in the New Ireland Forum initiative and of his support for a concerted attack on terrorism.

In early December 1984 Thatcher and FitzGerald met in Dublin at a European Community (EC) summit. Both agreed to exploratory talks between senior civil servants. The two respective cabinet secretaries, Armstrong and Nally, met early in 1985 and a ministerial meeting followed between the Northern Ireland secretary of state, Douglas Hurd, the Irish foreign minister, Peter Barry, and the British foreign secretary, Sir Geoffrey Howe. By the time Mrs Thatcher returned to Washington in late February 1985 serious Anglo-Irish talks were under way, buttressed by American willingness to underwrite such negotiations with an offer on extradition and a financial aid package, once an Anglo-Irish Agreement was in place.

Thatcher praised FitzGerald when the Irish government froze £1.7 million in a Bank of Ireland account and subsequently rushed an emergency bill through the Dáil in order to seize the money, allegedly intended for the IRA. A week later, nine RUC policemen were killed by an IRA mortar attack on Newry police station. A few days earlier, three IRA men were shot dead in Strabane by soldiers lying in wait.

At the annual St Patrick's Day celebrations in Dublin, Tip O'Neil assured FitzGerald and Hume of Reagan's financial support, once 'the ink is dry'. At the Northern Ireland Office, Chris Patten started a frantic exercise to determine if devolution was possible within Northern Ireland; he concluded it was not feasible in the short to medium term. By 22 March 1985, Douglas Hurd and Sir Geoffrey Howe were in Dublin to meet Peter Barry and Garret FitzGerald, and later that day the taoiseach spoke of 'novel structures'.[8] The *Mail on Sunday* developed a front-page lead the following weekend, speculating on 'a historic agreement'.[9] On Radio Ulster, Nicholas Scott attempted to play down the significance of FitzGerald's 'novel structures' and of the Dublin meetings; he said the paper's speculation 'was damaging because it raised expectations'.[10] The following weekend, Thatcher and FitzGerald met at an EC summit in Brussels, and the taoiseach was

---

[7] Official Summit Communiqué, Chequers, November 1984 (para.11).
[8] *Irish Times*, 23 March 1985.
[9] *Mail on Sunday*, 24 March 1985.
[10] *News Letter*, 25 March 1985.

reported to be convinced, at long last, that the prime minister was committed to an Anglo-Irish agreement.

But the prospects of an early agreement receded as the negotiations got down to discussing the crucial issues at stake. The British wanted a security agreement to defeat the IRA; sovereignty was inviolate. The Irish wanted far more. They sought Irish unity, but by consent. FitzGerald had shifted the focus away from the idea of the territorial unity of Ireland, towards the idea of reconciling its different traditions. Nationalists had to be weaned off the Republican cause by a demonstration that constitutional, non-violent, political action could achieve results. Irish influence had therefore to be apparent not only in matters of security and defence, but in issues affecting the administration of justice, the role of the RUC and the UDR, fair employment and better housing. The aspirations of the two sides were widely separated. The talks dragged on, and summit dates were cancelled.

The Northern Ireland local elections of May 1985 provided the spur London and Dublin required to redouble their efforts to strike a bargain. Sinn Fein won fifty-nine seats on seventeen of the twenty-six district councils in the province, polling 11.8 per cent of the votes. This was double what the opinion polls had prophesied, and only 6 per cent less than the SDLP figure. In Armagh, where Sinn Fein was the majority party, a Sinn Fein councillor was chairman of the council. Some, but by no means all, of the Sinn Fein councillors were also members of the IRA. Councillor Gerry Doherty was elected to sit in Derry's Guildhall, a building he once blew up. Councillor Tommy Carroll in Armagh had been sentenced to fifteen years' imprisonment for causing an explosion. Councillor Brian McCann in Craigavon had served a five-year sentence for possession of explosives and fifteen years for conspiring to cause an explosion. At Magherafelt, Patrick Toner was elected to represent Sinn Fein, having been jailed for three years for harbouring IRA men on the run. Gerry Adams had once pointed out that Sinn Fein and IRA are 'eggs in one basket', without any institutional relationship, but the 1977 IRA staff report defined the role of the political arm of the Republican movement as follows: 'Sinn Fein should come under Army organizers at all levels ... should agitate about social and economic issues which attack the welfare of the people. Sinn Fein should be directed to infiltrate other organizations to win support for and sympathy for the movement.'[11] Unionist-controlled councils began a campaign to suspend meetings and delegate the day-to-day running of the council's affairs to the town clerk; even Unionist councils with no Sinn Fein representative joined the boycott. Sinn Fein's success was an electoral threat to the SDLP, and a campaign

[11] *Listener*, 26 September 1985.

godsend to the Unionists. It also made the London–Dublin negotiations easier, since Sinn Fein was the common enemy.

Soon after the election two Northern Irish academics, Kevin Boyle
and Tom Hadden, completed a Penguin Special, called *Ireland: A
Positive Proposal*. They argued that the root of the present problem in the
province was the failure of the Republic and Britain to agree and
commit themselves fully to a single view on the constitutional status of
Northern Ireland. Proposals for allowing any exercise of power by the
Republic in the North could only be acceptable on the basis that any
joint powers should be administered in a reciprocal manner on both
sides of the border.

Ireland: A Positive Proposal was soon followed by a report prepared by
the Liberal-SDP alliance. Called *What Future For Northern Ireland?*, it
recommended an institutional recognition of the Irish dimension to
Northern Ireland politics. The report suggested a joint security
commission, a British-Irish parliamentary council and a Northern
Ireland assembly which would elect the executive. Detailed
consideration was given to the role of the RUC and the UDR and their
accountability to the local community and to the judicial system, and
the report urged that a commission on human rights be set up. It
concluded by suggesting that a confederal Ireland might be the means
to 'provide institutional recognition of the fact that, as well as the
political links, there are also deep personal and cultural inter-
relationships between our two countries'.[12]

Northern Ireland itself was in the throes of its annual marching
season, with a total of 1,897 Loyalist parades and 223 Republican
marches. In his report for the previous year, 1984, Sir John Hermon,
the RUC's chief constable had commented, 'I feel bound to say that the
objective of community reconciliation is not helped by the defiant
insistence of some sections of the community on parades and routes
regardless of circumstances'.[13] Policing the parades meant the
equivalent of 39,000 police shifts. Hermon decided that the marching
season of the summer of 1985 should see an end to such expensive and
potentially dangerous work for his hard-pressed force.

Hermon could not have foreseen that the 1985 marching season
would also coincide with the start of a province-wide campaign against
the London–Dublin talks, and that the RUC would be at the receiving
end of Loyalist anger and frustration. The chief constable knew,
however, that the Anglo-Irish discussions would cover aspects of the
RUC's policing of the province, and that he would have to fight for the
independence of his force. Hermon's relations with Commissioner

---

[12] *What Future for Northern Ireland?*, Alliance Commission, 1985.
[13] Chief Constable, RUC, *Annual Report*, 1984.

Wren of the Garda were strained. Four RUC officers had been escorting a Dublin-based Brinksmat bullion van when they were killed by an IRA bomb left on a farm trailer parked by the side of the Dublin – Belfast road in May 1985. Hermon claimed the bomb was triggered from across the border in the Republic. Commissioner Wren accused the RUC of using the media to put pressure on the Garda and a statement from the Irish Department of Foreign Affairs declared that the British government had accepted that the bomb was triggered in the North. Hermon felt isolated and threatened by the constant flow of leaks from Dublin which indicated that the Anglo-Irish talks were concentrating on the administration of justice, the accountability of the RUC and a role for the Irish Republic in security matters in the North.

In Castlewellan, in late June 1985, a Loyalist band parade was banned. A DUP councillor, Ethel Smyth, called for the ban to be defied; twenty-two people were arrested. Interference with Orange marches provided a genuine focus for Protestant anger. Loyalist paramilitaries and Unionist politicians saw an opportunity to express their mounting resentment of the London – Dublin talks by taking their protests to the grass roots and directing their anger at the RUC.

The Orange Order, which arranged the Loyalist marching season, was a huge, cumbersome 'rudderless ship', led by Revd Martin Smyth, MP. The higher ranks of the order were under the control of the OUP, but the bulk of its active members came from the DUP, the UDA and the UVF. *Fortnight* magazine described the Orange Order as 'a sleepy giant, an Official Unionist Gulliver pinned down by a lot of Paisleyite Lilliputians'.[14]

There was a major confrontation between the police and the order at the traditional Twelfth of July parade at Portadown. A thousand RUC officers, backed up by a battalion of the Queen's Own Highlanders, held the line and prevented the Orangemen from following the usual parade route, the first breach in a 170-year-old tradition. By the end of the marching season, 260 RUC officers had sustained injuries and a number of police families had been forced out of their homes by Loyalist attacks. Between 27 June and 9 August, 468 Loyalists and 427 Republicans were arrested on civil disturbance charges.

As the marching season drew to a close everybody took stock of the situation. The RUC had withstood the test and Hermon's leadership was secure. The Loyalists had been surprised by the firmness with which the Protestant-dominated police force had resisted Loyalist protests. Hermon's success on the streets helped to boost the sagging confidence of the Anglo-Irish negotiators. Mary Holland reflected some

---

[14] *Fortnight*, No. 223, 1985.

of the pessimism felt in Dublin when she reported that 'more and more voters in the Republic are beginning to wonder what on earth Garret FitzGerald thinks he's doing by trying to involve their government and police force in the Northern mess. Why doesn't he come home and run his own part of the country?'[15] Conor O'Cleary reported in the same issue of *Fortnight* that the British cabinet was evenly split on the Anglo-Irish talks; the crucial figure was Viscount Whitelaw. Ian Aitken in the *Guardian* identified Enoch Powell and Ian Gow as 'working hard behind the scenes to scuttle the Anglo-Irish discussions'[16] while *Fortnight* listed Sir John Biggs Davison, Michael Mates and Dr Brian Mawhinney, a Belfast-born Conservative, as constituting a hard core of anti-agreement back-benchers at Westminster.

The Times reported on 29 July 1985 that both London and Dublin denied a report that a draft agreement was under consideration by both cabinets. Whitehall sources emphasized an 'agreement was neither close nor certain'.[17] Dublin correspondents wrote of 'growing talk of a break with Britain and a return to a more confrontational policy over Northern Ireland'.[18] John Cole, political editor of the BBC, reported Whitelaw 'sceptical', Biffen 'nervous' and the lord chancellor 'determined not to have joint North–South terrorism courts'.[19] Julian Haviland, in *The Times*, reminded his readers that for the prime minister and the taoiseach 'the foundation of genuine peace for Ireland would be a prize of the highest value'.[20] It took John Cole to define the line between success and failure: 'the prize is when the Nationalists were to be content enough to return to full participation and Unionists were not so offended to withdraw, the booby prize is when the Agreement is not good enough to attract the Nationalists and worrying enough to send the Unionists over the top.'[21]

At the beginning of August 1985 a joint Unionist working party was formed in response 'to mounting concern' about the Anglo-Irish talks. A six-man team, made up of Peter Robinson, Ivan Foster, William Ross, Frank Millar, Peter Smith and Samuel Wilson, was to suggest 'strategies by which Ulster's interests within the United Kingdom could best be protected'.[22] The Unionist leaders, Molyneaux and Paisley, agreed on a joint policy and warned the British government 'that any attempt to involve the Government of the Irish Republic in the direction

[15] *Fortnight*, No. 221, 1985.
[16] Ibid.
[17] *Times*, 29 July 1985.
[18] *Fortnight*, No. 221, 1985.
[19] *Listener*, 15 August 1985.
[20] *Times*, 29 July 1985.
[21] *Listener*, 15 August 1985.
[22] *News Letter*, 3 August 1985.

or control of our affairs will meet with united Unionist opposition. Even a consultative role for the Irish Republic would be a violation of the Government's assurance of Ulster's right to self-determination ... it is clear to us that the wish of all Unionist people is to see our parties working together to resist this challenge.'[23] Peter Robinson supported the new Unionist accord – similar to the one which had secured eleven Westminster seats in the election of spring 1974 (see above p.11) – 'to work out a campaign of defiance in the event of Eire being given a say in Ulster's affairs'.[24]

The Unionist accord was reached after advice from back-bench Conservative MPs at Westminster that an agreement between London and Dublin was now more likely. The *News Letter* claimed 'the core of the discussions is not primarily concerned with real issues at all – but with international perception of them. Dublin now openly claims to be winning the international propaganda war against Mrs Thatcher and her Government ...'[25] Prime Minister Thatcher was in Washington at the time and the *News Letter's* comments were considered close to the truth. Negotiation on the core of the agreement was complete; what remained was the presentation of the text and the redrafting of its accompanying communiqué, which would cover all outstanding areas of dispute not previously resolved.

In Northern Ireland six hundred invitations were distributed to a meeting at Portadown on 7 August 1985 to establish a United Ulster Loyalist Front (UULF). The *News Letter* headline was 'Ulster Not For Sale' and the paper reported that Alan Wright, the UULF's convener, had said that 'we are very frightened that the constitutional process is going to fail us – the UULF would give unity of purpose, strong leadership and forceful, meaningful action'.[26] Peter Robinson, the deputy leader of the DUP, was reported to be present, as was Andy Tyrie of the Ulster Defence Association. His paramilitary organization was largely discredited within the Unionist camp because of its alleged involvement in serious crime. The organization's membership had declined since its heyday in the seventies, when it could claim a following of one hundred thousand. The one remaining effective faction within the organization was the Ulster Defence Force, a commando-type group of seventy paramilitaries under the leadership of John McMichael. The UULF was Alan Wright's creation and the impetus came from the events at Portadown on 12 and 13 July. Wright, an official of the Portadown lodge of the Orange Order, recognized the

---

[23] Ibid.
[24] *News Letter*, 1 August 1985.
[25] Ibid.
[26] *News Letter*, 8 August 1985.

significance of the RUC's blocking of the traditional parade route. If the RUC was prepared to stand up against Loyalist protesters, the Protestant movement required its own defenders, especially if its political leaders were to be outmanœuvred by London and Dublin. Wright gave an interview to the *News Letter*: 'our intention [was] to build up a massive organization of ordinary men and women . . . joined together in Ulster's hour of need . . .'[27] John McMichael used similar arguments: 'Since the sell out is initiated by Westminster, it follows that Westminster should be treated as an enemy. If the Government uses the police and army to enforce its hostile policy, then if Ulster is to fight, will it fight the Crown forces? I believe it is make your mind up time for Ulster loyalism . . . if some of the present Unionist leadership had been in power in 1912, Northern Ireland would never have come into existence.'[28]

On the evening of 18 August 1985, police homes on the Rectory Park Estate in Portadown were attacked by a Loyalist mob. A visiting Irish circus in Kilria was also attacked. At a public meeting in Portadown four days later the Official Unionist MP, Ken Maginnis, walked out of a gathering after a woman in the audience stood up to say that 'she would clap her hands if she heard of an RUC constable's death'.[29] Maginnis left as Paisley arrived. The DUP leader condemned the attack on the RUC but carried on with the public meeting.

In August 1985, Molyneaux and Paisley wrote a joint letter to the prime minister in which they said they were 'willing to contribute to a process of British-Irish discussions and co-operation'.[30] Their provisos were that United Kingdom sovereignty remained undiminished and that the Republic dropped its territorial claim to Northern Ireland. Molyneaux was to explain later that 'Mr Paisley and I said that if there was a devolved government at Stormont, we would follow the long established practice whereby Stormont ministers discussed such matters with Eire ministers. In that situation we would be in on the discussions rather than having the two governments going over our heads'.[31] The joint letter was the fruit of the six-man think-tank set up earlier that month. On the day the letter was posted to Downing Street, Nicholas Scott, deputy secretary of state at the Northern Ireland Office, gave an interview in which he said, 'we have recognized that it would be constructive for the Government in Dublin to have a consultative role over security and other matters in the Province'.[32] He also confirmed

---

[27] *News Letter*, 2 September 1987.
[28] *Fortnight*, No. 224, 1985.
[29] *News Letter*, 22 August 1985.
[30] *News Letter*, 2 November 1985.
[31] *News Letter*, 1 November 1985.
[32] *News Letter*, 29 August 1985.

that the Irish Republic would be consulted about matters affecting industry, agriculture and social policy in Ulster. This confirms the view that the central agreement was now in place, although Douglas Hurd hinted at major difficulties still outstanding when he said that 'the chances of an agreement were still 50–50. There will have to be a decision. It cannot be indefinitely delayed'.[33] In the mean time Hurd, in his last few days as secretary of state for Northern Ireland, concentrated on the agricultural crisis in the province. Potato yields were down 5 per cent and oil-seed rape and the flax crop had suffered badly from the wet summer. Paisley appealed for subventions from the EC disaster fund.

On Friday 30 August Molyneaux and Paisley met Thatcher and Hurd in London. The two Unionist leaders said they were 'profoundly anxious about the secrecy'[34] of the Anglo-Irish talks. They resented not being consulted, especially since they were aware that John Hume and his SDLP colleagues were in constant contact with the Dublin negotiators. Molyneaux and Paisley repeated their willingness to contribute to a dialogue with Dublin once the conditions outlined in their letter of 28 August were accepted. They urged the prime minister to 'put pressure on Eire to abandon its territorial claim to Northern Ireland';[35] they also warned of the dangers of a Loyalist backlash.

Four days later Douglas Hurd became home secretary and the Northern Ireland Office had a new secretary of state, Tom King. The leader of the British side of the negotiations was the foreign secretary, Sir Geoffrey Howe, aided by Sir Robert Armstrong, the cabinet secretary, and Sir Alan Goodison, the British ambassador in Dublin. The British civil servants working on the day-by-day negotiations were David Goodall, a deputy under-secretary of state at the Foreign Office, and Chris Mallaby, who was on loan from the Foreign Office. On the Irish side, the details were negotiated by Sean Dolan, secretary of the Department of Foreign Affairs and a former ambassador to Washington, and Michael Lillis, the head of the Anglo-Irish section of the Department of Foreign Affairs. Peter Barry, the foreign secretary, headed the Irish delegation, with Dermot Nally, the government secretary, and Noel Dorr, the Irish ambassador to London, in active attendance. *The Economist* claimed that the Irish delegation reacted angrily to Hurd's transfer: 'the silence of the elected politicians in Dublin is deafening and appalled. After five years of discussing the future of Northern Ireland with Mrs Thatcher's government in London

[33] Ibid.
[34] *News Letter*, 2 October 1985.
[35] *News Letter*, 2 September 1985.

they feel it has treated their effort with contempt.'[36] Others, especially in Northern Ireland, saw the move as confirmation that a deal was already in place and that the driving force behind the initiative now came from the prime minister and the Foreign Office. John Cole advised Mrs Thatcher against investing too much personal capital in Ireland, recalling Cyril Connolly's condemnation of Ireland 'as that green cul-de-sac turned away from Europe, where the revolutions lead backwards and the present is invariably the victim of the past'.[37]

A previous secretary of state for Northern Ireland, Merlyn Rees, published a book, *Northern Ireland – A Personal Perspective*, the main thesis of which was that the hope of finding a peaceful solution in the province 'lies with the Northern Irish people, not with outsiders in Dublin and London talking by proxy'.[38] He also identified economic issues as being the most important factor in bringing peace: 'Failure to deal with the unemployment problem could, however, be the most important factor in destroying the improvements in the security and political situation.'[39]

The prime minister's reply of 13 September 1985 to Molyneaux and Paisley showed how far policy had shifted since Rees's days in the Labour government of Harold Wilson. She wrote: 'I am convinced that our present dialogue with the Irish Government represents our best hope of improving co-operation in a number of areas, including security ... I repeat my unqualified assurance that sovereignty over Northern Ireland will be undiminished.'[40]

Tom King's first move as secretary of state for Northern Ireland was to invite the leaders of all constitutional parties to talks at Stormont Castle. A meeting with the DUP leaders was arranged for 19 September. Two days earlier, King went to Dublin to meet his Irish counterparts. Paisley cancelled his appointment with the secretary of state, refusing to take 'second place to Dublin'. The Unionist leaders requested a further meeting with the prime minister. Replying to her letter of 13 September, the two leaders wrote: 'we specifically sought an assurance that you interpreted undiminished United Kingdom sovereignty over Northern Ireland as precluding any British-Irish machinery dealing only with Northern Ireland ... we take it that your omission to confirm this in your letter is deliberate ... you have failed to make *de jure* recognition of the right of the people of Northern Ireland to self-determination a condition precedent to consideration of Irish

---

[36] *Economist*, 14 September 1985.
[37] *Listener*, 5 September 1985.
[38] *New Society*, 1 November 1985.
[39] Merlyn Rees, *Northern Ireland – A Personal Perspective* (Methuen, 1985), 320.
[40] *News Letter*, 2 October 1985.

demands.'[41] This was possibly the most important letter in the whole Anglo-Irish debate. The Unionists' letter properly interpreted the significance of Mrs Thatcher's missing assurances; the agreement was in being. Once the Unionists understood this, their anti-agreement campaign was launched. The fact that the two Unionist leaders did not appreciate the situation until mid September 1985 shows that they were either confident in their cause, or isolated from the realities of Anglo-Irish affairs. By the time they woke up to the probability of an Anglo-Irish agreement, the London and Dublin partners had agreed on most of the crucial issues. Peter Barry recalled the difference between the tactics of the SDLP and those of the Unionists: 'when leaks appeared, the Nationalist leaders came to Dublin and knocked on our door and told us what they would wear . . . the Unionists . . . did not go knocking on the British leaders' doors at Westminster, because they thought when the Agreement came they would do as they have done over the past 100 years . . . that is say no.'[42]

The United Ulster Loyalist Front, under Alan Wright's leadership, set about organizing a network of local defence groups to combat the Anglo-Irish talks; they were to be called the Ulster Clubs. The *News Letter* noted in late September 1985 that 'the official Unionist and DUP working group has had two months and the Loyalist people are still waiting for leadership. If firm action doesn't come soon, they will take the matter into their own hands.'[43]

Informed leaks continued to appear in the Irish and British press. Northern Ireland papers were singularly unsuccessful in penetrating the wall of secrecy that surrounded the ongoing negotiations. *Panorama* claimed in late September that 'there does appear to have been agreement on most fundamental issues – the establishment of some form of Anglo-Irish Council with a permanent secretariat in Belfast which will act as a conduit for nationalist grievances and hopefully for their redress – suffice it to say that she [Mrs Thatcher] seems unlikely to shrink from adding Dr Paisley's scalp to those of Arthur Scargill and General Galtieri'.[44] Peter Taylor of the *Listener* added that he understood the Irish were insisting on changes in the most sensitive security areas, the police, the UDR and the Diplock courts and that Dr FitzGerald needed to produce evidence of real change to ensure that the agreement could be embraced by John Hume's SDLP. He concluded his report by saying that 'the common denominator in the calculations on both sides [British and Irish] is the political impetus which failure

---

[41] Ibid.
[42] *News Letter*, 7 March 1988.
[43] *News Letter*, 24 September 1985.
[44] *Listener*, 26 September 1985.

would give Sinn Fein and its *alter ego*, the IRA ... Sinn Fein's electoral success ... has provided both sides, in particular the British, with the critical impetus for agreement'.[45]

In Northern Ireland, the Unionists marshalled their forces in the assembly, and passed a motion calling on the government not to go through with the agreement. Peter Robinson said: 'the day the Republic is given any role in the governance of Northern Ireland, then that same day, I will cease to recognize or respect the validity or authority of the United Kingdom Government.'[46] The final report of the Northern Ireland Assembly Devolution Report Committee was published. Sir Frederick Catherwood had been invited by the assembly to write a report which would provide a working basis for negotiations. It recommended that the legislative and executive responsibilities previously transferred under the 1973 Act should be exercised by the assembly, with a devolved executive answerable to it. The proposals were contained on less than three pages and reflected the paucity of ideas and the despondent mood of the Unionists at this crucial time in their history. Their leaders were 'unprepared for arguments about constitutional questions and unused to justifying the Protestant political position'.[47] Sarah Nelson's excellent work on Unionism concluded that 'few Protestants have a clear and distinct sense of Ulster nationhood or can articulate just what an Ulster identity is'.[48] Hazel Bradford, chairperson of the Official Unionists, voiced the dilemma facing Ulster Protestants when she contributed to Channel 4's programme *Comment*: 'It is impossible to reconcile the Nationalist Republican dream of a United Ireland, Gaelic in culture, independent of Britain, with the British Unionists' democratic right to self-determination and full British citizenship ... if what we are left with in Belfast is a form of citizenship fundamentally different from that enjoyed by the rest of you, then can it be British citizenship at all?'

Molyneaux and Paisley met Thatcher again at Downing Street on 30 October 1985. The Unionist leaders warned the prime minister that neither they nor the Ulster majority would accept any agreement which would let the South have a say in the running of the province. If an agreement was signed they demanded that its validity and acceptability in the province be tested either by a referendum or by holding fresh assembly elections. A seven-page document was handed to the prime minister; it contained the main proposals of the OUP's *The Way Ahead*, the DUP's *Ulster – The Future Assured* and the Catherwood Report.

---

[45] Ibid.
[46] *News Letter*, 9 October 1985.
[47] Sarah Nelson, *Ulster's Uncertain Defenders* (Appletree Press, 1984), 30.
[48] Ibid., 12.

The day before the meeting between Mrs Thatcher and the Unionist leaders, the final negotiating session between Armstrong and Nally was concluded in Dublin. The British cabinet considered the deal at its meeting on 31 October and gave it a guarded blessing.

In Northern Ireland plans were well advanced for an Ulster Clubs rally at the City Hall in Belfast. Ken Maginnis, in a speech to Eglinton Unionists, attacked Alan Wright's plans to organize 152 clubs across the province: 'I fear the self-appointed selfseekers who will take our young people and exploit their frustrations just as they did in the mid-seventies. I fear the protection rackets, the intimidation, the drinking clubs with the spin-off for personal profit and ultimately the relapse into sectarian murder.'[49] At the rally, which was attended by represent-atives of the UDA, the UVF and the Independent Orange Order and by a crowd of 5,000, Wright promised 'to defend loyalist rights to remain within the United Kingdom, defeating the Anglo-Eire process and combating the erosion of the loyalist heritage by Irish nationalism'.[50] The Clubs were to be modelled on Carson's original Unionist clubs, and 'any deal with Dublin would be met by organized and determined resistance'.[51]

Meanwhile, London was experiencing last-minute doubts. *New Society* suggested that 'everyone is getting cold feet up to the armpits ... the basic problem is how to describe the outcome as a green victory to nationalists ... and an orange victory for Ulster Unionists'.[52] FitzGerald tried to calm the British negotiating team. He identified the cause of the doubts as 'loyalist paramilitary violence ... we must make the attempt. It involves some risk, but I believe the risk is not as great as some people would like us to believe.'[53] He conceded that the negotiators were walking a 'tightrope' in their efforts to judge the level of any Irish government dimension in the affairs of the North. The final package had to be 'very finely tuned', but he was sure that Mrs Thatcher had the political will to back it.

FitzGerald correctly identified the one person who could now swing the negotiations into an agreement. The decisive factor was whether or not the Conservative government was prepared to call the historic Ulster Unionist bluff and assert ultimate Westminster authority on the Irish question in the face of explicit threats that the majority in the province would seek to make it ungovernable if London had the slightest truck with Dublin. FitzGerald had watched Thatcher over the

---

[49] *News Letter*, 1 November 1985.
[50] *News Letter*, 4 November 1985.
[51] Ibid.
[52] *New Society*, 1 November 1985.
[53] *Times*, 2 November 1985.

years as she slowly engaged herself in the Irish question. They had been personally close since he befriended her at a conference in the Middle East, when she was a back-bench MP. The taoiseach had taken upon himself the 'unpromising task of seeking to persuade Mrs Thatcher to inform herself about the realities of the Irish question and to concentrate on it ... for Mrs Thatcher ... the attraction of going down in history as the Prime Minister who set Ulster off down a new and less hopeless road, combined with the prospect of reducing the £4 billion annual cost of the present policy for fortress Ulster, was decisive'.[54]

But FitzGerald had other problems. Charles Haughey, the leader of the opposition in the Dáil, was vigorously campaigning in the United States against the agreement, arguing that it 'perpetuated partition'. The Fianna Fáil leader sent his deputy, Brian Lenihan, to Washington in an attempt to dissuade the Reagan administration from supporting the Anglo-Irish talks. Haughey released the text of a letter in which he said that 'the draft treaty appears to be based on the mistaken premise that Northern Ireland is a normal democracy ... the treaty could be regarded as an attempt to legitimize the Northern Ireland state at a time when its institutions have broken down'.[55] There were also reports that the strong and influential Irish-American lobby in the Senate was likely to frustrate British attempts to make it easier to return terrorist suspects to British jurisdiction.

Aware of the difficulties at Leinster House, the taoiseach's office in Dublin, Molyneaux and Paisley convened a press conference at Enniskillen directly targeted at journalists from the Republic. Only seven turned up, none of them from the South. Paisley warned that 'the way ahead for Northern Ireland and Eire was to be one of either friendly co-operation or bloody conflict ... the Unionist population in Northern Ireland will not tolerate any dilution of the sovereignty of the United Kingdom Parliament over Northern Ireland. There can be no input into the government of this part of the United Kingdom whether that input is in the form of a consultative role for the Government of the Irish Republic, a structure for channelling advice from the Irish Government to the British Government ... or any other mechanism, however ingenious that may be devised to give the Republic of Ireland government a say in British policy and administration of Northern Ireland. Such joint machinery would constitute a clear infringement of British sovereignty over the Province.'[56]

Tom King, speaking to Belfast Rotarians, said 'the Anglo-Irish talks threatened no one but the terrorists ... people start getting all the old

---

[54] *New Statesman*, 22 November 1985.
[55] *Sunday Times*, 3 November 1985.
[56] *News Letter*, 5 November 1985.

phobias and fears out of the cupboard. The old emotions and prejudices reassert themselves'.[57] The *News Letter* carried a report that suggested that the Anglo-Irish secretariat was 'unlikely' to be based in Belfast, as the Irish Republic and the SDLP were demanding: 'It will most likely be a "moving target" between locations in London and Dublin.'[58] At the time this was taken to be a Northern Ireland Office leak to pacify the growing Unionist anti-agreement campaign. It was also an eleventh-hour attempt to get the Irish delegation to climb down on its insistence on the secretariat being based in Belfast. Dublin was being encouraged to resist British pressure by the SDLP; there had to be a 'physical presence' in Ulster.

At a press conference in Belfast, on the same day as King's address to the Rotarians, Paisley convened his weekly press conference and warned his audience that 'London was poised to do a sell-out deal with Dublin . . . a Sunningdale-style scheme . . . Unionists would resist this betrayal'.[59] The *News Letter* supported the DUP leader's statement: 'on the issue of unity there is simply no half-way house or gradualist approach that will be tolerated by Unionists.'[60]

The day after the Paisley press conference, Tom King and Sir Geoffrey Howe met Peter Barry and Dick Spring in London. The *Sunday Times* reported 'a last minute hitch . . . what they fell out over was the presentation of the deal'.[61] The meeting took place on the same day as the Queen's Speech at Westminster. The Loyal Address contained the following commitment on Northern Ireland: 'My Government will continue to support the security forces in enforcing the law and in working for the eradication of terrorism. They will seek widely acceptable arrangements for the devolution of power. They will seek to improve further their co-operation with the Government of the Irish Republic. Renewed efforts will be made to create and sustain employment, particularly by the encouragement of the private sector.'[62]

Mervyn Pauley claimed in the *News Letter* that the London meeting of ministers was only convened after Armstrong and Nally had reached 'an impasse over the wording of the agreement, with Eire wanting more specific terms to describe the role it will be given in Ulster'.[63] Pauley went on to report that FitzGerald was insisting that 'Eire's role in Ulster affairs be made clear in the text of the agreement, whilst London wanted

---

[57] *News Letter*, 6 November 1985.
[58] Ibid.
[59] Ibid.
[60] Ibid.
[61] *Sunday Times*, 10 November 1985.
[62] *News Letter*, 8 November 1985.
[63] Ibid.

the terms to be more ambiguous'.[64] Michael Jones, writing in the *Sunday Times*, saw the hastily convened meeting of ministers in London as follows: 'the Dublin Government, ever wary of opposition politicians who will accuse it of surrendering the Republic's commitment to Irish unity, want Thatcher to present the deal as an historical act ... Thatcher on the other hand is anxious to minimize Unionist fears of a sell-out ... saving the SDLP is largely what the talks are about as far as Dublin is concerned ... [FitzGerald] fears that if Sinn Fein gains the upper hand among Catholics in the North, it could wreck the South as well.'[65] The impression that the Republic was more eager to reach agreement than Britain started to gain some credence. There was also a strong hint that the prime minister might have been misled by her Anglo-Irish negotiating team. Sir Geoffrey Howe, Douglas Hurd and Sir Robert Armstrong were portrayed as negotiators out of sympathy with the Unionist cause: 'they have similar world views and similar personalities. None of them has any enthusiasm for the Union. They see Northern Ireland as an encumbrance – a drain on their economy and an obstacle in foreign relations. For them, part of the attraction of the deal is any faint hope it might offer that in time the Ulster Protestants may come to regard themselves as Irish. The tribal antagonism of Ulster politics leaves them cold and contemptuous – a contempt that has been inadequately concealed from Unionist politicians.'[66] Sir Robert Armstrong, the *Spectator* argued, had successfully persuaded the prime minister to call the Unionists' bluff; the eleventh-hour jitters occurred when Mrs Thatcher started worrying about the security situation in the North. After a period of comparative security the prospect of a Unionist backlash, a reorganized Loyalist paramilitary threat and an uncertain response from the RUC made an agreement uncertain as late as Thursday 7 November 1985. The cabinet discussion was reported to be inconclusive.

The role of the RUC would be central to any successful implementation of the Anglo-Irish Agreement. It was recognized that the Unionists were very likely to take their protests to the streets. The RUC had successfully withstood Loyalist attacks in Portadown, but at a price. Attacks on police homes and the danger that the force would be sucked into a political dispute that might affect its operational independence, worried the chief constable, Sir John Hermon. He did not have a good relationship with his Irish counterpart and did not relish the thought of being forced by an international agreement to co-operate and share sensitive intelligence information with a force which did not

---

[64] Ibid.
[65] *News Letter*, 7 November 1985.
[66] *Times*, 5 December 1985.

have his full respect. In Houston, Texas, in late October 1985, Hermon said that 'the Dublin Government had no interest in penetrating the IRA or the INLA ...' [67] This was calculated to upset the Irish and worry the British. Hermon was determined to be his own man, running his force free of the requirements of an international treaty; he felt threatened by all the rumours circulating regarding the agreement. His intervention had the desired effect. Mrs Thatcher, it was rumoured, thought that the agreement was likely to cause more trouble than it was worth.

The *Spectator* led the charge for the abandonment of the talks: 'British Governments seem incapable of recognizing either the invincibility of Unionist opinion or its potential for good ... Things have come to a pretty pass when 70 per cent of the elected representatives of a United Kingdom assembly can propose eminently democratic reforms and yet be excluded and ignored for the sake of negotiations with a foreign power ...' [68]

The Economist, a strong supporter of a deal between Britain and Ireland, reported that 'intelligence sources, backed by reliable Unionist information, cast doubt upon the gravity of the Protestant threat. Reports from the power stations, where Protestant workers have control of the switches, indicate no preparations for a strike. Nor is there evidence of coherent organization in the few large factories left in Ulster. The paramilitary Ulster Defence organization has been trying to muster its members for resistance, but has not worked up much excitement.' [69] This was written before the march on 4 November 1985; the turnout of 5,000 shocked the security authorities.

FitzGerald, according to Mary Holland, 'refused to feel patronized by the British in the week before Hillsborough'. [70] He refused to budge on what he regarded as the crucial questions – the location of the secretariat and the venue for the signing of the agreement. FitzGerald wanted the signing ceremony to be in Ulster. In Brussels on Friday 8 November 1985 the taoiseach internationalized the Anglo-Irish talks by saying that the aim of a 'peaceful united Ireland must take "second place" to the securing in the Anglo-Irish negotiations of a better deal now for both communities in Northern Ireland'. [71] Charles Haughey said on Irish television that FitzGerald's claim that unity had to wait on peace was 'politically absurd'. [72] Mary Holland advised the taoiseach 'to stop worrying about the Unionists, Garret, Mrs Thatcher will look

---

[67] *News Letter*, 22 October 1985.
[68] *Spectator*, 2 November 1985.
[69] *Economist*, 2 November 1985.
[70] *Irish Times*, 12 March 1987.
[71] *Irish Times*, 9 November 1985.
[72] *Irish Times*, 11 November 1985.

after them – your responsibility is the northern nationalists'.[73] Fitz-Gerald's target audience was elsewhere; he was appealing directly to fellow European heads of government and to the American administration. It was a last-ditch effort to settle any outstanding doubts regarding Irish aspirations in signing the Anglo-Irish agreement. It worked. The *Sunday Times* confirmed two days later that the agreement was now on: 'the two communities which coexist in that troubled province will be assured in a binding, internationally-registered agreement that their separate identities will receive fair and generous recognition in a system of administration supported by both national governments. It is a unique attempt to resolve a unique problem. Britain will retain full sovereignty – we are not talking of nudging Ulster into a united Ireland. There is no covert deal with Dublin to deprive Unionists of their British birthright . . . for the North's nationalist community . . . the way is open to forge a new relationship with the Unionist majority based on shared rights and responsibilities . . . both Dr FitzGerald and Mrs Thatcher are taking risks in seeking to break the log jam.'[74]

In Northern Ireland, the SDLP held their annual conference. John Hume, the party leader, said of the Anglo-Irish talks: 'we do not expect a final settlement or an immediate solution . . . we know the path of progress is long and stony . . . there are no instant solutions. There can only be a healing process.'[75] This echoed FitzGerald's Brussels speech and was in stark contrast to the speech of Seamus Mallon, the SDLP deputy leader. He was known to be closer to Haughey, while Hume was closer to FitzGerald. Mallon said it was a 'contradiction – to suggest that legitimate nationalist aspirations could be put on the back boiler'.[76] He called for the scrapping of the Ulster Defence Regiment and the publication of the Stalker Report.

Sinn Fein's annual conference, or *ardfheis*, was held in Dublin; Gerry Adams, the party leader, claimed that 'the current London Dublin talks are a compliment to you all . . . they are trying to resolve how best to isolate and defeat Irish republicanism, through a mixture of repression and appeasement'.[77] *The Times* reported that the Republican movement feared that 'the Ulster deal could mean steps to crush the movement'.[78]

The Unionists, according to Roy Bradford, prepared to 'go over the top'. Frank McGuinness's play, 'Observe the Sons of Ulster moving towards the Somme', was about to open at the Belfast Festival.

---

[73] *Irish Times*, 13 November 1985.
[74] *Sunday Times*, 10 November 1985.
[75] *News Letter*, 11 November 1985.
[76] *Irish Times*, 11 November 1985.
[77] *News Letter*, 4 November 1985.
[78] *Times*, 4 November 1985.

Bradford claimed: 'Ulster in a real sense is about to go over the top, to grapple with the perilous uncertain future ... the core of the Ulster Unionist heritage, its emotional engine, is essentially Protestant ... talk of Queen and country is not just cant and claptrap ... will the essential nature of the Unionist heritage ... be endangered by the coming agreement?'[79] Bradford was in no doubt that it would. FitzGerald's Brussels speech had obviously not reassured the Unionists, but it had won over Mrs Thatcher. On Monday 11 November 1985 FitzGerald told John Hume in Dublin that the agreement was in the bag. The taoiseach recalled: 'the most moving moment of this dramatic experience came when, on an evening very shortly before we went to Hillsborough, Hume, Mallon and McGrady and Hendron told us that they and their party were ready to back our efforts.'[80] Over the weekend, the British and Irish partners had agreed on the details of the agreement, the text of the communiqué and the location of the signing ceremony. The Irish newspapers started leaking the details of the agreement the following day.

In the House of Commons, Tom King confirmed that he had met Irish ministers on three occasions; the foreign secretary had accompanied him to all three meetings. The purpose of the talks 'had been to deepen our relationship with the Republic in ways that will benefit both communities in Northern Ireland, on the basis that there can be no change in the status of Northern Ireland as part of the United Kingdom without the consent of a majority there, and that there can be no derogation from sovereignty on the part of the Government of the United Kingdom'.[81] Enoch Powell had earlier accused the prime minister of treachery, a charge that Thatcher found 'deeply offensive'.

Ian Paisley, having digested the details of the agreement, wrote to Thatcher and FitzGerald. 'Having failed to defeat the IRA', he told the prime minister, 'you now have capitulated and are prepared to set in motion machinery which will achieve the IRA goal ... a united Ireland. We now know that you have prepared the Ulster Unionists for sacrifice on the altar of political expediency. They are to be the sacrificial lambs to appease the Dublin wolves.' To FitzGerald, the DUP leader said: 'You claim in your constitution jurisdiction over our territory, our homes, our persons and our families. You allow your territory to be used as a launching pad for murder gangs and as a sanctuary for them when they return soaked in our people's blood. You are a fellow traveller with the IRA and hope to ride on the back of their terrorism to your goal of a United Ireland. We reject your claims and

---

[79] *News Letter*, 11 November 1985.
[80] *Irish Times*, 9 February 1987.
[81] *Hansard*, 14 November 1985, 673.

will never submit to your authority. We will never bow to Dublin rule.'[82]

The *News Letter* thundered against the deal and in particular the decision to base the secretariat of the Intergovernmental Conference in Belfast – what it called the 'Dublin bridgehead in Ulster ... It is of primary importance that no room be found at Stormont or anywhere else in Northern Ireland for any advanced force whose stated purpose is to secure the downfall of the Province and its annexation by a foreign power. There can be no place for equivocation on this point by anyone in public or private life who values the link with the United Kingdom. It will not be sufficient to oppose ... it must be defeated.'[83]

The agreement was finally accepted by the British cabinet, at its meeting on Thursday 14 November 1985. The prime minister and the secretary of state for Northern Ireland refused to confirm the existence of an agreement or to speculate on its contents in the House of Commons later the same day.

The Anglo-Irish Agreement was signed by Prime Minister Thatcher and An Taoiseach FitzGerald at 14.00 hours on Friday 15 November 1985 at Hillsborough Castle, in County Down, Northern Ireland. A communiqué, the drafting of which had been a taxing exercise, gave details of the way in which the agreement would be implemented. The agreement itself was confined to thirteen clauses.

The signing of the agreement had something of the air of a rushed and risky marriage ceremony. Both partners had travelled from afar. The groom seemed happy and relaxed; the bride was strained and nervous, as though she had been up most of the night before wrestling with her doubts about the wisdom of this arranged, mixed marriage. Most modern marriage contracts have a get-out clause; this ceremony was no different. Article 2 provided for a review 'at the end of three years or earlier if requested by either government'.[84] Nobody at the ceremony asked if there were any objections to the marriage, but the faint sound of an 'Ulster says No' chant could be heard from the direction of the front gates of Hillsborough Castle, where thousands of protesters had been assembling since early dawn.

The two prime ministers penned their signatures to an agreement intended to bring 'lasting peace and stability – and reconciliation'[85] to Ulster's troubled people. There would be no change in the status of

---

[82] *News Letter*, 15 November 1985.
[83] *News Letter*, 14 November 1985.
[84] Article 2, Anglo-Irish Agreement, Section G.
[85] Preamble to Anglo-Irish Agreement.

Northern Ireland; Ulster was to remain British. But 'if in the future a majority of the people of Northern Ireland clearly wish for and formally consent to the establishment of a united Ireland, they will introduce and support in the respective Parliaments legislation to give effect to that wish.'[86] The Unionist veto was no more. A permanent secretariat of civil servants from London and Dublin was to be established and based at Maryfield, on the outskirts of Belfast, and this would serve the Intergovernmental Conference of Ministers which would meet 'on a regular basis ... to deal ... with (i) political matters; (ii) security and related matters; (iii) legal matters, including the administration of justice; (iv) the promotion of cross-border co-operation'.[87] Devolution for Northern Ireland was the declared political goal, but pending that development the Irish Government 'may ... put forward views on proposals for major legislation and on major policy issues'.[88] While the conference would have no operational responsibilities for policing in the province, it would consider '(i) security policy; (ii) relations between the security forces and the community; (iii) prisons policy'.[89] It would also seek to give a boost to public confidence in the administration of justice, and both partners committed themselves to consider further the 'possibility of mixed courts in both jurisdictions'.[90] In their jointly declared policy of seeking to 'recognize and accommodate the rights and identities of the two traditions in Northern Ireland', the partners at Hillsborough agreed to consider 'changes in electoral arrangements, the use of flags and emblems, the avoidance of economic and social discrimination and the advantages and disadvantages of a Bill of Rights in some form in Northern Ireland'.[91]

The agreement expressed the hopes and aspirations of the signatories; the only matters of substance agreed upon after twelve months of negotiations appeared in the joint communiqué which accompanied the agreement. The two main policy issues involved concerned the Republic's commitment to sign the European Convention on the Suppression of Terrorism and the priority given by Britain to 'Ulsterization' – the concept of RUC primacy over the armed forces in security matters. 'The essence of what has been agreed is in fact a process or a procedure. The choice of the word conference is intended to mean something more than consultation and something less than involvement in executive actions and decision making.'[92] The

---

[86] Article 1(c), Anglo-Irish Agreement, Section A.
[87] Article 2(a), Anglo-Irish Agreement, Section B.
[88] Article 5(c), Anglo-Irish Agreement, Section C.
[89] Article 7(a), Anglo-Irish Agreement, Section D.
[90] Article 8, Anglo-Irish Agreement, Section E.
[91] Article 5(a), Anglo-Irish Agreement, Section C.
[92] *Fortnight*, No. 230, December 1985.

agreement was drafted not in the precise language of constitutional lawyers but in the flexible language of politicians. Almost everything had been left out.

At the subsequent press conferences, Mrs Thatcher described herself as 'a Unionist and a loyalist', while Dr FitzGerald underlined the historical division between the two partners: 'the British Prime Minister and I have come to these negotiations with different historical perspectives and, as it were, with different title deeds. But we have been able to agree about what would and what would not happen in the future ... the agreement ... involves no abandonment of the nationalist aspirations, nor any threat to Unionist rights, but it does offer a prospect of progress towards peace and justice for Northern Nationalists and of peace and stability for Northern Unionists.'[93] Prime Minister Thatcher stressed the security reasons for the historic agreement: 'I [am] not prepared to tolerate a situation of continuing violence. I want to offer hope to young people.'[94] It was these 'internal contradictions'[95] that were to dominate press reaction to the agreement over the first four weeks of its existence. Conor Cruise O'Brien concluded that 'the Agreement was quite unlikely to bring peace and stability ... or to reconcile two traditions, one of which it outraged'.[96] The Loyalist *News Letter*, in an editorial headed 'Ulster Spirit will Prevail', thundered against the agreement: 'to stab the Loyalist people in the heart, and then to profess great concern for their safety and future well being is more than the majority of people will be prepared to accept ...'[97] The *News Letter* became the leading anti-agreement campaign leader. In the Republic, the *Irish Times* was equally committed to support of the agreement, which it called 'a reasonable deal. It is not a solution, it is a beginning.'[98] The *Belfast Telegraph* commented that 'consent is a recurring theme, but is it consent to the right to say "no" if it fails an electoral test? ... If this is the price of nationalist consent to participation in Northern Ireland, it has been fixed at an unrealistically high level.'[99] The *Irish News* called the agreement 'a historic step in the involvement of Britain in the affairs of Ireland'.[100] David McKittrick in the *Listener* called the Hillsborough accord 'probably the most significant political development since the

---

[93] *Ireland Today Special*, November 1985, 10.
[94] *Irish Times*, 16 November 1985.
[95] *Listener*, 21 November 1985.
[96] Conor Cruise O'Brien, *Passion and Cunning and Other Essays* (Weidenfeld and Nicolson, 1988), 211.
[97] *News Letter*, 16 November 1985.
[98] *Irish Times*, 16 November 1985.
[99] *Belfast Telegraph*, 16 November 1985.
[100] *Irish News*, 16 November 1985.

state of Northern Ireland was created in 1921'.[101] The *Spectator* called it a 'fraudulent prospectus ... British Government seems to think that their wish for peace will be father to peace itself'.[102] *The Economist*, under the daunting headline 'Fixing Ulster', claimed that 'Mrs Thatcher has won with no concessions of principle, a new sword for fighting terrorism ...'[103]

Whatever the aspirations of the authors of the agreement, the political response in Northern Ireland was immediate and devastating. While the two prime ministers were saying their respective farewells before leaving the province, local politicians were giving their first reactions to the agreement. Having hurriedly returned from the Loyalist demonstration at Hillsborough, where effigies of the prime minister and the Irish tricolour flag had been burned, Dr Ian Paisley said at a Unionist press conference that 'the time for talking is over, the time for action has arrived',[104] while the Official Unionist leader James Molyneaux spoke of 'the stench of hypocrisy, deceit and treachery'.[105] The Sinn Fein president, Gerry Adams, thought 'the formal recognition of the partition of Ireland ... a disaster for the nationalist cause ... [it] far outweighs the powerless consultative role given to Dublin'.[106] John Hume, the leader of the SDLP, said: 'We do not believe that a final settlement of the Irish problem has been reached. We do believe than an opportunity has been created ...'[107] The IRA murdered Constable David Hanson, the first victim of a new phase of the Troubles; the UDA threatened to kill anyone who collaborated with the Maryfield secretariat.

On her return to Downing Street, the prime minister released the text of an exchange of letters between herself and Ian Gow, who had resigned because the agreement 'will prolong and not diminish the agony of Ulster.'[108] In the Republic, Senator Mary Robinson of the Labour Party left the coalition government on the grounds that the agreement 'could not achieve its objective of securing peace and stability within Northern Ireland ... because ... it would be unacceptable to all sections of Unionist opinion'.[109]

The day following the signing of the agreement, the Northern Ireland Assembly met in a special session at Stormont to debate the motion 'that

---

[101] *Listener*, 21 November 1985.
[102] *Spectator*, 23 November 1985.
[103] *Economist*, 22 November 1985.
[104] *Times*, 16 November 1985.
[105] *Listener*, 21 November 1985.
[106] *Irish Times*, 16 November 1985.
[107] *Ireland Today Special*, November 1985.
[108] *Times*, 14 November 1985.
[109] *Irish Times*, 19 November 1985.

this House repudiates the Anglo-Irish Agreement ... and deprecates [it] as an intolerable derogation of British sovereignty'. The assembly called for a referendum on the agreement and invited the prime minister to address it. The first stage of the withdrawal of consent began; Unionists would not communicate with British ministers, and Unionist councillors withdrew from a tree-planting ceremony. Molyneaux and Paisley sought a judicial review of the agreement; Mr Justice Mann threw it out within a week.

Tom King held his own press conference and appealed to the people of Ulster to read the agreement and not to be misled. Press coverage in the Sunday weeklies was encouraging from the government's point of view. The *Sunday Telegraph* rejected Unionist charges of betrayal, while the *Mail on Sunday* said that 'Mrs Thatcher was a real champion of the people of Ulster ... it would have been easier to let the matter rest and watch the Province slowly bleed to death'.[110] Most of the current affairs programmes on television and radio gave the agreement extensive coverage over the weekend. On *Weekend World* the prime minister explained that the purpose behind the agreement 'was to mobilize everyone against the men of violence, because violence and democracy could not exist together'.[111] On *This Week Next Week* reference was made to Peter Robinson's statement that 'Ulster was now on the window ledge of the Union'.[112] All fifteen Unionist MPs announced their intention of resigning and precipitating a mini-general election in the province. The SDLP rejected an overture from Sinn Fein for a Nationalist electoral pact to oppose the Unionist pact. An off-duty UDR soldier, Sergeant Robert Francis Boyd, was killed in Derry.

World reaction to the Hillsborough Agreement was generally supportive and encouraging. The *New York Times* editorial said that 'London and Dublin are trying imaginatively to transcend what cannot be reconciled'.[113] The *Boston Herald* saw the accord as 'a calculated but worthwhile gamble for peace'.[114] The *Australian* called it 'a watershed in Anglo-Irish relations'.[115] European newspapers gave the initiative their fulsome support.

Meanwhile Dr Ian Paisley, preaching to a congregation of 3,000 at his church, likened Mrs Thatcher to 'Jezebel who sought to destroy Israel in a day',[116] while the moderator of the Presbyterian Church of Ireland, Dr Robert Dickinson, said in a letter to the prime minister that

---

[110] *Mail on Sunday*, 17 November 1985.
[111] *Times*, 18 November 1985.
[112] *News Letter*, 18 November 1985.
[113] *New York Times*, 16 November 1985.
[114] *Boston Herald*, 16 November 1985.
[115] *Australian*, 16 November 1985.
[116] *Times*, 18 November 1985.

he saw the agreement as the 'beginning of the process of edging Northern Ireland out of the United Kingdom – sovereignty has been impinged'.[117] On Monday 18 November local newspapers in the province carried an advertisement that declared: 'We will not have it ... the Anglo-Irish accord amounts to joint London–Dublin Government ... a Dublin Role means a Dublin Rule.'[118]

Attention now turned to the debates at Westminster and the Dáil. At Westminster, the prime minister reported on the Hillsborough summit. She claimed that the agreement had two principal features. The first was the 'binding international agreement that the status of Northern Ireland will remain unchanged so long as that is the wish of the majority of its people ... the second main feature is the establishment of an intergovernmental conference'.[119] She added that the conference would 'not be a decision-making body'.[120] Roy Hattersley, standing in for Neil Kinnock, wished the initiative well, noting that the opposition regarded the most important advances to be the 'reassertion by the Dublin Government of their acceptance that a change in Northern Ireland status could not come about without the consent of the people of Northern Ireland ... [and] the acknowledgement by the British Government of what was described in a previous summit as the all-Irish dimension'.[121] This bipartisan approach did not impress the Unionist representatives. Peter Robinson called the agreement an 'act of political prostitution',[122] while Harold McCusker recalled the desolation he felt, standing outside Hillsborough waiting for a copy of the agreement to be brought out to him:

> I shall carry to my grave ... the sense of the injustice I have done to my constituents down the years ... I exhorted them to put their trust in this British House of Commons, which would one day honour its obligation to treat them as equal British citizens. Is not the reality of this agreement that they will now be Irish-British hybrids and that every aspect of their lives will be open to the influence of those who have harboured their murderers and coveted their lands?[123]

Dáil Éireann debated the Anglo-Irish Agreement from 19 to 21 November 1985, approving its terms by eighty-eight votes to seventy-five. Taoiseach FitzGerald, opening the debate, appealed directly to the Unionists in the North: 'whilst as nationalists we retain our aspirations

---

[117] *News Letter*, 20 November 1985.
[118] Ibid.
[119] *Hansard*, 18 November 1985, 19.
[120] Ibid.
[121] Ibid, 20.
[122] Ibid, 27.
[123] Ibid, 29.

to Irish unity achieved by free consent . . . we repudiate formally, and do so now in an international agreement, any question of seeking the unity of Ireland otherwise than with the consent of the majority in Northern Ireland',[124] and he concluded by stating that 'what has motivated me . . . most powerfully towards seeking and securing this Agreement . . . has been the objective of ending the alienation of the minority in Northern Ireland – it would be impossible to end the alienation of the minority . . . unless there existed within the structures of the Government of Northern Ireland, a significant role for the Irish Government'.[125] The leader of the opposition, Charles Haughey, concentrated his attack on the legal and constitutional issues raised by the agreement: 'Irish Government is acting in a manner repugnant to the Constitution of Ireland . . . it is difficult to avoid the suspicion that the whole purpose of this exercise from the British point of view is to secure Irish Government backing for their security policies . . . Time will tell.'[126]

The Fianna Fáil leader had an unhappy and divided party to deal with; there were persistent rumours during the three-day debate that a dozen or more TDs (members of the Dáil) were threatening to vote against Haughey's decision to oppose the agreement. As it turned out, only one TD voted against the party line. Conor Cruise O'Brien suggested that Haughey felt 'jilted, spurned, upstaged and has had his clothes stolen'.[127] Closing the debate in the Dáil, Peter Barry, the permanent Irish ministerial representative in the Anglo-Irish Intergovernmental Conference, again tried to reassure the Northern Unionists: 'The Irish Government has no designs on the North. We have no designs to have dominion over the Unionist people. We recognize their identity, their Britishness, their ethos, and their sense of being threatened by Irish unity.'[128] The agreement was approved by a majority of thirteen.

An *Irish Times*/MRBC poll of 1,000 people in the Republic showed that 59 per cent approved of Hillsborough, 29 per cent disapproved and 12 per cent had no opinion.[129] The main conclusion here is that Haughey's concern that partition was 'copper-fastened' by the agreement did not seem to carry weight with the public. The agreement gave a much-needed boost to popular support for the coalition government, still trailing Fianna Fáil in the polls. The government's performance rating went up by 10 per cent, to 34 per cent, while only 32 per cent approved of Haughey's anti-agreement stance, as opposed to 56 per cent in favour.

---

[124] *Ireland Today Special*, November 1985, 16.
[125] *Irish Times*, 20 November 1985.
[126] *Irish Times*, 19 November 1985.
[127] Ibid.
[128] *Times*, 21 November 1985.
[129] *Irish Times*, 23 November 1985.

On the day that the Dáil gave its support to the agreement, Tom King was roughly manhandled by a scuffling crowd, pelted with eggs, and at one point punched in the chest by a demonstrator when he arrived at Belfast City Hall. Called a 'white-livered cur and a yellow-bellied coward',[130] the secretary of state had to make a dash for the safety of his armoured car, which sped away throwing protesting Unionists off its roof and bonnet.

Belfast itself was getting ready for the weekend rally convened by the Unionist leaders and supported by the Orange Order. The biggest rally since the days of partition was promised. The prime minister let it be known that she was prepared to meet a deputation of Unionists before the parliamentary debate the following week, but the pro-government *Economist* launched a scathing attack on the Unionist opposition on the morning of the rally. Under the headline 'Don't Cry for Ulster', the article commented: 'once more, the leaders of the Ulster Protestant community are biting the hand that is feeding them . . . the Protestant majority regards loyalism as implying the right to Britain's loyalty – the right to expect mainland Britain to send young men to die in mean streets made meaner by Protestant bigotry . . . Mrs Thatcher has had enough. From now on, unless the Protestant community can agree to a power-sharing devolution formula, acceptable to Catholics, the rights of the minority community will be represented at the direct rule table by Southern politicians and officials.'[131]

The rally outside the City Hall pledged the Unionists to 'unyielding opposition' to the Anglo-Irish Agreement, which was 'a violation of our fundamental rights as citizens of the United Kingdom. We call on our Parliament not to endorse the agreement without the approval of the people of Ulster, expressed through the democratic process.'[132] The organizers claimed a turn-out of half a million, the *News of the World, Sunday Times* and *Sunday Express* gave an estimate of 100,000 and the *Irish Times* said that 35,000 had been present. The fourteen Westminster MPs undertook 'to resign our seats in the United Kingdom Parliament by January 1 1986 if the Anglo-Irish Agreement is ratified by Parliament'.[133] Ian Paisley led the addresses from the platform and finished with the following peroration: 'British we are. British we shall remain. Now Mrs Thatcher says that the Republic must have a say in our province, we say, never, never, never, never, never.'[134]

---

[130] *Times*, 21 November 1985.
[131] *Economist*, 23 November 1985.
[132] *Times*, 21 November 1985.
[133] *News Letter*, 25 November 1985.
[134] *Irish Times*, 25 November 1985.

The following day a *Sunday Times*/MORI poll[135] conducted in Northern Ireland gave an early indication of the local reaction to Hillsborough. It showed that 75 per cent of Protestant Unionists interviewed would vote 'No' if a referendum were held on the Anglo-Irish Agreement; 65 per cent of Roman Catholic Nationalists, on the other hand, would vote 'Yes'. Of the Protestants interviewed, 10 per cent supported unilateral independence; 15 per cent were prepared to take part in a rent or rate strike, and 27 per cent supported industrial action. John Hume's SDLP received a 7 per cent rise in support after Hillsborough, the DUP gained 3 per cent and the Alliance 2 per cent, while Sinn Fein lost 2 per cent and the Official Unionists 10 per cent.

The day before the Westminster debate on the Anglo-Irish Agreement, Prime Minister Thatcher met a delegation of seven Unionists, led by the speaker of the Northern Ireland Assembly, James Kilfedder. The *News Letter* headline, 'Premier digs in',[136] indicated that little progress was made at the meeting. John Cushnahan, the leader of the Alliance Party, also had a meeting with the prime minister; his main concern was the lack of a mechanism through which the majority community in Northern Ireland could make its views known.[137]

At the House of Commons Mrs Thatcher, having sketched in the background to the agreement and the historic divisions between the two communities in Northern Ireland, placed security at the top of her list of priorities, while seeking to reassure the Unionists that 'the agreement does not affect the status of Northern Ireland within the United Kingdom ... We, the United Kingdom Government, accountable to Parliament, remain responsible for the government of Northern Ireland ... If the Anglo-Irish Agreement is to bring about a real improvement in the daily lives of the two communities in Northern Ireland, it must be matched by a determined effort on the part of all law-abiding citizens to defeat the men of violence ... For if democracy is the rule of the majority, the other side of the coin is fairness and respect for the minority.'[138] Then, in a clear message for the Unionists, she concluded: 'We shall not give way to threats or to violence from any quarter.'[139] Neil Kinnock confirmed the bipartisan approach to the Anglo-Irish Agreement, but made a pointed appeal to the Unionists: 'The terrorists ... will rely on the sworn enemies in the Unionist groupings to erode and erase the Agreement ... the gunmen alone cannot make the Agreement fail.'[140]

---

135 *Sunday Times*, 24 November 1985.
136 *News Letter*, 26 November 1985.
137 *Times*, 26 November 1985.
138 *Hansard*, 26 November 1985, 750.
139 Ibid., 751.
140 Ibid., 753.

James Molyneaux's contribution concluded with the comment that 'in 40 years in public life I have never known what I can only describe as a universal cold fury, which some of us have thus so far managed to contain. I beg the Prime Minister not to misjudge the situation . . .'[141] In the House of Lords, Lord Fitt appealed to the Government not to shut out the Unionist community, while Lord Moyola, formerly the Northern Ireland Prime Minister James Chichester Clark, said that 'the people of the Province were facing a desperately serious situation which I believe could produce a holocaust'.[142]

The secretary of state for Northern Ireland, Tom King, opened the second-day debate by referring to the fears of the Unionists and appealing to them to 'give this agreement a chance . . . if it can be made to work, all the people of Northern Ireland will be the gainers, and only the terrorists will lose'.[143] Ian Paisley expressed clearly the Unionist attitude to the agreement: 'I will not talk in the terms of this agreement, for this agreement is treachery.'[144] Harold McCusker stated that 'the people of Northern Ireland . . . would prefer to be governed by a Catholic Nationalist in Northern Ireland than a Minister from the Irish Republic and who lives in Cork'.[145] Nicholas Scott, the under-secretary of state for Northern Ireland, closed the debate with an appeal to the SDLP 'to participate positively and directly in the political process in Northern Ireland'[146] and encouragement to the Unionists to accept that 'the agreement imposes no solutions but provides a framework and a practical working solution to relationships between the United Kingdom and the Republic of Ireland'.[147]

The Unionists stayed only long enough to cast their votes against the motion to approve the Anglo-Irish Agreement. There were 473 votes in favour and 47 against; it was the biggest majority in the Thatcher era. As *The Economist* noted, it united 'not just Mrs Thatcher and her entire front bench, but also rallies Mr Heath, Neil Kinnock, David Steel and Dr David Owen in her support'.[148]

On the following day, the Irish Senate approved the agreement by 37 votes to 16, and FitzGerald wrote that 'the agreement threatens the merchants of violence . . . Mrs Thatcher and I are both fully conscious of the risks of doing something to tackle violence at its political

---

[141] Ibid., 767.

[142] *News Letter*, 27 November 1985.

[143] *Hansard*, 27 November 1985, 890.

[144] Ibid., 910.

[145] Ibid., 917.

[146] Ibid., 968.

[147] Ibid., 969.

[148] *Economist*, 30 November 1985.

roots, but we are convinced that the riskiest path is to do nothing at all'.[149]

The Anglo-Irish Agreement came into force on Friday 29 November 1985, following the exchange of notifications of their acceptance by the two governments.

---

[149] *Times*, 28 November 1985.

2

The mini-election, the strike and the RUC

The Unionist members of parliament, having mustered only forty-seven votes against the agreement at Westminster, withdrew across the Irish sea to prepare for the by-elections scheduled for 23 January 1986. Enoch Powell, after some early reluctance, agreed to join the Unionist mass resignation. Powell was defending a slim majority of 458 in Down South. John Hume (SDLP) and Gerry Adams (Sinn Fein) let it be known that they did not intend to join the mass exodus and that there would be no Nationalist-Republican electoral pact. On the Unionist side there was a joint manifesto, and only one Unionist candidate stood in each of the fifteen vacant constituencies. If there were no anti-agreement candidates standing in any constituency, a dummy candidate would be offered, to be identified as Peter Barry (the Irish foreign minister).

The political agenda of the Anglo-Irish Agreement had already been set in the joint communiqué at Hillsborough; the Intergovernmental Conference would initially be concerned with 'relations between the security forces and the minority community in Northern Ireland; ways of enhancing security co-operation between the two Governments; seeking measures which would give substantial expression to the aim of underlining the importance of public confidence in the administration of justice'.[1]

On Monday 2 December 1985 Chief Constable Sir John Hermon of the RUC went to Dublin to meet Commissioner Wren of the Garda. The four-hour meeting was a signal not only that a three-year personal rift between the two was at an end, but that the two professionals were reacting positively to the agreement's top priority, cross-border co-operation against the terrorists.

---

[1] Joint Communiqué, Anglo-Irish Agreement, 15 November 1985, para. 7.

Commissioner Wren's Garda was directly responsible to the minister of justice; Hermon's RUC was accountable to the Northern Ireland Police Authority, not to a government minister. The RUC's role in the implementation of the Anglo-Irish Agreement became a major issue of confidence for the chief constable and his serving officers. Nicholas Scott had already met the Northern Ireland Police Federation on the day the agreement was ratified, in an attempt to allay their fears. Hermon issued a memorandum to all RUC members before he departed for Dublin, stating that he did not intend to surrender the principle that the force should be free from political interference and direction. 'It is a powerful guarantee against political policing, which would be contrary to the public good ... but ... we must embrace the necessity of full accountability for the way in which we discharge our duties.'[2] Hermon's struggle with the secretary of state, Tom King, and with his own police federation over the interpretation of Article 9 of the Anglo-Irish Agreement was to be a major issue over the next nine months. The chief constable had a very low opinion of politicians and a naturally high respect for his serving officers. He became obsessively protective of the force, its reputation and its practices.

Local politicians sought to exploit what they considered to be political directives to the RUC in the Hillsborough accord. Ian Paisley suggested on ITV's *Weekend World* on 8 December 1985 that certain members of the RUC might consider resigning rather than 'implement Dublin laws'.[3] The IRA also identified the RUC as the linchpin of the agreement. If they could break the primacy of the police force in security matters in the province, there would be mayhem; on the other hand, cross-border co-operation between the two police forces could spell trouble for the terrorists. Two RUC policemen were killed in Ballygawley and four others were injured after an IRA mortar attack on Tynan police station in County Armagh. By the end of 1985, the IRA had killed twenty-three members of the RUC.

Tom King's first trip abroad after the Anglo-Irish Agreement was to Brussels as head of an Industrial Development Board visit seeking European investment in Northern Ireland. During an after-dinner speech to industrialists, the secretary of state made the unguarded observation that FitzGerald, by signing the Hillsborough agreement, had accepted 'for all practical purposes and in perpetuity that there will never be a united Ireland'. FitzGerald, at an EC summit in Luxembourg, said that King's 'remarks were inaccurate and singularly inappropriate, and are in fact, as everybody knows, a complete

---

[2] *News Letter*, 3 December 1985.
[3] *Irish Times*, 9 December 1985.

distortion of my position'.[4] Thatcher, also in Luxembourg, when asked if it had been unwise of Mr King to use the word 'never', replied 'I am sorry if it came out that way'.[5] Charles Haughey, back in Dublin, said that the 'in perpetuity speech' gave 'expression to the fear that the whole purpose of the agreement from the British point of view, was to secure the full backing of the Irish Government for their security policies, and to legitimise the RUC, UDR, the courts, and various controversial practices'.[6] King hurried back to London and made a statement of regret in the House. Merlyn Rees advised him to abide by the old saying: 'Whatever you say, say nothing.'[7]

The Northern Ireland Assembly voted to suspend normal sittings, the members of the Alliance Party voting against, and set up a committee to examine 'the implications of the the Anglo-Irish deal for the government and future of Northern Ireland'. The committee met twelve times to hear evidence between 10 December 1985 and 9 January 1986, despite warnings from the government that it was endangering the long-term future of the assembly. Nicholas Scott estimated the annual cost of the assembly to be £2.5 million. A fund was launched to raise money 'to pay for public education and a counter-propaganda programme'.[8]

The first Intergovernmental Conference took place at Stormont Castle in Belfast on Wednesday 11 December 1985. The British delegation was led by Tom King and the Irish by Peter Barry. Stormont was under heavy guard. Unionist notices in the press had summoned protesters to come to Maryfield: 'The House of Treason, Home of Peter Barry. Be there today for a lunchtime protest.'[9] The *News Letter* itself carried the headline 'You're not welcome Mr Barry', and an illegal Loyalist radio station broadcast threats to East Belfast shopkeepers, urging them to close their shops as a mark of opposition during Barry's visit. Outside Stormont a banner said 'Northern Ireland Assembly says No', while a hydraulic lift held Ian Paisley aloft, side by side with the statue of Carson. At lunchtime, 5,000 workers from Harland and Wolff and from Short Brothers marched to Maryfield. By the end of the Intergovernmental Conference, thirty-eight police officers were reported injured.

Most of the working session under the joint chairmanship of King and Barry had been spent agreeing procedure, with Hermon and Wren reporting on their earlier meeting in Dublin. A new code of conduct for

---

[4] *Irish Times*, 5 December 1985.
[5] *Times*, 4 December 1985.
[6] *Irish Times*, 4 December 1985.
[7] *Times*, 5 December 1985.
[8] *News Letter*, 6 December 1985.
[9] *News Letter*, 11 December 1985.

the RUC was promised, and the Irish delegation reported that security on the south side of the border had been strengthened.

The European Parliament in Strasbourg supported the Anglo-Irish Agreement; the voting figures were 150 for and 28 against, with 11 abstentions. The House of Representatives voted to support the agreement with 'appropriate United States assistance, including economic and financial support to promote the economic and social development of distress areas in both parts of Ireland'.[10] There was also less encouraging news. Short Brothers, who employed 6,587 people in the province, were warned that, since Roman Catholic employees remained at between 14 and 17 per cent of the work-force, they risked losing their equal opportunities certificate and with it lucrative American contracts. The Northern Ireland Office announced that an additional £30 million was to be spent on law and order, as well as £50 million extra in 1986–7 for industrial development in Northern Ireland. To pay for this unbudgeted extra public spending, £44 million was to be withdrawn from the Northern Ireland Housing Executive budget, a cut of 13 per cent, resulting in an estimated 2,000 lost jobs.

Another crisis was unfolding in the High Court in Belfast. The Harry Kirkpatrick supergrass trial was entering its final week. It was a multiple prosecution of twenty-seven people based on the evidence of a criminal who gave evidence against former accomplices. Kirkpatrick, the supergrass, had pleaded guilty to seventy-seven charges, including five murders, arising from his days as second-in-command of the INLA Belfast Brigade. He turned Queen's evidence and the trial started in January 1985. It was to last 100 days and at its conclusion the judge, Mr Justice Carswell, determined 500 verdicts on over 150 charges, finding 26 guilty. Some of the guilty men had been in detention for four years. Lord Gifford QC commented that he was 'witnessing a masquerade of judicial proceedings, a form of trial which was more appropriate to a totalitarian state'.[11] Mr Justice Carswell defended the Diplock court system – under which a single judge sat without a jury – saying that 'there was no difference in the standard of proof required or the type of evidence admissible between jury and non-jury trials'.[12] Some of the men found guilty were sent to prison for a minimum of twenty-five years. Three went on hunger strike. Peter Barry requested a special meeting of the Intergovernmental Conference.

At Westminster, Sir Peter Emery moved a writ for the fifteen by-elections in Northern Ireland, with the claim that 'this qualifies for the

---

[10] *Times*, 14 December 1985.
[11] *New Statesman*, 3 January 1986.
[12] *Times*, 19 December 1985.

Guinness Book of Records'.[13] Earlier in the week, Neil Kinnock paid a day-long visit to the province and had a rough passage at Harland and Wolff. Margaret Thatcher chose the same week to give the *Belfast Telegraph* an exclusive interview on the Anglo-Irish Agreement. In the course of the article she admitted that the Unionist protest 'had been much worse than we expected'.[14] During the preceding week she had been heavily lobbied by religious leaders from the province. The home secretary, Douglas Hurd, appealed to the Unionists to abandon their parliamentary boycott: 'it is a negative and destructive device . . . Unionists should think twice before condemning an agreement which the IRA are so energetically seeking to destroy . . .'[15]

The Unionist pact was undergoing some slight twinges of strain; there were reports that a number of leading Official Unionists were unhappy with DUP-led protests. Frank Millar, the chief executive of the OUP, seemed to recognize the danger of allowing the anti-agreement campaign to drift. 'We have got to bring this province rapidly to a crisis . . . the longer it goes on, the more likely [the agreement] is to gain acquiescence.'[16]

In the Republic, the first political realignment since Hillsborough occurred. Former Fianna Fáil deputies Desmond O'Malley and Mary Harney formed the Progressive Democrats and launched a direct challenge to Charles Haughey's Northern policy and to the coalition government's economic measures.

The second Intergovernmental Conference was held in London on 30 December 1985 and was concerned primarily with the supergrass system and hunger strikes at the Maze prison. The conference communiqué stated that 'both sides agreed that the present hunger strike was to be deplored as a wrong and wasteful attempt to bring about change in this area'.[17] All the participants at the London conference were aware that the Republican movement in Northern Ireland might exploit the situation in the run-up to the by-elections. The Irish delegation was also alive to the danger of being too closely identified with the British stance on hunger strikes.

In Northern Ireland, the security services took into custody eighteen prominent Sinn Fein members, including Martin McGuinness and Seamus Cassidy. Five hundred and fifty extra troops from the 2nd Battalion, the Royal Anglian Regiment were sent to Northern Ireland to counter IRA activity in border areas. They arrived as figures were

---

[13] *Times*, 14 December 1985.
[14] *Belfast Telegraph*, 18 December 1985.
[15] *Irish Times*, 16 December 1985.
[16] *Times*, 27 December 1985.
[17] *News Letter*, 31 December 1985.

published showing that there had been a drop of 30 per cent in terrorist explosions and shootings in 1985, with ten fewer deaths than in 1984. The fifty-four fatalities included twenty-three RUC officers, the worst figure since 1976. Two further officers were killed in the early hours of 1986; Constable James McCandlass and Reserve Constable Michael Williams died as a result of an IRA bomb in Armagh City. The IRA in a statement said that they 'chose what was considered a safe area for the enemy ... to demonstrate our capacity to strike whenever and wherever we so decide'.[18] Peter Barry condemned the murders as 'calculated, vicious, evil and obscene'.[19] Sir Myles Humphreys, chairman of the Northern Ireland Police Authority, urged all constitutional political leaders to give their full support to the RUC.

Loyalist paramilitaries reported a threefold increase in applications to join the UDA since Hillsborough, and Conor Cruise O'Brien warned that the accord had the capacity to 'stir up ... what used to be called extreme unionism and is now beginning to be called Ulster nationalism'.[20]

Councils were continuing their adjournment policy for the third month running. A banner was erected on Belfast City Hall that read 'Belfast Says No'. A hundred-strong core of Unionist marchers started a trek from Derry to Maryfield in Belfast. They were joined at various stages during the five-day march by all fifteen Unionist candidates at the forthcoming by-elections. The leaders of the Ulster Defence Association, Andy Tyrie and John McMichael, limped their way through the whole trek. It finished outside the headquarters of the conference secretariat, which was closely guarded by the RUC. James Molyneaux's speech was drowned out by shouts of 'SS RUC' and 'RUC scum'.[21] Paisley was absent from the meeting, which was attended by his deputy, Peter Robinson, Harold McCusker and Hazel Bradford, chairperson of the Official Unionists. They had to make a rapid exit from the platform when the police began to retaliate after attacks lasting more than twenty minutes. Two police cars were overturned and one set alight, twenty-three police-officers were injured, and a BBC camera was smashed in the subsequent riot. The *News Letter* appealed for discipline: 'the agreement has placed RUC officers in [a] difficult position ... attacks on the RUC cannot be condoned.'[22] Molyneaux released a press statement which said 'there can be no justification for violence ... I and my party condemn it

---

[18] *News Letter*, 2 January 1986.
[19] *Irish Times*, 31 December 1985.
[20] Ibid.
[21] *Sunday Times*, 5 January 1986.
[22] *News Letter*, 6 January 1986.

unreservedly'.[23] Robinson said: 'I do not justify it but I do understand their sense of anger.'[24] The *Sunday Times* underlined the worsening situation: 'it has not been realised yet, that it is now at its most dangerous point since the time, more than sixty years ago, when partition led to civil war.'[25] Paisley, in an election speech at Carrickfergus, said that 'Unionists must not allow themselves to turn against the RUC as a force because it is at present being manipulated by the Government . . . many members of the force did not agree with what they were being instructed to do . . .'[26] Unionists were not pleased by a speech by Bishop Cahal Daly: 'policies presently being adopted and planned by the Unionist political leaders . . . may be . . . a recipe for disaster and anarchy – a peculiar form of borrowing by Unionists from the stated aims of Republicanism.'[27] Bishop Daly also called for an urgent and radical review of the supergrass trials. This topic was the first discussed at the third Intergovernmental Conference held at Lancaster House in London on 10 January 1986. It was announced the same day that the hearing of supergrass-trial appeals would be brought forward. Four were outstanding; Lord Justice Lowry promised they would all be heard by a three-judge appeal court within six months. The communiqué from the Lancaster House Conference stated that the attorney-generals of Ireland and the United Kingdom would meet to discuss the administration of justice, in particular the use of uncorroborated evidence from informers and the working of the Diplock courts. Tom King also emphasized the need for an early review of extradition in the Republic.

In Northern Ireland the nominations for the by-elections closed. Forty-one candidates offered themselves for election; fifteen Unionists, five Alliance, four SDLP, four Sinn Fein, nine Workers' Party and four Peter Barry dummy candidates. The Unionists published a joint manifesto called *Solidarity*. It invited the electors of Northern Ireland to 'deny the Government the moral authority to implement this agreement. If their verdict is ignored we have undertaken to lead a continuing campaign of opposition embracing every form of legitimate political protest.'[28] Tom King commented: 'just to say "Ulster says No" is not good enough. Ulster can't just say no. Ulster must say "Yes" to something.'[29] He wrote to all political leaders in the province inviting them to give their views on the future for the province.

---

[23] *News Letter*, 7 January 1986.
[24] *News Letter*, 8 January 1986.
[25] *Sunday Times*, 12 January 1986.
[26] *News Letter*, 11 January 1986.
[27] *Irish Times*, 3 January 1986.
[28] Joint Unionist Manifesto, *Solidarity*, 1986.
[29] *News Letter*, 15 January 1986.

The SDLP, having rejected a Sinn Fein proposal for an electoral pact, concentrated on two constituencies, those of Enoch Powell and Jim Nicholson. Sinn Fein stood for a rejection of the Unionist veto, disbandment of the RUC and the UDR, the release of all political prisoners and an end to partition. John Hume had meanwhile succeeded in persuading the three hunger-strikers at the Maze to give up their fast and go to appeal on the Kirkpatrick trial verdict.

A Coopers and Lybrand poll of 2,000 electors revealed that 73.6 per cent thought it unlikely that Mrs Thatcher would change her mind over the Anglo-Irish Agreement, with 80 per cent of those questioned opposed to violent action as a means of protest. Sixty-nine per cent agreed in principle with power-sharing. A BBC poll revealed that 90 per cent of Loyalists were opposed to the pact.

During the run-up to the election the government announced a 12.5 per cent increase in public spending for the province over the next three years, with the figures for 1986–7 (£4.52 million) representing an increase of £250 million on previous estimates. A £65 million order was placed at Short Brothers for Ministry of Defence missiles.

In Amsterdam, Brendan McFarlane, Gerard Kelly and Anthony Kelly were arrested after an arms cache was found in a container. The three arrested Ulstermen had all escaped from the Maze prison in 1983. Their capture – with that of fourteen semi-automatic rifles, two hand-grenades, seventy-five rounds of ammunition and four drums of nitrobenzine – was to give added force to the extradition question. Britain was already reviewing its extradition laws to prevent the United Kingdom being used as a haven by international criminals. A White Paper recommended the ending of the rule that a prima-facie case must be established before a British court ordered extradition. The Anglo-Irish Agreement committed the Irish Republic to sign the European Convention on the Suppression of Terrorism, which would make the extradition of terrorists easier north and south of the border. Shortly before Christmas James Shannon, accused of murdering former Stormont speaker Sir Norman Strange and his son, and Dominic McGlinchey were released by Belfast courts after being extradited from the South. A mistake by the RUC allowed Brendan Burns, wanted for questioning about the murder of five British soldiers in 1981, to walk from a Dublin court after he had been detained on warrants issued by the RUC; Lord Chief Justice Lowry quashed fifteen warrants requesting his extradition. It was this issue that preoccupied the British partners at the Intergovernmental Conference. The Irish were concentrating on stopping supergrass trials and ending the Diplock courts.

In West Belfast an IRA sniper shot a British soldier and a car bomb killed part-time UDR soldier Victor Foster. The terrorists were exerting maximum pressure on the Unionist politicians in the run-up to the by-election. There was confusion among Unionists and their supporters. Brian Inglis claimed in the *Spectator* that 'Unionism is a sham, a figleaf to disguise what is in reality Orange nationalism . . .'[30] Martin Harris in *New Society* quoted the words of Captain Bob Mitchell of the Ulster Light Horse: 'Behind every Unionist politician brave or foolish enough to tamper with the *status quo* is always the voice of tradition, not-an-inch loyalism, ready to tear him down for treachery. Reform is constantly outflanked by reaction.'[31] The historian A. T. Q. Stewart claimed that 'the Foreign Office, an organization more sinister than the IRA, has created a device so ingenious that wherever the Protestants touch it, it will blow up in their faces . . .'[32] Conor Cruise O'Brien said that the Unionists 'are being disarmed in the presence of, and at the behest, of their hereditary foes.'[33] Norman Gibson stated that 'loyalism is conditional, what ultimately matters is the Ulster Protestant identity, in the end the union is expendable'.[34]

The mini-election drew a turn-out of 62.2 per cent. Seamus Mallon beat Jim Nicholson in Newry and Armagh, but Enoch Powell survived to fight another election in Down South. The Unionist electoral pact won 71 per cent of the poll, with 418,230 votes. The SDLP won 70,917 votes, up 11 per cent on the 1983 general election, while Sinn Fein polled 38,821, a drop of 12 per cent over the same period. The SDLP's share of the Nationalist vote was 64.6 per cent (up 7.2 per cent), with Sinn Fein down to 35.4 per cent. If the mini-election is taken as a referendum on the Anglo-Irish Agreement, 47.9 per cent of the electorate voted against the agreement, with 13 per cent in favour.

Tom King followed the mini-election with an appeal to the SDLP to 'become involved in constitutional politics in a much more effective way . . .'[35] Sinn Fein excused its disappointing vote by saying that its supporters did not see the election as vital; they had only fought it because the SDLP refused a pact. The prime minister let it be known that she was prepared to meet the Unionists on their return to Westminister, but the Ulster Clubs called on the newly-elected Unionist members of parliament to 'come home to spearhead a campaign of non-co-operation and civil disobedience'.[36] Paisley reacted angrily to a television declaration by Nicholas Scott that the agreement would

[30] *Spectator*, 4 January 1986.
[31] *New Society*, 17 January 1986.
[32] *Spectator*, 11 January 1986.
[33] Conor Cruise O'Brien, *Passion and Cunning and Other Essays* (Weidenfeld and Nicolson, 1988), 208.
[34] *Fortnight*, No. 232, January 1986, 4.
[35] *News Letter*, 25 January 1986.
[36] *Irish Times*, 25 January 1986.

remain: 'his act today is to say the ballot box ... doesn't matter ... he is inciting Protestants ... to turn from the democratic process to violence.'[37]

The fourteen re-elected Unionist members of parliament and the one new face – Seamus Mallon of the SDLP – took their oaths in a strangely troubled House of Commons. The government was in difficulty; Michael Heseltine had resigned over the Westland controversy and Leon Brittan's resignation came on the day following the Northern Ireland by-elections. The ensuing cabinet reshuffle brought an Ulsterman, Dr Brian Mawhinney, MP for Peterborough, to the Northern Ireland Office as under-secretary of state. This was seen by some as an attempt by the prime minister to placate the Unionists, since Mawhinney's local roots meant he had a deeper insight into and possibly a better understanding of the Unionist cause.

FitzGerald, Thatcher's partner at Hillsborough, had his own difficulties. The coalition's budget heralded a year of austerity, with VAT up to 22 per cent, inflation expected to run at 4.5 per cent and a budget deficit of 7.4 per cent of GNP. In addition the newly formed Progressive Democrats, although a breakaway faction of the Fianna Fáil opposition, were actually winning supporters from FitzGerald's Fine Gael camp. FitzGerald's response was to reshuffle his cabinet.

When the two premiers met in mid February 1986, both were badly bruised from their respective political maulings. In addition to the conflict over the Hillsborough Accord, another issue was to bedevil their relationship: Sellafield. After the second leak in a fortnight, FitzGerald called for an independent European inspectorate and Haughey demanded that the plant be closed. The House of Commons Select Committee on the Environment called for more stringent safety controls at Sellafield. *The Times* called the Irish Sea 'the most radioactive sea in the world'.[38] Thatcher, in her response to FitzGerald's suggestions, stated that the 'leaks had been relatively minor events ... exaggerated by the media'.[39]

The Irish government's major contribution to the Anglo-Irish discussions was their signing of the European Convention on the Suppression of Terrorism and their commitment to introduce new extradition laws at the earliest possible time. This was a significant step forward in the fight against terrorism, and a development which the Northern Ireland Office hoped would encourage the Unionists to accept an invitation to meet the prime minister; here was proof of the reciprocal aspect of the agreement. Tom King appealed to the SDLP to

---

[37] Ibid.
[38] *Times*, 20 February 1986.
[39] Ibid.

join in a round-table conference on devolution, stressing to the Unionists that John Hume did not have a double veto over political developments in the province. Ian Paisley and James Molyneaux agreed to meet the prime minister on Tuesday 25 February 1986.

Preparations for the Downing Street meeting operated at various levels across the Unionist party divide. A number of politicians discussed various options which included UDI, tripartite talks between Britain, Ireland and Ulster and a round-table conference of all constitutional political parties in the province. The bottom line was a clear indication from the prime minister that she was prepared to reconsider the Anglo-Irish Agreement. Here again there were various options, ranging from a total abandonment of the agreement to its temporary suspension or, most novel of all at this stage, the recognition that the agreement had to stay, but that an alternative agreement could be considered, running in parallel, but outside the sphere of influence of the Anglo-Irish Agreement.

The Unionists met at a North Antrim hotel on 6 and 7 February 1986 to plan their strategy. Molyneaux envisaged 'a series of meetings with the prime minister'.[40] Robinson saw the Downing Street summit as a make-or-break session: 'Mrs Thatcher will either dump [the agreement] or press the button for the most major political crisis that this province has seen ...' [41] At the Northern Ireland Assembly's special two-day debate on the agreement, Paisley hinted at the existence of a reserve plan. Calling on the prime minister to provide an alternative to Hillsborough, he said that 'Unionists would be prepared not to escalate their protest'.[42]

The United Ulster Loyalist Front (UULF), a Unionist umbrella organization that co-ordinated various anti-agreement activities, included representatives of the two political parties, the Ulster Clubs, the Orange Order and the Ulster Defence Association. The Ulster Clubs' spokesman, Alan Wright, spoke of instigating a campaign of civil disobedience. Andy Tyrie, the UDA's head of operations, launched a province-wide recruiting drive with the rallying cry: 'Ulster is fighting for its existence. Come forward now and be trained to do your share. Every fit man owes his duty to himself and to his country.'[43] The RUC, according to *Fortnight*, believed that the UDA was 'contemplating ambitious and large-scale paramilitary action against the Anglo-Irish Agreement ... a new and more violent

---

[40] *Irish Times*, 3 February 1986.
[41] *News Letter*, 5 February 1986.
[42] *Irish Times*, 6 February 1986.
[43] *Irish Times*, 27 January 1986.

strategy'.[44] Tyrie and his deputy, John McMichael, had access to the illegal Ulster Freedom Fighters and Ulster Volunteer Force. *Ulster*, the UDA magazine, put further pressure on the politicians by claiming that men like 'Molyneaux, [John] Taylor and Paisley are merely stalling in order to try to think of some "nice" tactics to employ in order to avoid using nasty unconstitutional methods which will confront our enemies on our ground in the way they fear and we understand'.[45]

The UDA, like the Official Unionists and the Democratic Unionists, was represented on the 1986 Workers' Committee, a planning group of twelve shop stewards under the chairmanship of Frank Leslie of Northern Ireland Electricity. They planned a doomsday strategy; if the Downing Street meeting failed, there would be a plan in place for a province-wide response – a strike. They divided the province into seventeen regions based on the parliamentary constituency boundaries. The local member of parliament was the convening officer, supported by the local Northern Ireland assemblyman, many councillors and other interested organizations. This last group included the Orange Order. Co-ordinating the strike was to be a local responsibility, but its running and planning was in the hands of Leslie and his colleagues. The maximum pressure was exerted on the government, and on the Unionist politicians.

The latter were also under pressure from county representatives in the province. Many of the Unionist councillors felt that they were bearing the brunt of the attacks on the Anglo-Irish Agreement, while the assembly was still active and Unionist members of parliament were drawing their Westminster salaries. Hazel Bradford, chairperson of the Official Unionists, put it bluntly: 'they would like some reassurance that they are not simply cannon fodder and that their action will not be in vain.'[46] Councillors were obviously worried at the increasing evidence of extra-parliamentary activity, and by the fear that Molyneaux and McCusker were being outwitted and outmanoeuvered by Paisley and Robinson. In addition, their best-laid plans were short-circuited by the government when commissioners were appointed to administer the rate. They were also being threatened by the High Court; Lord Justice Lowry ruled on appeal that Belfast Unionist councillors were 'unlawful' in not setting a rate. A week earlier, Mr Justice Hutton had ruled that they were 'abusing their power' during the four-month adjournment protest. They were also ordered to take the 'Ulster Says No' banner down from the City Hall. A deadline of 26 February 1986 was set – the day after the Downing Street meeting.

[44] *Fortnight*, No. 230, December 1985.
[45] *Fortnight*, No. 236, March 1986.
[46] *News Letter*, 14 February 1986.

Seamus Mallon's maiden speech in the House of Commons appealed directly to the Unionists to 'come and build with us, say "yes"'.[47] He was also responding to increased pressure from Prime Ministers Thatcher and FitzGerald, who had met the previous day to discuss the pending Downing Street meeting with the Unionists. Both leaders agreed that John Hume's reluctance to involve himself and his party in political developments in the province was a major obstacle. The following day Hume said he was willing without 'preconditions to talk to Unionists',[48] but within the safety net of the Anglo-Irish Agreement. The Northern Ireland Office was also increasingly worried about the lack of clear SDLP support for the RUC.

The strains and tensions within the RUC surfaced in January 1986 in an article by Alan Wright, chairman of the Northern Ireland branch of the Police Federation. 'The role of the police', Wright argued, 'is to maintain law and order among the civilian population... the last thing we want is a military style police force ...'[49] The policy of Ulsterization, the primacy of the police over the military, had been established in 1977. It meant that the RUC was at the sharp end of the fight against terrorism in the province. Wright's article was a direct challenge to that policy: 'the primacy of the police is one thing ... guarding the borders of our state ... is an army job ... it is the job of the military to seek out and destroy the enemy and to provide a secure environment for the operation of the traditional law enforcement agency.'[50] The seething disquiet in the force surfaced in an edition of *Out of Court* on BBC 2, which featured actors playing the parts of five RUC officers. They spoke of their fears: 'we are caught in the middle of being seen to try and impose an agreement which the large majority of people here don't want ... no police force in the world can stop that type of demonstration. Sheer weight of opposition would make policing very difficult, if not impossible.'[51] The pressure was apparent, not only in the list of police casualties – one hundred officers off work with injuries since Hillsborough – but in the higher-than-average number of applications from police-officers for jobs outside the force. A post of chief security officer for the Northern Ireland electricity service attracted forty-two applicants from the RUC, mostly middle and senior officers. *Spotlight*, the BBC Northern Ireland current affairs programme, highlighted the existence of an overstretched occupational health unit in the RUC which was dealing with an increasing number

---

[47] *Irish Times*, 21 February 1986.
[48] Ibid.
[49] *News Letter*, 25 January 1986.
[50] *Irish Times*, 5 February 1986.
[51] *Irish Times*, 20 February 1986.

of police suicides. Fifteen police-officers committed suicide in three years between 1983 and 1986, an average of five a year; they were mostly young, the average age being twenty-four. In the fifteen years after 1969, the average suicide rate in the force was one a year. Not surprisingly, the RUC refused to take part in the programme, arguing that the force was 'concerned that personal information, apparently obtained through police officers' confidential relationships with outside agents, was used as a basis for public comment'.[52] *The Times*, while recognizing the stressful nature of their work, warned the RUC of the implications of their internal divisions: 'if the RUC wishes to continue to call itself Royal, it had better be ready itself to enforce the laws of Her Majesty's government.'[53]

Signs that the government was alive to the dangers of an unstable RUC surfaced with a leak in *The Times* that the Ministry of Defence was considering sending an additional battalion of 550 men to Ulster. This extra manpower would bring troop numbers in the province to 10,200; numbers had already increased by 550 since Hillsborough, with the arrival of the Royal Anglian Regiment early in the New Year.

The IRA continued its campaign against the RUC; Constable Derek Breen was murdered at Maguiresbridge, together with a barman. Private John Early, a Roman Catholic UDR soldier, was killed at Belcoe in County Fermanagh in early February 1986. However, the arrest of five men in Roscommon and Sligo during late January 1986 and the discovery of 130 guns and thousands of rounds of ammunition, gave the security services on both sides of the border a much needed fillip. It was also the first positive confirmation of Libya's involvement with the IRA; the guns found were wrapped in Libyan army covers. The discovery of the cache was to have a significant impact on Irish public opinion. The rumour of a Gaddafi–IRA link was now fact. The guns may have been destined for Northern Ireland, but they had been hidden in the Republic. How many more of these secret arsenals were there in Ireland? Might they not be used against the Republic if the problems of the North spilled over into the South?

Preparations for the Downing Street meeting between Thatcher and Molyneaux and Paisley were accompanied by the placing of political markers by all concerned. King, the secretary of state, appealed to the Unionists to drop their anti-agreement stance and accept the offer of an alternative, parallel relationship with the government, outside the Anglo-Irish structure. Molyneaux promised that the Unionists would present the prime minister with an alternative plan for devolved government, but warned: 'if we are given the brush off, then to a large extent [we] would be seen in the Province as extinct volcanoes . . .

---

[52] *News Letter*, 21 February 1986.
[53] *Times*, 21 February 1986.

should Mrs Thatcher press the red button ... it would be the signal for certain factions to use methods which the politicians themselves would be powerless to prevent.'[54] This threat was given force by the decision of sixty cross-channel dockers at Larne harbour to vote for a one-day strike on Monday 3 March 1936, if the prime minister did not give a favourable response. The Ulster Clubs' leader, Wright, let it slip that a secret plan existed for a province-wide, one-day, all-out strike.

According to the local press, the strike committee's plan envisaged the closure of Aldergrove airport, Belfast Harbour airport and Larne harbour, and the stoppage of railways, buses, motorways, factories, shops, schools and filling-stations. There would be a reduction in electricity between 07.00 hours and 19.00 hours; government and local government buildings would be closed, and so would pubs. Agricultural machinery was to be deployed as barricades on the roads.

As Molyneaux and Paisley left for London, Peter Barry accused the Unionist leadership of deploying the 'big lie' to oppose the pact and to mislead a confused and frightened people. Leader writers in London and Belfast suggested that the government was likely to offer the two Unionist leaders a 'parallel structure', plus a Westminster Grand Committee, and an end to government by Orders in Council. Molyneaux, on arriving at Heathrow, added that the Unionist leaders would ask the prime minister to suspend the Anglo-Irish Agreement for three months.

The Unionist alternative, presented to the prime minister and Tom King on 25 February 1986, suggested devolution through a committee system, with seats assigned in proportion to party strengths. The local parliament would retain power in areas such as education, health, agriculture and social security, but it would have no legislative functions and there would be no power-sharing executive. The Unionist leaders also signalled their willingness to discuss the creation of an all-Ireland discussion council. This latter idea was being considered seriously in Dublin and London. The main thrust of the proposals reflected the split in the Unionist pact. The submitted plan bore the unmistakable imprint of the integrationist policies of Molyneaux and Enoch Powell. They wanted a closer relationship with Westminster, not a strong, devolved regional assembly. Paisley doubted if any devolved government was worth the candle if it had no responsibility for security. He, and his nearest political colleagues, also felt that they had the support of the electorate in the province for a wide-ranging protest. The government was on the run, the two prime ministers who had signed the Hillsborough accord were in a considerably weakened position, and he had everything to gain by not being sucked into talks about talks. He planned a speedy resolution to the crisis.

---

[54] *News Letter*, 24 February 1986.

At the Downing Street meeting, Mrs Thatcher agreed to consider the Unionist devolution proposals and suggested a further meeting within three weeks. She stressed the point that when devolution was agreed, all devolved powers would automatically be taken out of the London–Dublin sphere of influence. Mrs Thatcher also agreed to consider a round-table conference in Northern Ireland to discuss further devolution. The future of the Northern Ireland Assembly and the arrangements for handling Northern Ireland business in the House of Commons were also discussed. The secretary of state optimistically commented that 'suddenly there is the opportunity to look afresh at the range of different possibilities and opportunities'.[55] The government let it be known that the prime minister was to meet John Hume, Robert Eames, the new Church of Ireland archbishop, John Cushnahan and James Kilfedder, the Northern Ireland Assembly speaker, over the next couple of days. Molyneaux and Paisley flew back to Belfast. They reported to the strike committee, not to their political associations or their Westminster colleagues. They were heard in silence. The committee decided that what was on offer from the government was not enough to stop the momentum of the strike planned for Monday 3 March 1986.

The committee's decision, and the press statement of Molyneaux and Paisley that 'we now proceed to discharge our election mandate and withdraw the consent of the people of Northern Ireland from this Government',[56] was a shock to observers and, indeed, to the participants in the previous day's negotiations at Downing Street. Something had obviously gone seriously awry between the departure of the Unionist leaders from Downing Street, and their tired, unhappy demeanour twelve hours later in Belfast. According to Paisley, the prime minister had failed to meet the two basic Unionist conditions for further discussions: 'removal of the secretariat from Maryfield and no meetings of the intergovernmental conference during the devolution talks'.[57] Tom King and government briefings from London prior to the Downing Street meeting had both stressed the continuation of the Anglo-Irish structures. This had been known to the Unionist leaders when they accepted the invitation to meet the prime minister. Both leaders gave Mrs Thatcher the firm impression that a parallel alternative set of discussions was acceptable, without the prior abandonment of the Anglo-Irish Agreement. The strike committee soon changed that.

The strike plan was in place before the two Unionist leaders left for London. The Loyalist trade union leaders, the paramilitary

---

[55] *Times*, 26 February 1986.
[56] *News Letter*, 26 February 1986.
[57] *News Letter*, 27 February 1986.

representatives of the Ulster Clubs and the Ulster Defence Association were eager to test the depth and strength of opposition to Hillsborough. So was Peter Robinson, deputy leader of the DUP. Once he rejected the Paisley–Molyneaux report on the Downing Street meeting, the strike was on.

Press advertisements labelled 'A Call to Action' appeared in the local press, along with reports that the Unionist think-tank had actually rejected the prime minister's proposals. The names of Molyneaux and Paisley appeared on the advertisement, with Molyneaux stressing that 'there must be no violence in the course of this operation',[58] and Paisley adding that the strike 'must be a passive and voluntary demonstration'.[59] In the House of Commons, the prime minister stated that the strike would not deflect the government 'from its determination to implement the Anglo-Irish Agreement'.[60] The *News Letter* warned that 'the price paid for destroying the Pact should not be so high as to render impossible the work of rebuilding Ulster'.[61] *The Times* came to the defence of the government, encouraging it to 'face down a challenge to its authority ... Unionists are now embarking on the one course which is bound to weaken the Union ...'[62]

In the midst of reports of intimidation of shop-keepers, factory-owners and civil servants, the launch of Radio Free Ulster, a pirate radio service on FM 101, and the cancelling of all police leave, members of parliament like Merlyn Rees and Jeremy Hayes prophesised the end of the union between Great Britain and Northern Ireland. The Orange Order called on its 100,000 members to support the strike, while Short Brothers let it be known to all its employees that the works would remain open on Monday 3 March 1986. The twelve-hour strike was extended to twenty-four hours by the strike committee. Paisley heard about the change over the radio. Molyneaux cobbled together an eleventh-hour set of proposals, in a vain attempt to wrest the initiative back from the trade unionists and paramilitaries. He called for a temporary suspension of the agreement to allow talks to get under way. It was obvious that Molyneaux, like Paisley, had been 'running to keep up with the pace of events in Ulster'.[63]

Frank Millar, chief executive of the Official Unionists, added that he was prepared to talk to the prime minister without a commitment to suspend the Anglo-Irish Agreement, so long as 'she showed a

---

[58] *News Letter*, 28 February 1986.
[59] Ibid.
[60] *News Letter*, 27 February 1986.
[61] Ibid.
[62] *Times*, 27 February 1986.
[63] *Sunday Times*, 2 March 1986.

willingness to do so'.[64] This distanced the Official from the Democratic Unionists, and indicated the OUP's lack of enthusiasm for the strike. Molyneaux and Millar were worried by the course of events and by the high profile of Paisley and Robinson.

The Northern Ireland Institute of Directors advised their members not to join the strike, and the Northern Ireland Office confirmed that civil servants were expected to turn up for work. Chairman Brendan Harkin of the Northern Ireland Regional Committee of Industry said: 'at a time when our industrial base is rapidly diminishing and unemployment continues to rise, the last thing Northern Ireland needs is any action which will undermine the efforts being made to strengthen and develop our industrial base.'[65] Schools and colleges opted to regard the strike day as one of their optional days off, while factories rescheduled their shifts to accommodate the missing hours of the strike on late-night or weekend rotas.

The prime minister, in a letter to Archbishop Eames, aired her fears that 'the strike will lead to an erosion of support for the Union in the United Kingdom'.[66] Tom King, speaking on Radio Ulster, said: 'a lot of people are asking ... where on earth Unionist leaders are actually taking people at present'.[67] The inescapable conclusion was that the Unionists had, on Tuesday 25 February 1986, 'rejected too much too soon';[68] they had to contend with Mrs Thatcher and she had called their bluff. As *The Economist* commented: 'Mr Paisley and Mr Molyneaux ... now seem like moderates by contrast.'[69]

The strike started at midnight with pickets at Harland and Wolff. During the ensuing twenty-four hours 47 policemen were hurt, 57 arrests were made and 184 names were taken for possible future charges; 665 roadblocks were erected, of which 441 were cleared; 65 plastic baton rounds were fired; an unknown number of petrol bombs and 20 shots were fired at the RUC. Both airports were closed, sailings between Larne and Stranraer were cancelled, no trains ran, there were no bus services, country lanes were blocked by trees and the motorways closed by slow-moving convoys of farm machinery, some spreading slurry, others depositing nails and bolts on the tarmac. Radio Free Ulster kept up a service of strike news, summoning protestors to key locations for a pre-arranged rally or picket line.

Most of the shops in Belfast city centre inside the security barriers remained open but the number of customers was only a fraction of

---

[64] *News Letter*, 1 March 1986.
[65] Ibid.
[66] *Irish Times*, 1 March 1986.
[67] Ibid.
[68] *Times*, 3 March 1986.
[69] *Economist*, 1 March 1986.

normal trade. An estimated 4,000 strikers turned up at the City Hall for a rally to hear Peter Robinson, 'theatrically sombre in black tie and black cashmere overcoat, with a pile of empty coffins in front of him, compare Mrs Thatcher to President Marcos and Judas Iscariot, accepting the bribes of American silver to push a United Ireland into NATO'.[70] At Stormont, Fionnuala O'Connor noticed that people were allowed through road-blocks by showing passes with the red cross of St Patrick and the red hand of Ulster in the middle, signed by Peter Robinson.[71] The CBI reported that 'there was no production worth talking about in any of the big companies'.[72] At Short Brothers, only 14 per cent of the workforce showed up and machines closed down at lunch-time. Gallaghers had only sixty working on the shop-floor and their competitors, Rothmans, reported a 10 per cent attendance. Between 10 and 15 per cent, mostly white-collar workers, turned up at Harland and Wolff. The Saracens factory at Lurgan tried to stay open all day, but after a siege by 400 protesters the RUC escorted the work-force from the plant, firing plastic bullets to rescue an RUC crew trapped in their vehicle by the strikers. Shortly afterwards the factory was burned to the ground. The Belfast Chamber of Trade called the day of action a 'disaster day', while CBI chairman Tom Rainey reported the cancellation of a £38,000 order by an American company. A riot broke out in Belfast city centre after the Robinson rally; a Chinese take-away business was wrecked and a number of cars set alight. Once darkness came there were three separate attacks on police stations, and in Lurgan two police families were driven from their homes by rampaging Loyalist mobs.

Throughout the day, reports of police inactivity in the face of Loyalist harassment and intimidation kept circulating in media circles. By the day's end, there were 132 complaints against the RUC. Paul Valley reported: 'policemen sat in their squad cars and did nothing as convoys made up of dozens of tractors drove by.'[73] Sir John Hermon appeared on local television to explain that the RUC had kept the roads open on Sunday, 'removing literally hundreds of road blocks . . . at 7.00 a.m. on Monday the situation was stable. But from that time until ten or eleven o'clock there were literally thousands of protesters who came out . . . the police were not always in strength to deal with the particular situations.'[74] The conduct of the RUC during the strike set alarm bells ringing at Stormont, in Whitehall, in Dublin and at the headquarters of the UDA in East Belfast. If the RUC could not be relied upon to police

---

[70] *New Society*, 7 March 1986.
[71] *New Statesman*, 7 March 1986.
[72] *News Letter*, 4 March 1986.
[73] *Times*, 4 March 1986.
[74] *Irish Times*, 4 March 1986.

the province, what hope was there? The chief constable announced an urgent review of police operational tactics, and it was announced that disciplinary procedures would be taken against members of the RUC who manned barricades while off duty on the day of the strike. The Northern Ireland Police Authority gave its backing to the RUC, though recognizing that 'some errors in both deposition and judgement were made in the course of the day'.[75]

Molyneaux and McCusker said their party wanted nothing more to do with future days of action, and in a joint statement Molyneaux and Paisley said that 'looting, shooting, violence and intimidation are not acts of loyalty'.[76] Archbishop Eames and three of his bishops appealed to Unionist politicians 'to take a hard look at the price the whole community will pay for failure to honestly talk together about the future of Northern Ireland'.[77] Ken Maginnis, however, claimed that 'it was a successful day from our point of view ...'[78] and John Taylor commented 'should London not understand this message, then the next target of the Ulster majority must be Dublin'.[79] John McMichael threatened in the same newspaper: 'if Mrs Thatcher didn't listen, the next stage could be a campaign of civil disobedience.'[80] James Prior added the comment that it looked to him as if the political duo of Molyneaux and Paisley was in trouble. Other commentators saw hope in the collapse of the Unionist leadership: 'they must be the first boxers to win the first round and then decide to throw in the towel ... if they couldn't swallow a one-day strike and its side effects, they could certainly choke on the action needed to beat Mrs Thatcher.'[81]

The one-day strike was the first serious challenge to the Anglo-Irish Agreement. It succeeded in that it had an unsettling effect on the community; the Unionist politicians lost control of the strike and the paramilitaries gained ground. The security services took a hammering; the passive nature of RUC policing, however, disguised a major struggle both inside the force and between the chief constable and the Intergovernmental Conference. For once, local politicians and paramilitary leaders were a step ahead of most commentators and of the Dublin and London politicians in understanding the potential effect of this schism in the fight against the Anglo-Irish Agreement.

RUC primacy over the army authorities in the conflict in Northern Ireland went back to 1976. It was then that the 'Ulsterization' policy

---

[75] *Times*, 5 March 1986.
[76] *Irish Times*, 5 March 1986.
[77] Ibid.
[78] Ibid.
[79] *News Letter*, 4 March 1986.
[80] Ibid.
[81] *Fortnight*, No. 236, March 1986.

was clearly established. The regular British army and the locally recruited Ulster Defence Regiment were to function as back-up to the Royal Ulster Constabulary. The chief constable's operational independence of any political interference was regularly asserted and was actually guaranteed in Article 9(b) of the Anglo-Irish Agreement; there were nevertheless attempts to influence him. Hermon was acutely aware of the need to demonstrate his independence of action, not only to his fellow officers, but also to the two cultural communities in the province. He, more than anybody else, was alive to the political difficulties likely to arise from the inquiry by John Stalker, the deputy chief constable of Manchester, into the shooting of five unarmed civilians by RUC officers in 1982. Hermon alone received Stalker's first draft report; he sat on the recommendations for four months before passing the report to the province's director of public prosecutions on 13 February 1986. Sir John knew the likely timetable of events once the DPP had considered Stalker's report on a suspected cover-up of allegations of a 'shoot to kill' policy in 1982. It was all likely to come to a head in the summer, in the middle of the marching season.

Hermon held most politicians, local and national, in low esteem, blaming them for the crisis in Northern Ireland. He was firmly of the opinion that the RUC was the last bastion of law and order in the province. The force of 12,000 officers, only 10 per cent of whom were Roman Catholics, had been working for two years on a new code of conduct. Sir John guessed rightly that this would become an issue at the Intergovernmental Conference. The chief constable also knew that many of his officers would experience difficulties with the requirement to enhance cross-border co-operation (Article 9(a) of the agreement) and the apparent conflict with Article 9(b), which sought to guarantee the freedom of the chief constable's operational responsibilities from any interference by the Intergovernmental Conference. Hermon knew that this contradiction would lead to a public clash with the politicians of the Intergovernmental Conference. While this political in-fighting was going on, the RUC were at the sharp end of the community conflict on the streets, attacked from both extremes. There was talk of civil war.

According to the *News Letter*, 'hundreds of Ulster families are laying secret plans to escape civil war in the province. Businessmen are buying second homes in Great Britain . . .'[82] Molyneaux and Paisley issued a message to the RUC in the local press: 'None of us can run away from making a choice . . . we cannot sit back and allow you to be misled by false assurances that the Anglo-Irish Agreement does not interfere with the integrity of the RUC or involve a foreign power in directing your affairs . . . The Dublin government now have an equal say in "setting

---

[82] *News Letter*, 8 March 1986.

in hand" the work of the Chief Constable. This radically alters the role of the RUC officers who are employed and who took an oath to "truly serve" our sovereign. Now you are being asked to serve ... the Government of an Irish Republic which spawned the Provisional IRA and which still harbours the murderers of so many of your gallant colleagues ...'[83] On the same day a DUP assemblyman, Ivan Foster, released the text of a secret recording of a Northern Ireland Police Federation meeting in which one RUC officer said: 'the RUC must say no now ... I refuse to be the whipping stick for a foreign state who has harboured the terrorists who have murdered my friends and relations and my colleagues.'[84] Another said: 'the Anglo-Irish Agreement must go ... people we regarded as our friends are turning us out on the street ... we are being driven into police ghettos.'[85]

Sir John Hermon responded by stating that 'the RUC is not and will not be political in any way ... the independence of the Chief Constable is enshrined in law ...'[86] The Northern Ireland Police Authority stated: 'The only function which members of the Force have, concerns their duty to uphold the law as enacted by Parliament, in accordance with their oath of allegiance to truly serve our Sovereign.'[87] The *News Letter* advised Unionist leaders to 'endeavour to ensure that their legitimate protests are conducted within the law and do not involve confrontation with, or attacks on, the RUC'.[88] The warning came too late. During the week of the one-day strike, fifteen police homes were attacked, in Ballymena, Lurgan, Portadown, Belfast and, above all, in Lisburn. This was the territory of John McMichael, second-in-command of the UDA, and most of the 600 reported incidents of intimidation of policemen and their families over the next nine months centred on this area. The Unionist politicians continued their play-acting as leaders of the anti-agreement campaign by writing to the prime minister saying that they 'wanted to create the framework within which dialogue can take place'.[89] They still insisted that any talks about devolution should follow a suspension of the Anglo-Irish Agreement. The politicians were going through the motions; the paramilitaries were calling the shots. Molyneaux showed clear signs of regret at the course of events. He was 'horrified, shocked and disgusted at the intimidation and violence'[90] during the one-day strike. Paisley,

---

[83] *News Letter*, 7 March 1986.
[84] Ibid.
[85] *Irish Times*, 7 March 1986.
[86] *Irish Times*, 8 March 1986.
[87] *News Letter*, 10 March 1986.
[88] Ibid.
[89] *Times*, 11 March 1986.
[90] *Irish Times*, 4 March 1986.

Mary Holland of the *Irish Times* reported, 'appears to be physically and spiritually exhausted. He takes few decisions himself and leaves Peter Robinson to make the increasingly frightening running both on television and the public platform.'[91] While Molyneaux accepted the Northern Ireland Police Authority's statement on the role of the RUC, Robinson dismissed it as 'placemen appointed by the Government, doing their master's bidding'.[92] Within the force, Hermon moved quickly to bolster the morale of his officers. He set up a special squad to monitor Loyalist intimidation of police-officers and later an occupational health unit to deal with the trauma caused by the strains of policing.

The marching season was scheduled to start on Easter Monday. In 1985 1,897 Loyalist and 223 Republican parades had taken place; three were banned and twenty-three were re-routed. The Twelfth of July parade of Loyalists in Portadown had however been prevented for the first time in 170 years form marching down Obins Street through the Catholic enclave known as the Tunnel (see above p.19). The resulting riot had led to major damage and injuries to both RUC and loyalists. The marchers were determined that this year Portadown, the cradle of Ulster Loyalism, should be the test bed of Unionist anti-agreement resolve. Sir John Hermon, knowing how politically charged the whole issue of parade routes could be, suggested that an independent public tribunal be set up to consider the question of banning or re-routeing traditional parades. His suggestion fell on deaf ears. The Government sent an additional 550 soldiers – a battalion of the Royal Green Jackets – to the province; it did not intend to be intimidated.

The Northern Ireland Office went on the offensive. In a full-page advertisement in the local press the government stated that 'It is time to sort out the facts from the daily diet of fiction'. It was false to assert that the RUC would drop 'Royal' from its name and change the style and colour of its uniform. The UDR would not be disbanded. The Anglo-Irish Agreement did not represent Dublin rule, and the elected representatives of the province were not being neglected and ignored.

As the month progressed it became more and more apparent that the two Unionist leaders had yet again misjudged the mood of the activists in the province. Belfast City Council defied the law and decided to ignore both the government's deadline for striking a rate, and the High Court ruling on the 'Belfast Says No' banner. They voted to continue their adjournment policy by twenty-five votes to twenty-one. The mayoral chains of thirteen Unionist councils were hung on the barbed wire surrounding Stormont for the fourth Intergovernmental

[91] Ibid.
[92] *News Letter*, 11 March 1986.

Conference on 11 March 1986, while the Unionist joint working party put an advertisement in the local papers opposing the American administration's intention of giving financial backing to the Anglo-Irish Agreement.

The Unionist fight gained support from Conor Cruise O'Brien, who castigated Tom King for 'his stubborn infatuation with this Frankenstein's monster',[93] and who went on to prophesy the disintegration of the agreement. Cardinal Ó Fiaich declared that 'polarization between the communities has probably increased in the last six months'.[94] Columnists who before the one-day strike had argued that the government should offer a lifeline to the Unionist leaders now cautioned the prime minister against giving them an inch. The foreign secretary, speaking at a meeting in his constituency, said that 'it was deplorable that the people of Northern Ireland were being misled about the effects of the Anglo-Irish Agreement . . . it is simply not true that the Agreement amounts to joint authority; nonsense to assert that the Agreement is . . . a first step to Irish unity . . . it is no concession to the IRA terrorism . . . The British and Irish share so much and their cultures are so organically interlinked that the time is long overdue for us to put our differences behind us.'[95]

The Irish partner to the agreement was also experiencing some domestic problems over the selling of the agreement. The opposition leader, Charles Haughey, in a speech in New York to the Friends of Fianna Fáil, said that Hillsborough was 'unlikely to bring peace to Northern Ireland'.[96] Garret FitzGerald travelled to Washington for St Patrick's Day in the hope of witnessing the signing of the Aid Bill to Ireland. Unfortunately for him, a Foreign Relations Committee filibuster seeking amendments to the proposed extradition treaty with the United Kingdom meant that the authorization of the £170 million underwriting the Hillsborough accord had to be temporarily withheld. FitzGerald had to make do with an appeal by President Reagan to Americans 'not to give financial or moral support to Irish terrorists'.[97]

The shadow of extradition was beginning to threaten relationships. Ireland had signed the European Convention on the Suppression of Terrorism, but the first attempt to extradite Evelyn Glenholmes for terrorist offences ended in farcical failure. Glenholmes was wanted in connection with bomb attacks on Chelsea barracks, the home of the attorney-general, Sir Michael Havers, and an Oxford Street Wimpey

---

[93] *Irish Times*, 7 March 1986.
[94] *Times*, 31 March 1986.
[95] *Irish Times*, 15 March 1986.
[96] *News Letter*, 8 March 1986.
[97] *Irish Times*, 18 March 1986.

Bar. On Saturday 22 March 1986 Glenholmes, who had been detained ten days earlier in Tallaght, South Dublin, was released in the morning, rearrested and then released again in a 'Keystone Cops' sequence with Irish Special Branch. The original warrants issued by the DPP were found to be invalid. Douglas Hurd accepted that there had been incompetence in the DPP's office, but he criticized the Irish courts for refusing to allow an adjournment, and for refusing to accept a telephone call from Scotland Yard to the Garda as evidence that a fresh extradition warrant had been issued. As the British DPP ordered a disciplinary inquiry, Glenholmes disappeared. She was sighted, chased through Dublin and arrested once more. The court ordered her to be released again.

President Reagan's determination to make the extradition of terrorists to the United Kingdom easier was being frustrated by the well-organized Irish-American lobby in the Senate. But it was a delaying tactic – no more. In Northern Ireland another filibuster was also running out of time.

The Northern Ireland Office introduced an order to enable the government to appoint commissioners empowered to strike a rate for North Down, Ards, Larne, Belfast, Lisburn, Ballymena, Carrickfergus, Coleraine, Limavady, Armagh, Cookstown and Banbridge. The move came too late for many of the neighbourhood and community groups which depended on support from the councils. Fifty-four lay-offs from permanent jobs in the city followed the withholding of grants totalling £460,000 in the financial year 1985–6.

As Easter approached there were two crucial developments. The first was the prime minister's response to the letter of 7 March from Molyneaux and Paisley. Both Unionist leaders had fought shy of accepting Mrs Thatcher's invitation to a Downing Street meeting, preferring contact through correspondence. On 13 March 1986 they both took part in a Radio Ulster programme and said that 'there were signs which would become visible within a few days that talks with the government could be resumed on terms already outlined by the Unionist leaders . . .'[98] The *News Letter* commented that both leaders sounded 'unusually optimistic'.[99] Their optimism was ill-founded; when Mrs Thatcher sent her reply she flatly refused to suspend the Anglo-Irish Agreement, the bottom line of Unionist demands. Paisley reacted by claiming that Thatcher 'has closed the door on us in a tantrum, locked it, put up the chains and thrown away the key in her rage . . .'[100] Andrew Alexander in the *Spectator* warned: 'if Mrs

---

[98] *News Letter*, 14 March 1986.
[99] Ibid.
[100] *Irish Times*, 26 March 1986.

Thatcher does not want her legacy to be the destruction of the United Kingdom, then she needs to end the Hillsborough agreement . . . Hillsborough is as pregnant with danger for Britain as Munich once was.'[101] *New Society* took a different view: '[Mrs Thatcher] may feel that she has to lay the ghost of the successful Ulster Workers' Council general strike of 1974 . . . that Protestant stubbornness needs to be outfaced, brutally and in public.'[102]

That fight was not far off. The Easter Monday parade of the Apprentice Boys was normally held in Bangor, but on the day of the prime minister's reply to Molyneaux and Paisley the venue was switched to Portadown, the scene of the biggest riot in the 1985 marching season. The BBC got caught up in the marching row when it was announced that the Corporation did not propose to transmit live the main parade in Belfast on Saturday 12 July 1986 but intended instead to compile a province-wide round-up of the celebrations. The leaking of this decision was intended to maximize the BBC's discomfiture, coming as it did on the day of the prime minister's reply to Molyneaux and Paisley and the transfer of the Apprentice Boys' march from Belfast to Portadown. The BBC was accused of 'bowing to the orders of its political masters. . .'[103] Jim Wells, a DUP assemblyman, issued a statement 'warning BBC camera crews to keep away from Monday's Apprentice Boys rally in Portadown, for their own safety. . . I am not issuing a threat, I am merely offering the BBC some sound advice.'[104] The Apprentice Boys disassociated themselves from Wells's statement: 'we want nothing to do with comments of this calibre.'[105] Paul McGill of the National Union of Journalists summed up the situation: 'there is always a thin distinction between predicting violence and encouraging it.'[106] These developments led the chief constable to recommend to the secretary of state on Easter Sunday afternoon that the march in Portadown be banned. King agreed. Once his decision was made public, accusations of discrimination by the RUC against the Apprentice Boys started circulating. The situation was made worse by the violence that occurred at the end of a Republican march in Derry to commemorate the 1916 Easter Rising. A soldier was shot in the face. The RUC had made no attempt to ban the Republican march. In the early hours of Easter Monday, Paisley and Robinson assembled 3,000 marchers in Portadown and marched the Garvaghy route. Despite the secretary of state's ban, a parade had taken place at Portadown.

---

[101] *Spectator*, 29 March 1986.
[102] *New Society*, 28 March 1986.
[103] *News Letter*, 26 March 1986.
[104] *News Letter*, 28 March 1986.
[105] *Times*, 29 March 1986.
[106] Ibid.

The following morning advertisements appeared in the local press informing the readers of the ban in Portadown and the RUC's reasons for recommending the ban to the secretary of state: 'the parade had been taken over by paramilitary and subversive elements who were determined that there should be violence . . . there were plans to create confrontation with the police . . .'[107] The papers also carried the news that twenty-seven leading members of the UDA, including John McMichael, had been detained. The publicity had the effect of persuading the vast majority of the 20,000 marchers expected to take part in the Apprentice Boys' parade to stay away from Portadown, but a hard core did turn up determined to defy the ban. The RUC wore riot gear and a hundred extra troops were flown in by helicopter to help keep order. By nightfall no parade had taken place, but forty-nine people were injured, including thirteen policemen. One of the injured was Keith White, who died a fortnight later from injuries sustained when he was hit by one of 125 plastic bullets fired to quell the riot.

The secretary of state called the violence 'ludicrous mindless thuggery',[108] but most press coverage was devoted to the Paisley–Robinson parade. *The Times* leader said the march 'made the law look ridiculous and the authorities impotent',[109] while Seamus Mallon concluded that 'either there was a very obvious lack of forward planning by the police or there are those within the RUC who are not implementing the wishes of the Northern Ireland office'.[110]

Ian Paisley left the province and flew to the United States on a preaching mission; he and Robinson had successfully defied the law and the RUC. They had undermined the operational control of the chief constable and the standing of the RUC in the community. Despite the ban, a parade had taken place, and in spite of the order to stay away from Portadown some of the worst rioting in the seventeen years of the troubles had occurred there. Twice within the month the RUC had been outflanked, first during the one-day strike and now in Portadown. The RUC were on the run; the DUP assemblyman Ivan Foster advised that 'the public should shun them in places of business, social activities and in churches since they have sold themselves to serve a Chief Constable and a government whose only thought is the destruction of the Protestant people and their heritage'.[111]

On Easter Monday evening nine RUC homes were attacked; by the following Friday night a total of forty-five police families had been

---

[107] *News Letter*, 31 March 1986.
[108] *Times*, 1 April 1986.
[109] Ibid.
[110] *Irish Times*, 1 April 1986.
[111] Ibid.

driven from their homes. Molyneaux condemned the attacks, Robinson regretted but refused to condemn and John Taylor was reported to have said that 'the RUC could not expect to shoot plastic bullets at Protestants during the daytime and live peacefully in Protestant areas at night'.[112] Hermon met the Northern Ireland Police Federation, which subsequently issued a 'leave us alone' plea to the marauding mobs. It had no effect. A young police reservist was shot in the back at his home in North Belfast. Lady Hermon was attacked with eggs and tomatoes after visiting an intimidated RUC family in Lurgan. Seventeen shots were fired at an RUC landrover in North Belfast. A new welfare group was set up within the RUC and a commitment was given by the chief constable to improve communication between himself and the rank and file. The Irish Anglican bishops condemned the attacks and specifically targeted their comments at 'those who by their words or actions have engaged in, encouraged or condoned attacks on the homes and families of men who belong to a force that has suffered on behalf of this community for the past sixteen years'.[113]

The attacks on the RUC were understandably the lead stories, but Roman Catholic homes, particularly in Lisburn, were being systematically attacked by UDA and UVF mobs. 'It started on Easter Tuesday when the locals . . . returned from a parade in Portadown . . . the first stone through their front window was fired by a catapult. The second was a complete concrete breeze block . . . when night fell . . . they filled up the bath . . . father and mother would take it in turns to watch. Neither could sleep for longer than two hours.'[114] Between Easter 1986 and the end of the year 1,100 families applied to the Housing Executive for a transfer because of intimidation. John McMichael explained the UDA's reasons for attacking Roman Catholic homes: 'Every house, every street, every farm which is taken over by an Irish nationalist is a little bit less of Northern Ireland and a little bit more of Ireland.'[115]

John McMichael was a leading figure in the Unionist co-ordinating committee, a new anti-agreement body which included representatives of the DUP, the Ulster Clubs, the UDA and the 1986 strike committee; there was no representative from the Official Unionists. The committee met on Wednesday 2 April 1986; the following weekend, between Friday 4 April and Sunday 6 April, twenty-nine further attacks took place, forcing two RUC families to leave their homes before they were gutted by fire. The RUC raided UVF headquarters in East Belfast and

---

[112] *Irish Times*, 5 April 1986.
[113] Ibid.
[114] *Guardian*, 19 January 1987.
[115] Ibid.

took away computer tapes. Paisley cut short his preaching tour of the States and returned to Northern Ireland. The weekend press was dominated by reports of the worst week in the RUC's history. ITV's *Weekend World* featured an interview with an RUC officer who said that 'many of his colleagues were considering mutiny and resignations on a large scale'.[116] The *Sunday Times* reported that the British Inspectorate of Constabulary had concluded after a recent inspection that 'there was little likelihood of mutiny and mass resignations'.[117]

The decision to ban the Portadown march on Easter Monday had been a political one; the secretary of state alone can ban marches. The chief constable retains the operational control on every other aspect of public order, including re-routeing. Many newspapers speculated about why the chief constable had recommended a ban on the Portadown march. Hermon had already tried to distance his force and himself from the politics of parades; did he want the secretary of state to be involved at Portadown as a cover for his force, which was already bearing the brunt of the worst ravages of the anti-agreement protest? The riot certainly provoked considerable political reaction. The prime minister used the tide of support for the RUC in Britain to put Unionist politicians on the spot: 'All that is required for evil to triumph is that good men do nothing.'[118] The *Daily Mail* carried a front-page headline 'MPs plotting war on RUC' and the *London Standard* labelled the Unionist MPs as a group 'Ulster Thugs'. John Hume congratulated the RUC while castigating the Unionist members of parliament, and Des O'Malley praised the RUC while favouring a gesture to the North in order to lessen the level of violence. This message was also conveyed to the prime minister direct by Lord Moyola and Lord Brookeborough. Lord Fitt said on Radio 4 that 'some means must be found to involve the Protestant population . . . time is very short'.[119]

Paisley held a press conference on his return from America. 'I unequivocally and unreservedly condemn violence and these attacks on police homes and families. However it must be said that the RUC has been put in an impossible situation by having to implement decisions taken under the Anglo-Irish Agreement.'[120] He called for the immediate resignation of Sir John Hermon. Molyneaux, having been pilloried in the British press for the best part of a fortnight, felt dejected and demoralized: 'the reality is that Mr Paisley and I . . . have been overtaken by the people of Northern Ireland'.[121]

---

[116] *Irish Times*, 7 April 1986.
[117] *Sunday Times*, 6 April 1986.
[118] *Times*, 9 April 1986.
[119] *Times*, 10 April 1986.
[120] Ibid.
[121] *Times*, 11 April 1986.

The cabinet conducted a review of Northern Ireland affairs at its weekly meeting on Thursday 10 April 1986, and at prime minister's question time later in the day, Mrs Thatcher and Neil Kinnock maintained their bipartisan support for the Anglo-Irish Agreement and the RUC. Eldon Griffiths MP, the Police Federation's parliamentary representative, said that 'intolerable burdens were being placed on the RUC'.[122] He was speaking after a session of the Northern Ireland all-party committee in the House of Commons, where Alan Wright, the Northern Ireland Police Federation representative, was reported to have called on Hermon to stay away from the Intergovernmental Conferences: 'It is very hard to convince people that if someone is attending a high-powered political forum ... the RUC is not getting some political direction.'[123] The chief constable had already tried at the Intergovernmental Conference held on 12 March 1986 to get a clear statement in the official communiqué that he and the Garda commissioner were only present for that part of the meeting that fell within the definition of Article 9(a). Wright was fighting a rearguard defence of his chief constable within the Northern Ireland Police Federation's executive committee; he secured the smallest of majorities against moving a formal vote of no confidence.

Hermon was meanwhile attempting to re-establish contact with the Orange Order to discuss the traditional May Day parade through Portadown. He refused to give the Ulster Co-ordinating Committee negotiating rights and since they assumed control of the arrangements for the funeral of Keith White, the first Protestant victim of plastic bullets, policing was difficult and tense. White's father appealed for peace. By the end of the funeral day the security authorities estimated that damage done to property totalled £1 million. The Dunmurry Golf Club was set alight, as was a Roman Catholic primary school in Belfast, and seven RUC homes were petrol-bombed in Bangor, Dungannon, Kilkeel, Antrim and Belfast.

Hermon's problems with the Orange Order occurred because the order had lost all semblance of control over its own parades. It was concerned with the marching arrangements of the different lodges and their bands, and with their dress and parade standards. The actual control of the marches had passed first to the Ulster Clubs and then to the Ulster Co-ordinating Committee. Hermon's traditionally cordial relations with the Orange Order counted for nought in the new atmosphere which followed Hillsborough. The parades became protest demonstrations, not celebrations of a culture and an enjoyable day out.

In addition, the Orange Order had no influence over the activities of

---

[122] *News Letter*, 11 April 1986.
[123] Ibid.

the Independent Orange Order. One of their parades got out of hand in Portadown on Sunday 20 April 1986, when a thousand marchers attacked three RUC officers. This triggered a riot in nearby Lisburn and led to six RUC homes being attacked in Belfast. The day before, the DUP had held their annual party conference. Close ties exist between the DUP and the Independent Orange Order, and some commentators linked the riots in Portadown and Lisburn to the debate on the RUC at the DUP conference. A motion of no confidence in the chief constable was proposed by Cookstown barrister Alan Kane; Ethel Smyth, a County Down DUP councillor, said that the RUC were 'collaborators and mercenaries' who were 'selling their heritage ... they are the people who are putting us into an united Ireland at the point of a gun'.[124] Paisley deplored 'the political misuse and behaviour of RUC officers'.[125]

Four days later the IRA, having left the campaign against the RUC to the Loyalist paramilitaries, re-entered the conflict with the murder of Inspector James Hazlett. The same day the comments of three serving RUC officers were read by actors on Channel 4. One of them was reported to have said that 'the day is coming when the RUC will not carry out the instructions that come from Sir John's political masters ... there is no way I'm going to tackle the Protestant people who have looked after me for seventeen years'.[126]

The Unionist leaders attempted to wrest control back from the Ulster Co-ordinating Committee. They launched a twelve-point anti-agreement strategy, which included a clause urging 'officers of the RUC to press their professional body to act on the already expressed and growing reluctance of their members in policing an agreement that does not have community support'.[127] Far more important was the unconditional condemnation of the attacks on RUC homes and offices. As the *Irish Times* leader of the same day stated, 'Paisley and Molyneaux now know that they are riding a tiger ...'[128] Molyneaux had been disgusted with the course of events since the abortive meeting with Thatcher in February. He had a wider network of contacts than Paisley in Westminster among Conservative back-bench MPs and in the province through the well-structured Official Unionist party organization. He represented middle-class Unionism, whose views were aptly expressed by the former Lord Mayor of Belfast, Betty Bell: 'the RUC are our own fellow citizens who have protected us from IRA

---

[124] *Irish Times*, 21 April 1986.
[125] Ibid.
[126] *Times*, 24 April 1986.
[127] *Irish Times*, 24 April 1986.
[128] Ibid.

murder . . . don't turn on your kith and kin.'[129] Molyneaux also had
much influence among the hierarchy of the Orange Order; its head,
Revd Martin Smyth, was one of Molyneaux's closest political
colleagues at Westminster. Smyth was also the politician 'who had gone
furthest in distancing himself from . . . the paramilitary antics. Many
see him as the best hope for re-establishing dialogue between
Westminster and the disaffected Protestants.'[130] It came as no surprise,
therefore, when the Orange Order announced that it was cancelling the
May Day parade of the Apprentice Boys through Portadown because
'the politicians needed a breathing space'.[131] This was as significant a
development in the Unionist struggle with the Loyalist paramilitaries as
the Molyneaux–Paisley twelve-point strategy plan. It was a test of their
control over their respective supporters and an open challenge to the
paramilitaries to back off.

The chief constable recognized the signals and gave an interview to
the *Belfast Telegraph*, during which he sought to strengthen the hand of
some Unionist leaders by warning others of the dangers 'of supping
with the devil of paramilitary organisations . . . debasing the political
process by consorting with paramilitary elements of a mafia kind . . .
the upsurge in violence could not be blamed on Hillsborough . . . it is
blatant sectarianism'.[132]

Molyneaux and Paisley put their names to an advertisement calling
for a Day of Prayer on Saturday 3 May 1986. The Martyrs' Memorial
Church, Coleraine Town Hall and Lisburn Orange Hall were open all
day for 'prayers for the destruction of the Anglo-Irish Agreement and
the bringing about of a peaceful constitutional settlement'.[133] John
McMichael correctly identified the source of the brake on Unionist
street protests: 'Molyneaux and Paisley haven't a thought as to how to
defeat the Anglo-Irish Agreement . . . they are fiddling whilst Ulster
burns . . .'[134] For the first time since the one-day stoppage in March,
the Loyal Orange Institution of Ireland and the Grand Orange Lodge
went public in a series of press advertisements summoning their
members to a rally at Hillsborough to mark the first six months of the
Anglo-Irish Agreement. It was made clear that the UDA, the Ulster
Clubs and the Ulster Co-ordinating Committee would not be in charge
of this rally. It passed off peacefully. The RUC, together with the
Unionist and Orange Order leadership, had survived one of their most
testing times.

---

[129] *News Letter*, 11 April 1986.
[130] *Sunday Times*, 9 March 1986.
[131] *Irish Times*, 28 April 1986.
[132] *Belfast Telegraph*, 2 May 1986.
[133] *News Letter*, 2 May 1986.
[134] *Fortnight*, No. 236, May 1986.

While the Orange Order rally was assembling at Hillsborough on Thursday 15 May 1986, a senior officer in the Manchester Police made a minute of a talk he had had with a fellow officer; it had been mentioned that the deputy chief constable, John Stalker, had been to America at the expense of a businessman, Kevin Taylor. Within four days, Stalker was removed from the RUC inquiry he had started two years earlier. The decision to replace him with Chief Constable Colin Sampson of West Yorkshire, was made during the Police Federation conference. Sampson was also to conduct an inquiry into John Stalker. Those responsible for requesting Sampson to conduct both inquiries were Sir Lawrence Byford, HM Chief Inspector of Constabulary at the Home Office, Sir Philip Myers, HM Inspector of Constabulary for the North West, and Chief Constable James Anderton of Greater Manchester, Stalker's immediate superior. The Sampson inquiry was to consider the allegation that between 1 January 1971 and 31 December 1985 John Stalker, an officer in the Greater Manchester Police, associated with Kevin Taylor and known criminals in a manner likely to bring discredit upon the Greater Manchester Police.

The first Sir John Hermon knew about Stalker's problems was when Sir Philip Myers visited RUC headquarters at Knock in Belfast. Sir Philip also saw Sir Barry Shaw, the director of public prosecutions for Northern Ireland. Sir Barry had received the first part of Stalker's report from Hermon on 13 February 1986 and had requested Stalker to complete his inquiry. Stalker planned to interview Hermon on Monday 2 June 1986. On the preceding Wednesday, 28 May 1986, he was informed of the Sampson inquiry and sent on extended leave.

Stalker's inquiry was commissioned by Sir John Hermon in May 1984 to examine the way in which the Northern Ireland CID had conducted the investigations into the three incidents that had led to the deaths of Toman, Burns and McKerr on 11 November 1982, the fatal shooting of Tighe and the wounding of McCanley on 24 November 1982, and the deaths of Grew and Carroll on 12 December 1982. The three incidents involved the RUC's anti-terrorist squad; three IRA volunteers and two senior members of the INLA were killed, and so was a seventeen-year-old youth with apparently no paramilitary connections. Four RUC officers were subsequently charged, one with the murder of Grew, three others with the murder of Toman. All were acquitted. During the murder trials it was disclosed that the officers on duty had been given cover stories by RUC Special Branch officers in order to protect the identities of informants. Stalker's inquiry was to investigate the circumstances in which the three cover stories had been given to the CID and to see whether any criminal offence had been committed. He was also asked to examine the problems Special Branch officers faced when acting on information which they cannot reveal because of the need to protect an informant. Stalker was not commissioned to investigate the alleged 'shoot to kill' policy of the RUC, but that became the accepted shorthand to describe his two-year inquiry.

Kevin Taylor was a Manchester motor trader; in the early seventies he and Stalker lived 400 yards apart in Failsworth. By the time John Stalker was appointed to lead the Northern Ireland inquiry, his friendship with Taylor was on a firm footing. They had shared a cruising holiday in the Bahamas. Stalker attended Taylor's fiftieth birthday party and was his guest at the Manchester City Conservative Association's autumn ball on 23 November 1985. On 15 January 1986 Stalker told his chief constable, James Anderton, that he was distancing himself from Taylor.

Kevin Taylor, unbeknown to Stalker, had been the subject of surveillance by Greater Manchester Police since June 1984, a month after the start of the inquiry in Ulster. Taylor's association with members of the Quality Street Gang, a group suspected of dealing in drugs and of having contacts with known criminals in Spain, was the reason for the interest felt in him by the Drugs Intelligence Unit and the Manchester Police Fraud Squad. Taylor's home was searched on 9 May 1986 under a warrant issued in connection with an alleged conspiracy to obtain £240,000 from the Co-operative Bank by deception. On 15 May 1986, the day of the Hillsborough protest rally in Northern Ireland, a minute of the conversation between two senior Greater Manchester policemen reached Chief Constable Anderton's desk. The minute claimed that 'Taylor was saying John Stalker had been to his parties, and to America at his expense, that if nothing was done to put paid to the investigation by the Greater Manchester Police, then Taylor would "blow out John Stalker and associates"'.[135] Anderton contacted Sir Philip Myers; John Stalker's inquiry into the RUC was at an end. The political row was just starting.

The news that Stalker was off the RUC inquiry broke on 30 May 1986. Earlier in the week, Constable William Lawrence Smyth of the RUC and his colleague David Leslie McBride were killed by a bomb at Crossmaglen. The IRA also killed Major Andrew French in the same incident. There were three other victims of the IRA campaign within the same fortnight. The last thing the RUC required was a political storm over the Stalker inquiry. A conspiracy theory gained support, based on the known antagonism between Hermon and Stalker. The *Guardian* claimed that 'it was convenient to the force, to use no stronger word, that possible criminal proceedings against officers alleged to have

---

[135] Peter Taylor, *Stalker, the Search for the Truth* (Faber and Faber, 1987), 158.

followed a shoot to kill policy ... should be held in abeyance'.[136] The *Sunday Times* asserted that 'it was well known in police and political circles ... that Hermon had been bitterly critical of Stalker's investigation'.[137] Hermon issued a statement to the press warning them that 'he and his officers took strong exception to allegations published and broadcast during the past week'.[138] Not only were there allegations of a dirty-tricks campaign by the RUC to 'nobble' Stalker but also rumours started circulating that 'up to forty members of the RUC have been recommended to face criminal or disciplinary charges including murder and perjury'.[139] These attacks had the effect of helping to close ranks within the RUC. Alan Wright, the Northern Ireland Police Federation's leader, turned on those who 'attempted to use the federation as a "chisel" to split the force asunder ... the force has been quite literally the linchpin of stability, consistency and re-liability in a community at times apparently hellbent on self-destruc-tion'.[140] The official communiqué at the end of the sixth Intergovern-mental Conference at Stormont referred to 'a significant landmark in the development of co-operation between RUC and Garda'.[141] Later the same day, at the Northern Ireland Police Federation meeting, Tom King reiterated the assurance that 'the Agreement has no bearing on the Chief Constable's operational responsibilities'.[142]

Sir John Hermon was preparing for the biggest challenge to his independence and authority – the Twelfth of July parade in Portadown. The Portadown district master, Harold Gracey, had already announced that the lodges wanted to walk the traditional route through Obins Street and the Tunnel. The lodge decision was carried in most of the local papers. Hermon prepared for the worst. His officers had a foretaste of what might come when a two-hour riot flared in the village of Dunloy in County Antrim on the evening of the Intergovernmental Conference meeting. This disturbance followed a protest at Stormont by Paisley against Peter Barry's visit: 'Protestants have only one right left to them, that is to mobilise – resistance must be demonstrated in no uncertain manner.'[143]

The DUP leader was to repeat this threat a week later, when he was dragged from the Northern Ireland Assembly at two o'clock in the morning. Speaker Kilfedder had read out the official announcement

[136] *Guardian*, 5 June 1986.
[137] *Sunday Times*, 8 June 1986.
[138] *Irish Times*, 21 June 1986.
[139] *Sunday Times*, 20 July 1986.
[140] *Times*, 18 June 1986.
[141] Ibid.
[142] *News Letter*, 18 June 1986.
[143] Ibid.

that the royal assent had been given to the parliamentary order winding up the assembly. All seventeen DUP representatives, two Official Unionists and one Independent assemblyman sat tight when the Speaker and eight Official Unionists left the chamber.

The RUC baton-charged 200 Loyalist demonstrators on the steps of Stormont before carrying the protesting assemblymen out of the chamber. Paisley declared: 'We are on the verge of civil war because when you take away the forum of democracy you don't have anything left . . . if a Protestant backlash is the only thing that can destroy the Anglo-Irish Agreement then I will not stand in its way. Every man in Ulster, including every member of the RUC, is now to declare himself whether he is on the side of the lying, treachery and betrayal of the agreement, or whether he stands to defend to the last drop of blood his British and Ulster heritage.'[144] He warned the RUC men carrying him out of Stormont: 'You don't come crying to me if your homes are attacked. You will reap what you sow.'[145] On the same day the Ulster Clubs announced a picket of the homes of senior police officers and senior civil servants. They also disclosed that the Clubs' membership was 13,000, spread over forty-six clubs throughout the province. Paisley, taking part in Radio Ulster's *Behind the Headlines* programme, said he did not mean to advocate the use of the gun.[146]

The July marching season is spread over two weekends. On the first Sunday in July there is a parade to a church service. In Portadown this involves a march to Drumcree church. Traditionally this went through the Tunnel. Hermon resisted this, having successfully rerouted the same march a year previously through the Garvaghy estate. A security force of 800 policemen and 400 soldiers was in place to escort the church parade through the Garvaghy route. The RUC confined attendance to members of the Portadown Lodge. Gracey, the Portadown district master, accepted the RUC re-routeing and parade conditions; Alan Wright, his district chaplain and leader of the Ulster Clubs, did not. In the resulting riot twenty-seven RUC officers were injured, one receiving a dart in the neck. Plastic bullets were used to disperse the Loyalist protesters.

The following Saturday's Twelfth of July parade, the most important in the Loyalist calendar, now became the focus of speculation and of intense negotiations between the Orange Order and the RUC concerning the route of the Portadown parade. Would Hermon recommend its banning or would the Orange Order accept a re-routeing away from their traditional Tunnel route? Alan Wright, held

---

[144] *Irish Times*, 25 June 1986.
[145] *News Letter*, 24 June 1986.
[146] *News Letter*, 27 June 1986.

firm for the Tunnel. He was supported by Paisley, who summoned a press conference to express his support for Wright: 'The first great mobilization of Ulster Protestants must take place [in Portadown] on Saturday. Like the immortal thirteen at Londonderry, we must defend our heritage, our homes and our liberties.' He had a word for the RUC: 'the time has now come when they should follow the example of the British Army officers at the Curragh.'[147] The Orange Order let it be known that they opposed Paisley's plan. Molyneaux refused to go to Portadown and Smyth advised Orangemen to march in their traditional local parades and not go to Portadown.

Despite the traumas of the past six months, the RUC's *esprit de corps* was still strong. Hermon conducted secret talks with Smyth, Molyneaux and Portadown's Gracey, all members of the Official Unionist Party as well as of the Orange Order. On the eve of the Portadown march, seven of the eight local lodges agreed to a re-routeing of the parade along Garvaghy Road.

Paisley, Robinson and Alan Wright responded instantly. A force of 4,000 men descended on Hillsborough village and marched up and down the main street, all the main roads out of the village having been sealed by men in paramilitary dress armed with sticks and cudgels. Paisley said he was prepared 'to shoulder a rifle to save Ulster . . . they can call it sedition . . . they can call it incitement to violence . . . it will be over our dead bodies if they ship us down the river'.[148]

The following day, the Portadown parade followed the Garvaghy route; trouble only flared up on the return leg, when fourteen RUC officers were injured, eleven arrests made and one round of plastic bullets fired. It was less peaceful elsewhere. At Kilkeel, thirteen fishing nets belonging to Roman Catholic fishermen were burned; in Belfast an Orangeman thrust a pike into the chest of a spectator, while another split open a man's head with a ceremonial sword. In Rasharkin, County Antrim, twelve Roman Catholic homes were destroyed in a rampage by sixty Loyalists carrying cudgels, hatchets and pickaxe handles. During the day, although the vast majority of the parades passed off peacefully, 128 RUC officers reported injuries, 66 civilians were hurt, 127 arrests were made, 281 plastic bullet rounds were fired and 79 cases of intimidation were reported.

The RUC got little respite from the politicians. Peter Barry saw the re-routeing compromise as provocative: 'it is time the security forces stood up to the Unionist bullies and stopped intimidating marches through Roman Catholic areas.'[149] John Hume claimed the

---

[147] *Irish Times*, 10 July 1986.
[148] *Irish Times*, 12 July 1986.
[149] *Times*, 17 July 1986.

re-routeing 'was a boost for the bully boys and a breach of public undertakings given about provocative marches by the RUC'.[150] Tom King was reported to be furious with Barry and Hume, and Geoffrey Smith asked in *The Times*, 'has Barry forgotten how recently RUC families were being attacked by Protestant extremists?'[151] The *Irish Times* leader of the same day took a different viewpoint: 'the Anglo-Irish Agreement has taken a severe knock ... operational decisions have to fit into a framework of policy and principle ... it is not good enough.'[152] David McKittrick reported that 'privately, the Irish accused Mr King of something close to treachery, claiming he had assured them the Portadown march would be stopped'.[153]

Sir John Hermon took great pride in recounting his visit to Hillsborough Castle on the eve of the Portadown march, to inform the secretary of state of his compromise deal with the Orange Order. He left Hillsborough village just before Paisley and his supporters arrived to disrupt Tom King's sleep. Hermon saw his deal with Molyneaux as proof positive of his operational independence of the Intergovernmental Conference. He kept everybody in the dark until the last moment. If King had informally reassured Barry that the Portadown march would not take place that was his problem. Hermon had correctly interpreted the cause of the attacks on RUC homes at Easter as a direct response to the political decision to ban the march. The RUC was seen to be implementing that decision. This time he was determined to keep the Intergovernmental Conference politicians out of the dispute. There would be no ban if he could help it. Molyneaux understood Hermon's tactics, and persuaded Smyth and Gracey to ditch Wright and reject Paisley. The Portadown re-routeing was one of the most important events of the first nine months of the Anglo-Irish Agreement.

While thousands of Loyalists were marching on Saturday 12 July, an innocuous RUC press statement announced that Hermon had suspended two senior officers following a recommendation by Colin Sampson. Their suspension had been recommended earlier by John Stalker. Hermon rejected his advice in April 1985. There were no objections now.

---

[150] *Irish Times*, 14 July 1986.
[151] *Times*, 17 July 1986.
[152] *Irish Times* 17 July 1986.
[153] *Listener*, 21 August 1986.

3

Unionist disunity, terrorism and the first anniversary

After Easter the anti-agreement protest was organized on two distinct levels. The Ulster Co-ordinating Committee was in charge of demonstrations and public protests and a joint Unionist think-tank pondered the political options. A campaign of civil disobedience was launched: a rate and rent strike, economic sanctions against the Republic of Ireland, the resignation of Unionists from area boards and the adjournment of district council meetings. Westminster MPs were to continue to abstain from taking their seats in the House of Commons, and the Northern Ireland Assembly was to be the main forum for Unionist politicians. A public relations campaign against the agreement was launched in Britain; its first venture appeared in *The Times* on 1 May 1986. 'Northern Ireland is as British as Finchley' was the message superimposed over pictures of a defiant Mrs Thatcher. There were quotations from previous statements by the prime minister. The first, dated 29 July 1982, said: 'no commitment exists for Her Majesty's Government to consult the Irish Government on matters affecting Northern Ireland.' The second, made on 17 May 1984, declared: 'the constitutional future of Northern Ireland is a matter for Northern Ireland and this Parliament and for no one else.' The prime minister, the advertisement observed, 'appears to have changed her mind'.[1]

The Times advertisement was published by Belfast City Council, which, on the day the press campaign was launched, voted by twenty-eight to twenty-two to maintain its adjournment policy. The council was fined £25,000 by Mr Justice Hutton and given seven days to reconsider its decision. The adjournment campaign had started as a protest against Sinn Fein's presence in the council chamber and evolved into an anti-agreement tactic after the signing of the Anglo-Irish accord. The Northern Ireland Office prepared a report on Sinn Fein activities

---

[1] *Times*, 1 May 1986.

in the council chamber and decided against proscribing the party. Other means would have to be found of limiting its participation in the democratic system. Further consideration was to be given to the feasibility of demanding an oath renouncing violence. Sinn Fein's reply to Unionist strategy was to launch their 'Scenario for Peace', which called on the British government to repeal the Government of Ireland Act, announce their withdrawal and set a date for the convening of an all-Ireland constitutional conference.

Of far more immediate relevance to the situation in Ulster was the six-monthly report of the Northern Ireland Economic Council. The chairman, Sir Charles Carter, declared that 'this worsening of the economic situation is related to current political uncertainties'.[2] Urging a restoration of the housing programme, a reduction in the cost of electricity and more government orders for Northern Ireland, Sir Charles warned Tom King that 'the present situation could lead to a spiral of further depression and further violence, until the Province really does become ungovernable except by a massive military effort'.[3] As if on cue, Rothmans announced the closure of their cigarette factory at Carrickfergus, with the loss of 800 jobs. The May unemployment figure stood at 126,189, which represented 22 per cent of the population of the province.

The Unionist leadership of Molyneaux and Paisley was under intense pressure since the escalation of street protests in Portadown and the UDA attacks on RUC homes and Roman Catholic families. Attempts were made by the government to re-establish contact, especially with Molyneaux. Conservative back-benchers known to be sympathetic to the Unionists were encouraged to maintain their contacts, and every encouragement was given to a plan to launch a Friends of the Union group at Westminster. It was inevitable, given the siege mentality of political life in the province, that any new ideas would lead to divisions and quarrels within the Unionist alliance. It was already under considerable stress as a result of the activities of the Ulster Co-ordinating Committee and the part played by Paisley and Robinson in street demonstrations. It nearly came apart when five Official Unionists, including Lord Mayor John Carson, voted with the SDLP and Sinn Fein at Belfast City Council to abandon the adjournment policy and return to normal business. The decision was made in the face of a threat by a High Court judge to ban Belfast City councillors from public office for five years unless the boycott was stopped. The DUP councillors heckled the lord mayor and his Official Unionist colleagues as traitors and collaborators. A clear division between OUP and DUP thinking

---

[2] *News Letter*, 2 May 1986.
[3] Ibid.

emerged at the Northern Ireland Assembly, when Robert McCartney called for full-blooded integration. The OUP assemblymen labelled integration 'democratic direct rule ... devolution has kept us in limbo for sixty years'.[4] The DUP chief whip, Jim Allister, rejected integration, claiming it to be 'an unobtainable option ... a fraud and a deceit'.[5] Some columnists argued that there would be no break in the deadlock unless London or Dublin made a concession to the Unionists. The Ulster Co-ordinating Committee had a life of its own inside the DUP under Robinson's leadership, while the Official Unionists were split between street demonstrations and political intrigue on the one hand and integrationists and devolutionists on the other. The reality of the situation was that the Unionist leaders had lost control of the anti-agreement campaign. It also appeared that the Intergovernmental Conference ministers had failed to find a formula to bring the Unionists in off the streets. Those Unionists who were prepared to talk about talks were throwing their support behind the one option the government consistently rejected – integration. Columbanus Macness defined integration as 'a code word for denying Nationalists equality ... the Unionists are still a long way from swallowing the pill of according equality to the Nationalists'.[6]

The discipline of the Unionist members of parliament and the policy of abstention from Westminster was in some doubt when, for the second time in as many months, Northern Ireland MPs turned up to vote, this time on the Social Security Bill. Enoch Powell, Martin Smyth, Cecil Walker and John Taylor voted against the government's new bill. The Department of Social Administration calculated that the province would lost £44 million a year by its provisions. John Hume's SDLP estimated that social security payments represented 26 per cent of all household income in Northern Ireland. The Unionist quartet were described as 'backsliders' by Robinson, and Molyneaux, Paisley and Kilfedder met to tighten up discipline. There had been no such bickering earlier when the Unionist MPs joined a successful lobby against the Sunday Trading Bill. Paisley called that success 'divine intervention'.[7]

Archbishop Robert Eames did not invite any politicans to his enthronement. The paramilitaries however paid a visit to Armagh Cathedral and set fire to Ulster Television's outside broadcast unit. Eames joined a powerful lobby of clerical leaders, which included Cardinal Ó Fiaich and Dr John Thompson, moderator-designate of the

---

[4] *News Letter*, 1 May 1986.
[5] Ibid.
[6] *Fortnight*, No. 239, May 1986.
[7] *News Letter*, 16 April 1986.

Presbyterian Church. In a land where 83 per cent of the population claim to be regular church-goers, religious leaders have a certain status in society. Eames was an interventionist; before his enthronement he had called on Thatcher and FitzGerald to clarify certain sections of the Anglo-Irish Agreement, adding that the accord was a 'flawed, insensitive and ambiguous document'.[8] At his first synod, he said that there were limits to the right of political dissent; 'intimidation, mob violence, sectarian attacks went far beyond acceptable political protest'.[9] He also encouraged the authors of the Hillsborough accord to accept that they 'had a responsibility to create situations where constitutional political activity could take place'.[10]

Brass Tacks, a BBC2 current affairs programme, conducted an opinion poll of 1,060 people in the United Kingdom. Forty-two per cent approved of the Anglo-Irish Agreement, 32 per cent disapproved and the remainder were undecided or indifferent.[11] In the province, the opponents of the agreement read some hopeful signs into the 32 per cent return. It is likely that the street violence led people to blame the agreement for the nightly riots which they saw on television. The returns on the political future of the province were even more interesting; 26 per cent thought that it should be part of the United Kingdom, 24 per cent that it should be part of the Irish Republic and 35 per cent that it should be independent. This was a definite 'plague on all your houses' return. The 35 per cent return for independence coincided with a move led by one of the programme's participants, Peter Robinson, towards UDI for Ulster. Paisley's deputy was heckled by the programme's audience over the Loyalist attacks on the RUC. John Hume also appeared and said: 'if the government stands firm a new leadership will emerge from the Unionist community, one that wants to live in peace and harmony.'[12] Sitting next to him on the panel was Martin Smyth, the odds-on favourite to succeed Molyneaux, and the one Unionist politician who retained close personal connections with Conservative back-bench MPs and had, as head of the Orange Order, an alternative power base in the province. Gerry Adams's contribution to *Brass Tacks* was pre-recorded on film.

This network exposure coincided with a burst of activity by members of the newly formed group calling themselves Friends of the Union. There was a tour of Liverpool, Manchester, Edinburgh and Glasgow, a series of receptions took place at the Palace of Westminster, and a

---

[8] *News Letter*, 15 April 1986.
[9] Ibid.
[10] Ibid.
[11] *Irish Times*, 29 May 1986.
[12] *Irish Times*, 3 June 1986.

public relations agent was appointed in the United States. A week of protests was to be arranged in the province in the autumn. Meanwhile Paisley and Molyneaux set off on a series of 'Ulster Says No' rallies in Northern Ireland. In County Antrim Paisley suggested a boycott of goods from the Republic and urged Unionists not to socialize with supporters of the agreement. Molyneaux launched the campaign with the assurance that the 'Agreement was beginning to totter, crumble, it had already failed miserably in security'. Frank Millar, chief executive of the Official Unionists, said the new initiative was 'part of a longer-term plan to step up the political warfare against the agreement'.[13] But all was not well with the Unionist pact. There were reports of angry clashes, 'with members coming close to fisticuffs',[14] as the Unionist think-tank team struggled with the concepts of UDI, integration and devolution. *The Times* reported that the other Unionist organizing body, the Ulster Co-ordinating Committee, was 'discussing the feasibility of an all-out strike in the autumn'.[15]

Local politics is often more vicious than national politics. When Independent Unionist Jim Guy was elected as deputy mayor of Derry, DUP councillors called him a traitor. He was sent a note quoting Rudyard Kipling: 'Before a city's eyes, a traitor claims his prize. What need of further lies? We are the sacrifice.'[16] In Ballymena Borough Council, which was DUP-controlled, the Unionist pact was in trouble because the DUP refused to share the positions of mayor and deputy mayor with the Official Unionists. In Belfast, Sammy Wilson of the DUP was elected mayor in a contest with two other Unionist candidates, one of whom was known to be a Paisley nominee; Wilson was closer to Robinson. In his acceptance speech, Wilson made no pretence of representing all political opinion in the city: 'I am unashamed to be a Unionist and will do my best to rid this city . . . of two terrible cancers . . . Sinn Fein and the Anglo-Irish Agreement.'[17]

The cabinet's overseas and defence committee, with the prime minister in the chair, decided on 10 June 1986 to close the Northern Ireland Assembly. It had not been fulfilling its primary purpose of scrutinizing Northern Ireland legislation since the signing of the Anglo-Irish Agreement. It had failed to function as its author, James Prior, had intended since its inception in 1982. Eighteen members – thirteen from the SDLP and five from Sinn Fein – had absented themselves from the 78-member chamber from the beginning. The Alliance Party

---

[13] *News Letter*, 2 June 1986.
[14] *News Letter*, 31 May 1986.
[15] *Times*, 2 June 1986.
[16] *News Letter*, 3 June 1986.
[17] Ibid.

withdrew their ten representatives when the Unionists voted to suspend normal business and set up a committee to investigate the Anglo-Irish Agreement. Assembly members drew a salary of £19,000 and met regularly only on Wednesday afternoons. Their salary was the only source of income for some assemblymen; others, like Paisley, were the highest-paid parliamentarians in the United Kingdom, drawing salaries from Westminster, Stormont and Strasbourg. After the ratification of the Anglo-Irish Agreement, the Northern Ireland Assembly became the 'spearhead of the [Unionist] campaign'.[18] In January 1986 it published a scathing indictment of the Anglo-Irish Agreement. In mid March it recommended 'further measures of non-co-operation',[19] and on 15 May, six months after the signing ceremony at Hillsborough, fourteen DUP members took over the switchboard at Stormont and harangued all callers about the evils of the Anglo-Irish Agreement.

In moving the dissolution of the assembly, Tom King reiterated that 'devolution remains the Government's preferred option'.[20] He again extended an invitation to all constitutional parties in Northern Ireland to meet the government to discuss the future. John Hume welcomed the closure and repeated his 'willingness ... to sit down and discuss ... devolution'.[21] Enoch Powell was the only Unionist member to contribute to the debate. The secretary of state appealed to the Unionist MPs to return to the House and confirmed that the prime minister and he were prepared to consider ways to improve the handling of Northern Ireland business in the House. Ian Gow, a member of the Friends of the Union group, put the case for those Unionists who favoured integration as a solution: 'I would give to the twenty-six district councils ... modest additional powers ... there should be a regional council ... analogous to a county council in England ... legislation for Northern Ireland should be dealt with in this place ... in the same way as we now deal with legislation for Scotland and Wales ...'[22] The secretary of state responded: the Government do not support, and would not be prepared to suggest, integration as a policy for Northern Ireland.'[23] The speaker of the assembly flew to London on a 'Save the Assembly' mission involving the Queen and the Privy Council: 'dissolution at this critical time of constitutional uncertainty would remove the only elected forum in Northern Ireland where the Queen's loyal subjects can voice their deep concern.'[24]

---

[18] Cornelius O'Leary, Sydney Elliot and R. A. Wilford, *The Northern Ireland Assembly 1982–6* (Hurst, 1988), 91.

[19] Ibid., 192.

[20] *Hansard*, 12 June 1986, 507.

[21] Ibid., 510.

[22] Ibid., 1241–4.

[23] *Hansard*, 19 June 1986, 1218.

[24] *News Letter*, 19 June 1986.

The royal assent to the Bill dissolving the assembly was read out at the usual Wednesday afternoon session on 25 June 1986. The DUP filibuster was broken up in the early hours of the following morning with Ian Paisley prophesying 'hand to hand fighting in every street in Northern Ireland. We are on the verge of civil war'.[25] The twenty-four Unionist assemblymen retreated to Belfast City Hall where they held an 'alternative assembly'; Those attending observed the rituals of the House of Commons. This public charade failed to disguise the shambles within the Unionist pact. Molyneaux in particular was in a very exposed position. At an OUP press conference in early June he led everyone to believe that the government was about to allow the Hillsborough agreement to 'wither on the vine'. He was led to do so by encouragement from two quarters. Enoch Powell and Conservative back-benchers at Westminster, Gow and Biggs Davison in particular, led him to believe that during the debate on the renewal of direct rule the government would agree to integration and a Northern Ireland Grand Committee. Meanwhile, Peter Barry said in a debate in the Dáil that he was 'quite dissatisfied. I would want to see a lot more done more quickly with regard to the Conference.'[26] The Irish felt that King was lacking in enthusiasm for and commitment to the agreement. However, any lingering hopes Molyneaux had of a split at the intergovernmental level disappeared with the communiqué issued after the sixth meeting of the conference on 17 June 1986, which reported decisions on Irish voters, Irish street names and yet another police complaints procedure. Tom King's press conference, following the meeting with Barry, was agressively upbeat. He threw down the gauntlet to protesting loyalists by asking three questions: '(1) what is provocative about the Intergovernmental Conference, (2) what has the Agreement done to diminish Unionist interests and (3) what was offensive in the communiqué issued after the last meeting of the Dublin-London Conference?'[27] Molyneaux lost the chance to reply, because Robinson jumped in on Radio Ulster's *Behind the Headlines*. He answered: '(1) it legitimises Dublin's claim of jurisdiction over Northern Ireland, (2) our status has been altered, terrorism rewarded and the ballot box ignored, and (3) the communiqué committed the Government to finance the language and culture of a foreign state, which will dilute the Britishness and increase the nationalist ethos in Ulster.'[28]

Molyneaux got no concessions from the Northern Ireland Office and there were rampant divisions within his own party. One of his Unionist

---

[25] *Irish Times*, 25 June 1986.
[26] *Irish Times*, 5 June 1986.
[27] *News Letter*, 20 June 1986.
[28] Ibid.

colleagues at Westminster, Cecil Walker, published a document called *No Longer a Place Apart*, which recommended that the ten Official Unionist MPs abandon their boycott of Westminster. Molyneaux was also under intense pressure from Paisley, 'who was testing the water to see if there was a constituency for violent resistance'.[29] Molyneaux was worried that 'the medicine [Paisley's protests] is more dangerous than the disease [the Anglo-Irish Agreement]'.[30] The split in tactics between the OUP and the DUP reflected the degree to which Unionist party supporters regarded the various options as 'legitimate'.[31]

In the Republic Garret FitzGerald was also in a difficult and isolated position. He led a minority government with Labour, the minority coalition partner, distancing itself from Fine Gael's economic and social legislation. The 1981 crusade launched by FitzGerald to lead Ireland out of the shadow of de Valera's constitution with its claim to sovereignty over the whole of Ireland, and his own strongly-held views on the separation of state and church, received a crushing blow with the rejection of the divorce referendum on 26 June 1986. The proposed amendment to the constitution, which would have allowed divorce on the grounds of irretrievable breakdown when a couple had lived apart for five years, was lost. Some commentators saw in the defeat 'the clearest possible indication that enhancing ... attractiveness to Northerners is a very low-ranking item on the Irish national agenda'.[32] Stan Gebler Davies suggested that 'the people of Eire, faced with a choice between a Catholic state of their own and the faint possibility of a liberal united Ireland can be counted on to kiss Ulster goodbye every time'.[33] Dick Walsh of the *Irish Times* claimed that 'the Republic's claim to be regarded as a modern pluralist society has been severely damaged'.[34] Ian Paisley claimed the divorce referendum was the last nail in the coffin of the Anglo-Irish Agreement: 'the result has brought us back from the brink ... the civil war ... has receded as a result.'[35]

Margaret Thatcher and Garret FitzGerald had signed the Anglo-Irish Agreement to defeat terrorism, because 'violence and democracy cannot coexist'.[36] The intended target of the security forces of both countries was the IRA. The Loyalist backlash in Northern Ireland meant that the British government's thrust against the terrorists was blunted by the need to maintain law and order on the streets of the

---

[29] *Times*, 26 June 1986.
[30] *Listener*, 10 July 1986.
[31] *New Society*, 11 July 1986.
[32] *Times*, 30 June 1986.
[33] *Spectator*, 5 July 1986.
[34] *Irish Times*, 28 June 1986.
[35] *Irish Times*, 2 July 1986.
[36] *Times*, 16 November 1985.

province. The Republic's response was delayed by the need to retrain and restructure the Garda, and by difficulties connected with the process of extradition.

Each attempt at extradition since the Anglo-Irish Agreement had resulted in a humiliating failure for the British and Irish governments (see above p.68). Britain appeared to have more success elsewhere. In Holland, Brendan McFarlane and Gerry Kelly were fighting a losing battle against extradition to Northern Ireland. In the United States, President Reagan cajoled the Senate into supporting a revised extradition treaty that led to William Quinn's deportation to face a charge of murdering Constable Stephan Tibble in February 1975.

A six-point international agreement against terrorism was signed at the Tokyo summit of May 1986; there was to be an embargo on the export of arms to terrorist states, stricter control over diplomatic missions, improved extradition, stricter immigration control and the closest possible police and security co-operation. The European Community declared war on the IRA. Sean Hughes was arrested at Le Havre on 11 June 1986, and Harry Flynn, the alleged head of the INLA Council, was stopped in Paris in July. In Boston two IRA gun-runners, who hired Attorney-General Edwin Meese's private plane to smuggle arms to Ulster, appeared in court. The name of Patrick Ryan began to appear in connection with a missing £5 million which the authorities in Oslo were trying to trace. This ex-priest from Tipperary was also named by Interpol as the go-between in negotiations between the IRA and Libya. Commander Ahmed Jalloud, deputy to Gaddafi in Libya, told a group of West German MEPs that his country planned to 'resume aid to the Provisional IRA ... because of British co-operation with the US air raid'.[37] British security services had suspected since 1984 that Libya was supplying the IRA with weapons. They also suspected Ryan of being the IRA's banker in Europe, transferring large amounts of money between Swiss and Italian finance houses. Commander Jalloud's use of the word 'resume' in June 1986 confirmed intelligence reports, primarily from the United States, that the IRA had received shipments of arms from Libya in late 1984 and again in 1985. The discovery of the cache of arms stamped 'Libyan Armed Forces' in Roscommon and Sligo in January 1986 strengthened the hands of those in the security services who spoke of Ireland as a 'fortress island'. The Irish government instructed its ambassador in Rome to seek assurances from Colonel Gaddafi that 'his Government will not encourage the Provisionals or have contact with them, because such moves would be considered unfriendly'.[38]

---

[37] *Irish Times*, 18 June 1986.
[38] *Times*, 20 June 1986.

The Republican movement in Northern Ireland was under the control of the seven-man army council. The 'armalite and ballot box' strategy adopted in 1981 (see above p.14) gave Sinn Fein the chance to broaden community support for the Republican cause. By the time the Anglo-Irish Agreement was signed, Sinn Fein could boast 3 members of parliament (Sands, Carron and Adams), 5 assembly members, 56 district council representatives and a solid core of about 100,000 votes, some 10 per cent of the Northern Ireland electorate. It was Sinn Fein's success in the district elections of May 1985 that convinced Margaret Thatcher that the Hillsborough accord should be signed. The attack was to be two-pronged; terrorism was to be defeated by a security push north and south of the border, and terrorists were to be isolated from their host community by means of reforms that remedied major grievances.

The conflict in Northern Ireland conforms with all the standard definitions of terrorism. The IRA 'challenges the government's prerogative of the monopoly of armed force'[39] and attempts 'to impose [its] will by . . . a special kind of force designed to create an atmosphere of fear'.[40] Daniel Moynihan identified two features common to all terrorist organizations that certainly applied to the IRA: 'the principle of a self-appointed elite . . . and the principle that no one is innocent in politics – there are no innocent bystanders'.[41] Paul Wilkinson concluded that the key characteristics of political terror are 'indiscriminateness, unpredictability, arbitrariness, ruthless destruction and the implicitly amoral and antinomian nature of the terrorist challenge'.[42] To counter this, a government must convince the general population that it can protect them against the terrorists, while preventing 'the terrorists' political wing from making a display of political strength'.[43]

The security services had little to show for their sacrifices during the first six months of the agreement. Security successes took place for the most part outside the province. Patrick Magee's conviction for the Brighton bombing, McFarlane's extradition from Holland and the hunt for Ryan dominated the news in Britain, while the Loyalist backlash and the attacks on police homes and isolated Roman Catholic families occupied the attention of the public in Northern Ireland. Cross-border co-operation between the RUC and the Garda was improved, and the deployment of new battalions to the province meant that the

[39] Paul Wilkinson, *Political Terrorism* (Macmillan, 1974), 137.
[40] Benjamin Netanyahu, *Terrorism. How the West can Win* (Weidenfeld and Nicolson, 1986), 17.
[41] Ibid., 42.
[42] Wilkinson, op. cit., 17.
[43] Ibid., 140.

IRA's activities were curtailed. The IRA's chief victims continued to be the RUC, the UDR and the regular soldiers of the British Army. There was a marked decrease in IRA activity at the height of the Loyalist attacks on police homes, with a calculated enhancing of the terror campaign during the marching season.

A leading IRA terrorist, Seamus McElwaine, was killed by the security forces in April 1986 on his way to detonate a mine. The RUC uncovered an increasing number of IRA arms dumps. The Fraud Squad investigated cases worth £45 million and the RUC's anti-racketeering squad secured a growing number of convictions for extortion and illegal fund-raising. The RUC's successful penetration of the paramilitary cells was reflected in the increased incidence of punishment shootings. Frank Hogarty was shot dead on his return from London to Derry in May 1986; he was the third Derry informer to be executed within the year. The Droppin' Well pub murder trial in June 1986 sent four terrorists to prison for life, but other terrorist trials, which were based on the uncorroborated evidence of supergrasses, were collapsing on appeal.

The Loyalist paramilitary Ulster Defence Association was primarily a protection racket, operating on building sites and in gambling clubs and security firms. The ease with which first the Ulster Clubs, and then the Ulster Co-ordinating Committee, outflanked the UDA showed its irrelevance in the political struggle. The politicians were prepared to allow the half-hearted attempts of the UDA leaders, Andy Tyrie and John McMichael, to find a role for themselves in the anti-agreement campaign, trusting in the reassurances given by Peter Robinson and Alan Wright that they could do little harm. Their most important contribution to the struggle was the intimidation of police families and the attacks on Roman Catholic homes in and around Lisburn, John McMichael's UDA territory. It took others – the expelled DUP assemblyman, George Seawright, for instance – to politicize the remnants of the UDA's fighting force through links with the National Front and a UDA breakaway faction calling itself the Protestant Action Force. This group terrorized Roman Catholic residents in North Belfast, where three sectarian murders in one week in July 1986 led to riots on a new housing estate in Manor Street. Twenty-two families, Protestant and Roman Catholic, moved out and a peace line was built to seal one community off from the other.

Sectarian intimidation was also practised by the IRA, who issued death threats to workers involved in servicing security concerns in the province. The first victim was Seamus McAvoy, killed in his Dublin home in August 1985 for supplying portakabins to the RUC. Three other murders were carried out over the next twelve months, and on 30 July 1986 John Kyle was killed for supplying cement and sand to the security forces. 'Those who continue to refuse to take heed of this warning', read the IRA's statement, 'are in effect collaborating with our enemies ... they are part of the war machine.'[44] Second-hand car-dealers in Derry opted not to trade in former security cars. Laing issued a statement denying that they had ever carried out work for the security services and stopped work at RAF Aldergrove. Two dairies in County Down ceased to supply milk to local police stations. Blood transfusions were stopped at Whiterock army base for fear of threats by the IRA. In Newry, on the border with the Republic, one company withdrew its supply of fuel to the local police, while the council bin-men refused to collect rubbish from the army outposts in the town. On 26 July 1986, three men dressed as butchers walked up to an RUC patrol car parked in the town centre, shot all three occupants and threw a grenade into the car to frighten would-be rescuers away. These deaths brought to ten the total of RUC officers killed in the first seven months of the year; there had been 233 RUC deaths since the troubles started in 1969. The murder gang responsible for the Newry incident was believed to operate from across the border in County Louth. The first item on the agenda at the next meeting of the Intergovernmental Conference, originally called to discuss RUC handling of the Portadown march, now became cross-border co-operation and security.

A week later Peter Robinson led a mob of 200 supporters through the village of Clontibret, one and half miles south of the border with the Republic. The *Irish Times* commented: 'Peter Robinson wanted to find out what security was like on this side of the border. Now he knows.'[45] Robinson had not expected a Garda presence in Clontibret, but the RUC had reported the movement of vehicles in the province and the presence of large groups in Portglenone and Tandragee. Many were stopped at road-blocks, but thousands disappeared into side lanes. At Swatragh in County Londonderry 500 Loyalists invaded the village, parading in military-style formation up and down the one street. After two men had fired into the air, the group disappeared into the night. In Clontibret there was a similar show of military strength. When the Garda arrived on the scene they were set upon by the mob. One of the Garda officers 'fired five single shots from his revolver as his two colleagues discharged their sub-machine-guns over the heads of the mob'.[46] Peter Robinson and his colleagues 'attacked the police station, smashing the windows and the green communications box outside with cudgels, and daubed slogans ... on ... the station

[44] *Times*, 6 August 1986.
[45] *Irish Times*, 8 August 1986.
[46] *Guardian*, 14 January 1987.

and the Protestant village school'.[47] Robinson was arrested, detained overnight and subsequently charged on four counts of assault and causing actual bodily harm and seven other charges of causing malicious damage and of unlawful assembly. He refused water and food, and was released on bail of £10,000. On 10 August 1986 Robinson was escorted to the dais in Portadown by 'a colour party of twenty men wearing combat jackets and face masks'.[48]

The weekend also featured an illegal march in West Belfast to commemorate the fifteenth anniversary of internment; seventy marchers were arrested. Riots caused damage in Derry, Strabane, Kilkeel, Downpatrick and Keady, and Loyalist mobs went on the rampage in Portadown and Antrim. The Ulster Freedom Fighters released a video 'warning Roman Catholics working in Protestant areas not to turn up for work in the current climate'.[49] A fund to pay Robinson's legal fees was advertised in the local papers.

It was all too much for Molyneaux; he announced that he was abandoning his weekly press conference and would not be giving any more interviews. What particularly irked him was the media coverage given to the Clontibret invasion, the showing on network television of the Ulster Freedom Fighters (UFF) video and a leader in *The Times* which claimed that 'Mr Molyneaux appears unable to find a distinctive voice that is his own and meekly follows Dr Paisley's leadership'.[50] Molyneaux took umbrage: 'I have no intention of submitting to lectures ... on my duty to encourage yet another initiative in the aftermath of the predicted failure of the flawed Anglo-Irish Agreement.'[51]

Paisley, who had been on holiday in Canada, arrived back in the province in time to join the annual Apprentice Boys' march in Derry. He encouraged every available person to go to Dundalk to support Robinson. A two-hour riot broke out after Paisley had left Derry. Dundalk's main street showed the same scars two days later as Robinson's supporters retreated from the border-town court-room after the DUP deputy leader was remanded on bail until 2 October 1986. Petrol bombs were thrown at the Loyalists, and fourteen of their cars were smashed in the town's car park; they suffered further damage as they tried to escape.

Unemployment in Northern Ireland was running at 21.5 per cent. Sir Charles Carter, chairman of the Northern Ireland Economic Council, feared for the future and blamed political uncertainty and

---

[47] Ibid.
[48] *News Letter*, 11 August 1986.
[49] *Times*, 11 August 1986.
[50] *Times*, 8 August 1986.
[51] *Irish Times*, 12 August 1986.

terrorist activity for the deteriorating economy. The Anglo-Irish Agreement 'has made things much worse ... stimulated new unrest ... created political uncertainty ... inward investment is virtually at a standstill'.[52] Between March 1983 and March 1986 the number of jobs in Northern Ireland had fallen by 1.5 per cent, and the province received a subsidy of £1.5 billion a year. Unemployment blackspots highlighted the connection between terrorist action and a depressed local economy. Youth unemployment in West Belfast stood at 80 per cent and Strabane had a jobless rate of 52.4 per cent among men of all ages. Paddy Doherty, a strong Republican, went to Buckingham Palace to receive an award for his community work project in Derry and commented: 'once you stop looking for peace and start tackling the social and economic problems within the community, all of a sudden you get peace breaking out.'[53] His efforts, however, ran counter to the government's plan for a series of province-wide bodies rather than local task forces based on inner-city initiatives. The government feared sectarian control.

It faced a greater challenge in its attempt to outlaw discrimination in factories and family-owned businesses. Intimidation in the work place had 'now reached a level unmatched since the early 1970s, and it comes from terrorists on both sides'.[54] Twelve DHSS offices in the province closed down when 2,000 social security office staff stopped work in protest at threats to Roman Catholic colleagues. Short Brothers, the aeroplane and missile manufacturer, called in the police after twenty-four clocking-in cards belonging to Roman Catholic workers 'were removed and ripped up ... because they were IRA and republican supporters'.[55] Short Brothers was one of the key employers in the province, with a workforce of 6,587, only 14.8 per cent of whom were Roman Catholics. American defence contracts, worth £550 million, had been secured in March 1984 against a promise that the company would operate an affirmative-action programme on fair employment. A week before the Farnborough Air Show, the biggest shop-window for the company, the company's People's Loyalist Council called a thousand workers out on strike, after Sir Philip Foreman, the company chairman, sent a letter to all employees reminding them of company policy on the removal of flags, bunting, political posters and emblems from the factory floor: 'We must have an atmosphere within the workplace where all employees feel comfortable and free from intimidation.'[56] The dispute was settled when Short Brothers agreed to

---

[52] *Times*, 20 August 1986.
[53] *Economist*, 16 August 1986.
[54] *Economist*, 11 October 1986.
[55] *Times*, 18 August 1986.
[56] *News Letter*, 30 August 1986.

fly the Union Jack permanently over the factory; poppies and pictures of the royal family could be displayed 'sensibly'. At Farnborough the US Air Force announced that it was not taking up its option to buy thirty aircraft worth £300 million. The Northern Ireland Office published a consultative document on equality of opportunity in employment in the province, which proposed that public-sector employers should have a statutory duty to ensure equality of opportunity; private-sector employers would be given a certificate on signing a declaration on equality and their performance would be monitored. The trade union movement was also stirred into action by the intimidation at the DHSS and Short Brothers and published a campaign leaflet, *A Better Life for All*. The Irish Congress of Trade Unions was a Dublin-based movement; Loyalist workers from the 1986 strike committee led a demonstration against it when it held its annual conference in Belfast. Leaflets were handed out to delegates branding some of them as 'communists and republicans'.[57]

In mid August 1986, at the height of the sectarian campaign of intimidation, it 'seemed as though two sets of paramilitary groupings' were feeding off each other.[58] No sooner had the People's Loyalist Council at Short Brothers issued its threat to Roman Catholics than the INLA threatened Bass and Guinness, who between them employed 1,500 people. A fair indication of the effect of the unrest came with an announcement by Gallaghers of 700 redundancies at its Belfast plant. This followed closely on the heels of the closure of Rothmans at Carrickfergus.

Intimidation on the streets continued. In Lisburn 124 Roman Catholic and mixed families were attacked. The Housing Executive was able to offer alternative homes to only seventy-seven families. Most of those displaced wished to be rehoused in the Roman Catholic ghettos of West Belfast. They had tried living on mixed estates and now opted for the security of segregated communities. The RUC announced that 124 people had been arrested and charged with arson attacks since March 1986. The police 'had a record of a hundred reported intimidations, had discovered seventy-seven petrol bombs and confirmed that forty-three Roman Catholic homes had been fire-bombed in Lisburn alone since Easter 1986'.[59]

The sad summer of 1986 came to a close with a bombing campaign. There were eight incidents in the city on one day, 28 August. The Forum hotel, the railway station, the city hall and a city-centre pub were selected by the INLA as the targets of fire bombs or of hoax bombs. The

---

[57] *News Letter*, 2 July 1986.
[58] *Times*, 18 August 1986.
[59] *Irish Times*, 20 August 1986.

city centre came to a standstill. The campaign of terror was timed to coincide with the High Court appeal of INLA members against conviction on the uncorroborated evidence of supergrass Harry Kirkpatrick. It was to be the last of the supergrass appeals. The IRA killed a young electrician in Derry, exploded a bomb outside the police station in Newry and hijacked a bread van in Downpatrick. The van was loaded with bombs and left parked outside the town's police station. The IRA killed John Bingham, a leading UVF activist, whom they held responsible for five Roman Catholic deaths. He was given a UVF guard of honour at his funeral. The Protestant Action Force killed Raymond Mooney and Roy Webb in revenge for Bingham's death.

Ian Paisley was reported to be trying to control the carnage. Gerry Adams denied that the IRA had killed Bingham to provoke a Unionist backlash. Dr Cahal Daly accused all terrorists of 'following the gospel of Satan'.[60] He called on terrorists and those who supported them to discontinue their membership of the church. Many suspected that such appeals meant little to terrorists and their supporters, 'brought up to think of democracy as part of every day humdrum existence, but of recourse to violence as something existing on a superior plane, not merely glorious but even sacred'.[61]

The Unionist and historian A. T. Q. Stewart described the first year of the Anglo-Irish Agreement as one in which he had 'been governed from a heavily guarded bunker-like building . . . by men who are not responsible in any way to the population of Northern Ireland.'[62] Conor Cruise O'Brien said that 'the basis of the union seemed to be crumbling . . . we may . . . be already quite near the brink.'[63] James Naughtie observed that 'from Westminster, the depth of Unionist opposition was always underestimated, and from Belfast, there was imagined to be much more sympathy with the anti-agreement forces than ever existed'.[64] On one thing every commentator seemed to agree: Mrs Thatcher was not for turning. 'The idea that she always had an instinctive sympathy with Unionism was always a little misleading – there was common cause from time to time but never complete identification.'[65]

The ministers in the Northern Ireland Office could at least take some comfort from the fact that the agreement was still in place; the Sunningdale initiative only lasted for six weeks. Nevertheless, Tom King and his colleagues must have been worried by the reaction of the

[60] *Irish Times*, 1 September 1986.
[61] *Observer*, 12 December 1971.
[62] *Times*, 15 November 1986.
[63] *Irish Times*, 18 August 1986.
[64] *Fortnight*, No. 245, November 1986.
[65] Ibid.

Unionists. Government and Unionists were at loggerheads over the agreement, and the Unionists themselves were disunited and confused. Molyneaux lacked the political authority to keep his Official Unionist council under control and to give a lead to the few Conservative back-bench supporters at Westminster. His supporters back in the province were also alarmed by the ease with which Paisley seemed to be outflanking their leader. Molyneaux held the upper hand in terms of political representation, but once the members of parliament decided not to go to Westminster, his power declined. He and Paisley agreed 'to adopt separate anti-Agreement courses ... we concluded that opposition to the Anglo-Irish Agreement would be even more effective if we recognized that our two parties are different and draw their support from different sectors of the pro-Union population'.[66] This breach within the Unionist anti-agreement pact was to give the British government hopes of establishing a relationship with Molyneaux and isolating Paisley. The Northern Ireland Office announced that legislation would shortly be introduced to deal with incitement to hatred; there would be changes in the law relating to RUC control over public parades, a new complaints procedure would be instituted and the Irish language would be given recognition. The proposals, with the possible exception of the last one, were intended to encourage Molyneaux and enrage Paisley. The Northern Ireland Office, sensitive to Unionist feelings, was prepared to compromise on the language issue; it was considered 'reasonable to recognise and respect the interests which a comparatively small number of people in Northern Ireland have in the Irish language. To do more than this would, however, have serious administrative as well as political repercussions.'[67]

The International Fund for Ireland was launched to promote economic and social improvement and to encourage 'contact, dialogue and reconciliation between nationalists and unionists throughout Ireland'.[68] The £34 million available in the first year was to be invested in venture capital to stimulate private-sector investment, to improve communications and the quality of life and to ensure greater co-operation in the fields of education, research and the economy.

The issues given publicity at the ninth Intergovernmental Conference in October, the first since the July meeting between King and Barry, gave no grounds for an adverse Unionist reaction. The conference concerned itself with proposals for a Bill of Rights for the whole of Ireland, and a special conference on cross-border co-operation. The government was treading softly on issues on which Molyneaux was

---

[66] *Irish Times*, 4 November 1986.
[67] *Times*, 19 September 1986.
[68] *News Letter*, 25 September 1986.

known to be sensitive. King let it be known that he had 'asked the Dublin Government to remove Articles Two and Three' of the Irish constitution.[69] Molyneaux's confidence was slowly recovering. He received a major boost with the release of Thatcher's letter to FitzGerald on the issue of Diplock courts.

The Republic of Ireland had signed the Anglo-Irish Agreement in the belief that it would lead to changes in the administration of justice. Article 8 discussed the 'possibility of mixed courts in both jurisdictions for the trial of certain offences',[70] and the joint communiqué committed the signatories to 'seeking measures which would give substantial expression to the aim of underlining the importance of public confidence in the administration of justice'.[71] The Irish government wished in particular that the Diplock courts, where one judge sat alone without a jury, should be modified to allow three judges. Mrs Thatcher's letter of 4 November 1986 dismissed this possibility. She set out her reasons for rejecting the Irish proposal; any change would be an implicit criticism of the existing members of the Northern Ireland High Court. This was a view held forcibly by Lord Hailsham and Lord Lowry, the lord chief justice. The changes, if implemented, would be regarded as political rather than judicial. She also reminded the taoiseach that the Appeal Court already had three judges.

Tom King tried to ease the situation by listing some of the agreement's achievements in the field of justice. Three new judges had been appointed and a 50 per cent increase agreed in the size of the senior bar in Northern Ireland. The attorney-general had effectively stopped supergrass trials by insisting that there should be a reasonable prospect of conviction before authorizing court proceedings, and the lord chief justice had spoken against multi-defendant cases. The secretary of state emphasized that the government was 'determined to keep the number of cases without jury to a minimum'.[72] Mary Holland aptly summed up the Irish response: 'one year after Hillsborough the British have virtually reneged on Article 8.'[73]

The Irish partners to the agreement were in deep trouble at home. The *Irish Times* commented that 'Garret is now clinging to the Anglo-Irish Agreement like a drowning man to a leaking lifeboat'.[74] Two days later a motion of no confidence in his administration was lost by a majority of two. That gave him a six-month respite, since the Irish constitution does not allow the opposition to table a further no-

[69] *News Letter*, 13 October 1986.
[70] Anglo-Irish Agreement, Article 8.
[71] Joint Communiqué, Anglo-Irish Summit, 15 November 1985.
[72] *Irish Times*, 11 November 1986.
[73] *Irish Times*, 18 November 1986.
[74] *Irish Times*, 21 October 1986.

confidence motion within that period. But the sands of time were fast running out for FitzGerald, and the Anglo-Irish Agreement, once thought to be Fine Gael's salvation, began to look like its death knell. The partnership with Thatcher was not bringing returns fast enough to save FitzGerald's political skin, and there was no comfort to be found elsewhere: 'Private capital races out of the country ... Growth has stopped, investment has crashed, unemployment is surging, interest rates are over the moon.'[75] Expenditure on security was 'at least four times as much per capita ... as [in] the United Kingdom',[76] and a quarter of that expenditure was related to Northern Ireland. The promise of a breakthrough in Northern Ireland affairs as a result of the Anglo-Irish Agreement failed to materialize; the Irish team had little to show for their endeavours. Thatcher's rejection of the Diplock court reforms seemed to indicate that Ireland had all the burdens of co-responsibility for what was happening north of the border, but no authority to change things. The divorce referendum result seemed to indicate that FitzGerald had no power at home either. Conor Cruise O'Brien suggested that the agreement was 'a way of getting Britain off the hook of Northern Ireland'.[77] Stan Gebler Davies suggested that 'Dr FitzGerald had recently made it plain that he and his civil servants wish to clear out of Northern Ireland at the first available opportunity'.[78] There was certainly a strong feeling in Dublin by the autumn of 1986 that there was 'a question mark over the British Government's commitment'.[79]

FitzGerald could not even claim to have had much influence on John Hume and the SDLP. Mallon's success in the 1986 mini-election helped to harden the SDLP's stance. Hume, while declaring his willingness to join in discussions, made it plain that they had to be held within the parameters of the Hillsborough accord. The Unionists refused to budge until the accord was, at the very least, temporarily suspended. The Stalker suspension undermined a general move to support the RUC after their stance at Portadown in April, while the alleged inactivity of the police when faced with the one-day strike and the sectarian attacks on Roman Catholic homes in Lisburn stiffened Mallon's resolve not to be publicly associated with Hermon's call for community support for the RUC. The party adopted a wait-and-see attitude, content to watch while the Unionists were 'faced down ... the essential precondition for discussions on devolution ...'[80] Hume, declared Dr Cornelius

---

[75] *Economist*, 1 November 1986.
[76] *Listener*, 30 October 1986.
[77] *Irish Times*, 18 August 1986.
[78] *Spectator*, 15 November 1986.
[79] *Irish Times*, 18 August 1986.
[80] *New Statesman*, 21 November 1986.

O'Leary, 'has not tried primarily to bridge the gap between the two communities in the north ... instead he has engaged in talks with the British and Irish Governments ...'[81] Hume's links to Dublin now looked decidedly shaky. Haughey, FitzGerald's likely successor, was making strong anti-agreement speeches. Addressing a gathering at Bodenstown to commemorate Wolfe Tone, he devoted his speech to the situation in Northern Ireland: 'Northern Ireland is a failed political entity ... no attempt to shore it up with some kind of internal arrangement will succeed ... it is only when the power and influence of the London Government have been withdrawn from Irish affairs that the interests of all people on this island can be secured.'[82] The Anglo-Irish Agreement, Haughey argued, had achieved nothing: 'The position of the nationalists in the north is in fact seriously worsened ... sectarian assassinations are a stark reality and hundreds of nationalists are being ruthlessly terrorized and driven from their homes without any attempt being made by the police to intervene. Discrimination in employment has actually intensified and harassment of the security forces increased ... the abuse of human rights and the oppression of citizens are a daily occurrence there.'[83]

This forthright speech set off tremors throughout Ireland. FitzGerald accused Haughey of putting Catholic lives at risk: 'Mr Haughey's comments follow precisely the propaganda line that has been pursued in close parallel by the IRA and by extreme Unionists.'[84] The *Belfast Telegraph* said that 'Mr Haughey might be the best friend the opponents of the Anglo-Irish Agreement ever had'.[85] The *News Letter* reported that the Unionist leadership was uncertain how to react to Haughey's speech. Seamus Mallon said that 'we all must be very careful, because renegotiation could well wipe the slate clean ... and could be used by both the British and Unionists as a means of sliding out from their commitments and responsibilities'.[86] He went on to put the case for retaining the only all-Ireland development since partition; the agreement, he argued, had forced Unionists to redefine Unionism and had fundamentally changed the relationship between Northern Unionists and Westminster.

Haughey had a further reason for making his views on the agreement known so widely – he feared the repercussions of a plan by Sinn Fein to abandon its abstentionist policy in the Republic. Hitherto the party had held the view that it should not sit in the Dáil until Ireland was

---

[81] *Irish Times*, 4 August 1986.
[82] *Irish Times*, 13 October 1986.
[83] *Irish News*, 13 October 1986.
[84] Ibid.
[85] *Belfast Telegraph*, 13 October 1986.
[86] *Irish Times*, 13 October 1986.

united. If Sinn Fein won and took up seats in the Dáil, it was likely to
be at Fianna Fáil's electoral expense. Some observers suggested that Sinn
Fein could win up to 'half a dozen seats under Ireland's proportional
representational system . . . all at Haughey's expense'.[87] On 27
November 1986 the *ard fheis*, or annual conference, of Sinn Fein decided
by 429 votes to 161 to abandon the abstentionist policy. There was a
further split, into Provisional Sinn Fein led by Gerry Adams and
Republican Sinn Fein with Ruairí Ó Brádaigh as its head. Here was proof
that the Anglo-Irish Agreement had had a destabilizing effect on the
Republican movement. Adams called the agreement 'the new generator
of partition . . . it is an attempt to isolate and draw popular support away
from the republican struggle while putting a diplomatic veneer on British
rule, injecting a credibility into establishment 'nationalism' so that British
rule and the interests it represents can be stabilized in the long term'.[88]

The agreement posed a threat to the military and political fortunes of
the Republican movement. Cross-border security co-operation 'would
pose serious problems, at the very least of logistics and supply, to the
IRA'.[89] The Garda's discovery of the Roscommon and Sligo arms
cache was but one example of a new-found commitment in the
Republic. In the North, 'the organization became infiltrated by British
Agents and [was] suffering from informers, especially in Belfast'.[90]
Danny Morrison confirmed that this led in 1986 to 'very few
operations'.[91] The conviction of Magee, the extradition of Kelly from
Holland and of Quinn from America and the killing of Seamus
McElwaine all weakened the IRA operationally, but the organization
took advantage of the period of the Loyalist attacks on the RUC and
Roman Catholic homes 'to restructure and install a strong central
command . . . especially in Belfast'.[92] The comparatively low level of
activity was only the peace before the storm.

The first year of the agreement had been a disappointing one
electorally for Sinn Fein. The SDLP had rejected the proposal for a joint
Nationalist pact in the January mini-election, and Sinn Fein had
received 5,000 votes less than in the 1983 general election. The SDLP
benefited, especially in Armagh, where Seamus Mallon won the seat.
The decision to overturn the policy of abstention was a significant shift
in Republican tactics in the Republic. In reality, it was a struggle for the
leadership of the movement between the old guard, mainly based in the
Republic, and Gerry Adams and the northern command. Adams had

[87] *Sunday Times*, 26 October 1986.
[88] Gerry Adams, *The Politics of Irish Freedom* (Brandon Press, 1986), 105.
[89] Patrick Bishop and Eamonn Mallie, *The Provisional IRA* (Heinemann, 1987), 352.
[90] *New Statesman*, 20 November 1986.
[91] Ibid.
[92] Ibid.

prepared his case well. He got the General Army Convention to meet for the first time in seventeen years to support his motion. The central issue, according to Adams, was not absentionism: 'The problem we experience is that many republicans have long had a compartment-alized attitude to their republican activities whereby they pursue republican "politics" in isolation from their involvement in community groups, trade unions . . . we are seeking to change that.'[93] The Anglo-Irish Agreement could claim to have destabilized the Republican movement. In the Republic they feared the worst; one of the causes of the troubles in the North was spilling over into the South.

In Northern Ireland, the adjournment protest was under pressure. Most of the members of Belfast City Council were in danger of being disqualified from standing again (see above p.56). The council did not function as a proper body; the new lord mayor, Sammy Wilson, delegated council business to the General Purposes Committee, which then adjourned. However, the joint pressure of legal retribution and the weakening of the Unionist pact led a number of councils to abandon the protest. North Down returned to normal business; Mayor Bruce Milligan said that 'we do feel the strike tactic is dead'.[94] Carrickfergus Council, on the other hand, not only continued with the adjournment policy, but made local government administration impossible by preventing council officials from making decisions on day-to-day business. There was confusion, with accusations that some councillors were transacting business covertly. Molyneaux and Paisley met to 'put brakes on a slide back to normal business in council chambers',[95] but acknowledged that the rate strike had run its course. An advertisement in the *News Letter*, sent in by Molyneaux and Paisley, advised all who had withheld their rates in the campaign, 'which has been an outstanding success',[96] to settle their accounts in full before their debt was referred to the Enforcement of Judgments Office. The adjournment policy for district councils was to continue, as was the abstentionist tactic at Westminster. Opposition to the policies continued. Seven rebel Official Unionist councillors were expelled from the party for voting against Unionist policy. Others found themselves out-manoeuvred by their political opponents. A mix-up at Belfast City Hall resulted in some Official Unionist councillors voting with the SDLP and Sinn Fein, while in Craigavon two DUP members inadvertently voted with the SDLP, Sinn Fein and the Workers' Party to cause a tied vote. Six councillors from Belfast (Official Unionists and Independent Unionists)

[93] Bishop and Mallie, op. cit., 354.
[94] *News Letter*, 28 August 1986.
[95] *News Letter*, 24 September 1986.
[96] *News Letter*, 23 September 1986.

went to Castlereagh Council, which had a DUP majority, to object to the fact that it was carrying on its work while other councils closed down their services. The Castlereagh Council voted to exclude the visitors from the council chamber. Mr Justice Hutton put further pressure on Antrim, Coleraine, Lisburn and Castlereagh Councils when he awarded costs of £20,000 against them, ordered them to revert to normal business and declared their adjournment policy illegal. A fund was launched to help defray the campaign costs.

The alternative assembly ceased its play-acting on 15 October 1986. On the last day Maginnis argued strongly for non-violent civil disobedience; Robinson added that 'if civil disobedience fails we must be prepared to go further'.[97] He went on to state that he 'despised the House of Commons and the Prime Minister of the United Kingdom. They have both betrayed Ulster. You will never find any solution through them. It will only be found through Ulstermen.'[98] This was a public rejection of efforts by the Friends of the Union to bring Unionists back to Westminster, to agree to a round-table conference on devolution and to moderate their rhetoric. Molyneaux's leadership was under pressure; he would have to face an annual conference of his party before the first year of the agreement was out.

Stage-managed, high profile, DUP-inspired protests continued with increased vigour. As the anniversary of the agreement approached, there were plans for a repeat protest rally outside Belfast City Hall. Paisley had kept consistently to the policy that there would be no talks on devolution while the Anglo-Irish Agreement and the Maryfield secretariat were in operation. The word 'never', which he repeated five times at the Belfast rally in November 1985, meant just that. There was no scope for compromise. The Hillsborough accord had to go, lock, stock and barrel. However, he faced a challenge to his own position from his deputy, Peter Robinson. The struggle for ascendancy led to a marked escalation in the level of protest and the steady build-up of violence. After Robinson's invasion of Clontibret (see above, p.94) the Unionist pact was to all intents and purposes at an end; it was kept in place simply for show. Paisley had to try to re-establish relations with Molyneaux and to reassert his authority over Robinson. First, however, he had to appeal over their heads to his traditional supporters. He held a press conference at which he released details of a document purporting to be the minutes of a meeting between the chief constable and senior officers of the RUC. The paper included an assessment of Loyalist and Republican paramilitary groups; it was claimed that intelligence coverage of the IRA and INLA was good, but that 'similar

---

[97] *Irish Times*, 16 October 1986.
[98] Ibid.

penetration of loyalist groupings was essential due to the close alliance with political, paramilitary and subversive organizations'.[99] The document also claimed that the RUC knew of Loyalist plans to invade villages in the South, and to blow up sewerage plants in the North. Paisley finished the press conference by quoting a statement alleged to have come from one of the divisional commanders of the RUC; the Garda, according to the officer, 'promised much – delivered little'.[100]

Tom King moved to repair the damage done to relations between the RUC and the Garda. He said that 'the Garda needed help to develop its anti-terrorist techniques. Ireland had not faced this challenge before.'[101] He added that he was 'impatient for progress in cross-border security'.[102] Paisley's timing was uncanny. His ability to spot a problem and exploit it fully remains one of his greatest political assets. The Ulster Clubs started to picket the homes of so-called 'collaborators'. Robinson advocated UDI. The government had no influence and little contact with the DUP by this time. They were concentrating their attention on Molyneaux and his Official Unionists.

The Official Unionist party was battling for the soul of Unionism. The integrationists were fighting to 'bring to Ulster the fresh breezes of non-sectarian class politics as the major parties in Britain organized in Northern Ireland'.[103] The other wing of the party appealed to the 'tradition through which attainment to the Union was conditional on what was seen as Britain delivering its part of the bargain'.[104] Some wanted the accord abandoned, others wanted it suspended. Cecil Walker argued for an abandonment of abstention from Westminster. John Taylor hit out at the campaign tactics of the DUP: 'I am convinced that they do not yet recognize that such tactics are being totally ignored in Britain ... such has been the failure of the Ulster Says No campaign.'[105] At the Official Unionist conference – most of which was conducted in closed session, away from the prying press and media – an attempt to commit the party to total integration failed. Instead it decided on an all-out fight against the agreement, with no decision on either devolution or integration. Molyneaux 'called a temporary halt to the rethinking of political philosophy'.[106]

On Monday 10 November 1986, Ulster Resistance was born. Paisley waited for Molyneaux's party conference to end before launching what

---

[99] *Times*, 20 August 1986.
[100] Ibid.
[101] *Times*, 4 September 1986.
[102] *News Letter*, 17 October 1986.
[103] *Fortnight*, No. 243, September 1986.
[104] Ibid.
[105] *News Letter*, 17 October 1986.
[106] Ibid.

he called 'a disciplined force to resist the activities of the British and Irish Governments and the IRA to push us down the United Ireland road . . . it would be sad to see Loyalists die, but they would not be dying in vain as they are now'.[107] He gave plenty of warning of his intentions in an interview three weeks before the launch, calling for the mobilization of Ulster folk 'to do what Lord Carson did and that is to resist by whatever force they can muster'.[108] Molyneaux had commented that the idea of a citizen army 'would worry all right-thinking people',[109] and a group of Protestant clergy calling themselves the Referendum Group warned of 'civil war unless the Anglo-Irish Agreement is put to the ballot box . . . new armies are being formed, and, as a result, existing paramilitaries will be activated'.[110]

The Ulster Resistance rally was held behind closed doors at the Ulster Hall. The standards of nine Ulster divisions were dedicated as the audience 'resolved to band together to take whatever steps are necessary . . . embark on a province-wide recruitment of men willing and prepared to take direct action as and when required'.[111] Paisley was supported by Robinson, Alan Wright and Lord Mayor Sammy Wilson. The first show of strength by Ulster Resistance was at Kilkeel, where one thousand men marched through the village and Paisley was introduced as 'the head of Ulster's newest army'.[112] In Westminster the Queen's Speech said, 'My Government will continue through the Anglo-Irish Agreement to co-operate with the Government of the Republic of Ireland',[113] and promised a new bill to amend Northern Ireland legislation against terrorism. The SDLP called for a review of the incitement to hatred provisions, and the RUC warned that wearers of uniforms might be prosecuted. Paisley was centre-stage again: the 'archetypal demagogue was in the right place and at the right time, to articulate the well-founded instinctive suspicion of Ulster Unionists that they were being sold down the river'.[114] As Enoch Powell noted, Paisley had a 'habit of dealing in threats and the preference for a deliberately rough approach . . . it is a career that would be unthinkable in any English context'.[115]

The Ulster Clubs organized a province-wide torchlight parade on the eve of the anniversary of the signing of the Anglo-Irish Agreement; Alan Wright said that 'he and his followers wanted a more forceful

---

[107] *News Letter*, 20 October 1986.
[108] Ibid.
[109] *Irish Times*, 4 November 1986.
[110] *News Letter*, 4 November 1986.
[111] *Irish Times*, 11 November 1986.
[112] *Irish Times*, 13 November 1986.
[113] *Times*, 14 November 1986.
[114] *Spectator*, 22 November 1986.
[115] Ibid.

unionist leadership'.[116] The Harland and Wolff workers gathered at the Cornmarket at lunch-time on the eve of the anniversary. They had been crucial to the success of the one-day strike, but were reluctant to be used again in a further show of industrial muscle; redundancies were on the way. In Ballymena, forty Loyalists held an anti-internment rally, fearing a mass arrest of Unionists on the eve of the anniversary. In Hillsborough, the Orange Order rally drew a thousand supporters for a parade that had torches burning and drums beating. Molyneaux was present. Trouble was reported late at night at Lisburn, Lurgan and Carrickfergus and the police were called in to Short Brothers to investigate a hoax death-notice published in the *Belfast Telegraph*.

The UDA had refused to join in any organized protest. Throughout the first year of the Anglo-Irish Agreement the association had been excluded from the councils of Unionism, though it maintained its contacts with individual politicians such as Robinson. John McMichael had his own ambitions for his movement and was not going to allow anybody else to deploy the UDA's resources. Twenty minutes before the Belfast rally was due to begin, twelve UDA men wearing balaclavas appeared on the platform outside the City Hall and paraded back and forth. Demonstrators on the fringe of the large crowd started breaking into shops in the city centre. By the end of the afternoon 149 shops had been damaged and 14 of them looted. The rally audience was pelted with hundreds of golf balls. Paisley called for a round-table conference with Dublin excluded and the agreement suspended. Molyneaux assured his audience that 'we are through the worst of the crisis'.[117] Most of his supporters were trying to find a safe haven away from the rioters at the back of the crowd. Molyneaux also called on all Unionist councillors to resign from statutory bodies, to petition the Queen and to plan a more effective rate strike and television-licence strike. The rally broke up early. A hundred and ten arrests were made and twenty-seven civilians and forty-eight RUC officers were injured. Two people died. In Bridgwater, in Somerset, 400 marchers descended on Tom King's home in an anti-agreement rally organized by the Friends of the Union.

The first year of the agreement was over. There had been sixty-five deaths from violence that year, with terrorist groups claiming responsibility for fifty-five of them. The Republican movement killed three informers, two UDA members and ten civilians, as well as twenty-seven from the security forces: fourteen from the RUC, four from the army and nine from the UDR. The Loyalist paramilitary groups killed thirteen Roman Catholic civilians. The security services accounted for ten deaths.

---

[116] *News Letter*, 14 November 1986.
[117] *News Letter*, 17 November 1986.

4

Protests, feuds and elections

A week after Molyneaux's commitment to a hardening of the council protest, his Official Unionist Association rejected his plan by eighty-two votes to forty-four. Roy Bradford, a former member of the Stormont cabinet, said that 'this rejection shows up with unmistakable clarity the lack of a considered, clear-cut strategy . . . now publicly laid at the door of the leadership . . . the leadership of the DUP is one man, autocratic – the leadership of the OU is collegiate and exercised in erratic fashion by their senior Members of Parliament.'[1]

Molyneaux's public commitment to mass resignations at district council level came after the OUP annual conference and during the launch of Ulster Resistance and must be seen as his attempt to wrest the initiative back from Paisley and give his Unionist councillors a leading role in the anti-agreement campaign. The policy was unlikely to be popular. If 350 Unionist councillors were to resign, six councils would cease to function, since the opposition could not muster a quorum. In another twelve Unionist-controlled councils the opposition – SDLP, Sinn Fein and Workers' Party – would be able to take power. The eight Nationalist-controlled councils would continue to function as before. Frank Millar, the chief executive of the Official Unionists, came out against his party leader's policy: 'any unionist who walked out of a council and allowed republicans to take over would be guilty of treachery.'[2] Bradford added his support to the decision of the Official Unionist councillors not to resign; it was, he considered, 'neither fair nor logical to expect the poor bloody infantry to carry on fighting while their officers are carousing in the enemy tents at Westminster'.[3] This was a reference to the fact that Powell, Maginnis and Smyth had

---

[1] *News Letter*, 1 December 1986.
[2] *News Letter*, 19 November 1986.
[3] *News Letter*, 1 December 1986.

decided to take part in the House of Commons debate on the Northern Ireland (Emergency Provisions) Bill.

Molyneaux's predicament was made worse by the aggressive public stance taken by the DUP on the streets and in the council chambers. Paisley paraded at Portadown with 3,000 supporters of Ulster Resistance, many dressed in paramilitary uniforms. Robinson, the DUP's deputy leader, held the resignations of all the DUP members of Castlereagh council, pending clarification of the OUP's council policy. Once Robinson heard of the Official Unionists' volte-face, he resigned as mayor of Castlereagh in protest.

Official Unionist policy was explained by Jim Kirkpatrick, secretary of the party's Belfast City Hall group: 'I firmly believe that the adjournment campaign has run its full course and will do more harm than good ... by pursuing the adjournment policy we are handing the keys of the City Hall over to Sinn Fein.'[4] In addition to the political argument, most councillors were in danger of being disqualified from standing again if the High Court held them to be in contempt. Coleraine Borough Council voted to go back to normal business under threat of contempt proceedings. The DUP representatives walked out, leaving OUP councillors to vote with the opposition parties. In Belfast City Council the roles were reversed. Here the Official Unionists left the chamber, leaving the DUP in a minority position, outvoted twenty-two to fourteen on a motion to adjourn. The Offical Unionists had 'been instructed by ... party headquarters to try and avoid the imminent contempt of court'.[5] As Jim Wells of the DUP put it, 'confusion reigns in council chambers'.[6]

The adjournment protest was effectively at an end by mid February; Molyneaux admitted that he 'did not discount the possibility of the entire operation being terminated'.[7] This statement followed the announcement that North Down, Ards and Coleraine Councils had struck a rate. A week later Belfast City Council did likewise; the Official Unionist councillors abstained and the DUP hardliners were defeated by a combined SDLP, Alliance, Workers' Party and Sinn Fein opposition. Northern Ireland Office minister Richard Needham said he would 'quietly ignore'[8] the fact that the council had overrun its legal deadline by forty-eight hours. The council protest had lasted for fourteen months and had frustrated local government administration. The Northern Ireland Office had succeeded in appointing commissioners to set a rate,

---

[4] *News Letter*, 2 December 1986.
[5] *Irish Times*, 6 January 1987.
[6] *News Letter*, 22 January 1987.
[7] *News Letter*, 10 February 1987.
[8] *Guardian*, 18 February 1987.

but 45,000 ratepayers had withheld payment and been summoned for it in the financial year 1986–7. The funding of voluntary organizations and major new capital projects had been blocked. One such project, the new leisure centre in Cookstown, County Tyrone, would have employed thirty people in an area where 37 per cent of the population was out of work.

The failure of the council protest against the Anglo-Irish Agreement, which had evolved from Unionist demonstrations against the presence of Sinn Fein representatives in the council chamber created bitter enmity between OUP and DUP councillors. The proposal to effect a mass resignation from statutory boards such as the Northern Ireland Tourist Board, the Sports Council, the Housing Executive, the Police Authority and the Fire Authority met with more success. Unionist councillors were not in danger of losing their local power base by opting out of these province-wide, nominated bodies. Molyneaux, a JP for thirty years, signalled his support for the campaign by resigning.

The policy of abstention from the House of Commons also exposed the fragile nature of the Unionist accord. Molyneaux sought to explain the presence of Powell, Maginnis and Smyth at the debate on the Northern Ireland (Emergency Provisions) Bill by pointing out that it was a Bill and not an Order in Council, and therefore offered the first opportunity in twelve months to debate and move amendments. The DUP's chief whip was unimpressed by this delicate distinction; he said that 'the move would be interpreted . . . as something of a return to normality by Unionists and the beginning of coming to terms with the Anglo-Irish Agreement'.[9] The pressure to abandon the abstentionist policy was intense. Roy Bradford suggested that Unionists study Parnell's parliamentary tactics: 'let the members go back to Westminster and make a bloody parliamentary nuisance of themselves.'[10] The appeal went unheeded; Paisley, Smyth and Maginnis were removed from House of Commons Select Committees for refusing to engage in normal parliamentary activities.

The Unionists were not alone in their troubles. FitzGerald, threatened with defeat in the coming general election, travelled to London in an attempt to speed up the pace of change and save his own political skin. On 28 November 1986 he told King that the implementation of the Irish Extradition Bill was conditional on British action with regard to Diplock courts in Northern Ireland. He explained that the European Convention on Terrorism would be pushed through the Dáil in December 1986 and the Senate in January 1987, but would

[9] *Irish Times*, 18 December 1986.
[10] *News Letter*, 1 December 1986.

not be ratified until there was progress on Diplock courts, cross-border security and the relationship of the security forces with the minority community.[11]

The government's response was to publish the draft of a new Public Order Bill and to present a bill to amend the Northern Ireland (Emergency Provisions) Act of 1978. Both measures went to the heart of the community conflict in the North. The Public Order Bill repealed the Flags and Emblems (Display) Act (Northern Ireland) of 1954 and brought the laws in Northern Ireland into line with legislation in the rest of the United Kingdom. It gave the police greater powers to impose conditions on parades and open-air meetings, and extended the notice period for intended marches from five days to seven days. The secretary of state was given the power to ban marches if he feared serious disruption to the community or undue demands on the security forces, and his decision could not be challenged in the courts. The new Emergency Provisions Act was to be the corner-stone of security policy in the province; it covered street and house searches and the arrest, interrogation and trial of suspected terrorists. It made no change in the Diplock court procedures.

The new Bill was published on the day a Labour Party deputation met FitzGerald in Dublin. They were persuaded by him of the strength of the case for having three judges in the Diplock no-jury courts. FitzGerald, however, made no headway at his meeting with Thatcher in London two days later and little progress was noted at the twelfth Intergovernmental Conference in Belfast on Monday 8 December. King admitted at the subsequent press conference that there were 'very real difficulties'.[12]

Further dificulties arose when Fianna Fáil introduced controversial amendments to the Extradition Bill and the Single European Act. The amendments concentrated on the issues of sovereignty and neutrality, two of the motivating forces of Haughey's political career. He proposed a *prima-facie* requirement as an additional hurdle in the Extradition Bill, and a reaffirmation of Irish neutrality in the Single European Act.

FitzGerald opposed the *prima-facie* amendment by arguing that if it were added to the new bill 'the country could become a haven for terrorists and criminals ... Ireland would have to denounce the convention on extradition which it had already signed and the resulting changes would make extradition impracticable in many cases'.[13] He recalled that the first Irish extradition law, introduced by Haughey in 1963, had not included a *prima-facie* requirement. He also reminded his

---

[11] *Irish Times*, 29 November 1986.
[12] *Irish Times*, 9 December 1986.
[13] Ibid.

Irish audience that the United Kingdom was trying to exclude the requirement from its laws. Instead of the *prima-facie* requirement, FitzGerald's government imposed its own checks and balances. The British attorney-general would have to send his Irish counterpart a note through the diplomatic channels, confirming that the extradited person would appear before a court on a charge and not be detained for questioning.

When Tom King announced that the British government was 'not presently persuaded' that the Diplock procedures should be amended,[14] the Irish government postponed the implementation of the newly passed Extradition Bill from 1 June 1987 to 1 December 1987. Anglo-Irish relations were at a very low ebb, and trust and confidence in the Anglo-Irish Agreement at breaking-point. FitzGerald survived a no-confidence motion by one vote, after summoning two TDs from their hospital beds. The Dáil went into Christmas recess knowing that when it reconvened on 28 January 1987 the first business of the new session would be a budget guaranteed to shatter the fragile Fine Gael–Labour coalition.

In Northern Ireland, unemployment at stood at 19.3 per cent. There were 800 redundancies at Harland and Wolff a week after the first anniversary of the Anglo-Irish Agreement. The government introduced an appropriation order to increase public expenditure in the province; most of it went to cover the Harland and Wolff subsidy. Ian Gow made much of the fact that the Northern Ireland Office was seeking approval for additional expenditure of £50.5 million with three months of the financial year still to go; parliament had already approved the expenditure of £70 million. He blamed the Anglo-Irish Agreement for increased costs and quoted Sir Charles Carter, chairman of the Northern Ireland Economic Council: 'Unhappily, the government's initiative in the Anglo-Irish Agreement, whatever its political or foreign policy virtues, has made things much worse for the economy'.[15] Nicholas Scott released figures that showed that public expenditure per head was 40 per cent higher in Northern Ireland than in the United Kingdom as a whole. Within a week an additional subsidy, to the value of £68 million, was released when the International Fund for Ireland came into operation on 12 December 1986; the government undertook to regard any monies from the fund as additional funding for the province.

The public subsidy to the province was increased by 6 per cent for the financial year 1987–8; the increased expenditure was to cover additional annual security costs of £40 million, £55 million extra for education and

---

[14] *Hansard*, 16 December 1986, 1083.
[15] *Hansard*, 4 December 1986, 1114.

£50 million extra for health. Thirty per cent of the total budget was taken up by social security payments. A further boost to the Northern Ireland economy came with the announcement, a week before Christmas, that the EC was to allocate £11 million in grants to the province. Another seasonal present came with the award of a £225 million contract by the Ministry of Defence to Short Brothers.

In Belfast an 800 lb IRA bomb demolished a number of houses near the Lisburn Road RUC station. The security services anticipated an orchestrated bombing campaign, following the split at the Sinn Fein annual conference. The new Republican Sinn Fein was expected to parade its fire power, and the INLA was thought to be eager to capitalize on what they saw as a weakening of Gerry Adams's position within the Republican movement. The security services were certain that the terrorists had considerable reserves of very sophisticated weaponry. In Newry, thirty civilians were injured when mortars fired at the town's RUC station missed their target, hitting surrounding houses. The IRA South Down brigade apologized, saying that its 'engineers would be checking to see why the missiles overshot the Edward Street RUC post'.[16] Bombs exploded in the Granville Arms in Mill Street in Belfast, and a grenade went off in a pillar-box in Queen Street. Hotels in Dungannon and Cookstown were extensively damaged by fire bombs. The RUC put this down to a combination of pre-Christmas activities by Republican Sinn Fein, the first tentative efforts of a new terror group called the People's Liberation Army and the IRA's reaction to the extradition of Brendan McFarlane and Gerard Kelly from Holland to Northern Ireland.

The security services had new leaders at the helm. The commander of the UDR was Brigadier Michael Bray, who held his first press conference to deny a DUP claim that the regiment had been slashed by 50 per cent and all recruitment stopped. A week later David Caldwell, who had served in the UDR sixteen years previously for five months, was killed when a bomb went off in his lorry. He became the forty-third UDR man to die since the beginning of the troubles.

The new chairman of the Northern Ireland Police Authority was Tom Rainey, chairman of Carreras Rothman (NI) and chairman of the CBI. He took over from Sir Myles Humphreys, who had served for ten years. Sir John Hermon had succeeded in distancing himself from the political manoeuvrings of the Intergovernmental Conference, preferring to have meetings with his Irish counterpart outside the conference sessions; neither police chief attended the Intergovernmental Conference held at Stormont on 8 December 1986. Cardinal Ó Fiaich, in a pre-Christmas interview on RTÉ, said that he could not

---

[16] *News Letter*, 2 December 1986.

advise Roman Catholics to join the RUC 'until affairs like the Stalker one are cleared up'.[17] The RUC called the cardinal's views hurtful, and the Police Federation, in a letter to Ó Fiaich, said 'we have lost 235 officers and another 5,900 have been injured . . . it is therefore deplorable that you . . . should so publicly distance the Church from our Roman Catholic members'.[18] Archbishop Eames said that 'all public leaders must recognise the dangers inherent in failing to give full backing to the Constitutional forces of law and order'.[19] Peter Barry entered the debate by encouraging Roman Catholics to join the RUC; Seamus Mallon advised them to wait. Lord Brookeborough labelled Ó Fiaich an 'evil primate', later to withdraw 'evil' and substitute 'irresponsible and bad'.

In the High Court in Belfast, two days before Christmas, a three-judge appeal court quashed the guilty verdicts on twenty-five of the original twenty-seven accused in the Kirkpatrick supergrass trial. Between November 1981 and November 1983 at least seven Loyalist and eighteen Republican supergrasses were responsible for the arrest of nearly 600 suspects. Fifteen supergrasses retracted their evidence and only ten trials took place; of the 217 defendants, 120 were found guilty, a conviction rate of 55 per cent. In five of the ten cases, 67 out of the 74 convictions were quashed on appeal. The overall conviction rate for the supergrass trials, taking the appeal verdicts into account, was 44 per cent.

The decision of the High Court in Belfast coincided with a pre-Christmas tour of the province by Mrs Thatcher. The BBC refused to carry a call from the Unionist leaders for Loyalists to protest against the visit, on the grounds that the corporation did not see it as its function to bring people out on the streets. During her visit, Mrs Thatcher said that 'the Agreement is coming to be accepted because the fears expressed about it have not been well-founded'.[20] Paisley claimed the prime minister came 'as a dictator, she can only move surrounded by a vast turnout of security forces,[21] and Gerry Adams called the visit 'a flag-waving stunt'.[22] The prime minister announced the ratification of the extradition treaty between the United Kingdom and the United States of America; the American bolt-hole for Republican terrorists was no more.

In Christmas and New Year messages, Cardinal Ó Fiaich told paramilitary groups that 'your methods are unchristian and sinful',[23]

---

[17] *Irish Times*, 22 December 1986.
[18] *News Letter*, 23 December 1986.
[19] Ibid.
[20] *News Letter*, 24 December 1986.
[21] *Irish Times*, 24 December 1986.
[22] *News Letter*, 24 December 1986.
[23] *News Letter*, 2 January 1987.

while Archbishop Eames warned that 'apathy on the part of people who feel unable to influence events is a subtle yet highly dangerous ingredient in our society today'.[24] Terrorist activity had accounted for seven more deaths in 1986 than in 1985; forty were attributed to the Republicans, thirty-seven to the IRA, three to the INLA and fifteen to the Loyalist paramilitaries. Ten RUC officers, eight UDR soldiers and four regular army soldiers were among the casualties. The Housing Executive released figures that showed the full force of the intimidation of the summer months; 1,118 families had left their homes, almost all as a result of Protestant paramilitary activity.

The Unionists put a brave face on their internal feuds and welcomed the New Year 'secure in the knowledge that the Anglo-Irish dictat is not going to endure' (Molyneaux)[25] and that 'this will be the year we bury the treacherous deal' (Paisley).[26] The *News Letter*, started fifty-six years before the French Revolution and published continuously during the reigns of nine monarchs, celebrated its 250th birthday by warning that 'in the New Year, Unionists must continue to say "No" loud and clear ... that the Agreement is so divisive in its construction and application that it will permanently prevent the two communities coming together'.[27]

The Unionists launched a province-wide petition calling for a referendum. Molyneaux, Paisley and eleven other Unionist MPs signed the petition on the table that Sir Edward Carson used to sign the 1912 Covenant against Home Rule. Petition day was to be Saturday 17 January 1987; the count would be held on Friday 23 January. The petition said that 'the Anglo-Irish Agreement puts the Queen's subjects in Northern Ireland under a different form of Government from those in other parts of the United Kingdom and in fear of being deprived of their rights and status as citizens of the United Kingdom' and requested 'a referendum to ascertain whether that agreement hath their consent or no'. Paisley declared that, if the petition was refused, 'we are fully justified in a total withdrawal of consent from government, and a vigorous energetic civil disobedience campaign'. Molyneaux defended door-to-door canvassing for the petition against SDLP and Alliance claims that there would be intimidation of those who did not wish to sign. The *Guardian*'s Ian Aitken saw the petition as further proof that 'Mr Paisley and his colleagues have succeeded in capturing the political initiative in the Province ... It is time to get going before the self-styled Doctor is left in possession of the field'.[28] This prospect was

---

[24] Ibid.
[25] *News Letter*, 31 December 1986.
[26] Ibid.
[27] Ibid.
[28] *Guardian*, 5 January 1987.

particularly unappealing with a general election in prospect and a hung parliament a possibility; a MORI – *Sunday Times* poll gave the Tories 39 per cent, Labour 38 per cent and the SDP – Liberal Alliance 21 per cent. 'The prospect of being held to ransom by the likes of Mr Paisley and his increasingly sinister DUP henchmen ... should encourage all three party groupings [at Westminster] ... to make clear to both sets of Unionists that the survival of the Agreement is not, and never will be, on the negotiating table.'[29] Attention was diverted from the campaign by the damaging split in the council chambers, the jockeying for position in the constituencies once the sniff of a general election was in the air, and the Clontibret raid trial of Peter Robinson.

Robinson's trial on four charges of assault and causing actual bodily harm and seven charges of causing malicious damage and of unlawful assembly ended abruptly when he changed his plea to guilty to the charge of unlawful assembly. The presiding judge at the special criminal court said that the Clontibret attack was a serious criminal act which justified a substantial term of imprisonment. The Loyalist presence in the Irish border village was grossly offensive, provocative and cowardly. Robinson was sent first to Portlaoise gaol and then transferred overnight to Limerick prison. The following day he was fined £15,000, made to pay £2,588 in damages, and bound over for ten years on a surety of £10,000. A freedom fund was launched in the north to help defray his legal expenses. Robinson, according to the judge, 'lacked the courage either to dissociate himself from the mob or to try to discourage them from stopping cars and terrorizing their occupants'.[30] Robinson returned north to little of the hero's welcome given him in August after his earlier court appearances in Dundalk. His change of plea saved him from a prison sentence but severely undermined his position; he lost credibility because he had climbed down and admitted guilt. The DUP's loss was Molyneaux's gain. Paisley was now ready to talk, and Molyneaux held the upper hand.

The Official Unionist councillors, who had thwarted the DUP's plan for a mass resignation by district councils, led the withdrawal from the statutory bodies and now actively encouraged their members of parliament to go to prison rather than pay fines incurred in the civil disobedience campaign. Molyneaux's deputy, Harold McCusker, was imprisoned for a week for failing to pay a £50 fine for non-payment of his road tax; the importance his party attached to this symbolic gesture was apparent when the BBC received an official complaint regarding its lack of coverage of the arrest and imprisonment. McCusker's detention was the first fruit of a new OUP policy of putting their Westminster

---

[29] Ibid.
[30] *Guardian*, 17 January 1987.

leaders in the forefront of their campaign against the agreement. As McCusker explained from prison: 'I have consistently rejected violence by unionists ... because ... there was a more effective alternative ... to deny the Stormont Castle regime the moral authority to govern us by the withdrawal of consent and presence from all the institutions of state.'[31] Molyneaux and his party had regained the momentum and the control of the anti-agreement campaign. McCusker and his Westminster colleagues went to the City Hall to reveal the final figure for the referendum petition. The total of 441,035 was about 16,000 short of the Unionist vote at the mini-election a year earlier, but still represented a substantial body of public opinion; Molyneaux claimed that it 'would shake the Government into realizing how strongly people in Northern Ireland wanted to vote on the Agreement'.[32] Tom King rejected the call for a referendum. Paisley retorted: 'it is the Government that is saying no, no, to a referendum, no to consultation, no to the ballot box, and no to equal rights for the Ulster people.'[33]

On the day the petition results were announced, the IRA unleashed a bomb blitz on Belfast and Lisburn. The city-centre terror campaign expected in the run-up to Christmas arrived late, but caused millions of pounds worth of damage. Republican Sinn Fein was thought to be responsible for a botched mortar attack on a joint Army–RUC base at Crossmaglen. As in the Newry attack, the mortars missed their intended target, demolishing a Gaelic Athletic Club pavilion and digging craters in the pitch. The INLA shot and injured David Calvet, a leading DUP politician. On the same day the IRA killed police reservist Constable Ivan Crawford in Enniskillen. A fortnight later Major George Shaw, the highest ranking UDR officer to be killed for some years, was shot at his home in Dungannon.

The INLA was divided by feuds between the old guard, most of whom had recently been released from gaol following the Kirkpatrick supergrass appeal, the current generation of INLA leaders, who were deeply implicated in criminal activities such as extortion, intimidation and racketeering, a breakaway faction calling itself the People's Liberation Army, and the Irish Republican Socialist Party, the political wing of the INLA. Thomas McCarten was the first victim of the INLA vendetta. He was killed on the eve of the Kirkpatrick appeal. Thomas Powers and John O'Reilly were next, killed in a bar in Drogheda where they had gone to meet fellow INLA terrorists to arrange a restructuring of the organization. Powers was the first of the old guard to die; released at the Kirkpatrick appeal, his freedom lasted for twenty-eight days.

---

[31] *News Letter*, 27 January 1987.
[32] *Guardian*, 31 January 1987.
[33] *News Letter*, 7 February 1987.

Mary McGlinchey, held responsible by the security authorities for 'more than 20 killings',[34] was shot dead at her home in Dundalk; she was linked to the murder of at least three INLA men between 1982 and 1985. Tony McCluskey's body was found on an isolated road a few feet inside Northern Ireland; he was assassinated for giving 'information about the identity and whereabouts of one faction of INLA to another group'.[35] The People's Liberation Army killed Michael Kearney for hiring out guns to criminals involved in armed robberies. The organization also warned 'old guard' and 'current INLA leaders' of their intention to assassinate up to twelve more men who, they alleged, 'were resisting orders to disband and are involved in racketeering and gangsterism'.[36]

The extent of paramilitary involvement in fraud was revealed at the trial of Francis Duffy and Bernard McKeaveney, who admitted cheating the Inland Revenue of some £200,000 by misusing tax exemption certificates, the money being handed over to the INLA. Both were gaoled for two years. At their trial Mr Justice Nicholson said that most of the houses built in Belfast over the past ten years had been controlled by the IRA and the UDA. He accused the Housing Executive of turning a blind eye to the loss of millions of pounds of taxpayers' money to paramilitary groups. The RUC disclosed that recently the 'paramilitaries had switched their attention to acting as employment agencies. The current tactic was to approach a subcontractor with the offer of a number of plasterers for a job. Each plasterer would pay the agency a fee. If a contractor didn't employ the plasterers he was threatened. He paid up.'[37]

Nicholas Scott disclosed that 140 prosecutions for tax evasion were already pending. The RUC had set up a special squad to deal with the frauds and they were 'beginning to choke off the supply of funds' to the paramilitaries.[38] The following day, the *Irish Times* published a photograph showing UDA officers handing out free EC food. Captain Alan Hart of the Salvation Army confirmed the UDA's involvement in the distribution of EC surplus beef and butter. The *Irish Times* alleged that the IRA were distributing foodstuffs from the same source in the Nationalist ghettos.

The Ulster Defence Association's last public show of strength had been at the rally held at City Hall, Belfast, on the eve of the anniversary of the signing of the Anglo-Irish Agreement. The association's

---

[34] *News Letter*, 2 February 1987.
[35] *Guardian*, 6 February 1987.
[36] *News Letter*, 20 February 1987.
[37] *Guardian*, 12 February 1987.
[38] Ibid.

paramilitary activities were overshadowed by the launch of Ulster Resistance, but the Housing Executive's report indicated the extent of its intimidation of Roman Catholic families at the height of the marching season. The UDA was far more involved in racketeering and gangsterism than in military campaigning or political activity and this led to rifts in the leadership. Andy Tyrie, the organization's head, was apolitical; his interest was in the administration of the business side of the organization – racketeering. His deputy, John McMichael, had political ambitions. He regarded the UDA's supporters as storm troopers to be deployed under political guidance, preferably his. On 29 January 1987, McMichael launched his political manifesto, *Common Sense*. The document called for a constitutional conference to be convened by the secretary of state to discuss elections to an assembly under a written constitution. There would be a bill of rights and a new supreme court. The 78-member assembly would be appointed by proportional representation. The chief executive would be selected from the largest party and other positions on the executive would be determined by the proportion of votes won by each party. John Hume welcomed the document as 'a constructive attempt to break the deadlock'.[39] The *News Letter* called it a 'step towards a just solution'.[40] The Northern Ireland Office said that 'it was a sign that some of the people in Northern Ireland are turning their minds to the question'.[41] The document was dismissed as 'irrelevant' by Molyneaux and Paisley. Paisley rejected the concept of power-sharing; Molyneaux thought the document 'not only impractical but also dangerously reactionary'.[42]

McMichael was pleased with the warm reception given to his plan by the supporters of the Anglo-Irish Agreement but dismayed by the reaction of the Unionist politicians, which was more important to his personal ambitions. It showed that he was still regarded as an outsider by the Unionist establishment. The significance of the rebuff to McMichael and therefore to the political wing of the UDA was not lost on the association's divisional commanders. The UDA became a criminal, sectarian, mercenary organization. It ceased to be a movement.

Readjustments were taking place in the Loyalist paramilitary hierarchy. Ulster Resistance, a working-class, Belfast-based organization, competed for members with the Ulster Clubs, a rival federation of local cells. The UDA was marginalized by its criminal activities. The Ulster Freedom Fighters became the active service unit of the Loyalist

---

[39] *Irish Times*, 30 January 1987.
[40] *News Letter*, 30 January 1987.
[41] *Irish Times*, 30 January 1987.
[42] *Fortnight*, No. 249, March 1987.

paramilitary cause. It was the UFF that planted eighteen incendiary devices in Dublin and Donegal, causing more than £2 million worth of damage south of the border during the run-up to the Irish general election.

On Tuesday 20 January 1987 the coalition cabinet in Dublin failed to agree on the budget proposals. Dick Spring and his three Labour colleagues resigned and FitzGerald submitted his resignation to the president. The general election was to be held on 17 February 1987. Unemployment in the Republic was running at 19.6 per cent, despite a high emigration rate. The national debt stood at £22 billion and public borrowing was 10 per cent of the national income. There had been disagreements and divisions within the cabinet and the referendum on divorce had been a serious miscalculation.

Haughey's Fianna Fáil Party was expected to win, although 22 per cent of the electorate – an unusually high proportion – claimed to be undecided. The Anglo-Irish Agreement was hardly mentioned during the campaign. Haughey said in a pre-election broadcast that he did not wish to make the North an issue in the election: 'from the very start we said our objection was to the constitutional implications, but if those who believed in the Agreement could make progress under it, we would not inhibit or interfere with them in any way.'[43] He added, however, that if elected taoiseach he would make significant changes in the new law on extradition.

In London the home secretary, Douglas Hurd, announced that he had referred to the Court of Appeal the cases of six Irishmen gaoled for life for the Birmingham public house bombings of 1974. This was an issue close to the heart of the Anglo-Irish relationship: 'in Irish eyes a reopening of the Birmingham case is one of the central tests of the Hillsborough Agreement.'[44] Hurd said that he had decided on the referral after considering new information about the scientific evidence and after a former officer had made allegations of police intimidation and violence in obtaining confessions.

In Northern Ireland Tom King suggested to the Unionists that the four-week Irish general election campaign meant that there would be no meetings of the Intergovernmental Conference and 'part of the work of the permanent secretariat at Maryfield ... would also be suspended. This is an opportunity which meets the requirements which Unionists have laid down ...'[45] This attempt at encouraging the Unionists to get involved in discussions fell on deaf ears and also upset the Dublin government. Peter Barry fired a broadside at King: 'all aspects of the

---

[43] *Guardian*, 19 January 1987.
[44] *Guardian*, 21 January 1987.
[45] *Guardian*, 23 January 1987.

work of the conference, including the joint secretariat at Maryfield, operate on a continuing basis, irrespective of the political situation in either jurisdiction.'[46] In other words there was no question of a suspension to accommodate the Unionists.

The Prevention of Terrorism Act had its origins in the Birmingham pub bombing of 1974. Rushed through parliament at the time, the Act required annual renewal. Two full-scale reviews of its operation had been carried out. Sir Cyril Philips provided an annual review of the Act in advance of each year's renewal debate. His 1987 report took issue with the need for exclusion orders, the sanction under which the Home Office had powers to remove people, including citizens, from Britain or the United Kingdom. There were 240 accumulated exclusion orders in operation, but only three had been newly introduced in 1984 and seven in 1985. Sir Cyril Philips suggested that the orders, which struck at the right of the individual to leave and move around in his own country, be now phased out. Lord Colville QC, a Tory peer, also prepared a report for the Home Office, and recommended that all anti-terrorist laws be scrapped and replaced with new measures better able to deal with international terrorism. He also echoed Sir Cyril Philips's concern about the exclusion orders which 'could cause hardships in some cases'.[47] Lord Colville suggested a tightening-up of immigration procedures. The annual report of the Standing Advisory Commission on Human Rights, a Northern Ireland statutory body, also supported doing away with the exclusion orders. They also recommended that the European Convention on Human Rights be incorporated into the law of the United Kingdom and proposed that all terrorist cases in the non-jury Diplock courts be heard by three judges. The secretary of state rejected all these proposals. Strip-searching was also to continue.

These were issues at the heart of the Anglo-Irish Agreement's commitment to 'seek measures which would give substantial expression to the aim of underlining the importance of public confidence in the administration of justice'.[48] The British government was not to be rushed into any radical change of policy.

A *Daily Express*-MORI poll of 1,000 people gave strong support for the 'troops out' campaign in Northern Ireland. A total of 61 per cent of those interviewed wanted the troops brought home. There was no clear view on what would happen afterwards, but when asked to decide on the future of the province, 29 per cent wanted Northern Ireland to remain part of the United Kingdom, 29 per cent supported UDI, 21 per cent favoured a united Ireland and 15 per cent had no opinion. When asked

[46] Ibid.
[47] *News Letter*, 30 January 1987.
[48] Anglo-Irish Agreement Joint Communiqué, para. 7.

what was the most important question facing Britain, less than 0.5 per cent of those polled chose Northern Ireland. According to a *Guardian* leader, this meant 'that most of us simply don't care ... you have a British electorate which is happy to leave matters to the Northern Ireland people themselves ... but it wants rid of the cost and dangers of Northern Ireland'.[49] Seventy-five per cent of those interviewed 'felt the future of the province should be decided by its people, preferably by referendum'.[50] This was the week in which Molyneaux and Paisley presented to the Queen the petition asking for a referendum on the Anglo-Irish Agreement.

Charles Haughey polled 44.2 per cent of the Irish electorate and won eighty-one seats in the Dáil; he was three short of an overall majority. FitzGerald's Fine Gael won fifty-one seats, O'Malley's Progressive Democrats fourteen, Spring's Labour Party twelve, the Workers' Party four; there were four Independents. Sinn Fein won no seats; they polled 1.8 per cent of the vote.

The two leading parties suffered their poorest election returns since the 1961 campaign. FitzGerald's coalition partner, the Labour Party, lost only two seats, but the greatest gains were made by the Progressive Democrats, who in six weeks increased their representation from four to fourteen. A middle-class party which did not claim to have its origins in the Irish Civil War, it stood for the separation of church and state, supported the Anglo-Irish Agreement and was no fan of the new taoiseach. Charles Haughey's first task was to secure from a minority party the support he needed to give him a majority in the Dáil. It took three weeks.

On Thursday 19 February 1987, the day the Irish election result was announced, the draft of the Public Order (Northern Ireland) Bill was published and laid before the House of Commons. It dealt with 'a number of aspects of public order in the province with regard to processions and public meetings, stirring up hatred or arousing fear – and the repeal of the Flags and Emblems (Display) Act (Northern Ireland) 1954'.[51] The issue drew the Unionist members of parliament back to Westminster for the debate on 10 March 1987 and gave the Unionist pact a brief respite from its internal contradictions. Unionist opposition to the Anglo-Irish Agreement was criticized by the moderator of the Presbyterian Church in an outspoken attack which echoed what the Irish Anglican hierarchy was saying. Dr John Thompson said that 'refusal to pay taxes, to attend parliament regularly, or to meet British ministers, while accepting all the benefits that accrue from the

[49] *Guardian*, 11 February 1987.
[50] *News Letter*, 11 February 1987.
[51] *Hansard*, 10 March 1987, 219.

United Kingdom Government is both counter-productive and morally questionable ... no real attempt has been made to influence either Government or public opinion ... small wonder our image is tarnished ... the majority of political leaders ... have not responded positively to changing times'.[52]

Dr Thompson's address indicated how far the Presbyterian Church in Ireland had shifted its position since the Hillsborough summit. His timing could not have been better. That same day the Unionist leaders announced the setting-up of a task force to canvass opinion on 'securing support for a continuing campaign against the Anglo-Irish Agreement and [to] ascertain what consensus, if any, existed about alternatives to the Agreement'.[53] With the council protest in disarray, the Unionists were under pressure to be seen to be doing something. McCartney's campaign for integration and equal citizenship was splitting Unionist membership, and the UDA's *Common Sense* document, although dismissed by Molyneaux and Paisley, was given a generous reception by the other political parties and by some columnists. The Unionists also knew that a British general election was not far away, and they needed to be in a position to offer realistic alternatives in their joint manifesto. Saying 'no' was obviously not enough.

The task force was set up after a conference of all the Westminster Unionist MPs except John Taylor. Backbench Conservative members of parliament and members of the Friends of the Union group were also instrumental in getting the Unionists together, following a meeting Gow and his colleagues had with the prime minister in early February. She gave no indication of being prepared to alter her stance on the Hillsborough Accord, and her statement following the Irish election result killed stone dead any hopes the Unionists had that Haughey's success would lead to a weakening of the Anglo-Irish relationship: 'the Agreement was made between two sovereign countries and not political parties.'[54]

The composition of the task force reflected the majority status of the OUP partner in the Unionist pact. There were two Official Unionists, Harold McCusker and Frank Millar, and one member of the DUP, Peter Robinson. The balance of power within the Unionist pact had altered dramatically after Clontibret and the launch of Ulster Resistance. Fifty-fifty representation was replaced by an arrangement that reflected the parliamentary strength of the Official Unionists at Westminster, where they had ten members to the DUP's three. Molyneaux's guiding hand was behind the launch of the task force. It

---

[52] *News Letter*, 24 February 1987.
[53] *Fortnight*, No. 254, September 1987.
[54] *Guardian*, 25 February 1987.

is highly unlikely that either he or Paisley had any inkling of the hot potato its members were to land on their desks four months later, just in time for the joint Unionist election manifesto.

In the mean time, the Unionist leaders had other problems to sort out. Belfast City Council was fined £25,000 by Mr Justice Hutton for deliberately disobeying the order to resume normal council business, while Castlereagh was threatened with a fine of £10,000. The next stage would be the fining of individual councillors and possible disqualification if payment were refused. Molyneaux wanted to bring this phase of the protest to an end, since it would damage his own position in the Official Unionist council, which was opposed to the adjournment policy; he also feared kamikaze tactics from DUP councillors.

The UDA's document *Common Sense* was followed by *Forward to Victory*, a statement of policy by the Ulster Clubs. The two Loyalist paramilitary groups were still attempting to present themselves as part of the political dialogue. The press reaction to *Common Sense* had worried Molyneaux. The Ulster Clubs' political manifesto did not receive the same support. It suggested a Northern Ireland grand committee, made up of members of the Unionist political parties, the UDA, the Orange Order, the Ulster Clubs, the Apprentice Boys and the Workers '86 Committee. Policies would be prepared on external affairs, education, the environment and local government. The Northern Ireland Police Authority would be invited to give its allegiance to the grand committee, taxes would be withheld from the British government and the workings of the social services agencies in the province would be disrupted. The purpose of the venture was 'to sustain the much-talked-about withdrawal of consent, provide a necessary focus for the allegiance of the Ulster people, and allow the deep-rooted resentment and rejection of the agreement to be channelled into constructive and effective action'.[55] The Ulster Clubs' initiative was a failure and the movement's ultra-militant stance was also increasingly unpopular. The Loyalist paramilitary campaign against the Anglo-Irish Agreement suffered from the Robinson débâcle at Clontibret. The strategic link between the Unionists and the paramilitaries was seen to be weak, and without a political leader of the stature of Robinson the paramilitaries became sectarian mobs or criminal protection racketeers.

The Unionist boycott of Westminster was all but over before Tom King rejected the petition calling for a referendum: it would only 'serve to identify the majority ... democracy isn't just about the rule of the majority. It's about respect for the position of the minority'.[56] The secretary of state explained that referenda could only be justified if there

---

[55] *Irish Times*, 3 March 1987.
[56] *Guardian*, 5 March 1987.

were changes in parliamentary and ministerial powers. The Anglo-Irish Agreement involved no changes in his powers or in the status of the people of Northern Ireland. Molyneaux rejected this interpretation: 'it is not open to denial that Her Majesty's Government has entered with a foreign state into an international agreement of which the provisions relate not to the United Kingdom as a whole, but to one part of it only.'[57] Paisley said that 'constitutional resistance to the Agreement was over'.[58] What he meant was that a campaign of civil disobedience was now fully justified; what happened in fact was that Paisley and his Unionist colleagues at Westminster went back to the House of Commons. By so doing they abandoned their protest, rejected the call from the likes of the Ulster Clubs to 'pull out of Westminster and lead the civil disobedience campaign themselves',[59] and gave Molyneaux a taste of tactical success as the Unionist leader.

It was the government's new legislative programme that forced the Unionist members back to Westminster. Legislation that directly affected the Unionist and Loyalist way of life was in danger of being implemented with little or no opposition, amendment or debate from the Unionist side. The first cracks in the united opposition occurred with the Northern Ireland (Emergency Provisions) Bill in December 1986. Three Official Unionist members of parliament turned up for that debate; all fourteen Unionist MPs were back for the Public Order debate on 10 March 1987. The Order became law on 2 April 1987, the Unionists having already announced that there would be a day of defiance a week later. The RUC issued a statement explaining its interpretation of the repeal of the Flags and Emblems Act: 'underlying the Force's approach to the display of flags and emblems is the desirability of creating an atmosphere in the community in which flags are flown with dignity and respect and are not used for provocative defiant or offensive purposes ... no action should be taken either to remove a Union flag or direct its removal without approval from this HQ.'[60] A non-provocative approach was to be adopted.

Margaret Thatcher sent Molyneaux a letter calling on him to respond positively to an invitation to talks. She also expressed surprise that Molyneaux should object to the new public order legislation: 'the only significant departure is that parade organizers should give police reasonable notice.'[61] This was a pointed reference to a much-heralded protest to be led by Molyneaux and Paisley against the new Public

---

[57] *News Letter*, 6 March 1987.
[58] *Guardian*, 5 March 1987.
[59] *News Letter*, 6 March 1987.
[60] *News Letter*, 1 April 1987.
[61] *Guardian*, 3 March 1987.

Order Act. There had been an early disagreement between Molyneaux and Paisley regarding the scope of the day of defiance. The OUP leader denied that he had agreed to joint demonstrations. He wanted a low-key, orderly protest meeting. The paramilitary groups were not invited and John McMichael warned that 'Mr Paisley will learn quickly that Ulster people will no longer be used like Pavlov's dogs by people who have not the courage to fight, nor the intelligence and integrity to find a settlement'.[62] McMichael expected Loyalists to stay away from the day of defiance protests.

There was a change of mood in the province. A *News Letter* editorial claimed that 'those who operate on a political level of unionism are increasingly finding themselves isolated because of a trend which has become apparent at other levels among people who wish to behave as if everything is normal throughout the province'.[63]

The Unionist members of parliament paraded illegally on Friday 10 April when they presented a petition objecting to the new public order legislation to the RUC in Belfast. The chief constable had already explained the police plan of action: 'marchers would be informed the parade was illegal and names would be taken for possible prosecution – arrests would only happen if there was violence.'[64] There was no violence, and from the point of view of the organizers the march was a failure. Two hundred supporters turned up in Lisburn to hear Molyneaux warn against splits in the Unionist opposition. Paisley led a march of 'several hundred' in Ballymoney; he 'was grieved by unionists who had not turned out to support the demonstrations'.[65] Robinson drew several hundred in Belfast, and McCusker more than a thousand in Lurgan. The Unionists claimed the day of defiance was never meant to be more than a token protest, but several DUP members read the political situation correctly and blamed Molyneaux and the OUP. Ivan Foster suggested that 'the DUP would mount a more successful campaign against the Anglo-Irish Agreement without the straitjacket of the unionist pact'.[66]

The strains within the DUP were exposed at a party executive meeting a few days after the day of defiance. Fifty members walked out after Paisley threatened to resign unless the executive agreed to support his no-contest general election strategy. It was a 'hot and heavy four-hour meeting'[67] that finally broke up with Paisley in an 'angry table-thumping mood'.[68] If Robinson had been sure of grass-roots support,

---

[62] *News Letter*, 11 April 1987.
[63] Ibid.
[64] *Irish Times*, 11 April 1987.
[65] *News Letter*, 13 April 1987.
[66] Ibid.
[67] *Irish Times*, 15 April 1987.
[68] Ibid.

the executive meeting would have offered an opportunity of toppling Paisley, but once he fell from grace there was no effective electable leader to muster an anti-Paisley lobby. Paisley survived, but with a deeply divided and bitter party. Molyneaux also had dissension in the ranks. McCartney's integration and equal citizenship campaign was a niggling distraction. Molyneaux had hit out at the 'spectacle of unionist gladiators going for each other . . . I have begged the mavericks to desist from their internecine strife'.[69] A general election would bring the issue to a head, but the Unionists were in no condition to fight an election. The task force report was still in preparation, the various anti-agreement protests were in confusion, there was open warfare within the party structures and the Intergovernmental Conference had restarted after a change of government in the Republic. No wonder David Burnside, a leading member of the Friends of the Union, said that 'Unionism was at its weakest, most disorganized and least influential position of any period in its history'.[70] The change in the public's attitude to the Anglo-Irish Agreement was demonstrated during the parades of Easter 1987. The main Orange Order parade at Carrickfergus complied with the new Public Order Act and gave the required seven days' notice to the police. At Portadown the marchers avoided Catholic areas. It was a considerable contrast to the events of 1986.

Charles Haughey took three weeks to put together a majority administration in the Dáil. Garret FitzGerald, the outgoing taoiseach, offered his party's full support if the Anglo-Irish Agreement were allowed to continue untouched. The new taoiseach replied by 'accepting that the Anglo-Irish Agreement was an accord . . . accepted as binding . . . Ireland and Britain are so much involved with each other . . . governments must strive to have the best possible relationships'.[71] FitzGerald resigned as party leader and Alan Dukes was elected leader of Fine Gael.

Haughey went to Washington for the annual St Patrick's Day parade. Reagan's 'support for the agreement was spelled out forcefully to Haughey, who accepted the first instalment of US aid under the development fund set up as part of the Hillsborough Agreement'.[72] The president added that 'the time has long come when people of goodwill . . . should draw the line and let the perpetrators and supporters of violence and mayhem know that they will no longer be tolerated'.[73] Reagan officials recalled that eighteen months earlier,

---

[69] *News Letter*, 20 March 1987.
[70] *Irish Times*, 16 March 1987.
[71] *Irish Times*, 7 March 1987.
[72] *Guardian*, 25 March 1987.
[73] *Irish Times*, 17 March 1987.

when Fianna Fáil was in opposition, Haughey and Lenihan had tried to persuade American government ministers to withhold their support for the pending Hillsborough Agreement. There was no doubt that the St Patrick's Day meeting with President Reagan was a difficult one for Haughey. FitzGerald and John Hume were present to witness and help the taoiseach through this difficult manœuvre.

In the Irish Supreme Court, Raymond Crotty won a three-to-two majority verdict for his argument that the Single European Act compromised Ireland's constitutional commitment to neutrality. The Haughey government would have to conduct a referendum to amend the constitution. Ireland's sovereignty and constitutional status were being challenged by its association with its European partners. How much longer would it be before the Anglo-Irish Agreement constituted the same threat? Christopher McGimpsey, a Northern Unionist, saw his chance and asked the High Court in Dublin to rule on the unconstitutional nature of the Anglo-Irish Agreement in relation to Articles 2 and 3 of the Irish constitution of 1937.

The Intergovernmental Conference in Belfast on Thursday 21 April 1987 was the first with Brian Lenihan as co-chairman. He had met Howe in Brussels and King in London for informal talks before travelling to Belfast. His style was likely to be different from Peter Barry's, more relaxed and concentrating on fewer issues, which he identified as job discrimination, the operation of security forces, in particular the UDR, and the release of EC monies to aid Northern Ireland. King and Lenihan agreed that there was 'substantial room for practical improvements on the ground between the RUC and the Garda'.[74] A new security task force was agreed.

This cross-border initiative had already surfaced at the Westminster debate on the Northern Ireland (Emergency Provisions) Bill on 8 April 1987. Nicholas Scott, opening the debate, revealed that there are 'roughly 300 road crossings between Northern Ireland and the Republic of Ireland. Of these, approximately 100 are closed'.[75] The government sought parliamentary approval to close more cross-border routes. The minister of state promised a substantial reduction in the delays in cases coming to trial. He disclosed that for the first six months of 1986, the average 'waiting time between remand and committal was about thirty-three weeks, and the average time between committal and trial was twenty-seven weeks',[76] a total waiting-time of sixty weeks. The government proposed a time limit of 110 days from the date of the first remand. The secretary of state successfully resisted attempts to

---

[74] *Irish Times*, 22 April 1987.
[75] *Hansard*, 8 April 1987, 314.
[76] Ibid., 325.

outlaw internment; it was still an option should the security situation deteriorate.

In Northern Ireland, on the same day as the Emergency Provisions Bill debate at Westminster, IRA volunteer Laurence Morley was buried. He had been shot dead by the UVF, and his funeral had been postponed for two days because of a huge RUC presence designed to stop any military takeover of the funeral. During that time, there were twenty-six bomb scares and sixteen vehicle hijackings, with riots during the hours of darkness. The cortège, with an estimated 6,000 mourners, took seven hours to travel from the Ardoyne to the Milltown cemetery. Sir John Hermon explained that the police had received information 'which indicated that the funeral would be taken over by Sinn Fein and the Provisional IRA and used as a paramilitary showcase'.[77] Dr Cahal Daly appealed to the RUC to rethink its funeral policies, while condemning the IRA: 'the honour and dignity extended to a body of a dead man were affronted by the bombs ... which were deliberately planned by the paramilitaries to coincide with the funeral ... the massive and disproportionate police and military build-up served simply to inflame emotions and very many moderate people in the Catholic community have been dismayed at the spectacle of the RUC being seen to walk into a trap cleverly but predictably set for them by the paramilitaries'.[78] A day later Constables Fred Armstrong and Robert McLean were killed when the IRA shot them at the quiet seaside town of Portrush. They died on the day of the publication of the chief constables's annual report for the previous year, 1985. It had been an 'extraordinarily' difficult year according to Sir John Hermon, with 12 members of the force killed, 14 stations wrecked by bombs and a massive increase in intimidation of RUC oficers, leading to 500 attacks on police homes and the setting up of an emergency housing unit to help rehouse police families. That phase of the current troubles was over. The force now faced an even deadlier enemy, an IRA active service unit out of control. Its base was Derry and in six months of 1987 it equalled the number of RUC fatalities for the whole of 1986.

The INLA, which contained the 'truly wild men of the republican movement',[79] was also out of control. The organization had been formed by Seamus Costello in 1974, following a split in the official IRA. The INLA killed Airey Neave at the House of Commons in 1979. It was responsible for the killing of 63 people in 1981, 48 of them members of the security forces. A year later, 11 were killed at the Ballykelly disco bombing. In 1982 Dominic McGlinchey, a prominent member of the

---

[77] *News Letter*, 9 April 1987.
[78] *News Letter*, 10 April 1987.
[79] *Listener*, 7 May 1987.

faction, attempted to take over the IRA Army Council and ordered the chief of staff to leave. He introduced a system of direct military rule under which the punishment for all crimes was death and the general headquarters staff under the chief of staff became the sole authority. McGlinchey, permanently on the run, was unable to take day-to-day control of the organization and it broke up into various factions which competed for position by carrying out spectacular atrocities or shows of sheer bravado. One of the factions was led by Gerard Steenson, who was released with Powers, McCluskey and Kearney after the Kirkpatrick supergrass trial. All four were dead by mid March 1987. Steenson, head of the Belfast division of the INLA, was assassinated for having tried to disarm the movement and hand its territory and its arms over to the IRA.

Also in March, Thomas Maguire was found shot in the head on a border road in south Armagh. The gun that shot him was used six days later to kill Fergus Culan. Both men were from Newry and the INLA faction responsible for both assassinations claimed that they had been police informers, responsible for fifty arrests and the discovery of thirty-five arms dumps. In all, the INLA feud left twelve dead. The killing was brought to an end by order of the IRA and the mediation of Fathers Jerry Reynolds and Alex Reid. A number of Republicans who had been prominent in the movement in the early sixties were drafted in to supervise the disbanding of territory committees and the handing over of arms to the IRA.

The IRA had its own internal distractions. Following a meeting of the General Army Council in the autumn of 1986, and the split at the Sinn Fein *ard fheis* which led to the launching of the breakaway Republican Sinn Fein (see above p.103), the military structure of the movement was reorganized. The security authorities had successfully penetrated the old cell structures and the army council disbanded all local commands. Authority was vested in a central committee which included Gerry Adams and Martin McGuinness. Certain local commanders resented losing power, especially since it was thought likely that the new divisional commanders would be political appointees. This fear seemed confirmed when Paddy Adams, brother of Gerry, was made head of the Belfast IRA command.

The incidence of punishment shootings, always a reliable indicator of changes within the IRA, rose sharply in March 1987. The revamped unit in Belfast had also made its presence felt. Three policemen were injured when a car bomb exploded outside Roselawn Cemetery as Reserve Constable Peter Nesbitt's remains were about to be buried. Nesbitt had been killed at a bakery explosion in the Ardoyne. The IRA explained that the bomb had been placed at the cemetery because of 'police brutality at funerals of republican paramilitaries over the past

four years'.[80] The front of the newly built but still unopened Smithfield
market centre was destroyed by a bomb; an empty shop on the Dublin
road was set on fire and thirty-six bomb hoaxes caused chaos in Belfast.
In south Armagh John Chalmers, a lorry-driver, was killed instantly
when shot by two gunmen. He had swapped a shift with his son-in-law,
who worked for the UDR: a case of mistaken identity.

In Derry, the security authorities detected signs of a rift in the local
command; a rogue active service unit was in operation. It struck on 23
March 1987; Leslie Jarvis, a civilian instructor at Magilligan prison,
was shot dead when returning to his parked car. Two RUC officers
went to investigate and were killed instantly when Jarvis's booby-
trapped car exploded. When Gerard Logue, an IRA 'volunteer' in
Derry, blew himself up at an arms dump, his funeral brought the city to
a standstill with four bomb alerts. A checkpoint at Culmore stopped a
car containing packages of explosives timed to explode during Logue's
funeral. At a house on the Creggan estate, 900 rounds of ammunition,
158 magazines, radios, detonators and bomb-making equipment were
found. At the funeral, two hooded gunmen emerged from the porch of
St Columb's Church to fire a volley of shots over Logue's coffin. Dr
Edward Daly, bishop of Derry, banned the bodies of IRA men from
churches in his dioceses; requiem mass for IRA men would be held in
the absence of their remains. Daly declared that 'we cannot permit our
church grounds to become battlefields – they are not freedom fighters
– they have repeatedly demonstrated that they respect neither God nor
man'.[81] These strong words drew an immediate response from Martin
McGuinness, leader of the Republican movement in the north-west; he
said the IRA would 'review' the situation, seen by some as clear
evidence that the Derry IRA cell was out of control. This view seemed
to be confirmed when twelve masked men, armed with an assortment of
guns, staged a military display in the Creggan estate. The divisional
commander of the RUC branded the IRA killers 'mad dogs' when they
shot Sergeant Tom Cooke as he left the Derry Golf Club, the fifth RUC
man to be killed in the north-west within a month. The demand for a
security review was becoming urgent. There had been no significant
increase in security resources since the winter of 1985–6, when a
thousand extra troops had been sent to the province.

The Loyalist paramilitaries were rearming. There had been a break-
in at the UDR base in Coleraine; 170 rifles and pistols were stolen and
driven away in a UDR van. It was an inside job by Samuel Ferris and
Keith McCelland, two serving lance-corporals in the UDR who were
also members of the UDA, supplying arms to the Ulster Volunteer

[80] *Guardian*, 14 March 1987.
[81] *Guardian*, 27 March 1987.

Force. In Glasgow, Andrew Robertson was gaoled for twelve years after being found guilty of plotting to supply arms to the UDA. In Belfast Cyril Rainey, a part-time UDR soldier, got twelve years for his part in the killing of Lennie Murphy, the so-called Shankhill Butcher.

On the Republican paramilitary side, the first evidence of their possession of semtex was found in mid February 1987; one hundred pounds of semtex, with detonators and timers, was discovered in two arms caches in Delamere Forest, Chester, and Trentabank Forest, Macclesfield. In 1978 a CIA double agent had sold twenty-two pounds of semtex to Colonel Gaddafi of Libya; the link with Libya had been confirmed a year earlier, with the discovery of arms in Roscommon and Sligo.

In Ulster Iain O'Conner, the first British soldier to die for six months, was killed on his first week of service in the province. His Land-Rover took a direct hit from two IRA bombs in the Divis Flats complex in Belfast. A part-time UDR soldier, Jim Oldman, was shot dead, and Reserve Constable George Shaw died at Ballynahinch RUC station. There were two further RUC deaths when Constables Armstrong and McLean were shot at Portrush.

In Reindahlen, the BAOR headquarters in West Germany, thirty-one people were injured when a bomb exploded outside a mess where a party was being held. In the United Kingdom, letter-bombs were sent to Bernard Ingham, the prime minister's press officer, and to two other senior civil servants.

At Easter the Orange Order marches went off without trouble, but Gerry Adams led a Republican march to commemorate the Easter rising of 1916. It was declared an illegal parade by the police under the terms of the new Public Order regulations. Adams said that 'the British will only be talked out of Ireland through the rattle of machine guns and the roar of explosives'.[82] Politics was to take a back seat. The columnist John Cole commented that 'there now exists, in tiny segments of both Catholic and Protestant communities, a great stench of evil . . . no one has produced an intellectually convincing way of dealing with the IRA'.[83]

In the following week RUC Inspector David Ead was killed by the IRA in Newcastle, his colleague Tom Cooke died after being shot at Derry Golf Club, UDR soldier William Graham was shot dead in Pomeroy and Lord Justice Gibson and his wife were killed by a bomb. Lord Justice Gibson was the second most senior judge in the province. He and his wife, who was president of the Irish Girl Guides, were returning north after a holiday in the west of England. They crossed by

---

[82] *Irish Times*, 20 April 1987.
[83] *Listener*, 23 April 1987.

ferry to Dublin and were escorted to the border with Northern Ireland by Irish Special Branch. It was while driving between the Irish frontier post and the military checkpoint at Killeen that the pair met their death. Gibson had been the judge at the trial of the three RUC policemen accused of the murder of three IRA men in the 1982 shooting incident which became the subject of the Stalker-Sampson report. He had commended the policemen for their courage in bringing the 'three deceased men to justice, in this case the final court of justice'.[84] The IRA did not forget.

Tom King was under increasing pressure to be seen to be doing something to halt a murderous campaign intended, as he saw it, 'to undermine the morale of the security forces, to increase tension and hatred between the communities, and thus to provoke over-reaction from some unionists'.[85] The Police Federation appealed for government action; the RUC said that 'there is an overdue need for people ... in positions of power and influence, to say clearly ... that these organizations stand totally condemned and that the good of the community lies in support for the lawfully constituted democratic forces of law and order'.[86] The chief constable, Sir John Hermon, flew back from the United States to conduct a security review. He was determined that if new resources were to be made available, they should go into strengthening the RUC and not into increasing the number of soldiers in the province.

The IRA killed William 'Frenchy' Marchant, the UVF's second-in-command. His funeral was attended by Cecil Walker MP, Alan Wright of the Ulster Clubs, John McMichael of the UDA and Tommy Lyttle of the 1986 Workers' Committee. Six different RUC stations were attacked over the first weekend in May. Finbarr McKenna, an IRA activist, died when a blast bomb he was trying to throw at the RUC station on the Springfield Road exploded prematurely. Fifteen vehicles were hijacked and set on fire after his funeral and fifty masked men attacked the Barnsley Road RUC station twice in one evening with petrol bombs; they succeeded in destroying the church next door.

The RUC–Garda security task force set up at the Intergovernmental Conference on 21 April 1987 had an early success. The Garda discovered a giant underground bunker in Cavan, and 2,700 lb of homemade explosives were found in a horse trailer, the largest find in the province for years. Attention now turned to London and a special parliamentary debate on Northern Ireland security. It was to be the first occasion in sixteen months for some of the Ulster Unionists to contribute to a Westminster debate.

---

[84] *Irish Times*, 27 April 1987.
[85] *News Letter*, 28 April 1987.
[86] *Times*, 25 April 1987.

Opening the Northern Ireland security debate, the secretary of state, Tom King, said that the initial objective of the IRA was 'to undermine the morale of the RUC, to spread disaffection among the Army and to create reluctance and unwillingness to serve in Northern Ireland'.[87] He attributed the increased level of violence to Sinn Fein's disappointing performance in the Irish election and to the split between Sinn Fein and Republican Sinn Fein. King announced an increase in the RUC reserve; UDR part-time members were to be called to voluntary permanent duty for the next few weeks. The secretary of state for defence agreed to provide additional support; this was interpreted to mean further SAS deployment in the province. The Ministry of Defence had agreed to supply additional helicopters. The secretary of state also referred to measures to stop the flow of cash and resources to the terrorists.

James Molyneaux, the leader of the Official Unionists, appealed to the government 'on humanitarian grounds, to review and recast the Government's political and security strategies ... as long as [the Anglo-Irish Agreement] is perceived by all sections of the community to be designed to lead to the embodiment of Northern Ireland in some form of an all-Ireland state, the terrorists' organizations, whose object that has always been, will be encouraged to maintain and even redouble their efforts'.[88] Ian Paisley, making his first contribution at Westminster for eighteen months, recalled the launch of Ulster Resistance: 'men from across the province ... came to the conclusion that the Government and the House had not the will to win the war, and that they would sell us down the river ... I have come to the same conclusion ... If the right hon. gentleman pushes us down that crimson road, marked with tombstones instead of milestones and littered with democratic principles that should have been upheld, he will find that the Ulster people will not stand for it.'[89] Seamus Mallon of the SDLP drew attention to the failure in the province 'to identify a political problem or to seek a political solution to it. We should not confuse a security solution with what is essentially a political problem'.[90] 'The problem', he argued, 'cannot be solved by repression or by force, by strengthening repressive legislation or by increasing the police or the army. It will be solved only when we win the battle for the hearts and minds of the people in a political way.'[91] Nicholas Scott, the minister of state in the Northern Ireland Office, closed the debate by stating that 'the IRA is a

---

[87] *Hansard*, 6 May 1987, 736.
[88] Ibid., 756.
[89] Ibid., 762.
[90] Ibid., 764.
[91] Ibid., 768.

dedicated, ruthless and cynical terrorist organization, operating with no standards or rules. We must be equally professional, but we must not abandon the standard appropriate for a liberal democracy to protect itself against an onslaught by a terrorist organization'.[92]

Two days later an SAS unit wiped out the East Tyrone brigade of the IRA. Eight terrorists were killed, and one civilian died in the crossfire. It was 'the biggest military reverse for the IRA since the Black and Tan days of the 1920's'.[93] Among the dead were James Lynagh, the IRA's top assassin, wanted for six years by the RUC, and Patrick Kelly, commander of the IRA's East Tyrone brigade. The innocent civilian killed by a stray bullet was Anthony Hughes. Riots occurred elsewhere in the province. Two hundred petrol bombs were thrown at the police in Belfast. Twenty vehicles were hijacked and a rocket-launcher was discovered in a youth club in West Belfast.

Lynagh was buried in the Republic, in County Monaghan. A colour party of six men and two women dressed in full paramilitary uniform escorted the coffin and three hooded gunmen fired a volley of shots over the cortège. A plain-clothes gardai fired a warning shot into the air when his car was manhandled over a wall into the river four feet below. The gardai escaped through the car's back window.

In the North, the RUC issued a statement on the force's funeral policy. In future, the RUC would only liaise with the family and clergy with the 'objective of avoiding any police involvement or intrusion in what should be a private occasion of grief'.[94] There would be a deliberate effort to 'let it be seen that the RUC are not going to physically intrude or impose themselves on the funeral or burial'.[95]

The terrorists were under renewed pressure from the Catholic Church and the police. Before long, pressure from the leaders of Sinn Fein was added. Prime Minister Margaret Thatcher had called an election for Thursday 11 June 1987.

The first casualty of the British general election was the report of the Unionist task force. Molyneaux and Paisley agreed that it should be shelved for the time being. Both leaders knew that they were merely postponing the inevitable row which would occur when the report was published. None of the rumoured conclusions of Robinson, Millar and McCusker surfaced in the joint Unionist election manifesto, *To Put Right a Great Wrong*. It recommended that the Anglo-Irish Agreement be suspended, the Maryfield secretariat closed and separate talks held between the British prime minister and the Unionist and Nationalist

---

[92] Ibid., 809.
[93] *Sunday Times*, 12 May 1987.
[94] *Irish Times*, 11 May 1987.
[95] Ibid.

parties. There would be no return to normal Westminster attendance and no negotiations until the agreement was put into cold storage. 'Unionists will not negotiate in the cage of the Agreement',[96] said Paisley, who was hoping for a hung parliament in which the Unionist group could negotiate away the Anglo-Irish Agreement in exchange for their support at Westminster.

The task force report was rumoured to be moving towards an 'acceptance that the precondition of the Anglo-Irish Accord being dropped before Unionist talks was now outdated'.[97] This was political dynamite, since it undermined Unionist tactics since the signing of the agreement at Hillsborough eighteen months earlier. The report's three authors were also thought to be backing a devolved, power-sharing executive which included responsibility for security. They suggested a constitutional conference in two parts, the first between London and Belfast and the second between London, Belfast and Dublin. They accepted that an 'Irish' dimension existed on such issues as the promotion of co-operation and friendship within the island of Ireland. Their deliberations ran counter to the high-profile campaign of the anti-agreement Unionists – full-page press advertisements, paid for by the levy on council rates – and undermined a series of press briefings and lobbying sessions in London, Birmingham, Glasgow and Manchester. The sting of the report was in its final conclusion. If all else failed, consideration should be given to moving towards 'an independent Northern Ireland, on the basis of dominion status with constitutional guarantees for the minority'.[98] This 'last gasp' option was unlikely to please the Unionist leaders but its message was very clear: settle within the Anglo-Irish Agreement or get out.

Robert McCartney was forced to get out of the OUP, and Jim Allister chose to get out of the DUP in the run-up to the general election. McCartney was called before the Official Unionist Council and told that his presidency of the Campaign for Equal Citizenship was incompatible with the rules and constitution of the OUP. He was also accused of describing Ulster's political parties, including his own, as consisting of people who had 'pledged themselves to Lilliputian sectarian politics . . . adopting Micawber's policy of hoping something would turn up . . . perhaps hoping that God was a Unionist'.[99] He was found guilty of attacking his party's members of parliament by suggesting that if they went back to Westminster it would not really matter, as they had nothing to say. He was thrown out of the party, and

---

[96] *News Letter*, 22 May 1987.
[97] *Irish Times*, 21 April 1987.
[98] *Times*, 4 May 1987.
[99] *News Letter*, 20 May 1987.

his North Down Official Unionist constituency association was expelled by a thirty-three to one vote of the OUP executive. McCartney was nominated by the debarred association as their 'Real Unionist' candidate against the sitting Popular Unionist, James Kilfedder, the former speaker of Stormont. He had also been a member of the OUP, but had left the party in the seventies.

Jim Allister resigned from the DUP and from public life because he was opposed to the continuation of the Unionist electoral pact. When Paisley refused to break the pact with Molyneaux, Allister left, saying that 'Unionist unity is so devoid of substance and real meaning that we are told that its entire existence is dependent on the automatic return of fourteen individuals to Parliament'.[100] Allister took with him ten members of the Newtownabbey branch and a similar number of supporters from the Ballymoney branch in County Antrim. Paisley stemmed the haemorrhaging by going round each branch pleading for unity, at least during the election campaign. The election attracted a large number of candidates overall: 77 stood in 17 constituencies.

The Conservative manifesto upheld the Anglo-Irish Agreement: 'it continues in precisely the terms in which it is drafted',[101] with the government working towards a devolved government including Roman Catholics and Protestants. The Labour Party also gave its support to the agreement, but added, 'we believe in a united Ireland, to be achieved peacefully, democratically and by consent'.[102] Labour emphasized the need for economic renewal to combat 'record unemployment and social deprivation' in the province. The Labour Party's Northern Ireland policy suffered from the inability of the party's national executive to agree on the details of its policy review paper on the province. Difference of emphasis appeared between the front bench spokesman, Peter Archer, and his deputy, Stuart Bell. At the annual conference in the autumn of 1986, a draft policy document was withdrawn when the national executive rejected it. The conference itself rejected a motion condemning the Anglo-Irish Agreement and calling for a British withdrawal from Northern Ireland. Peter Archer conceded that 'Labour did not have a strategy for Northern Ireland for when it came into office'.[103]

His deputy, Stuart Bell, had shared a fringe conference meeting with Tommy Carroll, a convicted car bomber and now a Sinn Fein councillor. Bell was barracked for saying that 'the perpetrators of violence are not democrats, let alone socialists. They are murderers of Irishmen.

[100] *Irish Times*, 23 May 1987.
[101] *Irish Times*, 20 May 1987.
[102] Ibid.
[103] *Irish Times*, 2 October 1987.

The Anglo-Irish Agreement is a bridge to unity'.[104] The fringe meeting had Ken Livingstone in the chair, and Bell was opposed by Bernadette McAliskey and heckled by the 'Troops Out' campaigners. Bell committed his party to repealing the Prevention of Terrorism Act, phasing out the Emergency Provisions Act, stopping strip-searching, abolishing plastic bullets and strengthening the Fair Employment Agency.

Kinnock refused to meet Sinn Fein until the party denounced violence, but his front bench spokesman, Archer, met Republican representatives in mid January 1987, though he stressed that 'his party's willingness to talk to Sinn Fein did not bind it to establish a formal relationship with the Republican movement if Labour were returned to power'.[105] Labour-dominated councils in Camden, Harringay and Hackney and Islington continued to play host to Sinn Fein visitors, and Livingstone attended Kelly's extradition hearing in Amsterdam. A Labour co-ordinating committee recommended that a Labour government should commit itself to withdrawal from Northern Ireland within its first term of office. A plan put forward by Archer, to give support for steps towards a united Ireland, conditional on the consent of the majority in Northern Ireland, was ambushed by Kevin McNamara and Clare Short. They persuaded a working party to accept that a united Ireland could be achieved 'with a significant degree of consent'.[106] This did away with the in-built Unionist veto. Stuart Bell added to the confusion by giving details of a plan for devolved government. He suggested a new structure of local government with education, housing and the environment returned to local control, and a Northern Ireland grand committee, and said that any review of the Anglo-Irish Agreement should involve the Unionists. This last statement brought a quick denial from Archer, who distanced himself from his deputy's words by stating that Bell was not representing Labour Party policy. Some thought that Bell was trying to throw the Unionists a lifeline, while others interpreted his statement as an acknowledgment that Labour was prepared to negotiate away the Anglo-Irish Agreement if the election led to a hung parliament. The party leader, Kinnock, rejected this option during an election interview on RTE: 'there will be no change of attitude with a change of government.'[107]

The same commitment to the Anglo-Irish Agreement was given by David Owen and David Steel in their joint Liberal–SDP manifesto, which proposed 'a confederated relationship between the United

[104] *Times*, 19 September 1987.
[105] *Guardian*, 26 January 1987.
[106] *Guardian*, 5 February 1987.
[107] *News Letter*, 1 June 1987.

Kingdom and the Republic of Ireland'[108] in the long term, with a devolved power-sharing assembly in the short term. David Steel suggested that by the 1989 European elections there would be an alliance between the Liberal–SDP alliance, the Alliance Party in Northern Ireland and the Progressive Democrats in Ireland.

The SDLP's manifesto was called *Keep Building*. Defending two seats and hopeful of winning two more (those of Enoch Powell and Gerry Adams), the party demanded changes in the Diplock courts. It claimed the Anglo-Irish Agreement was a better decision-making process than any since 1920. Austin Currie, once Stormont's youngest member, said that from the Nationalist point of view 'a continuation of Maggie Thatcher in power would be to our advantage . . . the best possibility of a solution depended on an agreement between the Republican party in the South and a Conservative government in Britain'.[109] He hoped that the election result would isolate the two Ps of Paisleyism and Provisionalism. Gerry Fitt, one of the founder members of the SDLP, issued a pamphlet in which he expressed 'bitter resentment at the support given by the SDLP to one of the most disastrous British Governments ever'.[110]

Sinn Fein had fourteen candidates standing and was defending one Westminster seat, West Belfast. The party's manifesto reaffirmed the right of the IRA to engage in armed resistance and called for a British withdrawal from the province. Some observers claimed that Sinn Fein was only going through the motions of contesting the election. The poor results in the Irish election had given the military wing the upper hand. Gerry Adams's Easter speech, which had spoken of 'the rattle of machine guns and the roar of explosives', seemed to indicate a withdrawal into the party's West Belfast citadel, and its choice of candidates, in winnable constituencies in Mid Ulster and North Belfast, seemed to confirm that the electoral period of Provo strategy had ground to a halt. Nevertheless, keeping West Belfast for Gerry Adams was all-important.

For the political parties in Northern Ireland, there was only one issue in the election: the Anglo-Irish Agreement. The public, however, had different interests. In a Coopers and Lybrand poll of 1,000 people, 71 per cent said than the state of the economy was of greater importance as an election issue than the agreement. Despite the plans to spend £60 million on the Castle Court development in Belfast city centre and the £240 million Laganside project, unemployment stood at 19.3 per cent. Harland and Wolff made a further 500 redundant. Their labour force

---

[108] *Irish News*, 19 May 1987.
[109] *Fortnight*, No. 250, April 1987.
[110] *Irish Times*, 10 June 1987.

now numbered 3,750; twenty-five years earlier it had been 20,000. Labour Party 87, a merger of the Northern Ireland Labour Party, the Newtownabbey Labour Party and the Labour Party of Northern Ireland, placed its main emphasis on social and economic policies in its election manifesto, calling for an industrial plan, a regional development agency, and special help for workers' co-operatives. Throughout the 1950s and 1960s the Labour Party polled an average of 25 per cent of the vote, with its highest return in 1962 – 32.8 per cent of the vote. In 1987 its candidates would be lucky to save their deposits. Once the Troubles started, Unionist workers split according to cultural and religious traditions; 'social politics was killed at childbirth by constitutional fear and uncertainty.'[111]

Northern Ireland politics is not an extension of the arguments about defence or the welfare state. It is trapped within the confines of its own existing communal divisions, but because of the Anglo-Irish Agreement and its effect on political and social life in the province, what happened in Britain was of unusual interest in Northern Ireland in the 1987 election. The opinion polls suggested a Conservative win. Northern Ireland did not feature in the election until the last week of the campaign, by which time the polls had narrowed the gap between Conservative and Labour to 4 per cent. Douglas Hurd introduced the first split in the bipartisan policy on Northern Ireland by stating that he would be in real difficulties if he were a Labour minister: 'I would find myself having to explain that a significant part of my . . . parliamentary party is in sympathy with the terrorists.'[112] Tom King echoed FitzGerald's appeal before the Irish election: 'all responsible parties should speak with one voice against the evil of terrorism',[113] but added, 'Sinn Fein takes obvious encouragement from Labour's stance on Northern Ireland and on terrorism'.[114] This drew a reply from Paisley; King, he said, 'has ordered his civil servants of all ranks to talk to and co-operate with Sinn Fein. This is what he does in Northern Ireland . . . in England, he poses differently'.[115] Gerry Adams entered the row, stating that he had not met Kinnock, but had met Douglas Hurd and Willie Whitelaw. Kinnock said that he would 'not talk to Sinn Fein, and he would not come to a deal with Unionists in the event of a hung parliament'.[116]

The Unionist leaders campaigned in the expectation of a minority administration after the election. Paisley encouraged Unionist MPs to

[111] *Fortnight*, No. 250, April 1987.
[112] *Times*, 28 May 1987.
[113] *News Letter*, 1 June 1987.
[114] Ibid.
[115] Ibid.
[116] *Irish Times*, 1 June 1987.

have a 'shopping list of demands for when they found themselves in the position of power brokers'.[117] Molyneaux expected a Conservative lead of between thirty and fifty seats and said that 'Unionists will be sounding out opposition parties'.[118] John Hume predicted that the Unionist leaders would seek talks with the next prime minister, leading to negotiations involving all Northern Ireland's constitutional parties; 'they will not slam the door behind them this time', he said.[119]

The SDLP leader was taking his cue from an outspoken address by Archbishop Eames at the opening of the General Synod of the Church of Ireland in Dublin. Eames, who was rumoured to be closely involved in the Unionist task force deliberations, said that the 'Anglo-Irish Agreement should be replaced by a second agreement involving to a great extent all the constitutional parties concerned in Northern Ireland ... the new agreement would constitutionally and chronologically supercede the first ... it would be morally reprehensible if the newly elected governments of the United Kingdom and the Republic of Ireland were to sit back and say there was nothing they could do about Northern Ireland'.[120]

Chief Constable Hermon travelled to Dublin two days before the election for a three-hour meeting with his counterpart in the Republic, Commissioner Wren. Top of their agenda was the murder of Constable McLean, shot dead on his parents' farm in Donegal. Irish Special Branch had warned him that he was a likely target for an IRA active service unit based in Donegal. On the same day Private Joseph Leach of the 1st Queen's Lancashire Regiment was shot dead in Belfast. The IRA was not lowering its sights because an election was in the offing. There had been a noticeable drop in the level of violence by terrorists during previous campaigns. This time there was no let-up. Charles Watson was shot dead in Clough, County Down, and part-time UDR soldier Ivan Anderson was killed a fortnight into the election campaign. In Strabane, an off-duty UDR man driving a school bus full of children was shot, while in Castlecaulfield another part-time UDR man was critically injured. In Castlewellan, an off-duty RUC officer went berserk, firing at the Oak Grill Restaurant. He was set upon and severely beaten.

The strains and stresses of serving in the RUC surfaced at the annual general meeting of the Northern Ireland Police Federation a week before the election. Alan Wright said that 'fear generated by the security situation is the least cause of stress among the RUC. What

---

[117] *Irish Times*, 10 June 1987.
[118] Ibid.
[119] *Times*, 9 June 1987.
[120] *Irish Times*, 20 May 1987.

causes most stress in this force is the way the force is managed'.[121] Wright called on the government to 'adopt a more aggressive and realistic approach ... make a life sentence, a life sentence'.[122] He recommended an end to the 50 per cent remission on sentences, an end to a suspect's right to silence, and an increase in the detention time for interviewing, because 'this community is trying to fight a war with its legal arm tied behind its back'.[123] Terrorism was also the subject of lengthy debate at the Venice Economic Summit, the day before the election. All the nations present agreed to make no concessions to terrorists.

The general election returned Margaret Thatcher and the Conservative Party to power with a majority of 101. In Northern Ireland the only change occurred in County Down, where Enoch Powell's 37-year parliamentary career was terminated by Eddie McGrady's election as the SDLP's third representative at Westminster. There was little comfort for the integrationists; their two leading proponents, Powell and McCartney, were defeated. The Alliance Party and the Workers' Party polled 100,000 between them. The DUP's share of the poll fell by 8 per cent, although the number of votes cast stayed steady at just over 85,000. Sinn Fein retained West Belfast and a core support of 83,389 but slipped 3 per cent in its share of the vote. The SDLP gained a further seat and a 3.2 per cent increase in its share of the vote; it polled 64.9 per cent of the Nationalist vote, as compared with 35.1 per cent for Sinn Fein. The OUP increased their share of the vote – up 3.8 per cent to 276,220 – but polled 2 per cent less than in the general election of 1985.

The election in the province was conducted on issues arising out of the Anglo-Irish Agreement; 66.2 per cent of voters (44.4 per cent of the electorate) were opposed to the agreement and 33.7 per cent (22.6 per cent of the electorate) in favour of it. The most interesting result was in Antrim East, where Roy Beggs, the Official Unionist candidate, had the benefit of the no-contest pact with the DUP. The turnout was down to 55.2 per cent, the lowest in the country, but Beggs's majority, only 367 in the 1983 election, soared to 15,360. The DUP supporters in Larne, Glengormley and Rathcoole stayed away from the voting booths in protest at the no-contest pact forced on them and the DUP by Ian Paisley.

Molyneaux accepted that the 2 per cent drop in the Unionist vote was 'due to Unionist disquiet over the abstentionist policy at Westminster – it seems to have backfired'.[124] A public relations agency was to be

---

[121] *News Letter*, 3 June 1987.
[122] *Irish Times*, 3 June 1987.
[123] *News Letter*, 3 June 1987.
[124] *Irish Times*, 13 June 1987.

hired to help sell the Unionist cause. There was little doubt that Molyneaux intended leading his depleted parliamentary team back to the House of Commons. He had lost his most influential parliamentary colleague in Powell. For Paisley's DUP it was a disappointing and unsatisfactory election result. Internal disputes had weakened party cohesiveness. Paisley's hold on the party faithful was not as sure as in previous elections. Their share of the vote was down dramatically, reflecting the concern felt by their supporters about the flirtation with paramilitary activities.

It was the decisive Conservative majority of 101 seats, together with the negative response on the doorstep and on the hustings and the failure of traditional Unionist voters to vote that scuttled any plans the leaders of the Unionist pact had of prolonging their 'no' campaign. Molyneaux was positively pleading for a meeting with the prime minister when he said that 'unionism would favourably consider an invitation to dialogue with Mrs Thatcher'.[125] There were no hidden bargaining positions available to the Unionists, nor could the leaders ignore the existence of the task force report for much longer.

Enoch Powell left active politics; he was unlikely to be offered an alternative parliamentary platform in the House of Lords by a prime minister he had accused of treachery and called a Jezebel. Nicholas Scott, the Northern Ireland Office minister in charge of security, and a strong and committed defender of the Anglo-Irish Agreement, was replaced by John Stanley. Scott was no respecter of reputations and not easily bullied. His move across the Irish Sea, and the track record of his replacement, were of more than a passing interest to the Dublin partner in the Intergovernmental Conference.

FitzGerald said that Mrs Thatcher's success 'copper-fastened the Agreement'.[126] Haughey was more likely to be interested in the political implications of Lord Hailsham's move from the Lord Chancellorship. Hailsham was on record as being the major obstacle to mixed courts and to three-judge no-jury Diplock courts. He was also known to be strongly against Haughey's plans to introduce a prima-facie clause into the extradition arrangements between Britain and Ireland. The taoiseach had already ordered his attorney-general, Gerry Collins, to consider the feasibility of introducing the clause as an amendment. His fall-back position, should that option be unavailable, was to threaten to hold up the implementation of the new Extradition Act, scheduled for 1 December 1987. Haughey intended to bargain with Thatcher, linking reform in the administration of justice in Northern Ireland with the implementation of the Extradition Act.

---

[125] *News Letter*, 15 June 1987.
[126] *Irish Times*, 26 June 1987.

In the Queen's Speech, the new government committed itself to 'seek an agreed basis on which greater responsibility can be devolved to representatives of the people ... work unremittingly for the defeat of terrorism ... build upon the constructive relationships established with the Republic of Ireland, in security and other matters'.[127] Seeing no reference to the Anglo-Irish Agreement, Molyneaux commented that 'there was scope for negotiations'.[128] The General Assembly of the Presbyterian Church of Ireland indicated the drift of Loyalist Protestant thinking when it rejected a call for the suspension of the agreement at its meeting in June 1987. This was a significant indicator of a changed mood, since the same assembly, twelve months earlier, had certainly not conceded that the agreement was now a *fait accompli*. The Methodist Church went one step further than the Presbyterians and adopted at its conference a report accepting the framework of the agreement while urging all political leaders to pursue its devolution clause. The Anglican bishop of Connor encouraged Unionists to 'find the basis for a devolved administration with widespread acceptance, as provided for in the Accord'.[129]

All these views were in line with what the task force report was rumoured to be recommending. It also confirmed what the Coopers and Lybrand poll had disclosed just before the election. Integration and power-sharing were the most popular options, unilateral independence and direct rule bottom of the poll.

Between the election and the start of the parliamentary session, the IRA killed three security officers. Joe McIlwaine, a UDR soldier, was shot dead the day after the election. Nathaniel Cush, a former UDR officer, died three days later; his car was booby-trapped. In Carrickfergus an off-duty policeman, Sergeant Robert Guthrie, was caught and killed in the school playground. He became the eleventh RUC victim of terrorism in six months.

---

[127] Ibid.
[128] Ibid.
[129] *Fortnight*, No. 254, September 1987.

5

Talks, extradition and Enniskillen

In July 1987 the Unionist task force report, *An End to Drift*, was
published. It was in two parts, of which only the first was made public.
The second part was reported to be highly critical of the Unionist
leaders and their anti-agreement tactics. *An End to Drift* recommended
exploratory talks with the Thatcher government, to see if an alternative
to the Anglo-Irish Agreement could be negotiated. This was a
considerable advance on past negotiating positions, which had insisted
that there would be talks only when the agreement had been scrapped
or suspended. The authors rejected integration: 'we cannot believe that
constitutional security is to be found in a campaign to persuade mainland political parties to extend their organization to Northern
Ireland.'[1] They acknowledged that 'a policy of total integration continues to attract substantial support in the Unionist community –
however the Whitehall establishment is strongly opposed to such a
course'.[2] They went on to conclude that 'devolution is the more attainable objective'.[3] This brought the report into line with mainstream
Conservative thinking.

The report commented that 'we have no doubt that the Anglo-Irish
Conference is tantamount to joint authority',[4] but suggested that a
Unionist convention be set up to lead a renewed campaign which would
demonstrate the absence of consent to the Hillsborough accord.
Meanwhile discussions with the government should begin. Should these
talks about talks fail, Unionists should seek a new base for Northern
Ireland outside the present context – in other words, independence.

The Times called the task force report a giant leap forward in Unionist

---

[1] *Irish Times*, 3 July 1987.
[2] *News Letter*, 3 July 1987.
[3] Ibid.
[4] Ibid.

thinking: 'It would be churlish to underestimate the magnitude of the change in perceptions with which the authors of the report have come to terms.'[5] However, it doubted if much progress would result, chiefly because of the struggle over the control of security.

Molyneaux and Paisley gave the report 'begrudging acceptance'.[6] They claimed that 'the debate of the moment is concerning the willingness on the part of Her Majesty's Government to declare that it is prepared to seek a new agreement which will supersede the other. We must find out if that willingness exists or can be established'.[7] They were preparing for the first of the talks about talks with senior Northern Ireland Office civil servants. It took place on 7 July 1987 and was the first official contact since the Downing Street meeting with Mrs Thatcher in February 1986. The suggestion that Millar, McCusker and Robinson, the authors of the task force report, be involved in these deliberations was not accepted by Paisley and Molyneaux. The first meeting was a brief affair, to agree procedure. The second was arranged for the following week, immediately after the Twelfth of July parades. Paisley, meanwhile, effectively scuttled the task force initiative by declaring that the bottom line of all negotiations was that the Anglo-Irish Agreement cease to be implemented and the Maryfield secretariat cease its operations. Molyneaux said he 'wasn't wildly optimistic',[8] that anything would come of the talks about talks. Both Unionist leaders travelled to Westminster to meet the civil servants, Sir Kenneth Bloomfield and Sir Robert Andrews. The meeting lasted twenty minutes. Molyneaux said that a further meeting was unlikely until early winter. Paisley flew to the States for a holiday.

At Westminster the government had renewed the direct rule legislation for the province. The Labour front bench team was reshuffled and Kevin McNamara, MP for Kingston-upon-Hull North, replaced Peter Archer as Northern Ireland spokesman. He was known for 'his persistent advocacy of a civil libertarian stance on security issues, going back to his participation in the Campaign for Democracy in Ulster in the 1960s'.[9]

In Northern Ireland the marching season passed quietly. The Orange Order complied with the new seven-day notice requirement and did not attempt to challenge the RUC ban on their preferred route through Catholic areas. They held a religious service in the open in front of a high metal security screen erected by the RUC to block access to

---

[5] *Times*, 3 July 1987.
[6] *Irish Times*, 8 July 1987.
[7] *News Letter*, 8 July 1987.
[8] *Irish Times*, 14 July 1987.
[9] *Fortnight*, No. 254, September 1987.

Woodhouse and Obins Streets. Alan Wright was arrested for disorderly behaviour.

The last scheduled Intergovernmental Conference before the long parliamentary vacation occurred on 15 July 1987. It was only the second meeting since the Irish election in February. Peter Barry had complained about the infrequency of the meetings and the pace of reforms. Lenihan's view was that his first priority should be to give the Unionists 'time and space to change direction'.[10] The communiqué noted the Inspectorate of Constabulary's investigation into the management and organization of the RUC's élite anti-terrorist Special Branch and the HQ Mobile Support Units, and the promise of a new guide on fair employment in the early autumn, pending new legislation in the next session of parliament. The Irish representative formally withdrew the Stalker affair from the agenda of the Intergovernmental Conference. King and Lenihan agreed to make a joint application for the release of £80 million destined by the EC for the North and the Republic, currently held up by bureaucratic red tape. Britain apologized for a number of unauthorized incursions on Irish territory by security services from the North.

Near the border, an INLA renegade, Dessie O'Hare, nicknamed the Border Fox, attacked Elizabeth Nicholson and her two children as she drove out of the family farm on her way to shop. The terrorists were after her husband, Jim Nicholson, the former Unionist member of parliament. Elizabeth Nicholson was allowed to proceed to her shopping, and the Border Fox escaped.

Over the border in Belleek an IRA sniper shot Lance-Corporal Thomas Hewitt on his first day's patrol in the province. In Ballymena, the terrorists used a sledgehammer to break down the back door to Constable Norman Kennedy's home. They shot him at point-blank range. He had only recently moved to the house after being hounded out of his home by Loyalist mobs. In Portadown, the Northern Bank was raided by five men dressed as policemen; they got away with a quarter of a million pounds. The RUC believed a Loyalist gang from Belfast was responsible. In Boston, USA, three men who admitted smuggling seven tons of weapons and ammunition to the IRA in 1985 were gaoled for periods of between four and ten years.

The UVF and the IRA engaged in a tit-for-tat campaign of death in Belfast. The death of Dominic Jude O'Connor, a Roman Catholic, was avenged by the murder of John Tracey, a Protestant. Jim Keelan and Eddie Campbell were murdered by the UVF and the IRA shot dead Alan McQuintan and William Richard Magrath. Patrick Hammell was assassinated by the UVF; fourteen hours later the IRA shot Harry

---

[10] *Irish Times*, 16 July 1987.

Sloan. Some observers thought that a territorial dispute was the reason for the feud. Others saw it as a deliberate attempt at creating sectarian strife in order to goad the Unionists into retaliation.

In the House of Commons, the newly elected Ken Livingstone claimed that Airey Neave, the Conservative front-bench spokesman on Northern Ireland before his assassination by the INLA, had known of a plan by Captain Robert Nairac and three UDR volunteers to kill three members of the Miami Showband in 1975. The intention had been to undermine a ceasefire which had been negotiated between the Labour government and the IRA. Livingstone was repeating claims made earlier by Fred Holroyd and Colin Wallace, two former army officers who had served in Northern Ireland during the 1970s; they argued that a dirty-tricks department of MI5 had been working to destabilize Northern Ireland. Holroyd claimed that Captain Nairac had told him that he had killed John Francis Green, an IRA leader, in 1975. He also claimed that 'the SAS used Loyalist paramilitary groups to carry out murder missions across the border in the Republic'.[11]

The supporters of the task force report suspected a covert campaign against its recommendations in the first week of August 1987, during the run-up to the third round of talks about talks between the Unionist leaders and the Northern Ireland Office civil servants. Robert McCartney started the rumour that 'the so-called task force were secretly negotiating a deal with like-minded members of the SDLP'.[12] He was angry that the task force, while recognizing the support for integration among Unionist supporters, had rejected it as an attainable option. He charged the task force authors with being 'Ulster nationalists first, and everything else, especially British, next . . . their fight is not the maintenance of the Union, but the protection of Protestant interests'.[13] The charge that secret talks had taken place was developed further in the *News Letter*. The paper claimed that four meetings had been held, involving civil servants, Unionists and SDLP members. 'The real aim and objectives of these talks between the NIO and the two Unionists is to get rid of Molyneaux and Paisley as Unionist leaders.'[14] The *Irish Times* alleged that the *News Letter* was carrying on an 'orchestrated witch hunt against Millar',[15] and Molyneaux challenged the *News Letter* to 'oblige their anonymous sources to stand over the charges they freely and gratuitously make'.[16] The task force report was radical in its recommendations, and difficult enough to sell without the

[11] *Guardian*, 28 February 1987.
[12] *News Letter*, 3 July 1987.
[13] Ibid.
[14] *News Letter*, 15 August 1987.
[15] *Irish Times*, 12 August 1987.
[16] *News Letter*, 15 August 1987.

added handicap of suggestions of covert meetings with an opposition party regarded by many as the Nationalist enemy.

The newspaper articles appeared shortly after Paisley's return from holiday. During his absence abroad, Roy Bradford had suggested that the Unionists would 'accept power-sharing if the Government agreed to some change in or dilution of [the agreement]'.[17] Martin Smyth MP said that 'simple devolution is not on, a federal UK with a place for Northern Ireland would be perfectly workable'.[18] Archbishop Eames contacted OUP, DUP, SDLP and Alliance leaders to arrange informal talks. Everybody agreed except Paisley. He called the archbishop's idea 'unwise'.[19]

The London meeting between the Unionist leaders and the civil servants, Bloomfield and Andrews, took place on 11 August 1987. Paisley tried to distance himself from the recommendations of the task force report. He denied that the talks about talks were initiated by *An End to Drift*: 'our mandate for these talks comes from the general election and our manifesto when we said we would be going to see if there had been a change of heart on the part of the government.'[20] This statement was issued on the eve of the next meeting with Bloomfield and Andrews. It became obvious during the meeting that the government had not had a change of heart.

There was 'a general air of pessimism because of growing splits within Unionism'.[21] Paisley rejected all power-sharing: 'as for having John Hume and Seamus Mallon in the Government of Northern Ireland ... it's not on.'[22] Bradford tried to rally the dispirited Unionist ranks by publishing his blueprint for progress. It included a public commitment by the Unionists that they would accept in principle that the minority community should share in the administration of the province in proportion to its political strength and said that Unionists should meet Haughey without the involvement of the British government to discuss the establishment of an institutional link with Dublin. Bradford suggested that 'by offering such a package of power sharing plus an Irish dimension, Unionists would regain the high ground'.[23] The Northern Consensus Group issued a discussion paper entitled *Untying the Knot, a New Opportunity*. It urged a new administration bridging the political gap and with responsiblity for security: 'we believe that in practice the Anglo-Irish Agreement can be

---

[17] *News Letter*, 6 July 1987.
[18] *News Letter*, 27 July 1987.
[19] *Irish Times*, 12 August 1987.
[20] *News Letter*, 18 August 1987.
[21] *Irish Times*, 19 August 1987.
[22] *Fortnight*, No. 254, September 1987.
[23] *News Letter*, 31 August 1987.

"devolved away" even if symbolically it remains in existence.'[24] The Charter Group's Harley West was much nearer to understanding the Unionist split when he said that the task force report has been 'consigned to the rubbish bin, Unionists must expect to be misled into believing that all that is attainable is a local administrative Assembly without power and a Grand Committee at Westminster to rubber stamp the will of our political masters'.[25] This view supported the notion that the Unionist leaders did not seek a major change to the existing status quo. In the mean time they were happy to prolong the talks about talks.

One Unionist who was not content to play the waiting game was Frank Millar, chief executive of the Official Unionists and co-author of the task force report. He resigned, and his departure was a public admission that the debate about the task force proposals was over. He had emerged from an extremist family in sectarian North Belfast to become a voice of moderation; 'his experiences told him that consensus offered more than supremacy.'[26] The new chief executive of the Official Unionists was James Wilson, a councillor for eleven years and a former shipyard engineer.

Frank Millar was not the only political figure to opt out of public life in the province in the summer of 1987. Jim Allister and twenty of his supporters went before the election. Will and Pip Glendenning, Alliance councillors in Belfast, resigned and were replaced by two Sinn Fein representatives. John Alderdice replaced John Cushnahan as leader of the Alliance Party. Nigel Hamilton, general secretary of the DUP, and John Kennedy, of the SDLP's research unit, resigned, as did Peter Smith, honorary secretary to the Official Unionists. Peter Robinson's resignation as deputy leader of the DUP was to follow shortly.

The secretary of state, Tom King, felt confident enough of his position to visit Belfast city centre for the first time in eighteen months. Next day, he met Paisley and Molyneaux for the first time since the Downing Street meeting of February 1986. King met the two leaders to try to avert a breakdown in the talks about talks with the Northern Ireland Office civil servants. There was an impasse. King, aware of the splits and strains in the Unionist pact, played for time and suggested an adjournment. However, he made no attempt to keep secret the fact that the Unionist leaders had broken their own nineteen-month ban on meeting government ministers. Alan Wright, who had been campaigning to stop the talks about talks, said that 'it was absolutely astonishing that the two leaders could find time to sit down with their arch-enemy'.[27]

---

[24] *News Letter*, 7 September 1987.
[25] Ibid.
[26] *Fortnight*, No. 255, September 1987.
[27] *Irish Times*, 15 September 1987.

King travelled to Dublin to meet Haughey and Lenihan, who seemed more concerned about a plan to use the North Sea as a dumping-ground for Sellafield waste and the closure of the Liverpool–Dublin ferry than about North–South affairs. They were angry about a press briefing given by Deputy Chief Constable Michael McAtamey, which resulted in reports critical of the Garda in *The Times*, the *Daily Mail* and the *Mail on Sunday*, but welcomed a new community relations unit set up under Brian Mawhinney and an additional £250,000 earmarked by the Northern Ireland Office for youth organizations in the province. The meeting ended with 'an exchange of views on how they saw changes in the administration of justice'.[28]

Charles Haughey had successfully guided Ireland's most austere economic policy to date through the Dáil. Fine Gael had abstained on the budget vote rather than face the prospect of another election. Hospitals were to close, school-building programmes stopped and welfare payments were tightened. The first goal was to stabilize the national debt, standing at one and a half times the national income. The 'national question' took second place to the economy.

A poll on unification held by the Market Research Bureau of Ireland and an *Irish Times* poll seemed to confirm the weakening interest in the 'national question'. Forty-nine per cent of the population of the Republic believed that unity with the North would never be brought about; only 39 per cent had thought so in 1963.

In Northern Ireland, 40,000 copies of the new guidelines on fair employment were printed and circulated to all employers. The document had no legal standing, but was an important indicator of government thinking. It gave employers an opportunity to amend their recruiting procedures before new legislation was introduced. Firms refusing to conform could be denied government contracts and, following the introduction of new legislation, government grants. The new guidelines suggested that the current declaration of intent was to be replaced by a declaration of practice which would act as a licence, renewable at regular intervals and depending on performance. The guidelines suggested an end to word-of-mouth recruitment and unsolicited applications. All vacancies were to be advertised and the number of candidates from under-represented minorities increased. Selection should be solely on the basis of merit, though affirmative action should also be taken where necessary.

The new guidelines did not go as far as the MacBride principles, which supported reverse discrimination and quota recruitment. Sean MacBride, the Nobel Peace Prize winner, had attracted considerable support for his ideas in the United States. No American company had

---

[28] *Times*, 17 September 1987.

as yet signed the MacBride principles but they posed a threat to companies like Harland and Wolff and Short Brothers. The possibility that they might be accepted in the United States led the Northern Ireland trade unions and the local Confederation of British Industry to support the government's new employment guidelines.

The Northern Ireland Committee of the Irish Congress of Trade Unions (ICTU) had been moving towards a policy of equal opportunity since 1986. Liam McBrinn, president of the Trades Council, declared that 'the level of intimidation, sectarianism, discrimination is something the trade union movement cannot just turn a blind eye to'.[29]

In the summer of 1987, the Fair Employment Agency ruled in favour of a Catholic worker at Mackie's textile engineering firm. The worker had complained that the display of Loyalist flags and emblems interfered with his ability to do the job. At Short Brothers, two thousand workers failed to return to work after the management took down flags and bunting on 1 July 1987. King left for the States, to promote the government's guidelines, to persuade American companies not to sign the MacBride principles and to search for new jobs and inward investment.

The Industrial Development Board in Northern Ireland attracted investments worth £311 million in 1986. It had also created 4,187 new jobs, at a cost of £9,000 per job. The Department of Economic Development identified six weaknesses in the Northern Ireland economy: lack of enterprise, poor quality, poor productivity, the peripheral geographical position, the large public sector (which accounted for 70 per cent of local employment) and the unfavourable political situation. In July 1987 a report identified areas for improvement; it suggested a more positive attitude to self-employment, weekly starter grants for small-scale projects and a 'total quality' campaign. Public funding should be used as a catalyst to improve competitiveness and the public sector should obtain a higher proportion of goods and services from local firms.

King's visit to the States started off well with the announcement that two textile companies were to invest £6 million in the province. Arrangements had also been made for the investment of £54 million from the International Fund for Ireland. Tourism had attracted 824,000 visitors to the province in 1986. A survey by the Northern Ireland Tourist Board indicated that 35 per cent of all holiday-makers came out of curiosity, to see for themselves if the province lived up to its media image. The French and West German visitors, in particular, claimed that the sectarian ghettos of West Belfast and the Bogside were their favourite haunts. Only 5 per cent of the 5,000 questioned were put

---

[29] *Fortnight*, No. 251, May 1987.

off by the presence of armed soldiers in the street and only 9 per cent commented unfavourably on the Troubles.

The IRA had already targeted hotels in the province; in August they returned, blowing up the Landsdowne Court Hotel on the Antrim Road and destroying the Barday Restaurant in Shaws Bridge. Tit for tat killings continued; the UVF killed Michael Power and the IRA Stevan Megrath. In late August two Special Branch officers, Detective Constable Stanley Carson and Detective Constable Michael Malone, were shot dead at the Liverpool bar opposite the Liverpool–Belfast ferry terminal. The death of an off-duty RUC man, Reserve Constable Finlay, brought the total of murders in the first nine months of 1987 to seventy-one; twenty-six were members of the security forces and forty-five were civilians.

In Wiltshire, Special Branch detectives arrested two men and a woman near the grounds of Tom King's country home. Their arrest followed several days of police surveillance. Inspector John Jones of Avon and Somerset Police said they 'were treating the matter as one of national security'.[30] The three Irish suspects were held under the Prevention of Terrorism Act.

In London Peter Imbert, the Metropolitan Police commissioner, and James Anderton, chief constable of Greater Manchester, called for the removal of a suspect's right to keep silent. The proposal had been one of the Northern Ireland Police Federation's submissions to the Northern Ireland Office in April 1987. The home secretary, Douglas Hurd, asked, 'is it really in the interests of justice . . . that experienced criminals should be able to refuse to answer all police questions . . . [31] It was thought an amendment might be made to the Criminal Justice Bill, to revise 'a fundamental principle of English justice, that it is for the Crown to prove guilt and not for the accused to prove innocence'.[32] The proposal had been debated at length and rejected in 1972 and again in 1984. The lord chief justice, Lord Lane, and the retiring DPP, Sir Thomas Hetherington, were known to support the idea that a court should be able to comment on or draw inferences from the fact that a defendant had been silent when questioned by police. The *Guardian* called the proposal 'another disturbing example of the Government's indifference, not just to the civil liberties of suspects, but also to the principle of balance in criminal procedures'.[33] Within a year the right to silence was withdrawn. The announcement came while the trial of the three Irish people arrested at Tom King's Wiltshire home was in

---

[30] *Guardian*, 1 September 1987.
[31] *New Statesman*, 25 September 1987.
[32] *Times*, 21 September 1987.
[33] *Guardian*, 17 September 1987.

progress. The three accused opted not to give evidence, and retain their right to silence; they were all found guilty.

The home secretary ordered a new police investigation into the case of the Guildford Four, Paul Hill, Gerard Conlan, Patrick Armstrong and Carole Richardson, all of whom had served twelve years. It was alleged that the prisoners' confessions might have been secured by police violence and threats against them by certain policemen. Two Irishmen, Joe O'Connell and Brendan O'Dourd, convicted for their involvement in the Balcombe Street Siege, had admitted playing a part in the Guildford bombing.

The referral of the Guildford case and the granting of leave to appeal to the Birmingham Six were political acts, intended to influence the Irish government's stance on extradition. For Mrs Thatcher, the importance of the Anglo-Irish Agreement lay in the successful extradition of suspected terrorists from the Republic. It would also be a 'sizeable trophy with which to impress the Unionists. The Anglo-Irish Agreement will be seen to be working in its law enforcement and security dimension'.[34]

The Irish government's quid pro quo for extradition, according to Garret FitzGerald, was the implementation of changes in the administration of justice in the North: the reform of the Northern Ireland court system and a new code of conduct for the RUC, who would also accompany all UDR patrols. FitzGerald's intervention 'led to consternation in London and Dublin'.[35] King and Lenihan, both in the United States, denied such an understanding. Neither had been in office at the time of the alleged understanding, which FitzGerald claimed 'amounted to a contractual obligation'.[36]

When Lenihan and King met in Dublin prior to their visits to the States, both agreed that job discrimination was top of the agenda, but by the time Lenihan returned from the States he confirmed that 'reforming the system of justice in the North was the main item on the agenda of the next meeting of the Anglo-Irish Conference'.[37] Cardinal Ó Fiaich added to the pressure on Lenihan by claiming that 'members of his church in Northern Ireland would feel "betrayed" if Dublin authorized altered extradition procedures in advance of changes in Ulster's controversial single-judge terrorist courts system'.[38] King's response reflected the gravity of the situation: 'I would be very concerned if extradition was not implemented. It is a very important issue.'[39]

---

[34] *Irish Times*, 15 August 1987.
[35] *Fortnight*, No. 257, December 1987.
[36] *Times*, 23 September 1987.
[37] *Irish Times*, 3 October 1987.
[38] *News Letter*, 5 October 1987.
[39] *News Letter*, 6 October 1987.

The second round of talks about talks between Molyneaux, Paisley and King passed with little comment. John McMichael summed up the situation: 'Paisley totally rejects the concept of any form of government other than majority rule and Molyneaux has absolutely no commitment to devolution. We therefore have two political leaders who are talking with the Government, and they have no policies to negotiate with.'[40]

Peter Robinson's resignation as deputy leader of the DUP caused shock and surprise in Ulster political circles. It was known that relations between Paisley and his deputy had been strained since the publication of the task force report, but few outside observers imagined that the schism would result in Robinson's departure. His resignation was thought by some to be inevitable once Paisley rejected power-sharing and then went on to exclude Robinson and the other two authors of the task force report from any contact with the Northern Ireland Office. Others thought the resignation a calculated political gamble. The Unionist leadership was in confusion and Robinson had nothing to lose by cutting free. He might even be able to reappear as the sole leader of a realigned Unionist movement. If all else failed, a break from party politics gave him the opportunity to repair his links with supporters in the UDA.

The Loyalist paramilitary organization had itself been shaken to its foundations by the television programme *Roger Cook Reports*, which claimed that £15 million a year ended up in the hands of terrorists. Eddie Sayer, a senior member of the UDA, said that 'political ideals came second, crime comes first'.[41] He was dismissed from the UDA and John McMichael started an internal investigation into the criminal activities of the organization. Within three months he was killed by a car bomb.

Molyneaux and Paisley each gave £5,000 to help defray the £36,000 bill which the twenty-four Unionist councillors on Belfast City Council had incurred as part of their anti-agreement protest. The Unionist leaders' contribution covered the costs of those councillors who were unemployed. The others would have to pay up or face disqualification for five years. The Northern Ireland Office introduced a discussion document, *Elected Representatives and the Democratic Process in Northern Ireland*, which reflected 'the widespread public concern over the role and activities of elected representatives whose attitude to terrorist violence appears incompatible with a genuine commitment to constitutional politics'.[42] It discussed the proscription of terrorist organizations, an extension of the period of disqualification for those who served gaol

---

[40] *Guardian*, 9 October 1987.
[41] *Irish Times*, 19 August 1987.
[42] *News Letter*, 13 October 1987.

sentences for terrorist offences, an oath of allegiance and a declaration of support for the fight against terrorism. *The Times* argued strongly in its support. The *Spectator* said that 'the declaration, quite simply, is basic necessity for decent local government'.[43] Republican Danny Morrison said that Sinn Fein councillors would adopt the 'de Valera option' with regard to the oath; they would simply go through the motions of endorsing the declaration. The government's initiative was of more importance to Unionist councillors, whose adjournment protest was becoming ineffectual. They could at least persuade themselves, if nobody else, that they had forced this concession from the Northern Ireland Office.

The Unionist leaders were less satisfied with the new RUC code of conduct. They saw this as having been forced on the police by the Intergovernmental Conference. In fact, it was being drafted before the Anglo-Irish Agreement was signed. *Professional Policing Ethics* was presented to the Police Federation as an extension of the code of conduct of the Metropolitan Police, but it was dragged into the political debate between London, Belfast and Dublin. The code was to be incorporated into the new confidential RUC manual and bound the RUC officers to be sensitive to Roman Catholic as well as Protestant traditions.

Supporters of the Anglo-Irish Agreement began to see some of the benefits of the accord emerging from the bureaucratic pipeline. The International Fund for Ireland, an end to supergrass trials, a new code of conduct for the RUC, the fair employment initiative and the oath against violence all pointed to the start of a new era in Northern Ireland. The Irish language and integrated schools had received substantial new funding and the worst of the Unionist protest was over. The leaders were talking to the secretary of state, the members of parliament were back at Westminster, and the last of the local councils, Carrickfergus, had brought its adjournment protest to an end. Security, however, remained a problem. Despite the increased investment in policemen and regular soldiers, there were more fatalities, the incidence of bombings and shootings was on the increase, and intelligence indicated that a major restocking of the terrorists' arsenals was taking place.

Meanwhile, the Anglo-Irish Agreement was facing new difficulties. At the annual gathering in Bodenstown to commemorate Wolfe Tone, Charles Haughey threatened to renege on one of the central tenets of the whole agreement – extradition. In a carefully drafted speech, Haughey said: 'The first duty of a sovereign, democratic state is to protect the life, liberty and the fundamental rights of its citizens. To hand the citizen over to another jurisdiction is something that should only be undertaken with great care and scrupulous regard for all circumstances. It is clear that at present many Irish people are questioning whether or not Dáil

---

[43] *Spectator*, 17 October 1987.

Éireann should agree to submit Irish citizens to a system of justice in which a large section of the community in the North has not as yet been persuaded to place its confidence.'[44] From a ceremony which commemorated one of Ireland's most famous Protestant leaders, the taoiseach appealed directly to the Northern Unionists: 'It is surely time that the two traditions in this country entered into direct dialogue with each other on the possibility of creating structures . . . which would move us nearer to the establishment of peace with justice for all.'[45]

The deadline for any agreement was 1 December 1987. That was the date on which the Dáil would be asked to decide on the implementation of the Extradition Bill which had been passed a year earlier. When Haughey succeeded FitzGerald he had immediately ordered his legal officers to consider the introduction of a prima-facie requirement to the Extradition Bill. Haughey's options were, therefore, a further post-ponement or a toughening of the conditions under which extradition could be operated. Either decision would be opposed by Britain.

The dispute centred on Article 8 of the Anglo-Irish Agreement and Paragraph 7 of the joint communiqué. Article 8 concerned the administration of justice and stated that 'the two Governments agree on the importance of public confidence in the administration of justice. The Conference shall seek . . . measures which would give substantial expression to this aim, considering *inter alia* the possibility of mixed courts in both jurisdictions for the trial of certain offences. The Conference shall also be concerned with policy aspects of extradition and extraterritorial jurisdiction as between North and South.'[46] Paragraph 7 of the communiqué added: 'Against this background, the Taoiseach said that it was the intention of his Government to accede as soon as possible to the European Convention on the Suppression of Terrorism.'[47]

FitzGerald claimed that it was 'only Mrs Thatcher's prior and personal agreement to reform the province's courts that had secured his signature to the Agreement'.[48] In November 1986 the British prime minister wrote to the taoiseach rejecting the concept of three-judge courts and the Irish Extradition Bill was put on the shelf. Civil servants had been trying to find a way out of the impasse. The lord chancellor, Lord Hailsham, held that 'if the United Kingdom Government forced upon the Northern Irish judiciary a system which they were unwilling to accept that would be politicization of the judicial system'.[49]

---

[44] *News Letter*, 12 October 1987.
[45] *Irish Times*, 14 October 1987.
[46] Anglo-Irish Agreement, 15 November 1985, Article 8.
[47] Anglo-Irish Agreement, Joint Communiqué, para. 7.
[48] *Economist*, 3 October 1987.
[49] *News Letter*, 28 August 1987.

Suggestions were floated that a new senior legal officer be established in Northern Ireland; others suggested the appointment of two lay assessors to sit with single-judge Diplock courts. Ian Aitken claimed that 'the opposition seems to have as much to do with the *amour propre* of the Ulster judges as with objective matters of law'.[50] The *Independent* claimed the Diplock courts were 'an affront to the legal traditions of the United Kingdom'.[51]

Lenihan flew to London on Saturday 17 October 1987 to meet King and Douglas Hurd, the home secretary. Hurd was steering the Criminal Justice Bill through the House of Commons and one of the major issues of debate was his intention to abolish the need for countries wanting to reclaim their criminals to demonstrate a prima-facie case. The London discussions were continued in Belfast a week later when the Intergovernmental Conference met. The resulting communiqué mentioned the new RUC code of practice, and referred to measures against terrorist racketeering and cross-border smuggling. There was no disguising the major issue. Tom King said that 'the Irish Government have made a commitment and it is obvious that if the Extradition Act does not come into effect, this would raise serious reservations'.[52] The Anglo-Irish Agreement was in great difficulties. The *Economist* commented that 'the Irish would probably settle for an acceptance of change in principle, and a promise to work on the details ... The British are hunting desperately for a form of words that would fall short of getting them committed to getting rid of the courts'.[53]

The prime minister added to the difficulties by stating that 'the future of courts in Northern Ireland is a matter for the United Kingdom government and is not a bargaining factor'.[54] The *Irish Times* concluded that 'if the British now feel that they cannot change the Diplock system, the Irish Government is entitled to take the view that there has been a breach of faith'.[55] The *Guardian* supported this line, adding: 'Failure to deliver progress on so fundamental a matter of public confidence strikes at the very heart of the Anglo-Irish Agreement.'[56] Tom King rejected FitzGerald's claim that the introduction of three-judge courts had been promised and added that 'failure to ratify the Act would have very serious implications for Anglo-Irish relations'.[57] Four days later FitzGerald addressed the Liberal Club in London; there had

---

[50] *Guardian*, 19 October 1987.
[51] *Independent*, 13 October 1987.
[52] *Irish Times*, 22 October 1987.
[53] *Economist*, 30 October 1987.
[54] *News Letter*, 23 October 1987.
[55] *Irish Times*, 6 October 1987.
[56] *Guardian*, 19 October 1987.
[57] *Times*, 31 October 1987.

been 'no specific Diplock court pledge'.[58] There was no British commitment to introduce three-judge Diplock Courts. The Anglo-Irish relationship was on the rocks because of a rumour. FitzGerald's credibility plummeted, but the one who was caught in the maelstrom was Haughey. This game of political roulette was played against a background of unprecedented developments elsewhere. In London the Birmingham Six appeal had started, with the Irish government represented in court and Irish papers giving a verbatim account of the case. In Brittany Adrian Hopkins, a bankrupt travel agent from Bray, County Wicklow, was arrested on board his boat, the *Eksund*. In Derry, two coffins were deposited outside St Eugene's Cathedral to await a requiem mass which had been forbidden by the diocesan bishop. In Dublin Sinn Fein's annual conference was under way.

Adrian Hopkins had flown to Amsterdam in early September 1987. There he purchased a Swedish motor boat called the *Eksund*. On 3 October he flew to Malta to join up with the crew who sailed the boat to Libyan territorial waters, where American defence satellites observed the transfer of arms and ammunition to the *Eksund*. When the boat was boarded by French customs and security officers off the port of Brest, they discovered a crew of five Irishmen and 150 tonnes of arms, ammunition and explosives. The Panamanian-registered trawler, reportedly bound from Malta to Kiel, was booby-trapped with plastic explosives. On board were Hopkins, Henry Cairns, a bookshop owner, also from Bray, and three others from Donegal and Mayo. They were carrying false passports.

In Derry two IRA terrorists, Edward McSheffrey and Patrick Deery, were killed when a bomb they were priming exploded prematurely. In the same week a 2,000 lb bomb was found in Derry, a 3,000 lb bomb in County Tyrone and a big cache of explosives in Tommebridge. Gilbert McNamee, the IRA's most sophisticated bomb-maker, received a 25-year sentence.

The families of McSheffrey and Deery requested a requiem mass. Bishop Edward Daly refused to lift his ban on requiem masses being held while the remains of IRA men were in the church. A Republican vigil was held outside the bishop's palace in an attempt to get him to change his mind. The dead terrorists' families informed the bishop that the two coffins would be presented for mass at the door of the cathedral. The bishop was at the Birmingham Six appeal hearing. The coffins were allowed into the precincts of the cathedral 'under protest, to avoid unbecoming scenes'.[59] On the procession to the cemetery six hooded gunmen appeared and fired a volley of shots over the two coffins. In the

---

[58] *Irish Times*, 4 November 1987.
[59] *Times*, 31 October 1987.

subsequent riot, as the police attempted to arrest members of the colour party, one of the coffins was upended and crashed to the ground.

In Dublin the Sinn Fein Conference was overshadowed by the deaths of thirteen active-service-unit members in twelve months. The *Eksund*'s arrest, McNamee's imprisonment, the possibility of extradition, the 'choking' of the cash supply and the anticipated oath of allegiance for those holding public office did not leave much scope for Gerry Adams to present an upbeat account of the year's activities. Sinn Fein had done badly in both Irish and British elections. Adams said the movement 'must face the reality of its political isolation – most people will not struggle, never mind vote, for abstract things. They will not fight for ideas'.[60]

Elsewhere in the Republic, the security forces were on full alert searching for Dessie O'Hare, the Border Fox. He and two accomplices kidnapped a Dublin dentist, John O'Grady, the intended victim being O'Grady's father-in-law. O'Hare was a free-lance assassin, brought up in south Armagh. In November 1986 he was released after serving an eight-year gaol sentence in the Republic. He acted for a time as a contract killer for the INLA but was expelled for free-lancing on his own account. He kidnapped O'Grady on 14 October. The dentist's family agreed to pay a ransom of £1.5 million, but only after they had been sent a small box containing the tops of O'Grady's little fingers. Before the money was handed over, a routine search found O'Grady. He was released, but O'Hare and his two associates escaped. O'Hare was on the run with a reward of £100,000 for his capture. He took time to contact the *Sunday Tribune* and tell them 'the gang badly needed the ransom to fight the British'.[61]

In Fermanagh, people were assembling to remember another British battle. It was Remembrance Sunday in Enniskillen.

> I will, with permission, Mr Speaker, make a statement on yesterday's terrorist attack at the war memorial in Enniskillen. This occurred shortly before the parade arrived for the formal wreath-laying ceremony. I should explain to the House that the normal procedure in Enniskillen is that the parade forms up and marches to the war memorial where the act of remembrance takes place, then marches to the Cathedral for the Remembrance Day service.
>
> At 10.45 a.m., as spectators were gathering near the war memorial, a bomb exploded in the St Michael's reading room, outside which a number of people were taking up their normal vantage point. No warning whatsoever had been given. The explosion demolished the gable wall, which fell, crushing the waiting spectators. Eleven people were killed and

---

[60] *Guardian*, 2 November 1987.
[61] Ibid.

more than sixty injured. Of the injured, twenty-one were detained in
hospital overnight, of whom four are very seriously injured. Among those
killed are three elderly couples, a young nurse and an off-duty
policeman.[62]

Tom King's statement to a packed House of Commons recorded the
worst atrocity in the province since the discothèque bombing in
Ballykelly in December 1982, when seventeen people died. The
secretary of state added: 'In all the tragedy of the terrorist campaign,
this outrage stands out in its awfulness. To perpetrate such an outrage
against people, for many of whom the occasion was already one of
sorrow and remembrance, betrays a total lack of human feeling.'[63]
Paisley called the attack 'a diabolical deed by hell-inspired monsters'.[64]
John Hume called the massacre 'probably the most deeply provocative
act to have been committed against the Unionist people'.[65]

A Protestant paramilitary group went looking for revenge in Belfast.
Five Catholics were sprayed with gunfire from a passing car, Thomas
Ferguson was attacked and Alan Lambert, a nineteen-year-old science
student at the University of Ulster, was shot in the back of the head.

Presidents Reagan and Gorbachev and Taoiseach Haughey all sent
their condolences to Prime Minister Thatcher. The Ulster Clubs
encouraged her to 'send in the SAS'[66] and Peter Robinson said that 'it
is only when the Ulster people take on and defeat the IRA that there will
be peace in Northern Ireland'.[67]

Gerry Adams 'extended sympathy on behalf of the Republican
people . . . I do not try to justify yesterday's bombing. I regret very
much that it happened'.[68] The Provisional IRA issued a statement
'deeply regretting what had occurred and the catastrophic consequences
of the explosion'.[69] The *Republican News* conceded that the movement
'was shocked and shaken by the blast – we do not attempt to excuse
or defend the action'.[70] Paul Corrigan, the Sinn Fein leader on
Fermanagh District Council, said, 'I won't condemn bombings in
general. I support the right of the IRA to wage military action against
the occupation forces.'[71] A member of the West Fermanagh brigade of
the IRA phoned a Belfast radio station to warn security services that an

---

[62] *Hansard*, 9 November 1987.
[63] Ibid.
[64] *Guardian*, 9 November 1987.
[65] *News Letter*, 9 November 1987.
[66] *Irish Times*, 9 November 1987.
[67] *Guardian*, 9 November 1987.
[68] *Times*, 9 November 1987.
[69] Ibid.
[70] *Times*, 13 November 1987.
[71] *Times*, 11 November 1987.

unexploded 150 lb bomb lay concealed in a village eighteen miles from Enniskillen. It was primed to explode at the same time as the Enniskillen bomb.

Gordon Wilson was trapped in the rubble with his daughter Marie. On Radio Ulster the morning after the tragedy he recalled how he felt in the shattered masonry for her hand. He heard her ask five times, 'Are you all right, Daddy?' Her last words were 'Daddy, I love you very much'. Wilson spoke of forgiveness and reconcilation. Two thousand people attended an open-air service at the Cenotaph in Belfast and Roman Catholics and Protestants united in a special mass at St Michael's Cathedral in Enniskillen. Gordon Wilson was given an ovation as he entered the church. In London, the thirteen Unionist members of parliament led a parade from Temple Bar to Downing Street, where a letter was handed in at Number 10. In Dublin twenty books of condolence, containing 50,000 signatures, were collected and a minute's silence was observed at 6.00 p.m. on Sunday 15 November 1987. At all Catholic services, a statement from the Irish bishops was read to the congregation: 'There is no room for ambivalence ... the choice is between good and evil. It is a sin to join organizations committed to violence or to remain in them. It is sinful to support such organizations or to call on others to support them. There is no excuse for thinking that the present violence in Ireland can be morally justified.'[72] An ecumenical congregation of 3,000 heard the statement at St Patrick's Cathedral in Dublin. At three churches in Belfast, members of the congregation walked out in protest at the bishops' message.

Commissioner Wren of the Garda and Chief Constable Hermon of the RUC met to co-ordinate plans. Sir John Hermon claimed that 'the murder executives of Sinn Fein control the IRA ... the Provos intended to kill civilians'.[73] A senior Republican source told the *Guardian*, 'Enniskillen has been an absolute disaster for us – politically we have shot ourselves in the head'.[74] Ed Moloney commented in *Fortnight*: 'IRA violence acted as a midwife to the Anglo-Irish Agreement, and now, just when the Accord seemed to be at its weakest, IRA violence has rescued and strengthened it, while at the same time dealing a fatal blow to Provo ambitions in the Republic ... as long as it continues, IRA violence will always have the potential to destroy the carefully nurtured plans of Sinn Fein leaders.'[75] The *Spectator* said that Enniskillen 'may well be taken as an indication of the IRA chiefs' lack

---

[72] *News Letter*, 16 November 1987.
[73] Ibid.
[74] *Guardian*, 9 November 1987.
[75] *Fortnight*, No. 257, December 1987.

of control over their men in the field'.[76] Sinn Fein's *ard fheis* had met only a week before Enniskillen. A new war council had been elected from the twelve-man executive and it was thought unlikely that it would have sanctioned such an atrocity. Observers of IRA affairs recalled that the South Armagh Brigade had not observed the ceasefire of 1975. Adams's quick condemnation of the explosion seemed to support those who argued that an active-service unit was free-lancing without war council approval. Roy Beggs, the Official Unionist MP for East Antrim, named Charles Caulfield as the Enniskillen bomber. Caulfield lived in Monaghan town, a few miles south of the border.

A number of articles were written about the likely effect of the explosion on Sinn Fein's electoral fortunes. Brian Walden claimed that it 'dealt a severe blow to the credibility of the IRA. Its claim to be part of a rational political movement and not just a gang of murderous psychopaths will be harder than ever to sustain. But it would be a serious mistake to think that the IRA has been broken and that peace in Northern Ireland is just round the corner.'[77] Others tried to suggest ways in which the horror of Enniskillen could be used to wean supporters of the IRA back into constitutional politics. They concluded that the options were few. Ben Pimlott claimed that the IRA enjoyed three kinds of support. The first group had personal experience of British imprisonment: 'this ever-growing group is unpersuadable . . . but others might be detached.'[78] The second group saw Sinn Fein as the only party with the determination to get things done. The third consisted of young people, 'often aimless and nihilistic, who regard the IRA with a combination of fear and fascination'.[79]

The *News Letter* described the massacre as a 'cowardly and barbaric crime against humanity' but hoped that 'buried under the bloodstained rubble' was the Anglo-Irish Agreement.[80] The *Sunday Times* saw hope in the tragedy: 'the revulsion of most Catholics must be turned to resolve, the SDLP must declare its full support for the security forces, the Unionists must push at the British Government's open door and seek talks on a new way towards power-sharing.'[81]

The *Spectator*, in a leader titled 'React in Anger', said that 'the English lack the words because they lack the understanding, the love of blood so apparent in the Republican cause . . . the IRA believe, not unreasonably, that Britain cannot make up its mind . . . the best chance

---

[76] *Spectator*, 14 November 1987.
[77] *Sunday Times*, 15 November 1987.
[78] *New Statesman*, 13 November 1987.
[79] Ibid.
[80] *News Letter*, 9 November 1987.
[81] *Sunday Times*, 15 November 1987.

for Britain is to react in anger . . . and seize the moment to declare an end to constitutional experiment'.[82]

At the lord mayor's banquet at the Guildhall, the prime minister said that 'the best defence against terrorism is to make clear that you will never give in'.[83] The same day a special meeting of the Intergovernmental Conference was held in Dublin. The two partners agreed on Operation Mallard; Ireland committed 7,500 Garda and Irish army troops to co-operate with the RUC and British army troops in the North, in a joint security sweep. Enniskillen was the obvious reason for the special push and the nationwide search for Dessie O'Hare was also in progress. The real reason, however, was to be found in the transcripts of interviews with Adrian Hopkins in prison in Paris. He confirmed Interpol and American intelligence reports that at least four shiploads of arms and ammunition from Libya had been landed in Ireland. Somewhere on the island were 2,000 Kalashnikov rifles, forty tonnes of explosives and twenty partially-equipped missiles.

In the Republic, time was running out for one of the great cliffhangers of Irish politics, the Extradition Act. The Enniskillen bombing, the gruesome activities of O'Hare's gang, and the threat implicit in the description of the *Eksund*'s cargo tilted public opinion in favour of ratification. Neil Kinnock flew to Dublin to offer Haughey a commitment by the opposition to press at Westminster for a speedier reform of the administration of justice in Northern Ireland. Nicholas Fenn, the British ambassador in Dublin, met the taoiseach twice. His message was the same both times: do not tamper with the provisions of the Extradition Act. But Haughey knew, and everyone else acknowledged, that there would be changes. 'The Irish misgivings are not mere cussedness,' reported the *Guardian*; 'the opposition should not be misconstrued . . . it is not founded on softness towards terrorism. It is not specifically founded on dislike of the non-jury and single-judge Diplock courts in the North. It is founded on the appeal of the Birmingham Six.'[84]

Lord Chief Justice Lane and Lord Justices O'Connor and Brown sat for twenty-seven days listening to the appeal of the six Irishmen convicted of the bombing in which twenty-one had died and more than 160 had been injured thirteen years previously. Hugh Callaghan, Patrick Power, Gerry Hunter, Richard McKenny, Bill Power and Johnny Walker had been convicted at Lancaster Crown Court after a 43-day trial. The case had been referred by the home secretary to the Court of Appeal after *World in Action* broadcast a claim by Tom

---

[82] *Spectator*, 14 November 1987.
[83] *News Letter*, 17 November 1987.
[84] *Guardian*, 19 November 1987.

Clarke, a former Birmingham policeman, that he had witnessed ill-treatment of the men during questioning. Devon and Cornwall Police had conducted an investigation into allegations of ill-treatment by the Midlands Police. In all, there had been six court hearings examining all or part of the Birmingham case. Lord Lane said that the three judges would prepare their verdicts by the beginning of 1987. The case had saturation coverage in the Irish press and the debate on the Extradition Act was conducted against this emotive backdrop.

In Whitehall, Ireland's vacillation over extradition was regarded with mounting contempt. Haughey's parliamentary dilemma confirmed the worst fears of those who argued that the Republic was a haven for terrorists on the run from the police in the North. In the celebrated case of Dominic McGlinchey, the Irish Supreme Court had overthrown the long-standing constitutional protection awarded to people wanted for terrorist crimes if their motives were held to be political. So far, McGlinchey was the only person to be extradited to the North, and then re-extradited back to the Republic. The new Extradition Act not only incorporated into Irish law the European Convention on the Suppression of Terrorism; it significantly strengthened the precedents set by the Supreme Court. The Sunningdale Agreement of 1974 had also dealt with people accused of terrorist offences. The Irish government had agreed that people accused of offences committed in Britain and Northern Ireland could be tried in the Republic. The British authorities had been slow to use this legislation, creating a feeling in the Republic that the continuing demand for extradition had more to do with political than with security considerations.

The British government knew how difficult extradition could be made by a prima-facie requirement. The Criminal Justice Bill was an attempt to simplify the system, and Lord Caithness admitted during a House of Lords debate that 'the United Kingdom is widely regarded in Europe as the haven for serious criminals'.[85] Instead of the prima-facie requirement, the government proposed to demand from other governments a warrant, a statement of fact about the crime and evidence about the law under which the individual was to be prosecuted.

Charles Haughey was badly shaken by the suggestion that the Irish Republic had become a repository for an arsenal big enough to threaten his government and perhaps Irish democracy itself. He was also impressed by repeated urging from the United States that Ireland must do its full share in stamping out terrorism. He swallowed his instinctive and long-held misgivings over the passage of the controversial extradition law and he openly declared war on the IRA. A process was introduced under which the Irish attorney-general could form an

---

[85] *Times*, 21 October 1987.

opinion on whether or not to accept an extradition warrant, accompanied by a supporting statement from the British attorney-general. The amended Bill also stipulated that the extradited person would be tried only for the offence detailed in the extradition papers. Haughey accepted a constructive opposition amendment which provided for a review of the operation of the new safeguards, and thereby secured their passive support in the Dáil vote. The Extradition Act became law on 1 December 1987 by seventy-eight votes to twenty-six, with sixty-two abstentions.

What were described as 'intense diplomatic exchanges' took place in the days leading up to the Dáil vote. Tom King welcomed the ratification of the European Convention on Terrorism but regretted the proposal to give a role to the Irish attorney-general. Margaret Thatcher used stronger language to condemn the amendments, which 'made Britain the least favoured nation in Europe in seeking ... extraditions from the Republic'.[86] This criticism hurt the Irish, who regarded the new arrangements as a compromise and a climb-down from a previously held position. The British ambassador to Dublin indicated the depth of British impatience with the Irish changes, 'which we see as unnecessary ... rather hurtful'.[87] He went on to detail some of the problems. Irish law allows the detention of suspects for only forty-eight hours. The ambassador suggested that the new procedures made extradition more difficult within that time: 'on the British side, we are in despair that this will prove possible in practice.'[88] *The Times* rejected the new Bill and prophesied 'more muddles on courtroom steps. Handing the pivotal role in such cases to a political appointee is hardly the best way of guaranteeing visible impartiality'.[89]

Thatcher and Haughey met in Copenhagen in early December. The prime minister claimed that the taoiseach promised to review the new arrangements if they did not work. Molyneaux correctly interpreted the coolness between the two prime ministers as proof that the extradition row was the 'most serious rift with Dublin for a decade'.[90] It certainly gave the Unionists renewed hopes that the Anglo-Irish Agreement was on its last legs. They prepared for the fifth round of talks about talks with Tom King. Molyneaux had issued a five-point plan of action for the Unionists at a rally at Hillsborough in mid November, two years into the Anglo-Irish Agreement. He called for a return to basic unity which alone would see the Unionist community through the current

---

86 *Times*, 2 December 1987.
87 *News Letter*, 7 December 1987.
88 *Irish Times*, 7 December 1987.
89 *Times*, 5 December 1987.
90 *News Letter*, 2 December 1987.

problems. He suggested the return of internment for a 'mere 200 thugs, murderers and terrorists and a restoration of authority to your elected representatives'.[91]

The SDLP appointed a group of three – Austin Currie, Seamus Mallon and Sean Farren – to review possible discussion points with the Unionists. They too were acutely aware of the contradictions within the Anglo-Irish partnership and were in danger of being isolated, north and south of the border. John Hume was missing the direct contact he had had with FitzGerald; relations with Haughey were not as constructive. Hume felt a new affinity with the British Labour Party once Kevin McNamara became the front-bench spokesman on Northern Ireland. McNamara committed himself to working out a clear party policy on Northern Ireland. In one of his earliest speeches he denied that Labour was maintaining a bi-partisan policy with the Conservatives on Northern Ireland. He accused successive Conservative governments of being 'preoccupied with problems of violence and security leading to an increasing reliance on coercion. We must show that progress is achieved despite the violence rather than because of it'.[92] The general election campaign, in particular Tom King's attack on Livingstone and Douglas Hurd's taunts concerning the welcome given to visiting Sinn Fein supporters by Labour-dominated councils, indicated Conservative willingness to exploit Labour divisions. Those divisions became a rift after Enniskillen.

At the annual meeting of the Labour Co-ordinating Committee, Sean Rogers called on Kinnock and the national executive to take immediate action against Livingstone and his supporters, 'who are morally culpable for what happened in Enniskillen'.[93] Livingstone hit back, claiming that the Provisional IRA would 'win its struggle to drive Britain from Northern Ireland'.[94] Kinnock replied that 'anyone would think that the IRA is a liberation army. It is not. They, like the other paramilitaries, are a few hundred armed gangsters who commit political atrocities and spend the rest of their time in graft, corruption and protection rackets'.[95] At a national executive meeting a week later, Kinnock gave Livingstone a dressing-down in front of his colleagues. This failed to stop Livingstone opposing a motion on Northern Ireland which supported the Anglo-Irish Agreement, condemned the Enniskillen bombing and opposed the Sinn Fein 'bullet and ballot' strategy. In the House of Commons, Livingstone and seventeen other

[91] *News Letter*, 16 November 1987.
[92] Ibid.
[93] *Guardian*, 16 November 1987.
[94] *Times*, 16 November 1987.
[95] *Times*, 19 November 1987.

Labour MPs, including Tony Benn, tabled a motion calling on Britain to end its jurisdiction in Ulster and withdraw its troops. At the Parliamentary Labour Party meeting, Kevin McNamara said 'a rapid withdrawal of Britain from Northern Ireland would lead to a civil war and even a holocaust'.[96] Livingstone cited seven public opinion polls since 1971 that favoured withdrawal.

The IRA was under siege from Operation Mallard. Forty people were arrested in the North and two former Maze prisoners, Dermot Finnucane and Paul Brennan, were arrested in the Republic. Four large underground bunkers were discovered in Galway, Wicklow and Cork. The 55-foot bunker on a farm in Arklow was thought to be the storage place intended for the *Eksund* cargo. Martin McGuinness, vice-president of Sinn Fein, was arrested in Derry, in connection with 'a serious crime' and an active-service unit was apprehended on the Foyle bridge carrying a 40 lb home-made bomb. Paul Anthony Kane, another escaper from the Maze, was detained by the Garda in County Longford, released after forty-eight hours and then rearrested after a car chase. He was held in custody pending an application for his extradition. His arrest and detention were challenged in the Irish courts, which decided a few days before Christmas that he was lawfully held. This allowed the RUC to pursue its extradition claim, the first under the new Extradition Act.

In Belfast, riots were triggered by Kane's arrest. Twenty-five simultaneous bomb scares closed shops, theatres and the international airport. This was the first attempt by the IRA to put on a show of strength since Enniskillen. The fact that no ammunition or explosives were involved showed how effective Operation Mallard was in 'freezing' terrorist action. The Garda disclosed that 'so far this year 123 weapons, 10,000 rounds of ammunition, and 4,000 lb of explosives were seized in the South',[97] while the RUC had seized 247 weapons, 18,000 rounds of ammunition and 13,000 lb of explosives. They also warned that a further 40 tonnes of explosives, and over 2,000 weapons were still hidden somewhere on the island.

After some months of reorganization following the feud earlier in the year, the INLA struck twice before Christmas. George Seawright was the first victim; he was shot in his taxi shortly after his release from a six-month gaol sentence for disorderly behaviour during a City Hall demonstration against Tom King. Originally in the DUP, he was expelled for suggesting that Belfast City Council invest in incinerators 'to burn Roman Catholics and their priests'. He was known to have close contacts with the Ulster Volunteer Force and thought to be behind

---

[96] *Guardian*, 3 December 1987.
[97] *Guardian*, 24 November 1987.

the tit-for-tat shootings along the peace-line in Belfast. His murder was thought to be 'a reprisal for the murders of Roman Catholics in Belfast'.[98] Two days before Christmas John McMichael was killed when his ignition key triggered a bomb underneath his car. A UDA colour party fired a volley of shots over his coffin at midnight on Christmas Day and six thousand mourners attended his funeral, including the leaders of the OUP and the DUP and their deputies. The IRA justified the assassination of McMichael on the grounds that he was 'a paramilitary combatant'.[99]

The reward of £100,000 offered by the Irish authorities for the apprehension of Dessie O'Hare, the Border Fox, was not needed after all. After six weeks on the run he was wounded and captured at Urlingford, County Kilkenny, when he drove his car at a checkpoint manned by security forces. The manhunt for O'Hare exposed the weakness of the Garda. Both of his accomplices had been arrested and had then escaped. The *Economist* claimed the force was 'plagued by 3 C's – poor communication, poor command and poor control'.[100] The force was still tied closely to the Ministry of Justice. There was no independent police authority to check appointments and most of the money allocated to the Garda was spent on equipment rather than on better management. There was a change of commissioners; Wren was replaced by Doherty, and *Fortnight* magazine reported a change of attitude, 'a real feeling that the RUC and Garda are moving in on the common enemy of terrorism without the mutual suspicion which had bedevilled' relationships in the past.[101] Only a year earlier, senior members of the Garda were still praising the virtues of being a community police force. Now, with information from the *Eksund*, the experience of trailing O'Hare and the new commissioner's attitude, the Garda's 'tone and confidence has completely changed'.[102] The Extradition Act gave the relationship with the RUC a 'new backbone'. The RUC disclosed that in 1987 there had been a 50 per cent increase in deaths caused by terrorist activity. Ninety-three people died, compared with sixty-one in 1986; a quarter of them were terrorists, sixteen were members of the RUC, eight were from the UDR and three were regular soldiers. The IRA claimed responsibility for sixty deaths, the Protestant paramilitaries for a further fourteen. Reported shooting incidents numbered 600, compared with 385 in 1986; explosions went up from 173 in 1986 to 226 in 1987. The *News Letter*, in its end of the

[98] *Times*, 3 December 1987.
[99] *Times*, 24 December 1987.
[100] *Economist*, 14 November 1987.
[101] *Fortnight*, No. 258, January 1988.
[102] *Guardian*, 14 December 1987.

year review, said: 'Few people will be sorry to see an end to a year which has been marked by increased violence, bloodshed, injustice and despair in Northern Ireland.'[103]

---

[103] *News Letter*, 31 December 1987.

6

Fraud, justice and the Gibraltar shootings

Early in January 1988 *The Times*, reviewing Margaret Thatcher's eight years as prime minister, commented: 'this unbending lady has compromised often . . . on Rhodesia, on Ulster . . . what is astonishing is that she has preserved throughout the reputation for inflexibility, which she so loves.'[1] The Ulster reference was to her change of mind after the 1984 autumn summit, when she turned down the proposals of the New Ireland Forum. A year later she signed the Anglo-Irish Agreement and had steadfastly refused to concede an inch to Unionist politicians or Republican terrorists. The *News Letter* saw the prime minister in a different light: 'The Thatcher Government has endeavoured to shift the burden of grievance from one section of the Ulster community to another, and attempted to deceive both into believing that the agreement with Dublin offers tangible benefits.'[2] It was an attitude that gave rise to 'Unionist chaos and Provo discomfort'.[3] Fergus Pyle said that he had witnessed 'momentous things happening in the ramshackle edifice of Unionism',[4] while the *Irish News* reported splits in the Republican movement based 'on growing doubts about the chances of success through the armed struggle . . . the prospect of continuing war for decades to come, with no guarantee of a united Ireland at the end of it'.[5]

January 1988 also saw the return of Peter Robinson as deputy leader of the DUP. The *Irish Times* speculated that 'Molyneaux and Paisley had been forced to give in to the pressure from within their respective parties'[6] and set up a ten-man think-tank. Robinson came back into

---

[1] *Times*, 4 January 1988.
[2] *News Letter*, 4 January 1988.
[3] *Fortnight*, No. 256, November 1987.
[4] *Irish Times*, 1 January 1988.
[5] *Irish News*, 1 January 1988.
[6] *Irish Times*, 11 January 1988.

favour as a member of this group, which was to prepare a joint outline proposal for submission to the secretary of state. The talks about talks between Tom King and the two Unionist leaders were likely to be called off unless Molyneaux and Paisley 'came forward with more realistic ideas for the future government of the Province'.[7] The Unionist leaders were under sustained pressure to come up with a scheme of administrative devolution that would give the SDLP a share in local government. The Unionist Charter Group called for a commission to 'formulate a single cohesive way forward dedicated to firm commitment for a devolved government'.[8] The North Consensus Group called for 'a cross-community devolved administration with wide support and with responsibility for security'.[9] Both organizations stressed that it was important to stop feuding and identified the Unionist leaders as the main stumbling block.

A new profile of Ian Paisley by Clifford Smyth concluded that the DUP leader's political stand 'really helped to scare off Ulster's middle class Unionists ... the business and professional classes have largely opted out'.[10] Smyth then summed up the career of the voice of Protestant Ulster: 'Ian Paisley is really an articulation, a spokesman, rather than a leader ... reacting on an off the top of the head basis ... The great problem has been that the DUP has appalled opinion outside Ulster ...'[11]

Fortunately for the Unionists, the SDLP – Sinn Fein talks about talks diverted attention away from their difficulties; the *Independent* commented that the talks earned 'John Hume an alpha for political realism and Gerry Adams an alpha for cynicism'.[12] The talks were roundly condemned by *The Times*: 'they resurrect the question of what justification a democratic politician can find to sit down with a politician who is a front man for the terrorists. It is a question to which Mr Hume has found the wrong answer.'[13] The *Guardian*, on the other hand, concluded that Hume had nothing to fear but that 'Adams is in deep trouble on political and military fronts'.[14]

John Hume moved to arrange talks with Sinn Fein after Adams said in an interview in November 1987 that he now considered 'no military solution was possible in the North ... There can only be a political solution. It can be resolved with a bit of vision, a bit of courage and a

---

[7] Ibid.
[8] *News Letter*, 4 January 1988.
[9] *News Letter*, 5 January 1988.
[10] Ibid.
[11] Ibid.
[12] *Independent*, 6 January 1988.
[13] *Times*, 13 January 1988.
[14] *Guardian*, 14 January 1988.

wee bit of standing up for ourselves'.[15] The *Irish Times* supported Hume's initiative. Mary Holland revealed that Haughey knew of the SDLP–Sinn Fein meeting before it took place. There is no evidence that Tom King knew of the likelihood of Nationalist talks about talks. Hume defended the talks as a 'dialogue aimed at achieving an end to violence'.[16] Adams said, 'it was a good and proper thing that John Hume and I talked.'[17]

Unionist reaction was best summed up by Raymond Ferguson, a former OUP assemblyman for Fermanagh, when he said that 'Hume was certain to enrage the entire Unionist community ... his intervention would strengthen the resolve of the "do nothing" faction in Unionism at the very time that Unionist leaders were at long last applying themselves to putting forward alternatives to its supporters, or admitting that the Agreement was here to stay'.[18] Molyneaux called the talks 'very regrettable'.[19] Seamus Lynch of the Workers' Party said, 'It is hypocritical nonsense of Mr Hume to pass this off as part of an open-ended commitment to dialogue. He is engaged in an exercise which seems to give political credibility to the most vicious sponsors of terrorism in Northern Ireland.'[20]

Conor Cruise O'Brien spoke of the relationship between the SDLP and Sinn Fein in an address to the Friends of the Union at Westminster: 'it is not a purely adversarial one, it has many of the characteristics of a symbiosis ... Unionists generally regard the SDLP as conducting together with Sinn Fein a kind of combined anti-Unionist operation, on nice cop, tough cop lines.'[21]

The Nationalist – Republican talks started on the day that Archbishop Runcie claimed that he 'detected a new atmosphere of hope in the North',[22] following meetings with Cardinal Ó Fiaich and Archbishop Eames and the leaders of the Presbyterian and Methodist Churches in Ireland. The Hume – Adams talks effectively killed political dialogue in Northern Ireland for nine months; certainly they successfully pre-empted any Northern Ireland Office plans to conduct inter-party, cross-community talks in the province. They made talks about devolution difficult at the very time that the Unionists were finalizing their submission to Tom King. Molyneaux and Paisley presented the think-tank's devolution proposals on Tuesday 26 January 1988. They

[15] *Hot Press*, November 1987.
[16] *Fortnight*, No. 259, January 1988.
[17] Ibid.
[18] *Fortnight*, No. 259, January 1988.
[19] *News Letter*, 12 January 1988.
[20] Ibid.
[21] *Irish Times*, 8 January 1988.
[22] *Times*, 11 January 1988.

envisaged a Northern Ireland grand committee and an assembly run by executive committees, with the SDLP offered the chairmanship of such committees in proportion to the number of seats gained in the assembly. The committees would oversee all functions apart from security. The talks about talks between the secretary of state and the Unionists were now concluded.

It was the timing of the SDLP – Sinn Fein talks that aroused the most interest. Most observers concluded that there was little likelihood of Hume and Adams agreeing on a joint policy. Why therefore make them such a public issue just as the Unionists were at long last putting forward constructive proposals? The talks effectively sabotaged Tom King's devolution plans; they also gave Haughey room for manœuvre on an all-Ireland level – the 'totality of relationships within these islands'.

The taoiseach himself was under pressure to be seen to be doing something on the 'national question'. Peter Barry accused him of 'contributing to a slowing down in the pace of progress and change in Northern Ireland'.[23] Barry spoke of 1987 as 'a year of stagnation'. For Haughey it had been a bruising series of fights with the British and he suspected that the coming year was not going to be any easier. He had to find an alternative policy to the London – Dublin – Belfast triangle of discussions. He decided that the shortest route to success in 1988 lay between Dublin and Belfast. The Irish Supreme Court's ruling on the extradition of Robert Russell to the North helped the taoiseach's case. The Supreme Court decided that Russell, a member of the IRA, could not avoid extradition to Northern Ireland by pleading that his offences were politically motivated and aimed at ending British rule. The Republic was no safe haven for IRA terrorists on the run. The Unionists took note of this milestone in Irish legal history. A day later an ITN report claimed that the Provos had up to twenty surface-to-air missiles, part of a cargo ferried from Libya to Ireland before the *Eksund* voyage. The report claimed that Adrian Hopkins, the owner of the *Eksund*, made three separate trips to the Mediterranean to pick up Libyan arms. Most of the guns, ammunition and explosives were hidden in bunkers in the Irish Republic.

The secretary of state for Northern Ireland warned of a 'terror drive which is supported by Libya'[24] and his minister John Stanley met Gerry Collins in Dublin for security talks amid rumours that plans were afoot to seal the border area, to make it a war zone, and to prevent the transfer of arms across the frontier. Oliver Miles, the former ambassador to Libya, was appointed joint head of the Anglo-Irish secretariat. Security was now the priority issue for both partners in the Intergovernmental Conference.

---

[23] *Irish Times*, 8 January 1988.
[24] *News Letter*, 21 January 1988.

The chief constable of the RUC's report for 1987 recorded ninety-three deaths from terrorist activity, 'the worst loss of life in Northern Ireland since the hunger strike year of 1981. The deaths included thirty-one persons regarded by the police as known terrorists.'[25] Sixteen members of the RUC, three regular army soldiers and eight UDR members were murdered. There had been a noticeable shift in the pattern of terrorist murders during the year. Fourteen of the RUC fatalities occurred in the first six months of the year; in the second half of the year, civilians bore the brunt of the attacks. From July 1987 onwards Belfast became the centre of IRA activity; nineteen civilians were killed in the city between July and December 1987.

In his New Year message, Sir John Hermon warned that the IRA 'was poised to use surface-to-air missiles to attack helicopters and start an indiscriminate car bombing blitz . . . it will be their endeavour to . . . raise the level of violence, death and destruction'.[26] He based this prophesy of doom on intelligence reports of the interviews with the *Eksund*'s crew in France. Significantly, he added that 'the IRA are relying on diehards because they cannot trust younger men becoming involved'.[27] The botched attempts at attacking Newry and Crossmaglen at the end of 1987 supported his view that the Republican movement was short of both recruits and suitably trained operational terrorists. The chief constable's press conference was attacked by the *News Letter*, which said that 'the people of Northern Ireland do not see his role primarily as that of a weathercock predicting the most awful storms ahead . . . what they really want to know is what the security forces are going to do about it'.[28] This leader followed a claim by Paisley that the army was shortly to be given primary responsibility for security in the border areas. As usual, Paisley's contacts in the civil service were not too far off target. A border battalion was to be created from service men already in the province and based at Drummadd barracks in Armagh. It was to assume responsibility for sealing a strip of land twenty miles deep along the 280-mile border. This was a serious setback to the policy of Ulsterization, under which the RUC had supremacy over all security personnel in the province. The government decision reflected the alarm felt in security circles about the three shipments of arms from Libya to the Republic. The new battalion's job was to stop them arriving in the province. The move also represented a significant shift in policing tactics, away from fighting terrorists towards a greater emphasis on strengthening intelligence-gathering and the

---

[25] Chief Constable, RUC, *Annual Report*, 1987, 8.
[26] *News Letter*, 2 January 1988.
[27] Ibid.
[28] Ibid.

setting up of special task forces to hit the supply lines of terrorist organizations. The attack was targeted on all terrorists or paramilitary organizations. Hermon, in his New Year press conference, commented on the Ulster Defence Association as well as on the IRA; there were, he said, 'many sinister aspects to the organization . . . the outlawed Ulster Freedom Fighters [were] an integral part of the UDA'.[29] Five days later three leading UDA members, David Payne, James McCullough and Thomas Aiken, were arrested. Their cars, hired at Aldergrove airport, were found to be carrying 61 rifles, 30 automatic pistols, 11,500 rounds of ammunition and 150 anti-personnel grenades. It was subsequently confirmed that the RUC had been following this particular attempt at rearming the Loyalist paramilitaries since the bank raid in July 1987 at Portadown. The arms were purchased in the Middle East, part of a bigger delivery split between the UDA, the UVF and Ulster Resistance. Such was the mood of uncertainty and pessimism in the Loyalist paramilitaries that it was immediately assumed that either Ulster Resistance or the UVF told the police about the UDA haul. The discovery was but one example of superior counter-intelligence by the RUC.

The paramilitaries were clearly unsettled and possibly at their weakest for years. Punishment shootings give an indication of indiscipline within the organizations. A total of 124 punishment shootings were recorded in 1987, a trebling of the figure for the previous year. Obviously, all was not well with the paramilitaries, especially when the thirteen deaths in the INLA feud, the two UDA/UVF murders by their own men, and the six IRA executions from their own ranks were added to the score. Anthony McKiernan became the first IRA execution of 1988. William Kane was killed by the UVF and the IRA killed two UDA servicemen, Captain Timothy Armstrong and William Stewart. They died the week before the launch of an anti-terrorist video on local television in the province. 'You know you can stop it. Act now' was the title of the Northern Ireland Office commercial. It lasted for sixty seconds and was first played on Ulster Television on Monday 18 January 1988, in the prime-time slot during *News at Ten*. The commercial cost £170,000 to produce. It was set in a working-class area, and focused on a young man's private thoughts about the life he had led: 'All my life people have hated the police and the army. I was reared in streets filled with guns. I always looked the other way when the lads were having a go. Who cares? I thought. They left me with no job and no hope, they wrecked where I live.' The young man recalled incidents of paramilitary violence he had witnessed. He concluded the video by saying that he wanted 'the hoods off my back'.

---

[29] Ibid.

Going home, he dialled the confidential line to the police: 'I want a decent future.' While he waited for the answer, he looked across to his young wife, nursing their baby in her arms.

The BBC originally turned down the Northern Ireland Office's request to screen the commercial, on the grounds that it would have nothing to do with paid advertising. The IBA objected to the film because it 'appeared to focus on Republican terrorism alone'.[30] Ironically the filming took place in the heartland of Unionist East Belfast. A number of minor changes were made to the production, after which the IBA said that it was 'down the middle. We don't see it as biased one way or another'.[31] The BBC's local broadcasting council vetoed the transmission of the video, but a compromise agreement resulted in a fifteen-second public service announcement being transmitted three times daily on Radio Ulster and BBC Northern Ireland. Some BBC journalists 'expressed concern over the agreement . . . it represents yet another capitulation by BBC heads to pressure from Government ministers'.[32] The *News Letter* claimed it smacked of manipulation and political pressure: 'it is but a short step from giving in to official coercion, even when it is claimed to be in a good cause.'[33] The local NUJ branch said 'it would have preferred [if the BBC] had declined the government's offer. We would see it as the tip of a dangerous iceberg of government propaganda'.[34] The public service announcement was transmitted 112 times before the Board of Governors decided to bring it to an end in early March 1988. The actor who made the public service announcement and the BBC staff announcer who introduced the tape were both threatened by paramilitaries. The *Independent* claimed that the 'INLA had put both on its death list'.[35]

The television and radio advertisements were supported by a publicity campaign in the local press and on public hoardings. The number of confidential telephone lines was increased and the RUC reported a marked increase in the use of the facility. There had been a decline in the use of the confidential lines prior to the new initiative, although the RUC's overall detection rate continued to improve. It reached 43 per cent in 1987, the best since 1969. Nevertheless, all the major indices of terrorist crime increased during 1987. The chief constable declared anti-racketeering to be his priority in 1988, 'to eliminate the flow of funds to paramilitary organizations'.[36] A new task

[30] *Fortnight*, No. 260, March 1988.
[31] Ibid.
[32] *News Letter*, 25 January 1988.
[33] *News Letter*, 26 January 1988.
[34] *Fortnight*, No. 260, March 1988.
[35] *Independent*, 5 March 1988.
[36] Chief Constable, RUC, *Annual Report*, 1987, 10.

force was to be established to curb the endemic problem of gangsters running protection rackets in the province. The current RUC anti-racketeering squad was to be strengthened by a joint Inland Revenue, Customs and DHSS inquiry team; this was to be followed within a year by new legislation. The first step would be the Registration of Clubs Order, which would tighten up the granting and renewal of club licences across the province. In 1983 nearly 600 members-only clubs had been registered, with 254,270 members who bought over £27 million worth of drinks. Illegal slot machines netted £27,000 a year per machine, and pool tables contributed a share of their revenue to financing the paramilitary organizations. John Stanley said that 'we run a real danger in Northern Ireland of having a permanent Mafia situation . . . it is a multi-million pound business which is bleeding the initiative, wealth, enthusiasm and jobs of a generation'.[37] Alex Thomson claimed that 'loyalist and republican gang leaders were on first-name terms, meeting regularly in each other's territory to carve up the city, for cash'.[38] James Adams claimed that 'the Protestants have conceded expertise in building site frauds to the Catholic terrorists, the Catholics have allowed the UDA to dominate the security market'.[39]

Such a division of labour made the RUC's job virtually impossible, because their normal sources of inside information generally did not cross the religious divide. The standard rate each developer paid was £3,000 per site, with anything up to £400 per week from the builder on top of that. Thomson reckoned that 95 per cent of Belfast building sites were involved in the racket. The RUC estimated that 'construction frauds netted £40 million a year, giving an annual profit of £10 million to loyalist and republican paramilitaries'.[40]

Protection rackets and tax exemption certificates were a major source of cash. Elsewhere in the province, smuggling was the backbone of the terrorist economy. There was a profitable trade in pigs, grain, cattle and sheep across the border. At one time the Common Market paid farmers in the Republic a subsidy of £8 per animal exported to the UK, and a subsidy of £12 a ton when grain moved the other way, from the North to the South. Farmers who owned land that straddled the frontier became millionaires. The terrorist organizations cost the Dublin government alone a £100 million loss in revenue on cross-border trade. The twin tactics of the terrorists – armed might and economic sub-version – were to be tackled head on, not only by a reinforced RUC hit squad but also by a revamped Garda south of the border. A new

---

[37] *Listener*, 7 January 1988.
[38] Ibid.
[39] James Adams, *The Financing of Terror* (New English Library, 1986), 172.
[40] Ibid, 169.

Garda Advisory Group was established, made up of industrialists and other public figures, a new two-year training course was established and there was a higher educational qualification for entry into the force. There was also talk of setting up armed divisional task forces.

Co-operation between the RUC and the Garda was said to be excellent. Over the weekend of 24 January 1988 a number of British newspapers carried reports of a British intelligence briefing that claimed that a defrocked Irish Catholic priest was Gaddafi's link with the IRA. His name was Patrick Ryan. On Monday 25 January 1988 an IRA bomb killed Constable Colin James Gilmore, and Jack Kielty was murdered by two hooded terrorists. In Dunmurray a bomb caused £1 million pounds worth of damage.

In London, in the House of Commons, the attorney-general, Sir Patrick Mayhew, announced that no RUC officers would be prosecuted despite evidence that policemen had conspired to pervert the course of justice. Sir Patrick was making known the directions given by Sir Barry Shaw, the director of prosecutions for Northern Ireland, following investigations carried out by John Stalker and Colin Sampson (see above pp.77–9). His statement was to sour relations between London and Dublin and led to the opening of a new North–South relationship in Ireland. It was a major turning-point in Anglo-Irish affairs. It changed the tone and nature of the partnership launched at Hillsborough. It triggered a series of crises, each one serious in its own right, but made much worse by the changed atmosphere after Mayhew's statement. Coincidences became conspiracies.

Sir Barry Shaw instigated the court proceedings against the four policemen on the basis of information obtained during investigations into the three shooting incidents and concluded that on the evidence offered no criminal proceedings were warranted in the case of the shooting of Michael Tighe, but that the trials for the other two killings should proceed. After studying court transcripts of the evidence given under oath at the two trials, Shaw concluded that the initial CID reports on which he had based his decision to prosecute were suspect, since 'material and important facts had been omitted, and . . . matters which were untrue and misleading in material and important respects had been included'.[41]

The attorney-general announced that Sir Barry Shaw had decided after reading the Stalker–Sampson report that no further prosecutions were warranted. 'The Director has, however, concluded that there is evidence of the commission of offences of perverting or attempting or conspiring to pervert the course of justice or of obstructing a constable in the execution of his duty, and that this evidence is sufficient to require

---

[41] *Hansard*, 25 January 1988, 21.

consideration of whether prosecutions are required in the public interest'.[42] The attorney-general was consulted. Sir Patrick took into consideration 'matters concerning the public interest and, in particular, national security'.[43] He advised Sir Barry Shaw of his opinion and Shaw concluded 'that it would not be proper to institute any criminal proceedings'.[44]

Kevin McNamara, the Labour front-bench spokesman on Northern Ireland, called the decision 'incredible'.[45] Ken Maginnis welcomed the attorney-general's statement as being 'in the best interests of everyone'.[46] Seamus Mallon said it was 'a very sad day for those who believe in the process of justice in the North of Ireland'.[47] Stuart Bell asked 'why should we have cover-up rather than accountability?'[48] Ken Livingstone got himself expelled from the House for stating that 'the Attorney-General has reduced himself and the office he holds to the level of an accomplice to murder'.[49] Pressed to explain how he defined the public interest, Sir Patrick said that 'national security in Northern Ireland and elsewhere gives rise to considerations that affect the safety of people's lives. In judging the public interest, I, and any prosecuting authority, must balance one harm to the public interest against another.'[50] He confirmed that he had consulted, and that it was 'the right of those whom I consult to indicate to me matters that in their view bear upon the public interest'.[51] The attorney-general did not disclose the names of those he had consulted. He certainly had not sought the views of his Irish partners in the Hillsborough agreement. He had not even informed Dublin of the likely timing of his parliamentary statement.

The Irish government expressed 'deep dismay', adding that it was 'deeply concerned at the implications of this decision for public confidence in the administration of justice in Northern Ireland'.[52] The Fine Gael leader, Alan Dukes, described the Westminster statement as 'astounding'. Geraldine Kennedy of the Progressive Democrats called it 'unfortunate and disillusioning'. Labour's Dick Spring expressed 'serious doubts about Britain's commitment to the Anglo-Irish process and peace in Northern Ireland'.

---

[42] Ibid.
[43] Ibid., 22.
[44] Ibid.
[45] Ibid., 23.
[46] Ibid., 25.
[47] Ibid., 26.
[48] Ibid., 27.
[49] Ibid., 31.
[50] Ibid., 25.
[51] Ibid., 24.
[52] *Irish Times*, 26 January 1988.

In the province, Ian Paisley welcomed the government statement as an end 'to the political handcuffing of the security forces'. John Hume enquired 'what society can withstand the principle that national security transcends the cause of justice?' Gerry Adams claimed that 'the cover-up of murders extended from the RUC men involved to Mrs Thatcher'.

The first sign of the Dublin government's concern and anger came with an order to the Garda commissioner to cancel a meeting arranged with the RUC's chief constable. An emergency meeting of the Intergovernmental Conference was requested. The taoiseach said in the Dáil that 'it must be clear to any reasonable observer that the only persons likely to benefit from what has now happened are the paramilitaries. I would have thought that a decision to prosecute would be in the best interests of the RUC and that they would have welcomed action by the British authorities to uphold the principle that in a democracy ... the use of lethal force by the police must be the very last resort, that perjury, misleading statements to the authorities and other actions designed to pervert the course of justice should not be tolerated. Matters cannot be left as they are.'[53] Gerry Collins, the minister of justice, said that 'a very serious problem now exists in Anglo-Irish affairs ... these are damnably serious matters. They destroy the credibility of the RUC.'[54] He also added that 'anyone who believes there was a conspiracy to pervert justice but that there should be no prosecutions is not fit for public office'.[55] This led to a complaint from the British Foreign Office to the Irish ambassador in London. Irish opposition leaders alleged that Tom King had given a firm undertaking at the Intergovernmental Conference of December 1986 that prosecutions of RUC officers would follow the Stalker–Sampson report. The secretary of state denied the claim. He had, by all accounts, a serious difference of opinion with the attorney-general over the decision not to prosecute. He realized the importance the Irish partners to the agreement attached to the Stalker–Sampson inquiry. Tom King also knew that the SDLP would consider the attorney-general's statement to be a serious setback to their hopes of persuading the Nationalist community in the North to look upon the RUC as an impartial police force. The Unionists would welcome the DPP's resolution of a six-year-old problem. For the British government it was a case of fastening down the hatches and waiting for the storm, or storms, to blow over.

The Economist, under the headline 'Killings under the Carpet' said: 'Policemen have killed and lied about it. Ministers find it inexpedient to

[53] *News Letter*, 29 January 1988.
[54] *Irish Times*, 29 January 1988.
[55] *News Letter*, 29 January 1988.

prosecute them.'[56] The *New Statesman* claimed that 'the Attorney-General's statement will have done nothing to dispel the stink of corruption which hangs over the whole affair ... the fact is that the whole instinct of the British establishment is to cover up and refuse to admit to mistakes.'[57] The *Irish Times* claimed that 'the British Government has dealt with the Stalker–Sampson affair with unconscionable arrogance'.[58] Geoffrey Smith said in *The Times* that 'there is now an overriding obligation on the British Government to show that even if criminal prosecutions are not to be brought, it will not allow the security forces to take the law into their own hands ... there must be expulsions and names must be named.'[59] The *Independent* ran a series of commentaries on the crisis, concentrating on the problems of a 'liberal state menaced by an illiberal attacker ... how far should it employ illiberal methods such as imprisonment without trial, torture and murder, in its own defence? In Northern Ireland the most expedient as well as the most high-minded answer is never ... the authorities should therefore have gone to almost any lengths to show that justice has been done in the Stalker affair.'[60] The *Guardian* acknowledged that Stalker found no evidence of an overt shoot-to-kill policy but came to the conclusion that 'the cold-blooded killing of a young boy, followed by a conspiracy to conceal the truth, amounted to the action of a Central American assassination force'.[61] Conor Cruise O'Brien, in an article headed 'Casualties of the cover up', claimed: 'most people in Ireland, and I think many people in Britain as well, take Sir Patrick's statement to imply that there was indeed a shoot-to-kill policy operated by members of the security forces against IRA suspects in 1982; that senior figures in the security services approved it, covered up for it, and stifled inquiry into it and that the British Government, with the facts before it, approves and maintains the cover up.'[62] He reported that the Anglo-Irish Agreement was somewhat tarnished in the Republic, but that Haughey would 'not necessarily be inconsolable ... provided it were seen by citizens of the Republic to have broken down as a result of British treachery, and not of his own intransigence'.[63]

Four days after the Mayhew statement, Lord Lane announced that the appeal of the Birmingham Six had been rejected: 'the longer the hearing has gone on the more this court has been convinced the jury was

---

[56] *Economist*, 6 February 1988.
[57] *New Statesman*, 29 January 1988.
[58] *Irish Times*, 1 February 1988.
[59] *Times*, 4 February 1988.
[60] *Independent*, 6 February 1988.
[61] *Guardian*, 15 February 1988.
[62] *Times*, 27 January 1988.
[63] Ibid.

correct.'[64] The lord chief justice accepted that 'there was no doubt that the [Birmingham Six] had been violently assaulted in the prison'.[65] The Irish government 'learned of the decision with great regret and disappointment',[66] and Haughey added that 'the Birmingham Six judgement had fully justified his Government's decision to include special arrangements and safeguards in extradition'.[67] The *Irish Times* leader commented that 'British justice, as a concept, has not much of a record with hearts and minds here'.[68] *The Times*, on the other hand, commented that the 'ensuing row has more to do with politics than law. In Ireland the Birmingham Six Appeal is seen as a test case of the entire British legal system.'[69] Haughey was under pressure from groups such as the Irish Anti-Extradition Committee. The biggest rally since the H-block protests drew 5,000 marchers to Dublin to hear Tiernan MacBride say that it was 'impossible for any Irish person to get a fair hearing in Britain, and therefore, no Irish person should be extradited there'.[70] In London a Troops Out rally of 3,500 people heard Ken Livingstone repeat the same message. In Strasbourg the European parliament passed a motion condemning the attorney-general's decision. At Westminster 130 members of parliament put their signature to a motion calling on the home secretary to establish an independent review tribunal on the Birmingham Six appeal.

The first Intergovernmental Conference since the Mayhew statement and the Birmingham Six appeal decision met amidst a chorus of conflicting protests and advice for the participants. There were demands for a judicial review, 'John Hermon's head on a platter',[71] full publication of the Stalker–Sampson report, the release of the Birmingham Six and a United Nations investigation into security policy in Northern Ireland. The five-hour conference ended in deadlock, with Tom King admitting that there 'were very, very grave issues which do pose difficulties for us'.[72] Gerry Collins, deputizing for Lenihan, said the 'tatters of Anglo-Irish relations have been handed over to the Prime Minister to repair'.[73] The Irish delegation requested that the issues affecting confidence in the administration of justice, cross-border security co-operation and the Birmingham Six be considered by the full British cabinet.

---

[64] *Times*, 29 January 1988.
[65] *Economist*, 6 February 1988.
[66] *Times*, 29 January 1988.
[67] *Irish Times*, 4 February 1988.
[68] *Irish Times*, 29 January 1988.
[69] *Times*, 29 January 1988.
[70] *Irish Times*, 8 February 1988.
[71] *News Letter*, 5 February 1988.
[72] *News Letter*, 3 February 1988.
[73] *Irish Times*, 3 February 1988.

Meanwhile the Garda discovered two buried oil storage tanks packed with guns, ammunition and explosives, all clearly labelled with Libyan Army markings, at Malin Head, County Donegal. On the border, the RUC intercepted an ice-cream lorry carrying 2 rocket launchers, 13 warheads, 20 hand grenades, 15 rifles, 10,000 rounds of ammunition, 12 revolvers and a machine-gun. The load had been picked up in County Tipperary and shadowed all the way into the province. Despite the veto on meetings between the heads of the two police forces in Ireland, operational co-operation was obviously continuing. In North Belfast, another part of the Loyalist consignment of arms from the Middle East was uncovered. This hoard belonged to the Ulster Volunteer Force and included grenades, rocket launchers, rifles, pistols and ammunition. John Stalker, who had published a book on his experiences in Northern Ireland, stated that he had not uncovered any formal shoot-to-kill policy, but recalled that 'what I did get was a feeling that the atmosphere was raised to an extent and the adrenalin was flowing at such a level that the feeling was OK, dead or alive we'll be protected to some extent. We're soldiers really, in police uniforms, and we can probably justify deaths afterwards because we're in a war.'[74] He said he had recommended the prosecution of eleven RUC officers, naming Special Branch detective superintendents Thomas George Anderson and Samuel George Flanagan as the principal initiators in the cover-ups of the 1982 killings. Stalker also said that there was evidence of MI5 influence in the initial decision not to prosecute the RUC officers involved in the shooting of Tighe.

These revelations led to a statement from the RUC. The police spokesman said: 'Stalker has made it clear that he found no evidence of a shoot-to-kill policy. Let it therefore be stated once and for all, there was no such policy. It has been suggested that the RUC had a hand in Stalker's removal from his Northern Ireland inquiry. This is untrue. The RUC also rejects the accusation that the force obstructed his inquiry.'[75] The same day Tom King rejected a Labour Party demand for a judicial inquiry, whilst the attorney-general announced that the government did not propose to prosecute Stalker under the Official Secrets Act. In London, an informal meeting between King and Collins failed to break the impasse. The Irish partners had suggested a temporary suspension of the conference procedure, recognizing that Tom King required more time to prepare his considered response. The talks got nowhere and the Irish team of Gerry Collins and Ray Burke flew to Brussels to brief Taoiseach Haughey, who was scheduled to meet Prime Minister Thatcher at the EC summit.

---

[74] *Guardian*, 6 February 1988.
[75] *Irish Times*, 11 February 1988.

The Irish cabinet wanted the attorney-general to change his decision. The British made it clear that the attorney-general was independent of government and that there could be no government interference in legal matters. When the two leaders met in Brussels, the *Irish Times* noted that 'the only concession Thatcher made to Haughey was to go to the Taoiseach's room as opposed to summoning him to hers'.[76] Both leaders agreed that, despite the impasse over the Stalker affair, the Intergovernmental Conference should function as before on other issues. At St Anne's Cathedral in Belfast, the duke and duchess of York attended a service to dedicate a memorial window to the 252 RUC officers killed in the present troubles. They heard Archbishop Eames say: 'there is no alternative to a police force which is answerable to the community it serves and protects. There is no alternative to a police service which is seen to be fair and beyond reproach.'[77]

Earlier on that Sunday morning two speculative stories appeared in the press, both based on official briefings, one in London, the other in Dublin. Their leaking indicated the poor state of affairs between the two partners at Hillsborough. The British leak concerned a proposal to make the Prevention of Terrorism Act into permanent legislation. The Dublin story concerned the ten extradition cases held up because the British attorney-general was not complying with the new Irish extradition warrant requests. The stories broke on the eve of the next Intergovernmental Conference, arranged hastily following the meeting between Thatcher and Haughey in Brussels. Not surprisingly, King and Collins made little headway at their Stormont summit. 'London–Dublin relations were believed to be hanging by a thread last night after five hours of seemingly unproductive talks' claimed the *News Letter*.[78] At Westminster, the home secretary introduced the draft legislation for the renewal of the Prevention of Terrorism (Temporary Provisions) Act. Douglas Hurd confirmed that a new Act would be introduced in twelve months which would have no limit on its timespan, although its powers would have to be renewed annually. The exclusion orders – 111 in Britain, twenty-three in Northern Ireland – would remain in force. The Act allowed the detention of suspects for up to seven days in cases involving terrorist acts. The home secretary was aware of the Irish attitude towards the Act, which was rushed through parliament in the wake of the Birmingham pub bombings in 1974, and attempted to reassure 'the people of Northern Ireland . . . citizens of the Republic . . . and all Irish men and women living this side of the water . . . that the powers are not aimed at those innocent people, they

---

[76] *Irish Times*, 13 February 1988.
[77] *Times*, 15 February 1988.
[78] *News Letter*, 17 February 1988.

are aimed at their oppressors – the terrorists'.[79] *New Society* said that 'the cackhandedness of its timing is breathtaking'.[80] Alex Carlile MP claimed the home secretary's announcement 'has probably done more to worsen Anglo-Irish relations than any other declaration or activities of the past few weeks'.[81] The *Guardian*'s Hugo Young argued that the new Act 'corrodes our standing in the world and our entitlement to tell other countries how to behave'.[82] The Labour opposition voted against the renewal of the Act for a further twelve months.

Reaction to the Act in the Republic was hostile. Peter Barry claimed 'strong resentment among many Irish people living in Britain'.[83] The *Irish Times* leader said, 'it is difficult to avoid the conclusion that London, for whatever reason or reasons, wishes to make things as difficult as possible for [Haughey] at this time'.[84] When he opened the Dáil debate on Anglo-Irish affairs, the taoiseach said: 'With regret I have to conclude that no progress has been made on matters of grave concern to us . . . we were entitled under the letter and the spirit of the Anglo-Irish Agreement to be informed and consulted in advance of the Attorney-General's statement.'[85] With regard to Sir Patrick's refusal to co-operate with the new Extradition Act, Haughey disclosed that Mayhew had written 'that he would not provide any material relating to the evidence forming the basis for the British prosecuting authority's intention to prosecute'.[86] Of the Prevention of Terrorism Act, the taoiseach observed that 'its implementation had been discriminatory and insensitive and has caused widespread resentment among law-abiding Irish people who rightly or wrongly view it as racialist in its operation'.[87] He confirmed that the British government had indicated that there would be no changes on Mayhew's decision not to prosecute, no publication of the Stalker–Sampson report and no clemency for the Birmingham Six. Haughey finished his survey of Anglo-Irish affairs on a positive note: 'I want to emphasise . . . our determination to resolve to do everything in our power to defeat the men of violence.' He lifted the ban on direct contact between the Garda commissioner and the RUC chief constable: 'it would be immoral to end security co-operation.'[88]

Tom King knew the content and tone of the Dáil debate before he

---

[79] *Hansard*, 16 February 1988, 927.
[80] *New Society*, 19 February 1988.
[81] *Hansard*, 16 February 1988, 936.
[82] *Guardian*, 18 February 1988.
[83] *Times*, 17 February 1988.
[84] *Irish Times*, 17 February 1988.
[85] *Irish Times*, 18 February 1988.
[86] Ibid.
[87] Ibid.
[88] Ibid.

announced the disciplinary and management changes arising out of the attorney-general's decision on the Stalker–Sampson report. The secretary of state announced that Sir John Hermon had invited the chief constable of Staffordshire, Charles Kelly, 'to consider whether disciplinary charges should be brought in the case of RUC officers of chief superintendent rank and below, and if so what charges would be appropriate'.[89] The Northern Ireland Police Authority was to consider whether anyone within the top ranks of the force should face disciplinary hearings. King also announced that management reorganization had taken place in Special Branch. The *Guardian* defined King's statement as 'the closest the Government has yet come to vindicating one of the central issues of John Stalker's account of his inquiry, that normal police practices of criminal investigation were thrown to the wall because of the need to protect Special Branch informers'.[90] Kevin McNamara said the secretary of state's statement was 'a most amazing rehabilitation of John Stalker'.[91]

The taoiseach's view of the secretary of state's statement was that it was 'insufficient to meet the Government's demands'.[92] He lamented 'the historic inability in Britain to comprehend Irish feelings and sensitivities'.[93] The *Economist* supported him: 'taking the Irish seriously is something British Governments are not good at.'[94] *The Times* was critical of the British position: 'it appeared reactive, ill-prepared and ill-coordinated ... it appears to be time for the Prime Minister to take proper charge of government policy ... and show that British statesmanship can be organized and presented with the same grasp of essentials which Mr Haughey displayed.'[95] The *Irish Times* commented that the agreement 'never signalled a fusion of Irish and British attitudes towards the centuries-old problems that have embittered relations between the two countries'.[96]

Haughey was credited with having handled the difficulties of the past two weeks with style and effectiveness. The taoiseach prepared for his party's *ard fheis* in a confident mood. His keynote speech was a development of his address at Bodenstown the previous autumn, when he had raised the possibility of direct North–South talks. The obvious problems on the Dublin–London axis gave added impetus to a stronger Dublin–Belfast channel of communication. Haughey appealed directly

[89] *Hansard*, 17 February 1988, 977.
[90] *Guardian*, 18 February 1988.
[91] *Hansard*, 17 February 1988, 980.
[92] *Irish Times*, 18 February 1988.
[93] *Times*, 18 February 1988.
[94] *Economist*, 20 February 1988.
[95] *Times*, 18 February 1988.
[96] *Irish Times*, 20 February 1988.

to the Unionists: 'I would greatly wish to have an opportunity to hear at first hand from the representatives of the Unionist tradition.'[97] A fortnight earlier, Molyneaux had hinted at Unionist willingness to explore further the usefulness of North–South discussions when he claimed that '90 per cent of people in the North would be prepared to play their part in helping the Irish and the British to design a new agreement which could lay the foundations for a lasting understanding within the totality of relationships'.[98] Molyneaux used one of the taoiseach's favourite phrases when he spoke of the 'unique relationship' between the two countries, which 'could give rise to an agreement that covered differing social and moral attitudes, leading to less cause for friction between the supporters of each country in the North'.[99] Mary Holland interpreted this speech to mean that the Unionists 'accepted that Dublin does have a role in the future shaping of the North'.[100] Holland recalled a similar approach to FitzGerald in the early days of the Anglo-Irish Agreement, when Molyneaux had suggested that the taoiseach had a far better understanding than had Thatcher of the depth of emotion in the North. This line of approach was repeated, virtually word for word, by John Taylor, one of Molyneaux's parliamentary group. The *Guardian* attributed this North–South flirtation to 'the fear that Thatcher may just be about to do a U-turn, abandon Hillsborough and go for devolution with the Unionists'.[101]

The 1988 *ard fheis* was probably Haughey's first public expression of a new attitude on Northern Ireland, based on the premise that the Anglo-Irish Agreement required drastic changes if it were to survive the first three-year review. The current agreement brought with it too many problems, and his mind was turning towards a new alternative agreement, possibly confined to Dublin and Belfast. A joint Unionist statement confirmed the continued wish of Molyneaux and Paisley to keep the channels open between themselves and Haughey: 'it should be possible to study alternative proposals in the Intergovernmental Council.'[102] (The Council had been set up by Haughey and Thatcher after the Dublin summit in 1981.) There was even talk that the Unionists would support an Irish government office or consulate in the North in return for the 'gun of the Anglo-Irish Agreement [being] removed from our heads'.[103]

Discussion of these possibilities was disrupted by the shooting of

---

[97] *Irish Times*, 22 February 1988.
[98] *Irish Times*, 8 February 1988.
[99] Ibid.
[100] *Irish Times*, 10 February 1988.
[101] *Guardian*, 19 February 1988.
[102] *Irish Times*, 23 February 1988.
[103] Ibid.

Aidan McAnespie as he crossed the border on his way into the Republic. David Jonathan Holden, an eighteen-year-old Grenadier Guard, was charged with unlawful killing. The incident happened during the routine handover of weapons as servicemen changed shift. The British statement referred to the accidental discharge of a weapon and the ricocheting of the bullets off the roadway. Cardinal Ó Fiaich called the shooting 'murder'. Dublin launched its own inquiry and McAnespie's body was exhumed for a second post-mortem, authorized by a local coroner in Monaghan. In the House of Commons, the prime minister said that 'the Anglo-Irish Agreement does not allow any Southern Irish inquiry into events that occurred north of the border'.[104] The *Irish Times* advised the Dublin government to be cautious. Cabinet minister Ray Burke sought to reassure people in Northern Ireland that the inquiry 'was not a vote of no confidence in the RUC',[105] or a sidestepping of the Intergovernmental Secretariat.

The situation was exacerbated by a Ministry of Defence announce-ment, on the day of McAnespie's death, that the only British soldier convicted of murder in Northern Ireland since the start of the Troubles was now back with his regiment, having served only two years and two months of a life sentence. Ian Richard Thain had shot a roadie with the Bananarama pop group in August 1983. The Ministry of Defence said that Thain's actions had 'been a tragic error by a very young man, who had been allowed to rejoin his regiment to rebuild his life'.[106] The *Daily Telegraph* commented: 'what is incomprehensible is the man's recall to his unit, an act of ... stunning insensitivity ... it can only inflict further damage upon Anglo-Irish relations.'[107] The MOD minister who had authorized Thain's release on parole a year earlier was John Stanley, now Tom King's deputy at Stormont.

Four Unionist members of parliament were gaoled for refusing to pay fines for taking part in an illegal procession. Martin Smyth, Harold McCusker, William Ross and Clifford Forsythe went to the Crumlin road prison for four days. A substantial hoard of arms was discovered at the Portmarnock harness-racing track, to be followed by an equally significant find in County Meath a few days later. In the Castle Court development in central Belfast, two UDR soldiers were killed and three others injured when a bomb exploded under a hoarding fronting the new multi-million-pound shopping and recreation centre. In Dublin the Intergovernmental Conference met again on Wednesday 24 February. The *News Letter* claimed it was 'the most difficult of all

---

[104] *Economist*, 27 February 1988.
[105] *Irish Times*, 24 February 1988.
[106] *Economist*, 27 February 1988.
[107] *Daily Telegraph*, 24 February 1988.

Intergovernmental Conferences'.[108] The communiqué referred to a discussion on the new Northern Ireland Office proposals on equal employment opportunities. The meeting degenerated into a muddle when Lenihan denied a claim by King that the heads of the respective police forces would attend the next Intergovernmental Conference. 'Dublin calls King a liar,' commented the *News Letter*.[109] The fact that the Irish foreign minister publicly disputed the secretary of state's version of the discussions on this most sensitive of issues clearly indicated how raw were the nerves and how lacking the trust and goodwill of earlier months. Hermon was still *persona non grata* in Dublin.

The secretary of state made a point of seeking cross-party support for the RUC during his opening speech on the Northern Ireland (Emergency Provisions) Act: 'a great debt is owed to the RUC ... I hope that people throughout Northern Ireland will recognize the RUC as it is today and not dwell on the problems with which it has been faced in the past.'[110] The opposition voted against the renewal of emergency powers and called for a judicial inquiry into the Stalker–Sampson report. A few days later the Independent Commission for Police Complaints replaced the Police Complaints Board in Northern Ireland. The new commission would supervise cases involving death and serious injury and also any other complaint against the RUC that it chose to oversee.

At Crossmaglen, Brendan Burns and Brendan Morley blew themselves up when a bomb they were priming exploded. Burns was wanted by the RUC for at least twenty-five killings, which included those of Lord Justice Gibson and the sixteen soldiers at Warrenpoint.

In the Dáil, the taoiseach defended his commissioning of an investigation of the shooting of McAnespie: 'It must be clear to everybody that the shooting dead of an unarmed civilian going about his normal and legitimate activity in broad daylight, by a British soldier from an observation post along the border is a matter of utmost gravity.'[111] The opposition parties in the Dáil were of the opinion that the taoiseach had reacted too hastily and suggested that the report should be sent to the RUC. Fine Gael and the Progressive Democrats were more interested in pressing the taoiseach on his policies with regard to the Anglo-Irish Agreement, and in particular his views on devolution for the province. Haughey initially responded by saying that 'the Agreement was not written on tablets of stone. It was not immutable.'[112] He then added

---

[108] *News Letter*, 25 February 1988.
[109] Ibid.
[110] *Hansard*, 25 February 1988, 480.
[111] *Times*, 2 March 1988.
[112] *Irish Times*, 3 March 1988.

that 'no one can argue that there is anything in the Anglo-Irish Agreement which makes devolution a mandatory solution'.[113] In reply to a question from FitzGerald, the taoiseach said that he 'did not accept any solution, brought forward within the confines of the existing structures in Northern Ireland, would provide a lasting solution to the problem'.[114] He suggested the 'establishment of new, all-embracing political structures for the whole of Ireland'.[115] The taoiseach was accused by opposition TDs of not exploiting the opportunities available through the Anglo-Irish Conference and warned that the Dáil consensus on Northern Ireland might disappear. Haughey was creating for himself as much room for manœuvre as the situation allowed. He was in a powerful position on the domestic scene, felt he was in an advantageous position with regard to his British partners and was receiving favourable responses from the North and generous sympathy and support from abroad, particularly from the Irish-American lobby in the United States.

Tom King was caught between an intransigent British cabinet, an enraged Irish administration and a fiercely independent law officer. His talks about talks with the Unionists were over for the time being, but there was a realization in the Unionist camp that their role in Northern Ireland politics had changed. The secretary of state talked to the SDLP despite John Hume's parallel discussions with Sinn Fein. The Nationalist–Republican talks about talks were another example of how the Anglo-Irish Agreement had changed the face of politics in the province. A new Police Complaints Commission was in place and the changes in the Fair Employment (NI) Act 1976 would, King hoped, 'be the biggest social advance for the Nationalist community since the signing of the Anglo-Irish Agreement'.[116]

On the afternoon of Sunday 6 March 1988, two men and a woman were shot dead by British security services in the streets of Gibraltar. The IRA claimed all three as members of an active-service unit; they were all from Belfast. News reports from Gibraltar referred to 'a police operation to prevent a car bomb attack near the Governor's official residence'.[117] The *Independent* claimed that 'bomb disposal experts defused 440 lb of explosives in a Spanish-registered car'.[118] The *Guardian* and the *Daily Telegraph* referred to the defusing of a '500 lb bomb in a car'. The *News Letter* added the information that the bomb

[113] *News Letter*, 7 March 1988.
[114] *News Letter*, 3 March 1988.
[115] *News Letter*, 7 March 1988.
[116] *Times*, 3 March 1988.
[117] *Times*, 7 March 1988.
[118] *Independent*, 7 March 1988.

'was timed to explode tomorrow'[119] and the *Independent* said that 'the three suspects had reportedly intended to detonate the car by remote control'.[120] *The Times* claimed that 'British Special Branch officers had been in Gibraltar for over a week'.[121] The *News Letter* quoted an eyewitness to the shooting who claimed that 'policemen jumped out of a car and shot to kill without warning'.[122] The *Irish Times* carried an IRA claim that the three dead terrorists 'were unarmed'.[123] Ian Stewart, the armed forces minister, said, 'there was a car bomb found which has been defused ... the bomb was timed to go off during the parade'.[124]

In the confused circumstances following the shootings, British newspapers had to rely mostly on official briefings. The British security services knew of the IRA plot; it involved a car bomb, which was to be detonated by remote control on Tuesday 9 March 1988 at 11 a.m., as the Royal Anglian Regiment paraded in front of the governor's residence. The suggestion that the terrorists had been shot without first being challenged and that they might have been unarmed came from the two Irish papers.

There were riots in West Belfast that Sunday evening. The leader of the dead IRA unit was Daniel McCann, a butcher from the Birchmount area of the Lower Falls. His companions were Mairead Farrell, a student of politics at Queen's University, Belfast, and Sean Savage, also from the Republican ghetto of West Belfast.

The following day the foreign secretary, Sir Geoffrey Howe, informed the House of Commons of the terrorist plot to explode a car bomb at the weekly guard-mounting ceremony in Ince's Yard, an enclosed area where fifty soldiers and a large number of civilians normally assembled. Savage drove a white Renault 5 car across the border from Spain. McCann and Farrell entered Gibraltar on foot, rendezvousing with Savage at the parked Renault. Sir Geoffrey added:

> their presence and actions near the parked Renault car gave rise to strong suspicion that it contained a bomb, which appeared to be corroborated by a rapid technical examination of the car. About 3.30 p.m. all three left the scene and started to walk back towards the border. On their way towards the border, they were challenged by the security forces. When challenged, they made movements which led the military personnel operating in support of the Gibraltar police to conclude that their own lives and the lives of others were under threat. In the light of this

---

[119] *News Letter*, 7 March 1988.
[120] *Independent*, 7 March 1988.
[121] *Times*, 7 March 1988.
[122] *News Letter*, 7 March 1988.
[123] *Irish Times*, 7 March 1988.
[124] *Guardian*, 5 December 1988.

response, they were shot. Those killed were subsequently found not to have been carrying arms. The parked Renault car was subsequently dealt with by a military bomb disposal team. It has now been established that it did not contain an explosive device. Inquiries carried out by the Spanish authorities have matched keys found on one of the bodies with a Ford Fiesta car, subsequently found on the Spanish side of the border, which contained three false passports and items of equipment, including insulation tape, electrical screwdrivers, a number of pairs of gloves, wire and an alarm clock. A key was also found for a third car. The search is continuing for this car and for explosives. An inquest will be held in Gibraltar.'[125]

George Robertson congratulated 'those responsible on what appears to have been a well-planned operation'.[126] It took Harold McCusker to introduce the words 'shoot to kill',[127] and Eric Heffer to ask 'why those three people, who although accepted as members of an active-service unit of the IRA, were shot and killed when it was admitted that they were not carrying guns and had not planted any bombs in Gibraltar?'[128]

Reaction in Dublin to the foreign secretary's statement was immediate and uncompromising. Peter Barry declared that 'the rule of law cannot be flouted by those paid to uphold it'.[129] A day later the taoiseach added that 'we are gravely perturbed at the shooting dead of three unarmed Irish people in circumstances where it appears from reports that they could have been arrested'.[130] This view was also being voiced elsewhere. A *Daily Telegraph* editorial said that the government should explain 'why it was necessary to shoot dead all three terrorists on the street'.[131] *The Times* welcomed the intention to hold an inquest into the shootings, adding, 'on present evidence, however, there is no justification for special inquiries which might evoke parallels with the Stalker–Sampson inquiries'.[132]

In Gibraltar Peti Celicia, who lived in a second-floor flat opposite the Shell petrol station on Winston Churchill Avenue where McCann and Farrell were shot, was contradicting the foreign secretary's version of the events. She claimed that there was no challenge from the security personnel prior to the shootings. The Spanish police found approximately 64 kg of Semtex explosives, detonating equipment and 2 kg of

---

[125] *Hansard*, 7 March 1988, 21.
[126] Ibid., 22.
[127] Ibid., 24.
[128] Ibid., 25.
[129] *Irish Times*, 8 March 1988.
[130] *Irish Times*, 9 March 1988.
[131] *Daily Telegraph*, 8 March 1988.
[132] *Times*, 8 March 1988.

ammunition in the boot of a white Ford Fiesta hired on the day of the shooting by Farrell, and left in a car park.

In the House of Commons, Dr David Owen urged the prime minister to hold an inquiry into the shooting. Sixty Labour MPs signed a motion which said that 'the recent shootings in Gibraltar are tantamount to capital punishment without trial'.[133] Robert Kilroy Silk wrote that 'we are in danger, not only of being perceived to have double standards, but also of having a flexible attitude to the rule of law'.[134] The *Independent* said, 'it is regrettable that it was not possible to arrest the three IRA members.'[135] The *Daily Telegraph* claimed that 'the MOD were still insisting at 9.00 a.m. on Monday (the day following the shootings) that a suspected bomb had been dealt with. Was it human error, or someone's attempts to dress later truths in instant clothing?[136] The *Sunday Times* claimed to possess evidence that 'categorically denied the terrorists were shot without mercy'.[137] The terrorists had been killed 'because their response to the challenges from the SAS were considered aggressive'.[138] The paper cast doubts on Peti Celicia's assertions: 'It is unlikely that she would have been in a position to have heard the challenges.'[139]

More information regarding the terrorists and their movements was divulged. McCann was first picked up on 5 November 1987 when he arrived in Málaga, travelling on an Irish passport in the name of Reilly. On 15 November Savage and McCann and a woman companion, travelling under the name of Mary Parkin, flew from Málaga to Madrid and then back to Dublin. By mid February 1988 Parkin was back in Spain, crossing the border into Gibraltar on two successive Tuesdays, 23 February and 2 March, to observe the military parade.

On Wednesday 2 March 1988 Savage, the bomb-maker, slipped out of Belfast to Dublin to catch a plane to Brussels and then on to Barcelona. He travelled on a passport in the name of Brendan Coyne. He arrived in Málaga on Thursday 3 March 1988 and booked into a hotel in Torremolinos. That afternoon McCann was stopped and questioned by British soldiers as he crossed the border between Northern Ireland and the Republic. The following day he checked into the same hotel as Savage in Torremolinos. Savage drove a thousand miles to fetch the explosives from another part of Spain. Security officers claimed that he met Patrick Ryan on Friday 4 March 1988.

---

[133] *Times*, 11 March 1988.
[134] Ibid.
[135] *Independent*, 8 March 1988.
[136] *Daily Telegraph*, 8 March 1988.
[137] *Sunday Times*, 13 March 1988.
[138] Ibid.
[139] Ibid.

Farrell's arrival in Spain went unnoticed until she met McCann and Savage at Marbella on the morning of Sunday 6 March 1988. Spain's élite anti-terrorist squad tailed Farrell's red Ford Fiesta and Savage's white Renault 5 to the border with Gibraltar. Farrell and McCann sat in the parked Ford car on the Spanish side of the border, while Savage drove the Renault into Gibraltar. His two companions waited an hour and a half and walked across the frontier to join Savage. All three were shot on their return journey, Farrell and McCann outside the Shell station on Winston Churchill Avenue, Savage under an old ilex tree in Landport Ditch.

In Ireland, Republican leaflets invited supporters to honour the dead by turning out to witness the arrival of the three coffins at Dublin airport. Gerry Adams and two former IRA chiefs of staff, Seán MacStiofáin and Seamus Turomey, headed the cortège as it left the airport for Northern Ireland. A further five thousand watched in silence as the convoy of cars passed through Dundalk at 9 p.m. on Monday 14 March 1988. The funerals were arranged for St Patrick's Day. Local papers in the province carried full-page advertisements from the RUC explaining its funerals policy. The statement was directed at the families of the three dead terrorists: 'we wish you to bury your dead in peace. We ask you to state publicly and without qualification that the funerals will take place within the law and give the RUC a public assurance that this will be adhered to. If you do so, the RUC will respond accordingly. If, however, there is no such unqualified response, or if it becomes evident that the Provisional IRA is determined to take over these funerals and to defy the law, then the RUC will have no choice but to do its duty, distasteful as it is in such circumstances.'[140]

At the border, during a symbolic handing over of the coffins to Northern Ireland, Jenny McGeever, a contract RTÉ broadcaster, recorded the Sinn Fein leader, Martin McGuiness, remonstrating with the RUC over their insistence that the Irish flags that draped the coffins be removed on entry into the province. The recording was transmitted on RTÉ and McGeever was sacked for contravening the ban on broadcasting Sinn Fein interviews.

In the North, the media recorded masked IRA men firing a volley of shots over a makeshift shrine in memory of the three terrorists. The army shot dead Kevin McCracken, an IRA sniper. Andy Tyrie, the head of the Loyalist UDA, resigned after losing a vote of confidence. He had earlier been warned to get out in seven days. Before the week was out, he discovered a bomb attached to the chassis of his car. His time was up after fifteen years at the helm. The following day Charlie McGrillen was shot dead by the UFF; the Loyalist paramilitary group

---

[140] *News Letter*, 15 March 1988.

warned that it intended to 'step up retaliatory and pre-emptive strikes against those it believed to be republican paramilitaries'.[141]

At the requiem mass for Farrell, Revd Raymond Murray alleged that 'she was barbarously assassinated by a gunman'[142] and Father Tom Toner said at the mass for Savage and McCann that 'people in high places are gloating over these murders'.[143] Ten thousand mourners followed the coffins to Milltown Cemetery. The RUC, following approaches from the Roman Catholic bishops, Sinn Fein and the SDLP, decided to adopt a low profile at the funerals. Intelligence reports indicated a serious danger of revenge attacks on the police following ten days of riots and unrest in West Belfast. The danger was readily acknowledged by the Catholic hierarchy in the area and the RUC agreed to accept their assurances that the emotionally charged occasion was best handled by the community itself, 'in the hope that this whole distasteful problem of paramilitary funerals would be resolved now and for the future'.[144]

The burial at the Republican plot was held up when it was discovered that the graves had not been dug deep enough. It was as the last coffin was being lowered that the shooting started. David Sapsted, a *Times* correspondent, described the scene:

> A shot rang out, sounding more like a child's cap pistol than a real gun. Inevitably those of us crowding round the rear of the Republican burial plot assumed the IRA was, despite earlier assurances, staging a final paramilitary salute to its Gibraltar dead. Another shot was quickly followed by two blasts fifty yards away which sent puffs of black smoke and earth into the air and which shook an estimated 10,000 people to their souls ... More shots followed and a middle-aged man some twelve feet from me fell to the ground, a widening crimson patch appearing on his trouser leg. 'Get down. For God's sake get down,' yelled a Republican steward near by. Women screamed and men shouted in a cacophony of panic. I crouched and numbly asked a colleague what was happening. 'Mortars,' he said. 'You'll hear them coming over.' They were not mortars. They were grenades. Four blasts shook the air, before an even more frightening sound rolled over the cemetery, a primordial chorus of hundreds of youths racing past me in pursuit of the attacker. It was a human foxhunt and the hounds were not to be thwarted.[145]

Michael Anthony Stone, a Loyalist paramilitary reject, killed three mourners, critically wounded a further four and left fifty others injured before he was rescued from the 'human foxhunt' by the RUC. Gerry

---

[141] *Guardian*, 15 March 1988.
[142] *News Letter*, 16 March 1988.
[143] *Guardian*, 26 March 1988.
[144] *Times*, 17 March 1988.
[145] Ibid.

Adams alleged RUC collusion with Stone; the RUC denied the charge. The chief constable explained that the occupants of a white police van seen on the motorway near the cemetery 'fled in fear of their lives as they observed a large crowd moving rapidly towards them'.[146] In the House of Commons, Tom King appealed for an end 'to this mad and awful cycle'.[147] Peter Robinson blamed the media for heightening the tension, 'treating the three Gibraltar terrorists as if some altruistic head of state had died'.[148] King agreed that 'television has a great responsibility in deciding what to show'.[149]

Serious rioting occurred in Belfast, as well as in the Creggan and Bogside areas of Derry. At Westminster Seamus Mallon called for the proscription of the UDA. Father Des Wilson said, 'For the rest of my life, in my own way, I will work for the removal of the British Government from this country ... West Belfast has been under the most ferocious attack ... we have had enough ... we have borne insult, derision, force ... and it must stop.'[150]

On Thursday of the same week, Kevin McCracken was buried at Milltown cemetery. Sinn Fein stewards used walkie-talkies and searched the bags of the mourners as they entered the Republican plot. Sir Eldon Griffiths said ordinary people would be horrified at any thought of no-go areas for the police force in the province.

On the following day, the funerals took place of Charles McCrillen, a Roman Catholic shot dead by the UFF, and Thomas McErlean, one of the three killed at Milltown Cemetery. That evening bride-to-be Gillian Johnston was killed by the IRA West Fermanagh brigade. The IRA admitted a blunder, saying that the attack was aimed at her brother. Ken Maginnis, the local MP, said she was 'shot because she was a Protestant, and for no other reason'.[151]

On Saturday 19 March 1988 the funerals of the other two mourners killed at Milltown Cemetery, John Murray and Kevin Brady, took place. The secretary of state gave an account of what happened in the House of Commons:

> Just after midday on Saturday, following the funeral service ... the cortège moved off along Andersonstown Road towards the Milltown Cemetery. At that point, a civilian car attempted to reverse away from the cortège ... its way was blocked, both backwards and forward, by taxis accompanying the funeral ... A number of those in the funeral cortège immediately set upon the car with the obvious intention of pulling

---

[146] *News Letter*, 19 March 1988.
[147] *Irish Times*, 18 March 1988.
[148] *News Letter*, 17 March 1988.
[149] *Times*, 18 March 1988.
[150] *News Letter*, 18 March 1988.
[151] *News Letter*, 21 March 1988.

out the two occupants. Photographs indicate that at this point the driver of the car leaned out of his window and fired one shot in the air – the only shot which both occupants fired in the course of the attack upon them. After only a moment's pause the crowd resumed the onslaught on the car, some of them smashing at it with iron bars, and eventually succeeded in hauling out both occupants.[152]

A witness at the scene described what happened next: 'I heard the man whimper like a lame dog as he lay on the ground being kicked, punched, battered and jumped on. Blood spurted from deep wounds, flesh hanging loosely from within the gashes. The crowds were shouting, "kill him, kill him now".'[153] Mary Holland, an *Irish Times* correspondent, was also present as the other occupant of the car 'passed within a few feet of myself and dozens of other journalists. He didn't cry out, just looked at us with terrified eyes as though we were all enemies in a foreign country who wouldn't have understood what language he was speaking if he called out for help.'[154] The two men were dragged into Casement Park. A taxi took them to a nearby piece of wasteland where, an eyewitness said, 'across the street I heard an execution squad finish their work. Eight shots rang out and then another two or three.'[155] Father Alex Reid was first on the scene and tried to give the kiss of life to one of the men. He then administered the last rites. Mary Holland called an ambulance and recalls one of the female bystanders saying, 'He was somebody's son. God have mercy upon him.'[156]

The two victims were corporals in the Royal Corps of Signals, Derek Woods and David Howes. The secretary of state was at a loss to know why they were in Andersonstown. The initial attacks on the car were recorded by television crews working for the BBC, ITV, RTÉ and the French television service. The pictures showed Republican stewards marshalling the cortège and then the reaction of the accompanying mourners when the soldiers' car tried to escape from the funeral procession. The pictures were transmitted within an hour of the attack. The *Sunday Times* commented: 'it was the television coverage of the attack that fuelled much of the outrage at the killings. Its immediacy meant that by the time the IRA realised how damaging the broadcasting of the violent scenes would be, dispatch riders were already tearing down the Falls Road ... the IRA's attempts at censoring had failed.'[157] The *Sunday Times* 'Insight' team put together a montage of pictures from the scene and claimed to be able to identify the IRA men

---

[152] *Hansard*, 21 March 1988.
[153] *News Letter*, 21 March 1988.
[154] *Irish Times*, 23 March 1988.
[155] Ibid.
[156] *Times*, 21 March 1988.
[157] *Sunday Times*, 20 March 1988.

who led the attack as Clecky Clarke and John McAvoy.[158] *The Times* said, 'the daylight nightmare of the lynch mob set new levels even for two decades of criminal violence and terrorism in Northern Ireland.'[159] The *Sun* carried the headline 'Scum of the Earth'. The *Mirror* called for a troops-out policy; the *Economist* simply said 'God Save Ireland'. Dr Cahal Daly appealed to Roman Catholics to leave the IRA: 'For God's sake, for Ireland's sake, let them leave the organizations now before still more grievous harm is done.'[160] He added,

> the evil of the IRA is often disguised with a mask of romantic rhetoric and militaristic mock ritual. For a ghastly half-hour on Saturday the mask slipped. The real face of IRA violence was shown and it was horrible to see ... there was certainly an element of fear of another Loyalist attack like that at Milltown Cemetery a few days earlier. Then the maniac face of the elemental lust to kill took over ... people would not have taken iron bars in their hands to batter soldiers ... if they had not first taken hatred into their hearts ... condemnation of the IRA is not a political matter ... it is a spiritual one ... the activities of the IRA are killing the souls of those involved in it or actively supporting it.[161]

Cardinal Ó Fiaich, Archbishop Eames, Dr William Fleming of the Presbyterian Church and Revd William Hamilton of the Methodist Church went to Stormont Castle to meet the secretary of state and called on 'all sections of our community to turn to God as the author of our faith. We call for repentance and forgiveness'.[162]

For the second time in five days Tom King went to Westminster to deliver a statement on shootings in Northern Ireland. The central issue was one of policing paramilitary funerals. Government and opposition parties at Westminster had been consulted before the arrival of the Gibraltar coffins in the province, and had agreed to the new policing tactic of allowing the mourners to organize their own funeral arrangements. Following the Andersonstown killings, Tom King announced that the chief constable of the RUC was conducting an urgent review of his paramilitary funeral policy. King rejected the accusation that the RUC had abandoned the policing of West Belfast to the IRA and Sinn Fein: 'there is no question of tolerating any suggestion that the IRA, Sinn Fein or anybody else will set up some alternative police force.'[163] John

---

[158] *Sunday Times*, 27 March 1988.
[159] *Times*, 22 March 1988.
[160] *Times*, 23 March 1988.
[161] *Sunday Times*, 27 March 1988.
[162] *Irish Times*, 22 March 1988.
[163] *Hansard*, 21 March 1988, 29.

Cole commented that the 'television pictures of IRA stewards equipped with walkie-talkie radio would have aroused envy in the CIA'.[164]

The television pictures of the attack were now central to the whole debate. The transmitted footage was already in the public domain, but the broadcasting authorities refused initially to hand over the untransmitted footage when approached by the RUC. The security services had at their disposal films transmitted on the networks and local television, as well as an independent feed from a security helicopter hovering overhead, but they also sought access to the pictures not shown on television, footage rejected mostly because it was out of focus, or repetitive. The BBC had forty-nine seconds of unused footage.

The initial approach from the RUC was in the nature of an enquiry as to what footage was left untransmitted. There was no request for it to be surrendered. The BBC does not automatically

> allow access to untransmitted film, when to do so would damage BBC editorial policy or endanger people who work for the BBC. If the camera crews are seen as gatherers of evidence for the security services their days are numbered. It is to protect against that threat, that all broadcasting organizations insist that interested parties . . . seek a court order first to view the material, and secondly to ensure its surrender to court officials . . . No public service broadcaster can be on the side of terrorism – but he has the right to deploy every last breath of the legal process to protect his sources, his colleagues' safety and his editorial independence.[165]

In the House of Commons, the prime minister said that 'everyone, the media included, has a bounden duty to do everything that he can to see that those who perpetrated the terrible crimes that we saw on television and that disgusted the whole world are brought to justice. Either one is on the side of justice in these matters, or one is on the side of terrorism.'[166] *The Times* supported the prime minister's stance against the BBC's policy of withholding the untransmitted film: 'the policy bears the marks of a sound principle applied too rigidly . . . television news executives, reporters and camera crews are citizens first and news people second . . . that independent news organizations can somehow exist independent of the rule of law and those who enforce it, is an absurdity.'[167] The *Independent* agreed with the Corporation: 'the BBC is right to pause . . . the Prime Minister was being misguidedly simplistic . . . journalistic 'no go' areas would be created.'[168] The

---

[164] *Listener*, 31 March 1988.

[165] Arwel Ellis Owen, 'The Anglo-Irish Agreement, a broadcaster's experience' (First Guardian Lecture, Nuffield College, Oxford, 1989), 21.

[166] *Hansard*, 22 March 1988, 194.

[167] *Times*, 23 March 1988.

[168] *Independent*, 23 March 1988.

paper suggested that a judicial authority should be responsible for deciding if the material should be released. John Gorst, MP for Hendon North, said the release of footage was 'a matter which Parliament should decide ... if an issue affecting public order and therefore the public interest arises, any material which is taken by the media must by law be made available to the police'.[169] Patrick Cormack, MP for Staffordshire South, explored the possibility of a Select Committee using its powers to obtain the film. William Ross, MP for Londonderry East, tried unsuccessfully to obtain an emergency debate on the BBC's refusal to hand over to the RUC 'the record of the vile and ugly murders that we saw in full on television'.[170]

The following day, the BBC handed over to the RUC the forty-nine seconds of untransmitted film, having been served notice that failure to comply would have meant the arrest of John Conway, BBC Northern Ireland's news and current affairs editor, under Section 11 of the Prevention of Terrorism Act and Section 13 of the Northern Ireland Emergency Provisions Act. The Corporation's director-general, Michael Checkland, said: 'the BBC has never set itself above the law. In dealing with this matter we have been concerned with the difficult and dangerous position of our crews in Northern Ireland.'[171] In Lisburn, a BBC news crew withdrew from a memorial service to the two dead soldiers, having been threatened by Loyalist paramilitaries and advised by the police that their safety could not be guaranteed.

The RUC could have used powers under the Prevention of Terrorism Act to acquire the untransmitted film on the afternoon of the shootings. The *News Letter* suggested that the whole controversy was a device of the 'faceless NIO media manipulators'[172] to deflect attention from the issue of policing funerals. Molyneaux hinted at a similar conspiracy. Others suggested that the Northern Ireland Office was 'out to get' the BBC because of its refusal to transmit the anti-terrorist video advertisement. What the government did was to short-circuit a well-established legal process. Their reaction seemed to confirm the view that the government saw no role for the media 'unless it was as an accessory to the armour of the state'.[173]

The prime minister met the coffins of Corporals Woods and Howes at RAF Northolt, where they were handed over to the custody of their families. At the Cenotaph in Belfast, 5,000 people attended a service to honour the two dead soldiers, and to hear the Lord Mayor ask the world not to 'judge Ulster's decent people by the scum of humanity who

---

[169] *Times*, 23 March 1988.
[170] *Hansard*, 22 March 1988, 197.
[171] *Times*, 24 March 1988.
[172] *News Letter*, 25 March 1988.
[173] Owen, op. cit., 21.

carried out this barbarous act of butchery'.[174] The RUC issued a statement abandoning its low-profile policy on paramilitary funerals. The chief constable was in County Londonderry, attending the funeral of Constable Clive Graham, killed by the IRA two days after the Andersonstown massacre. In Belfast, John Hume and Gerry Adams met and working documents were exchanged.

In London, Tom King and Brian Lenihan met at an emergency Inter-governmental Conference. The previous meeting had been the most difficult since Hillsborough. It had broken up in disarray, with Dublin denying that they had agreed to have Sir John Hermon present at the next conference. The revulsion which followed the killings at Andersonstown and Milltown had momentarily overcome the anger and distrust felt in Dublin over the Gibraltar shootings, the McAnespie incident, the British objections to the Extradition Act, the permanent Prevention of Terrorism Act and the attorney-general's decision not to prosecute RUC officers. Security was back on top of the agenda, and the chief constable of the RUC was invited back to the conference. During a six-hour meeting the parties condemned the recent violent outrages and discussed the new Police Complaints Commission. Tom King's disciplinary moves in his follow-up statement on the Stalker–Sampson investigation and the fair employment proposals were also considered, as was a recommendation to free up to thirty-four youths convicted of terrorist offences while under the age of eighteen. West Belfast, the scene of the recent shootings, was discussed; there were plans to invest up to £10 million in local Enterprise Development Units, health promotion projects, a new adult community centre, 500 new jobs and a new job market on the Falls and Shankill Roads. There was also a significant breakthrough in the extradition log-jam, with Lenihan speculating that 'extradition would be working normally in a matter of a few days'.[175]

The Anglo-Irish Agreement seemed to be back on the rails after a very shaky three months. There was a consensus that if the agreement could survive the traumas of the winter and spring of 1988 it could survive anything. The Dublin–London relationship, however, was not as close and united as it had been prior to the new Irish Extradition Act. The extradition of terrorists from the Republic was one of Margaret Thatcher's strongest reasons for agreeing to sign the Anglo-Irish Agreement. The 'least favoured country in Europe' taunt upset the Irish, but they failed to grasp the genuineness of Mrs Thatcher's anger and frustration. The 'special relationship' established by Thatcher and FitzGerald now counted for little. Irish sensibilites were no longer a major consideration in Downing Street.

[174] *News Letter*, 24 March 1988.
[175] *Irish Times*, 26 March 1988.

7

Talks, the media and terror

Between 15 and 27 February 1988 an opinion poll, commissioned by Ulster TV and *Fortnight*, and conducted by Coopers and Lybrand, interviewed 1,000 people across Northern Ireland. All respondents were asked whether in their opinion the Anglo-Irish Agreement had benefited the two communities in the province. One in four Protestants thought that the Catholic minority had benefited, and over a third of those thought they had 'got all they wanted'. Only 16 per cent of Catholics agreed; an overwhelming 81 per cent of minority respondents could detect no benefit to their community from the agreement. This negative response was particularly apparent among young, working-class Catholics. Of the small number of Catholics who thought they had benefited from the agreement, only 60 per cent said they had obtained 'more say'.

Protestant views regarding the benefits of the agreement to their community were even more worrying for the government. Only one in twenty-five Protestants thought that it had been of benefit to them. Of that 4 per cent, less than a third – 1 per cent overall – thought there had been any improvement in cross-border security. A very strong core of Unionism was still firmly opposed to the Anglo-Irish Agreement, but the will to turn opposition into action was weakening. Protests were less than half as popular amongst Protestants as a whole than they had been a month after the Hillsborough accord was signed.

The poll also attempted to gauge the effects of the events of the previous six months, a period which included the Enniskillen bombing, the attorney-general's statement on the Stalker–Sampson investigation and the Birmingham Six appeal, on the expectations of the people of the province. They found that Enniskillen had had a major influence on both communities, but that the rejection of the Birmingham Six appeal and the attorney-general's decision not to prosecute RUC officers had adversely influenced the Catholic community's response and had more than cancelled out the effect of the Enniskillen atrocity.

Nevertheless, more people saw hope for the future in the reaction to Enniskillen and in the talks about talks than in any other development. This was in stark contrast to the two issues promoted by the governments in London and Dublin as the successes of the agreement: better security (the capture of the *Eksund*) and better community relations (fair employment and the RUC codes of practice). Following the Gibraltar, Milltown and Andersonstown shootings, the only grounds for hope for the future were the talks about talks, between Unionists and the Northern Ireland Office, between the SDLP and Sinn Fein, and possibly between the Unionists and Haughey.

Speaking at a meeting of the governing body of the OUP a week after the Andersonstown shootings, Molyneaux gave a broad hint that his party would be prepared to play a role in building links with Dublin. The same weekend, Eddie McGrady MP broke ranks to say that the SDLP should not be talking to Sinn Fein while the IRA violence continued.[1] Peter Robinson expressed some of the Unionist frustration with the SDLP – Sinn Fein talks when he said that 'Hume was engaged in a rescue mission of the IRA'.[2] The Campaign for a Devolved Government published a pamphlet called *A Better Deal Together*, which recommended an end to direct rule, a setting aside of the Anglo-Irish Agreement, a referendum on devolved government, a bill of rights and ministerial involvement for Catholics in a new administration at Stormont. At Westminster, Livingstone and Benn sponsored a Bill to end British rule in Northern Ireland by 1990.

At Stormont, Tom King met John Hume at the start of talks about talks between the Northern Ireland Office and the SDLP. *The Economist* summed up the delicate nature of the political situation in the province when it said that 'what is needed now is a skilful chef to blend them together without the mixture curdling'.[3] The UTV–*Fortnight* poll provided valuable additional information on the public's response to talks about talks. Integration was the most popular option, but there was a marked split between the number of Protestants in favour (47 per cent) and the low Catholic return (9 per cent). The Protestant return reflected a 12 per cent increase in support for integration since December 1985.

The option commanding cross-sectarian support was, as ever, devolution with power-sharing. This attracted nearly a quarter of the respondents overall. Nearly twice as many Catholics as Protestants supported this option; indeed, more Catholics supported devolution and power-sharing devolution (31 per cent) than opted for a united

---

[1] *Times*, 29 March 1988.
[2] Ibid.
[3] *Economist*, 26 March 1988.

Ireland (25 per cent) or joint Anglo-Irish authority (12 per cent). Given the huge Protestant commitment to integration, the Anglo-Irish Agreement appeared to have failed to increase Protestant support for power-sharing. Molyneaux's strategy of creeping integration seemed to be in tune with Protestant opinion, although there were still disagreements within the Unionist ranks.

McGrady had already provided proof that the SDLP was engaged in an internal dialogue regarding its talks with Sinn Fein. He was against them, but his parliamentary colleague, Mallon, argued strongly for Sinn Fein involvement in inter-party talks. This option was rejected by the Unionists and by the prime minister: 'Ministers of this Government will have no contact whatsoever with Sinn Fein and will not deal with enquiries from them.'[4]

Splits appeared between the SDLP and Sinn Fein regarding the purpose of their talks about talks. The *Sunday Times*, citing SDLP leaks, said that what was 'under discussion is not a limited ceasefire but the once and for all renunciation of the gun component of the Provos' Ballot and Armalite strategy'.[5] This drew a strong rebuttal from Martin McGuinness at an Easter Rising rally, when he said that 'the discussions with the SDLP were not about an IRA ceasefire – there was no military agenda ... SDLP was not Sinn Fein's go-between for contact with Tom King ... the talks with SDLP aimed only at finding out if the two sides had common ground in nationalism.'[6]

The Republican movement was also undergoing changes; there were suggestions that Martin McGuinness was now head of the IRA. He was less interested in political discussions, and the tone of his Easter rally speech fuelled speculation that either the talks with the SDLP were nearing breakdown, or McGuinness was engineering such a collapse.

In his Easter message, Archbishop Eames expressed a 'hope that a growing number of people really want to see an end to the violence'.[7] Cardinal Ó Fiaich urged people 'to put a stop to your sinful campaign of violence'.[8] David McKittrick in the *Independent* suggested that little was likely to happen: 'the hope exists, not in political circles, but in ... journalistic quarters ... open intransigence is momentarily out of fashion and dialogue is, ostensibly at least, the name of the game.'[9]

At a farm auction on the Fermanagh–Cavan border, part-time UDR Corporal William Burleigh was killed by a car bomb. In the Republic, Dessie O'Hare and his gang were sent to prison for a total of 122 years.

---

[4] *Hansard*, 12 April 1988.
[5] *Sunday Times*, 3 April 1988.
[6] *News Letter*, 4 April 1988.
[7] Ibid.
[8] *Irish Times*, 4 April 1988.
[9] *Independent*, 8 April 1988.

In the House of Lords, the judicial committee rejected an appeal to allow the Birmingham Six leave to appeal against the refusal of the Court of Appeal to quash their convictions. The RUC's code of conduct was made public seven months after its circulation within the force. It stated: 'it is not the business of the RUC to concern itself with religion or politics.'[10] In Dublin, extensive reorganization of the Garda was approved by the minister of justice.

Peter Robinson appealed to Unionists to take 'command of events rather than watch them from the sidelines'.[11] The party was being marginalized, with the Northern Ireland Office encouraging a drift towards a united Ireland; no pressure was being put on the SDLP to commit itself to devolution. He ended his speech with an undisguised attack on the low-profile tactics of the Unionist leadership: 'opposition felt but not expressed, or sincere opposition without protest, were tantamount to acquiescence, and acquiescence is the brother of surrender.'[12] This speech reflected Robinson's utter disillusionment with the Unionist anti-agreement pact.

Sammy Wilson developed Robinson's argument on the SDLP's policy on devolution. He posed three questions: was the SDLP prepared to accept Northern Ireland as part of the United Kingdom; was the SDLP prepared to play its part in a devolved administration based on a widespread acceptance within Northern Ireland; would the SDLP be prepared to give its full support to all the institutions of state, including the police?

These contributions by Robinson and Wilson were important markers for the future. They did not expect an immediate reply from Hume, but they were establishing parameters for future Unionist–SDLP discussions once the Sinn Fein talks were out of the way. They also reflected Unionist fears that Hume had lost any enthusiasm for devolution.

Robinson's speech did elicit a quick response from Tom King. Three days later the secretary of state wrote to the two Unionist leaders inviting them for fresh talks. On his desk at Stormont was a copy of a speech Haughey was to deliver a few days later in New York.

The taoiseach called for a constitutional conference arranged by the two Hillsborough partners, but said that 'dialogue now between representatives of the different traditions could be a beneficial forerunner of such a conference'.[13] He suggested direct contact between himself and the Unionists in the North. The *Irish Times* interpreted his speech as meaning that Haughey was 'not bent on

---

[10] *News Letter*, 16 April 1988.
[11] *Irish Times*, 15 April 1988.
[12] Ibid.
[13] *Irish Times*, 22 April 1988.

keeping the Agreement in existence for its own sake, that it is replaceable and he is willing to see it replaced. In the mean time the Agreement stands.'[14]

In the House of Commons, Prime Minister Thatcher signalled her displeasure at the New York speech: 'the defeat of terrorism requires unstinting effort and effective co-operation across the border. We shall continue to press for that and to seek reassurances from the Irish government that [Haughey's] speech does not mean they are backing away from their responsibilities.'[15] What angered Thatcher was a reference in the speech: 'Democratic Parliaments today have cause to be concerned about the control and methods of operation of their own and others countries' intelligence services and security forces.'[16]

The British foreign secretary, Sir Geoffrey Howe, went out of his way to respond sympathetically to Haughey's speech. Having already issued a statement to the effect that the Foreign Office understood that the taoiseach's speech 'may have been dictated by the nature of his audience', Howe added, 'I do not underestimate the hurt felt by the Irish in recent months. I know that many of them believe that the English are insensitive and do not understand them. As a Welshman, I can easily follow the argument, although I am unwilling to endorse it. Let me make it clear that, for our part, any hurt is not intentional. It is not calculated. There is no conspiracy.'[17] Howe's speech was directed as much at the Irish-American audience in New York as at the Irish. The Foreign Office feared a resurgence of support for Noraid and other pro-IRA lobby groups. It also worried about Haughey's apparent shift from a determination to work within the Anglo-Irish Agreement to his current attitude, which might undermine hard-won American administration support for the agreement.

Unionists in Northern Ireland were confused by the 'tough cop, nice cop' routine of Thatcher and Howe. They were also alarmed by Haughey's reported preference for a federal Ireland. The *News Letter* thought his speech 'too green' and suggested that the talks process was undermined. Paisley said the New York speech was a 'stupid insult to Unionist people'.[18] Molyneaux kept quiet. Finton O'Toole speculated that the OUP leader understood Haughey's tactics to be that 'he will not ditch the Agreement, neither will he pursue it vigorously . . . if the Unionists had the imagination to come up with an alternative to the

[14] *Irish Times*, 25 April 1988.
[15] *Times*, 23 April 1988.
[16] Ibid.
[17] *Independent*, 25 April 1988.
[18] *News Letter*, 26 April 1988.

Agreement . . . they will find a Taoiseach who . . . has dealt himself a very free hand'.[19] An *Economist* – MORI poll of a sample of 2,027 respondents aged over eighteen in 175 constituencies between 11 and 15 March concluded that people in Britain were losing interest in Northern Ireland.[20] The poll was conducted after the Gibraltar shootings but before the Milltown and Andersonstown killings. Nearly half those interviewed favoured either independence (29 per cent) or a union with Ireland (19 per cent). The support for Northern Ireland remaining part of the United Kingdom was weakening, down 3 per cent to 27 per cent. The events of the last three years had done little to clarify opinion regarding the future of the province, since the biggest shift in preferences occurred in the 'Don't know' section, up 7 per cent to 25 per cent.

The British government was increasingly irritated by the Irish reaction to events. Norman Tebbitt, the former cabinet minister and close confidant of the prime minister, wrote: 'it is time the politicians, including the most passionate republicans in Ireland, tore away the misty romanticism in which they have clothed the common thieves, blackmailers and bloody psychopaths of the IRA . . . I say in sadness that I need reassurance that Mr Haughey is prepared to pay the price to defeat terrorism.'[21] Peter Jenkins in the *Independent* expressed a British reaction to the problem of how to cope with Northern Ireland: 'the province is one large "no go" area. It is a no go area for trial by jury, no go for ordinary rule of law, no go for the local democracy which is practised in all other parts of the UK. That is the problem, the British way of life won't go in Northern Ireland.'[22]

Extradition continued to be a bone of contention between the Republic and the United Kingdom. Sir Patrick Mayhew was still concerned that the new Irish Extradition Act conferred 'improper judicial powers on his Irish counterpart. He is further concerned that any evidence supplied could be challenged in an Irish court . . . the Irish authorities have also been unable to guarantee the confidentiality of information provided.'[23]

In the province, an ambitious plan to build the largest luxury liner in the world was unveiled by Ravi Tikko of Global Tankers and John Parker of Harland and Wolff. The £260 million project was dependent on a £100 million government grant and would guarantee employment to the East Belfast yard for four years. The project was launched as the

---

[19] *Fortnight*, 26 April 1988.
[20] *Economist*, 26 March 1988.
[21] *Sunday Express*, 13 March 1988.
[22] *Independent*, 22 March 1988.
[23] *Irish Times*, 8 April 1988.

Northern Ireland Office was considering the privatization of Harland and Wolff; there was considerable annoyance up at Stormont Castle at this pre-emptive strike.

Douglas Hurd disclosed that a Home Office working group was preparing legislation to allow the courts to freeze assets and confiscate investments accumulated by terrorist paramilitaries. A special task force set up in Northern Ireland to investigate allegations of fraud by DHSS claimants led to a walk-out by civil servants when the INLA threatened staff in Derry. The value of welfare state benefits to deprived communities in places like the Creggan and the Bogside soon forced the INLA to withdraw the threat. In County Tyrone, the IRA killed UDR soldier Edward Gibson and claimed responsibility for the death of a British army soldier in Carrickmore.

Up at Stormont King met Hume for the second of their talks about talks. The secretary of state was reported to be talking about a return of powers over education, housing and the environment to a locally elected assembly. He also indicated a willingness to back a package of proposals to help develop West Belfast and support integrated schools and the teaching of Irish. Hume was expected to reply that 'devolution on its own was not a solution to the Northern Ireland situation';[24] he was now considering a 'federal Ireland' as the more realistic option. Although both sides agreed to meet again, there were reliable reports that Tom King walked out of the talks, muttering that the Northern Ireland Office had succeeded in bringing the Unionists 'to the park only to find that the SDLP didn't want to play ball any more'.[25] Hume flew to Tennessee to receive an honorary degree, and at the ceremony continued the wooing of Ulster Unionists started by Haughey at Bodenstown nine months earlier: 'In the Unionist community, with its British identity and a rich Protestant heritage, there is tremendous pride in their tradition. Pride in their service to the Crown, pride in their industrial achievements and work ethic, and pride in their maintenance of their faith ... Can such pride not be fashioned into self-confidence instead of archaic supremacism?'[26]

Molyneaux, Paisley and King had their first formal meeting since January 1988. The local press carried suggestions that if King did not respond favourably to the Unionists' proposals all talks would be over and the anti-agreement campaign would resume its protests. Whatever Tom King told Molyneaux and Paisley, it certainly made an impression; after the meeting Paisley said, 'it was like the man who

[24] *News Letter*, 27 April 1988.
[25] Private interview, Head of Programmes, Northern Ireland.
[26] *Irish Times*, 2 May 1988.

landed on the moon, a first short step'.[27] The *Irish Times* noted the lack of the 'usual bombast or threats that tended to intrude on similar occasions in the past'.[28] Molyneaux claimed that King had told both Unionist leaders that he was prepared to discuss their proposals without any preconditions. He interpreted that to mean that 'Mr King is prepared to consider an alternative to the Agreement'.[29] This seemed to confirm John Hume's view that King was attempting to outmanœuvre the Haughey–SDLP initiative on an all-Ireland agreement.

Four days later Molyneaux set the cat amongst the pigeons by saying on ITV's *Weekend World* that he sought direct contact with Haughey: 'I think it would be unfair to Mr Haughey and to me to engage in summitry at this early stage . . . I think an exchange of ideas on paper would be the first step.'[30] Confusion reigned. John Cole said that 'consultation is like a four-ring circus, with no one sure whether the performance will eventually merge into one big ring, or whether there will be a fifth circus that no one thought about'.[31] Haughey said he hoped 'to respond very positively . . . to Mr Molyneaux's suggestions for preliminary contact'.[32] The *Irish Times* suggested that what was happening was 'an emerging formula for the development of a process outside of and parallel to the Anglo-Irish Agreement'.[33] Mary Holland interpreted Molyneaux's statement to mean that the OUP leader had 'brought the Unionist community to this rendezvous with history'.[34] Peter Barry said that 'the weekend has been, from the point of view of an Irishman, the most hopeful seventy-two hours we have seen for many years, in fact possibly ever. I think that we all should be very careful that we don't destroy those chinks of light that are now appearing.'[35] Archbishop Eames, opening the General Synod of the Church of Ireland in Dublin, said he detected the 'first signs of a new and more hopeful chapter to our troubled history'.[36] Mary Holland gave Eames a lot of the credit for 'steering the Unionists to the table' with Haughey.[37] The archbishop had met the taoiseach on a number of occasions, and was known to have Molyneaux's ear.

The question that preoccupied most politicians and commentators

---

[27] *Irish Times*, 12 May 1988.
[28] Ibid.
[29] *News Letter*, 12 May 1988.
[30] *News Letter*, 16 May 1988.
[31] *Listener*, 16 June 1988.
[32] *Irish Times*, 16 May 1988.
[33] Ibid.
[34] *Irish Times*, 18 May 1988.
[35] Ibid.
[36] *Times*, 23 May 1988.
[37] *Irish Times*, 25 May 1988.

immediately after the *Weekend World* programme was whether or not Molyneaux represented anybody apart from himself in extending the invitation for talks to Haughey. On the same programme Peter Robinson had suggested that King convene a meeting between the Unionists and the SDLP. A few days later Paisley added a caveat to his deputy's suggestions: 'meetings with the SDLP would have to await the end of the Sinn Fein talks.'[38]

The joint Unionist policy committee met twice during the week following the *Weekend World* programme to review Molyneaux's statement and to prepare for a further meeting with Tom King scheduled for Thursday 26 May 1988. Molyneaux was suddenly centre-stage. Because he was not an impressive public speaker, he was often underrated by political commentators. Roy Bradford, in the *News Letter*, was confident that the OUP leader knew what he was about: 'Molyneaux ... realizes the delicacy of the situation ... he has kept his balance amazingly well on the tightrope between constitutional opposition and violent confrontation.'[39] Fionnuala O'Connor, in *Fortnight*, was more critical: 'Molyneaux's non-policy has recently been hailed as brave and innovative ... over the past three years his strategy has been to say as little as possible and allow the Agreement to be pulled apart by its own contradictions. This passive approach has driven others to distraction – or out of politics altogether ... Mr Molyneaux has not deviated one inch ... he has no more conciliatory ideas now on a relationship with Dublin than he had three years ago.'[40]

Within a week it was apparent that Molyneaux had not been presenting a joint Unionist policy statement on North–South dialogue; he was freelancing. Paisley put the record straight a day before the Unionists' talks with Tom King, when he said that the 'Dublin government would have no say whatsoever and no place at the conference table'.[41] Sammy Wilson added that 'Mr Molyneaux can do much to clear the air by making a clear unequivocal statement as to where he stands ... [does] he intend to talk with Charles Haughey outside the arrangements agreed with the DUP?'[42] Paisley reiterated his understanding of those arrangements: 'a devolved government must be set up in Belfast *before* talks could be held with the Republic about relationships between the two parts of Ireland.'[43]

King, Molyneaux and Paisley agreed at their London meeting to bring the present phase of talks to an end. This was a temporary

---

[38] *Irish Times*, 17 May 1988.
[39] *News Letter*, 26 May 1988.
[40] *Fortnight*, No. 262, May 1988.
[41] *News Letter*, 26 May 1988.
[42] Ibid.
[43] *Irish Times*, 26 May 1988.

suspension while the SDLP–Sinn Fein talks were completed. The *Irish Times* concluded that the 'opening of multilateral discussions between the constitutional parties of Northern Ireland seems at last in sight'.[44] The *News Letter* broke off a series of articles attacking Molyneaux's flirtation with Dublin to caution against making any concessions to the SDLP: 'far too much time has been wasted on trying to bring a reluctant, weak, vacillating SDLP horse to the well.'[45]

The *News Letter*'s campaign against North–South discussions received a boost from an unexpected quarter. Dennis Goghlan, the political correspondent of the *Irish Times*, quoted an official source as saying that the Dublin government had sent Molyneaux position papers setting out a framework within which talks could take place. There were also reports that Molyneaux had met Alan Dukes and Dick Spring in London. Goghlan's article was to the OUP what the Zinoviev letter was to the Labour Party. Molyneaux 'categorically denied that he had exchanged position papers with the Taoiseach'.[46] Haughey did nothing either to help Molyneaux or to deny Goghlan's story. Molyneaux had gone too far for the Unionist 'not an inch' brigade in Northern Ireland. Paisley, with the full backing of the joint Unionist policy committee, said on RTÉ that there would be no discussions with Dublin before devolved government was in place in Northern Ireland, no talks with the SDLP until the talks with Sinn Fein were over and no talks with the government until the agreement was suspended. Mallon summed up the common reaction to the DUP's statement: 'for Unionists to make suspension of the Agreement a precondition is in effect closing off their options for dialogue.'[47]

Whatever the reasons for the crossed wires between Dublin and Belfast, the courtship between Molyneaux's Unionism and Haughey's Republicanism had been a fascinating affair, long and arduous. Marriage was never contemplated by either party, the dowries would have been too demanding, but the flirtation did help to develop new thoughts and nurture lost contacts. It also had a beneficial effect on the ardour of other would-be suitors. Tom King invited the Unionists up to Stormont for talks. King was far more eager to have the Unionists on his side than either Molyneaux and Paisley realized at the time.

Gerry Adams, after a nudge and a wink from Haughey, met Hume three times and exchanged documents, but no agreement was reached. Hume held that the British government, by signing the Anglo-Irish Agreement, had indicated that Britain had no long-term interest in

---

[44] *Irish Times*, 27 May 1988.
[45] *News Letter*, 27 May 1988.
[46] *Irish Times*, 2 June 1988.
[47] *Irish Times*, 7 June 1988.

remaining in Northern Ireland and argued that the way ahead was to convince the Unionists that their long-term interests were best served by a settlement within the island of Ireland. Sinn Fein sought a statement of intent from the British that they intended to withdraw from Northern Ireland; until that assurance was forthcoming the IRA campaign would continue. John Hume's view was that the terrorists only hardened the resolve of the British to stay in the province. The SDLP leader's purpose in engaging in talks with Sinn Fein was to bring the IRA military campaign to an end. The Republican movement was split between the Adams faction and the military arm of the movement. Adams argued that only substantial political support could secure for Sinn Fein a seat at any future conference table; failure to find common ground with the SDLP would create problems. He wanted an all-party, all-Ireland conference convened by Haughey, and failing that an all-Nationalist conference, another New Ireland Forum, but this time with Sinn Fein at the conference table. The military wing wanted to keep traditional Republicanism outside a pan-national grouping. They rejected the argument that the IRA was an electoral liability, and wanted to intensify the military threat. John Hume saw the differences within Sinn Fein as tactical; to Adams, they represented the fundamental principles of Republicanism.

The day after Tom King had said that SDLP–Sinn Fein talks were of 'no help at all in trying to get sensible dialogue going in Northern Ireland',[48] the IRA killed six soldiers at Lisburn.

At the end of April 1988 Thames Television produced a network edition of *This Week*, called *Death on the Rock*. It investigated the Gibraltar shootings and featured interviews with eyewitnesses to the shootings whose versions of the events differed from those previously given by the foreign secretary in his statement to the House of Commons on Monday 7 March 1988. On the evening of Tuesday 26 April 1988 the foreign secretary, Sir Geoffrey Howe, phoned Lord Thomson, chairman of the Independent Broadcasting Authority, and 'asked that the showing of *Death on the Rock* be postponed until after the inquest'.[49] Sir Geoffrey gave as the principal reason for his request the fear that the broadcast might prejudice the inquest. The IBA consulted David Kemp QC, whose opinion was that it would not. On the day of transmission David Glencross, director of television at the headquarters of the IBA, phoned the Foreign Office to notify them of the authority's decision to transmit the programme at 9.00 p.m. After discussions between Sir Geoffrey Howe and Glencross, the Foreign Office issued a statement: 'we are not quarrelling with the content of the programme or

---

[48] *News Letter*, 15 June 1988.
[49] *Windlesham–Rampton Report*, 130.

seeking to get it stopped. Our concerns are not based on the possible embarrassment of the Government or threats to national security. We are simply saying that showing it before the inquest could prejudice the proceedings.'[50] The IBA also issued a statement which said that the authority 'considers that the programme is a responsibly made documentary which assesses and analyses the role of the terrorists and the SAS in a thorough manner . . . the events of the Gibraltar shooting have already been the subject of wide journalistic investigation. The IBA believes that it would be unreasonable to deny further reporting of them to television'.[51]

The first important claim made by the programme *Death on the Rock* was that the three terrorists were tailed to the Gibraltar border by Spanish security officers who were in contact with the British authorities in the colony. The next controversial contribution was by Carmen Proetta, who claimed to have been an eyewitness to the shooting. In a sworn affidavit she said that McCann and Farrell 'had their hands in the air at the moment they were shot by the SAS . . . the British soldiers fired the first shot without warning . . .'[52] This version was confirmed by Stephen Bullock, a British lawyer, who was walking with his wife and baby son; he added that the terrorists were shot at very close range.[53] Savage died after the other two, at a corner in Landport Ditch. An unidentified woman eyewitness claimed Savage ran past her, pursued by a second man who had a gun in his left hand.[54] She did not hear any warning of any kind given by the man with the gun. She further claimed that Savage was shot three or four times more, as he lay on his back on the ground. This was confirmed by Kenneth Asquez, who withdrew his statement during the inquest, claiming that he had been pressured into giving an untrue account of what he had seen by an intermediary acting for *This Week*. Thames Television invited Lord Windlesham and Richard Rampton QC to 'conduct an inquiry into the making and screening of *Death on the Rock*'.[55]

A selection of headlines in the national press on the day following the transmission of *Death on the Rock* gives a flavour of the controversy that followed: '"Trial by TV" row over IRA killings film' (*The Times*); 'Defiant ITV angers Ministers' (*Daily Telegraph*); 'Storm at SAS Telly Trial' (*Sun*); 'Fury over SAS "Trial" by TV' (*Daily Mail*); 'TV slur on the SAS' (*Star*). In the *Daily Mail*, Geoffrey Levy stated the programme was 'woefully one-sided', and reflected its makers' belief that the

[50] *Times*, 29 April 1988.
[51] Ibid.
[52] *Windlesham-Rampton Report*, 53.
[53] Transcript, *Death on the Rock, Report*, 55.
[54] Transcript, *Death on the Rock, Report*, 56.
[55] *Windlesham-Rampton Report*, 3.

terrorists had been murdered 'with the summary justice of an execution without trial'.[56] Conversely William Holmes, writing in *The Times* on the same day, felt that the programme was a 'significant, thoroughly responsible and serious examination of a most disturbing case', and that it was in no sense a 'trial by television', but on the contrary 'simply raised questions and suggested that they required deep examination'.[57] The prime minister, interviewed on Japanese television, said that 'the place to have trials is in a court of law. Trial by television, or guilt by association, is the day that freedom dies.'[58] Sir Geoffrey Howe called the programme 'grossly and wholly improper'. The *Independent* claimed the government was 'involved in yet another petty but disturbing attempt to impose its version of prior restraint on the media'.[59] It argued that the foreign secretary's approach was 'seriously flawed. If potential members of the jury in Gibraltar are susceptible to comment in this country, then surely Sir Geoffrey would have been more tentative when delivering his initial version of events to the Commons.'[60]

At Question Time on May Bank Holiday the prime minister quoted from the Salmon Report: 'One would not wish to see in this country the horror of trial by press, television and radio. We have so far escaped them only because of the high sense of responsibility on the part of the press, television and radio and because of the law of contempt ... on this occasion, neither Thames Television nor the IBA demonstrated that high sense of responsibility to which the judge referred.'[61] It took Peter Jenkins, in the *Independent*, to complete the quotation: 'we have no doubt but that the solid advantages of freedom outweigh the remote risk of the tribunal being improperly influenced by such comment.'[62]

Sir Geoffrey Howe released the text of a letter he sent to Lord Thomson, in which he expressed his deep regret and serious disquiet at the IBA's decision to allow the transmission of Thames Television's production. Hugo Young in the *Guardian* rejected what he supposed to be the government's case against the broadcast, 'that when it comes to terrorists and the forces who struggle against them, the media have no useful or even valid role to play, unless as accessories to the armoury of the state ... the media serves this country best by standing up for the values which leaders under pressure downgrade'.[63]

The news that BBC Northern Ireland had a further television

---

[56] *Daily Mail*, 29 April 1988.
[57] *Times*, 29 April 1988.
[58] Ibid.
[59] *Independent*, 29 April 1988.
[60] Ibid.
[61] *Times*, 4 May 1988.
[62] *Independent*, 11 May 1988.
[63] *Guardian*, 5 May 1988.

programme on the same issue, scheduled for transmission in Northern Ireland a week after *Death on the Rock*, leaked out the day after the May Bank Holiday. The prime minister commented: 'I would prefer to think that we could rely on the television authorities to uphold the rule of law, which, after all, is the fundamental safeguard of the freedom of us all. One cannot agree with the rule of law and then flout its conditions. I hope that we will be able to persuade them that that is the predominant issue.'[64]

Michael Checkland, the director-general of the BBC, decided that the programme should be broadcast. He wrote to the foreign secretary, saying that 'the shootings and their aftermath were of special significance to the people of Northern Ireland ... much of the evidence was already in the public domain. It was part of the BBC's continuing commitment to a proper presentation of all facts relating to issues which affected people in the province.'[65] Dr Colin Morris, the BBC controller in Northern Ireland, added: 'Everybody wants to harness [the media] to their war chariots, the Government, the politicians, the paramilitaries and a fiercely sectarian public opinion ... the truth is democracy's best ally in the battle against terrorism.'[66] The *News Letter* strongly supported the BBC's stance: '... at the heart of the ongoing Gibraltar controversy is the Government's determination to launder the news.'[67]

Sir Geoffrey Howe saw a video copy of *Spotlight on Gibraltar* and said: 'it does concern me deeply, because it did contain the very features about which I have warned ... precisely calculated to contaminate the evidence and influence unhelpfully the way in which the inquest will be conducted.'[68]

Lord Scarman attempted to answer the foreign secretary's criticism: 'there is no trial imminent in the UK which could be prejudiced by the broadcast. There is no public inquiry set up, or even promised in the UK. The broadcast could not be stopped as a contempt of court or as a threat to any judicial proceedings pending or promised in the UK.'[69] Bernard Ingham, the prime minister's press officer, launched a counter-attack on the press: 'there is nothing wrong with the British media that a renewed respect for facts, objectivity and fairness rather than false gods of invention and malice would not cure.'[70] In Gibraltar Eric Thistlethwaite, the colony's attorney-general, took out an injunction

---

[64] *Hansard*, 5 May 1988, 1016.
[65] *Times*, 6 May 1988.
[66] *Guardian*, 5 May 1988.
[67] *News Letter*, 6 May 1988.
[68] *Times*, 7 May 1988.
[69] *Times*, 9 May 1988.
[70] Ibid.

to prevent local press, radio and television from reporting evidence about the killings. Lord Thomson replied to the foreign secretary's letter of 4 May 1988 by asserting that 'the issues as we see them relate to free speech and free enquiry which underpin individual liberty in a democracy. The right of broadcasters and the press to examine events of major public concern is well established and should be preserved.'[71]

The argument was to be resumed at the inquest in Gibraltar. Broadcasters in Northern Ireland had clashed with the government on three separate occasions in four short months: the anti-terrorist video, the untransmitted film of the Andersonstown killings, and now *Death on the Rock* and *Spotlight on Gibraltar*. There were clear signs of dissatisfaction with the way broadcasters handled terrorist-related stories.

Other pressing issues demanded consideration in May 1988. The IRA killed three RAF servicemen in two separate attacks, one in the Netherlands, and the other in Germany. The leaders of the IRA had noted public reaction in Britain to the murders of Corporals Howes and Woods at Andersonstown and now directed their military offensive away from the RUC and the locally recruited UDR, to concentrate on British army personnel in the province, in England and on the continent. The enhanced co-operation between the RUC and the Garda, and the success of the joint British army and Irish army search and arrest operation immediately after the Enniskillen bombing had forced the Republican movement to postpone its planned offensive in Ireland. The internal rift between the IRA and Sinn Fein was also an important factor in redirecting the military offensive and striking at the heart of British involvement in Northern Ireland. A British withdrawal was the goal and the way to achieve it was by influencing British public opinion.

The campaign started in Roermand in the Netherlands, close to the border with the Federal Republic of Germany. In the early hours of Sunday 1 May, three members of the Royal Air Force were sleeping off the effects of a day's drinking. They were sitting in a private car with British number-plates. An attack from an automatic weapon left SAC Ian Shinner dead, and his companions injured. Shortly afterwards a bomb destroyed a car in Neuw-bergen killing SAC John Baxter and SAC John Reid, and seriously injuring SAC Andrew Kelly. All three served at RAF Laarbruch. The IRA claimed responsibility for both incidents, adding, 'Disengage from Ireland and there will be peace. If not, then there will be no haven for your military personnel.'[72] In the House of Commons the secretary of state for defence, George Younger, revealed that immediate steps had been taken 'to strengthen still further

---

[71] *Windlesham-Rampton Report*, 138–9.
[72] *Times*, 2 May 1988.

the security of British forces in Germany and the Netherlands'.[73] The IRA attacks on European bases were not new. Eight British bases in West Germany were bombed in one night in 1978. The following year Sir Richard Sykes, the British ambassador in the Netherlands, was killed. In August 1979 a bomb placed under a bandstand in Brussels injured eighteen people.

A meeting of the Intergovernmental Conference in Dublin condemned the attacks and developed security proposals aimed at controlling cross-border smuggling in Ireland. The British disclosed plans to introduce legislation to confiscate illegal funds accumulated by paramilitary groups, and the Dublin High Court decided *not* to return £1,750,816 to Alan Clancey, a Dublin and New York pub-owner, believing it to be 'laundered money' on its way to the IRA. The same day, the RUC announced that paramilitary groups had been involved in 249 attempted or actual bank robberies in the first five months of the year. This frightening average of two bank robberies a day reflected operations involving more than £500,000.

Extradition arrangements between the UK and the Republic of Ireland were finally agreed on 13 May 1988. They had been at a standstill since the new Irish Extradition Act had passed through the Dáil shortly before Christmas 1987. The British attorney-general agreed to a 'case by case' basis, with Britain providing a full summary of a case against a suspect, but without the names and addresses of prospective witnesses. This fell short of the general agreement in principle to which the Irish thought Mayhew had agreed. They were further angered by the claim that the Irish attorney-general had modified some of the stipulations in the earlier exchange of correspondence. There was obviously still room for confusion. The Supreme Court decided that Paul Kane was properly detained by the High Court after his arrest in Cavan. The proceedings for his extradition, requested by the RUC, could now get under way. The following week another member of the IRA, wanted by the Metropolitan Police on a charge of conspiring to cause an explosion and possessing explosive substances, was arrested outside Portlaoise prison. Patrick McVeigh had served five and a half years of a seven-year sentence for arms smuggling. He was rearrested on his release to be the first test case for the new extradition arrangements.

In the province, three Catholics were killed by a Loyalist group in Union Street, Belfast; the Protestant Action Force claimed responsibility. SDLP councillor Brian Feeney claimed that a 'murderous gang comparable in bestiality to the Shankill Butchers was on the loose'.[74] At the Royal Ulster Show Ground thirteen people, three of them

---

[73] *Hansard*, 3 May 1988, 725.
[74] *Times*, 16 May 1988.

children, were injured when a bomb exploded under an RUC recruiting caravan. The showground was packed with visitors to the annual agricultural show. In Crossmaglen Corporal Derek Hayes and his dog Ben were killed when a bomb exploded under their feet. A week later, UDR soldier Michael Davey was killed in Castlederry and a Loyalist gang shot dead William Totten, a Roman Catholic. In Gibraltar, Felix Pizzarillo, the colony's coroner, was informed that he would be allowed to see the 'rules of engagement' drawn up for the SAS team by the Ministry of Defence. The same day, in Dublin, District Justice Jarlath Ruane released Patrick McVeigh on a technicality of identification. The first test case under the new Extradition Act failed miserably, as far as the British authorities were concerned. Mrs Thatcher was reported to be 'utterly dismayed'. The *Irish Times* said, 'somebody somewhere has blundered.'[75] *The Times* commented, 'the Irish Republic seems unable to keep its side of the bargain.'[76] The Irish government appealed to the High Court. The British attorney-general expressed 'profound frustration and surprise [at] a very grave setback'.[77] Tony Marlow, MP for Northampton North, suggested that 'members of the Irish judiciary are bent by their own republicanism, bullied by the IRA'.[78]

Patrick McVeigh was a free man again. In the United States Edwin Meese, the attorney-general, signed the papers which would extradite Joseph Doherty to Britain, where he had been convicted in 1981 of the murder of a British soldier. In Northern Ireland Bobby 'Squeak' Seymour, a UVF leader, was murdered by the IRA. David McLean, one of Seymour's colleagues in the UVF, had earlier been given concurrent life sentences of more than 400 years, having admitted forty-four offences which included three murders and six attempted murders.

On the evening of Wednesday 15 June 1988 Lisburn borough council, in conjunction with the YMCA, organized a half-marathon charity race, together with a shorter fun run. Some four and a half thousand people took part, among them six soldiers from Ebrington barracks in Derry. The soldiers travelled to Lisburn from Derry in a transit van and parked it unattended in the leisure centre car park where the runs started and finished. At the end of the race the soldiers climbed back into the van and left the car park. Nine minutes later all six were dead, killed by an explosive device attached to the underside of the van. Eleven civilians, including an eighty-year-old man and a two-year-old child, were injured. The IRA had launched its summer offensive, which was to leave fifty-eight people dead.

---

[75] *Irish Times*, 14 June 1988.
[76] *Times*, 14 June 1988.
[77] *Hansard*, 14 June 1988, 199.
[78] Ibid., 207.

The Lisburn fun run explosion increased the pressure for internment to be reintroduced. Alan Wright of the Northern Ireland Police Federation said it 'would help to divorce the terrorists from the community they exploited'.[79] The prime minister and Tom King rejected internment as an option, although the secretary of state confirmed that selective detention was 'not ruled out'.[80] Paisley made a moving address in response to an interruption from Mr Dykes, the member for Harrow East: 'He does not follow the coffins; he does not meet the widows and orphans; he has never put his hand on the curly head of a little girl or boy who will have no father, no mother and no succour from a father or mother.'[81] William Green, a miner and father of one of the Lisburn bomb victims, said 'he would like to see the rest of the lads brought back home before it happens to someone else's son'.[82] Yet another security review got under way, with the new GOC, Lieutenant-General Sir John Waters, under pressure to tighten security arrangements. The feeling was that the six deaths at Lisburn could have been avoided if the most elementary and basic security precautions had been used.

Douglas Hurd disclosed that the so-called 'godfathers of terrorism' were to be targeted by a new law which would make it illegal to hold, launder and control funds that could be used by the IRA or other terrorists. Two of the IRA's top terrorists, Patrick McLaughlin and Liam McCotter, were found guilty of plotting a terror campaign in Britain and sentenced to twenty years and seventeen years respectively. Their arrest was a serious setback to the IRA campaign.

In Belfast an Intergovernmental Conference resolved 'to reaffirm the determination of the two governments to work together for the defeat of terrorism by further enhancing cross border co-operation on security matters . . . and effective extradition arrangements'.[83] Security was again top of the agenda, with political dialogue taking a back seat. Nicholas Fenn, the British ambassador in Dublin, commented that the Anglo-Irish Agreement was 'one of those rare diplomatic instruments which changes the game thereafter . . . the Agreement had transformed for the better relations between Dublin and London'.[84] A sign of that change was a speech by Martin O'Muilleoir at a Sinn Fein meeting in Dublin that same week, when he was reported to have said that 'the IRA was becoming an electoral liability'.[85]

---

[79] *Times*, 8 June 1988.
[80] *Hansard*, 16 June 1988, 582.
[81] Ibid., 580.
[82] *Times*, 16 June 1988.
[83] *News Letter*, 18 June 1988.
[84] *Irish Times*, 22 June 1988.
[85] Ibid.

In south Armagh, an army helicopter made a forced landing after a tailpiece went missing. The IRA claimed that one of their units had shot the helicopter down. A week later they admitted responsibility for planting a bomb in a school bus in Lisnaskea; five schoolgirls and the driver, a part-time member of the UDR, were injured. The IRA statement said that an inquiry would be held. The security authorities also discussed the wisdom of having a well-known UDR soldier driving a school bus along a regular route in an area known to harbour an active-service unit.

At RUC headquarters in Knock in East Belfast, Sir John Hermon announced his retirement as chief constable, a post he had held for ten years. Before he made the announcement he received the Charles Kelly report on allegations of conspiracy to pervert the course of justice arising out of the Stalker – Sampson inquiry. Twenty officers were to face disciplinary proceedings. Sir John's announcement came in the week the Northern Ireland Police Authority met and decided by a majority of one not to discipline the chief constable and two of his senior staff over the Stalker – Sampson report.

Amnesty International released a report on a six-year investigation of the killing by the security forces of forty-nine persons, nineteen of them unarmed, since 1982. It called for a wide-ranging judicial inquiry and criticized the long delay in holding inquests in the province. In Gibraltar, Felix Pizzarillo announced that the inquest into the IRA deaths would be held on 5 September. He also ruled that the SAS men, if they appeared at the inquest, would have to be visible to the jury, the lawyers and the coroner.

Between Pizzarillo's announcement on 4 July and the opening of the inquest in early September, thirty-six people were to die in terrorist-related incidents, an average of four a week. By the time the inquest opened, the British cabinet was holding an emergency meeting on the crisis in the province, and the troubles had blown the SDLP – Sinn Fein talks apart. Ken Strange, a taxi-driver, died when he was caught in the crossfire between an IRA unit and the RUC. Terry Delaney, a Catholic, was chased through Dromore village, County Down, and shot dead at point-blank range by a Loyalist gunman who later accused Delaney of being an IRA intelligence officer. In the Falls Road, Eamon Gilroy and Elizabeth Hammill died when the wall of a local swimming pool was blown out by an IRA bomb. In the follow-up operation Warrant Officer John Howard became the four-hundredth soldier to die in the province when he stepped on a booby-trap bomb. Gerry Adams made his fifth 'apology' in as many months for the deaths of Gilroy and Hammill, who were local residents in West Belfast. In Pomeroy, County Tyrone, Seamus Wood, an IRA volunteer, died when a mortar-bomb he was priming backfired. Wood became the twenty-first IRA member to die in sixteen months, the highest casualty rate in twenty years. John Hume gave Gerry Adams a position paper that catalogued the cost of violence in Northern Ireland in terms of deaths: 'Republicans have killed five times as many people as all of the security forces put together, and thirty times as many as the RUC.'[86]

Patrick Ryan was arrested in Brussels. The ex-priest was believed by Interpol to be one of the IRA's leading bankers, arms suppliers and bomb-makers. In Duisburg in West Germany nine soldiers suffered minor injuries when two bombs exploded. In the Irish Republic, the Garda found a Russian-made machine gun which could fire armour-piercing shells over a distance of two miles. At Jonesborough in County Armagh four armed and masked men visited the home of William Bergin and his wife Jean. They were told to get out within seven days. Bergin, a retired RAF man, left for England.

On the Dublin – Belfast road, a 1,000 lb bomb killed three members of the Hanna family. The roadside explosion was intended to kill Judge Ian Higgins and his family as they returned to the province from a holiday in the USA. The Hanna family had arrived at Dublin airport on the same Aer Lingus flight. The IRA excused the operation by saying the Hanna family were 'victims of mistaken identity'.[87] Brendan Davidson, a member of the IRA, opened his front door to a man dressed in a policeman's uniform. He died, the victim of a 'fake policeman' from the UVF. In south Armagh Sergeant Michael Mathews of the Parachute Regiment died from his injuries after an IRA bomb blast. At the Northern Ireland Office, John Stanley was given a knighthood and sent to the back benches. The armed services minister, Ian Stewart, moved to Stormont as deputy to Tom King.

The next attack came in Britain. Lance-Corporal Michael Robbins died when a bomb exploded at Inglis barracks in north London, near the prime minister's constituency. Again lax security precautions were highlighted by the subsequent review. It was the IRA's first successful operation in Britain since the Brighton bomb in 1984, and was followed by a warning 'telling all civilians to stay away from military installations'.[88] Within a week, five more people were to die and ten were injured. Lance-Corporal Roy Buller, a UDR soldier, was killed in front of his wife whilst out shopping in Belfast. The same day DC John Warnock was killed when a bomb exploded under his car in Lisburn's Sloan Street. In Cookstown off-duty soldier Raymond McNichol was shot dead in his car. In Belleek, County Fermanagh, William Hassard and Fred Love were killed as they drove home through the village after

---

[86] *News Letter*, 20 August 1988.
[87] *Times*, 25 July 1988.
[88] *Times*, 2 August 1988.

routine maintenance work at the local police station. The Ulster Unionist Council met in emergency session to consider the deteriorating security situation. They called for an immediate return of internment. Paisley threw out a challenge to Tom King: 'Get tough or quit.'[89]

At Rattingen barracks in West Germany three servicemen were injured when a bomb exploded near the perimeter fence. The Lambeth Conference passed a motion proposed by Archbishop Eames condemning all forms of violence in Northern Ireland: 'we are not talking about freedom fighters or exponents of liberation theology. We are talking about a calculated campaign of murder by an organization condemned outright by the Roman Catholic Church.'[90]

At Dublin post office Frank Sutcliffe, a customs officer, was charged with being a member of the IRA when he turned up to collect a parcel from Amsterdam containing a sniper rifle, a decoder, a transmitter and an encoder. He was released on £10,000 bail. Twenty miles away in Newcastle, County Wicklow, ammunition and firearms were discovered in a wall. In the Ardoyne district of Belfast Seamus Morris, a student, and Peter Dolan, a lorry-driver's mate, were killed by a Loyalist gang firing from a moving car. At a Belfast hospital a soldier died from injuries sustained three weeks earlier.

In Ostend Warrant Officer Richard Heakin was shot dead at the wheel of his stationary car three minutes from the ferry terminal. Martin McGuinness, vice-chairman of Sinn Fein, said: 'It is highly encouraging to the nationalists that the people now paying the price are ranking members of the British Armed Forces . . .'[91] He then added the following significant statement: 'it would be unrealistic to imagine that the IRA could win militarily, but they have the ability to outlast the political will of the British.'[92] The military struggle was an aid to the political goal of a united Ireland. When the political discussions pointed to a possible agreement on something less than a united Ireland, the IRA applied extra pressure to force a rethink. Devolution meant defeat for the Republican cause. The purpose of the terror campaign was not only to sabotage the various talks about talks in Ireland, but to force British public opinion to react in an angry show of desperation and either pull out of the province, or reintroduce internment, what Tom King had called 'the best recruiting sergeant of the IRA'.[93]

Internment had last been introduced in 1971, when 1,981 people

---

[89] *News Letter*, 3 August 1988.
[90] *Times*, 6 August 1988.
[91] *Times*, 15 August 1988.
[92] Ibid.
[93] *Hansard*, 16 June 1988, 582.

were detained over a period of fifty-two months. The prime minister, Edward Heath, vowed never to use the power again because of the international reaction, 'which was very damaging to us'.[94] Paisley claimed in 1975 that 'detention without trial threw the entire Roman Catholic population into the hands of the IRA'.[95] Conor Cruise O'Brien was a strong advocate of internment: 'Terrorists declare themselves to be in a state of war with the society in which they move. Governments would be well advised to treat that declaration seriously, rather than treating the terrorists as actually members of the society against which they have declared war.'[96] Ken Maginnis, while accepting that the way internment was handled in the 1980s was unfortunate, claimed that intelligence was now far better: 'there are about 400 people who would select themselves.'[97] The prime minister and Tom King rejected the clamour for internment, but worse was to follow.

A Catholic quantity surveyor, Michael Laverty, was shot dead, and a Protestant greengrocer and ex-UVF member, Fred Otley, was killed by the INLA. A parcel bomb was sent to Ken Maginnis, and a young RUC policewoman lost her left foot after an explosion in Lisnaskea. A substantial supply of arms was found in the grounds of the Royal Victoria Hospital in Belfast. In Dublin, seventy mortars packed with semtex were discovered by the Garda.

On Saturday 20 August 1988 soldiers were arriving back at Aldergrove airport after leave. They left in a bus for their barracks in Omagh. Near Ballygawley an explosion blew the bus across the road and into a ditch. Eight soldiers were killed. A local doctor recalled the evening: 'When I got there, there were bodies scattered all over the place. They were lying in ditches, in the fields. There were some hanging out of the buses . . . I went round and sorted out those I could do something for and those that were dead. They all had major head and limb injuries of varying degrees . . . There were only two who were unconscious. One poor fellow had crawled into a cowshed to take cover and died on a bale of straw. We got to him as he just breathed his last. He was only a young fellow.'[98] *The Times* claimed the East Tyrone brigade of the IRA was responsible for the attack. Ken Maginnis said he could name the perpetrators. The prime minister cut short her holiday and flew back to Downing Street. Tom King was put in charge of a security review that involved the chief constable of the RUC, the GOC

---

[94] *Guardian*, 22 May 1988.
[95] *Independent*, 8 August 1988.
[96] *Times*, 3 May 1988.
[97] *News Letter*, 3 August 1988.
[98] *Guardian*, 22 August 1988.

and Archie Hamilton, the armed services minister. Security lapses were blamed again. The *Sunday Times* claimed that 'British intelligence agents provided detailed advance information about the current IRA terrorist campaign which was ignored by members of the security forces in Northern Ireland . . .'[99]

The IRA had killed more British soldiers in the first eight months of 1988 than in any comparable period since 1979. The figure went up to twenty-seven the following day, when naval officer Alan Shields was killed by a car bomb in Belfast. The same day a massive car bomb caused damage to Belfast city centre. It seemed at the time that nothing could stop the IRA; they could strike at anyone, any time, anywhere. A fear that the security authorities could not contain the terror gained momentum. The *News Letter* said, 'Enough is enough, the IRA has thrown down the gauntlet to the Prime Minister. If she fails to respond in a resolute way she will be condemning many more innocent people to slaughter and mutilation.'[100] The *Independent* said that the situation 'demands political leadership by Mrs Thatcher, Mr King and others. They must say that the reason the IRA is going to lose, no matter how long the struggle lasts, is that Northern Ireland is going to remain part of the United Kingdom'.[101] Enoch Powell called for a U-turn from the prime minister: 'only when and if there is undeniable evidence that Britain has at last abandoned its fatal . . . operation of ditching Northern Ireland can there be a respite and a remedy . . . words will have to be eaten.'[102] BBC Northern Ireland postponed the showing of a trio of plays from the province, one of which involved a series of terrorist killings. The BBC said it 'was inappropriate to show the series now'.[103]

Speculation mounted about Tom King's security review. Internment was on the agenda, but most commentators thought it an 'end game' ploy; once it was used there was no other option left. The secretary of state was 'caught between counterproductive repression and unpalatable reform'.[104] Mrs Thatcher said the government was about to tighten up regulations to prevent funds reaching terrorists, as well as setting up an anti-racketeering body. Tom King said that 'the IRA and Sinn Fein are fascist organizations, and if fascism is a political manifestation which must be resisted at all costs, then we have a positive duty to remove its exponents from our midst'.[105] Some commentators read

---

[99] *Sunday Times*, 28 August 1988.
[100] *News Letter*, 22 August 1988.
[101] *Independent*, 22 August 1988.
[102] *Times*, 22 August 1988.
[103] Ibid.
[104] *New Statesman/Society*, 12 August 1988.
[105] *Guardian*, 27 August 1988.

into these words a commitment to reintroduce internment. Others felt they reflected a determination to let the SAS loose on the terrorists.

In the middle of these crises, the London–Belfast leg of the Anglo-Irish triangle seemed to be working overtime. Little was heard of contacts between London and Dublin, or between Dublin and Belfast. The two prime ministers met at an EC Summit and the respective attorney-generals met to review the extradition arrangements. Haughey was under intense pressure from within his own party to abandon the extradition arrangements with Britain.

In the last full week of August, the agreement had its best security boost since Operation Longstop in November of the previous year. Gerard Harte and Robert Russell were extradited from the Republic to Northern Ireland, the first extraditions since 1984. The significance of this was reflected in the ferocity of the subsequent riots in the province. No fewer than 27 shootings, 21 bombings, 88 hijackings, 193 attacks on soldiers, 43 arrests and dozens of hoax bomb calls seriously disrupted life in Northern Ireland over the weekend of 27 and 28 August. The government offered rewards totalling £100,000 for information leading to convictions.

Two days later, three IRA terrorists were shot dead by the SAS on the road between Omagh and Carrickmore. The *Guardian* called the operation an 'army ambush'. The *Star* said: 'SAS rub out IRA rats.' The *Evening Standard* said: 'Serves them right.' The *Daily Mail* said: 'Justice has been done for our boys.' According to an eyewitness, the SAS had plenty of time to arrest the three IRA men, and 'opened fire on the back of the car'.[106] Tom King, in a radio interview, said that according to military sources the 'IRA gang had shot first'.[107] The taoiseach, chairing his first cabinet since the summer recess, called for a full report on the shootings through the Intergovernmental secretariat. His intervention was considered 'unhelpful' by Molyneaux: 'It would have been prudent to wait for the result of the official investigation ... it was a gesture ... which could be interpreted as giving solace to the IRA.'[108] The Labour Party's deputy spokesman on Northern Ireland affairs, Tom Marshall, called for an assurance that the incident would be properly investigated by the RUC and 'that the security forces operated within the rule of law'.[109]

Colonel J. C. Wakerly wrote: 'It is as though there is some misguided sense of British fair play obliging the authorities to ensure even-handedness and balance between the terrorists and the soldiers so that

---

[106] *Irish Times*, 2 September 1988.
[107] *Times*, 5 September 1988.
[108] *Irish Times*, 1 September 1988.
[109] Ibid.

neither side is seen to have an advantage in the game.'[110] John Spicer of Selwyn College, Cambridge, pointed out that the Criminal Law Act of 1967 allows a citizen to use 'such force as is reasonable in the circumstances in the prevention of crime . . . there is no room for pre-planned killings . . . if a soldier shoots a terrorist and he dies . . . the offence is murder'.[111] The secretary of state explained that soldiers, in addition to the rule of law, also operated under rules of engagement: 'If a threat is perceived by a member of the security forces [he] is absolutely entitled to take action to defend himself.'[112] The *Guardian* said that 'the question is simply one of the inescapable responsibilities of owing your allegiance to a democratic state committed to the rule of law and not to a terrorist conspiracy'.[113] Colonel Wakerly argued for a policy that stated that SAS units were in the field and that they would kill terrorists engaged in offensive operations. Revd William McCrea supported the same argument: 'The Government must take the war into the terrorists' den and rid our society of the IRA vermin. To put it bluntly this is the proper type of internment.'[114]

At the Londonderry border post on the road to County Donegal, a bus travelling from Letterkenny in the Republic was found to be carrying twenty-five pounds of semtex and four mortar tubes. At a border crossing in Aachen, West German police stopped a car and found two assault rifles, two revolvers and Gerard Hanratty and Terence McGeough, both of whom had been on the run from the British police since 1982. Another IRA active-service unit was demobilized.

In Derry, Sean Dalton climbed through a window into the flat of a neighbour who had been missing for a few days. Outside on the balcony was another neighbour, Sheila Lewis. Having checked the flat, Dalton opened the front door and triggered a booby-trap bomb. Both good Samaritans died in the explosion. The Derry Brigade of the IRA said that 'the operation was designed to inflict casualties on members of the British Army search squad . . . it went tragically wrong'.[115] Martin McGuinness apologized on behalf of the Republican movement. He defended the armed struggle but said that the IRA 'had a grave responsibility to ensure as much as is humanly possible that civilians are not endangered'.[116] This was a significant statement of policy by a Republican leader who was acutely aware of the morale-sapping effect of such military mistakes on the movement's host community.

The following day the talks between the SDLP and Sinn Fein were

---

[110] *Times*, 5 September 1988.
[111] *Times*, 1 September 1988.
[112] *Times*, 5 September 1988.
[113] *Guardian*, 1 September 1988.
[114] *News Letter*, 31 August 1988.
[115] *Irish Times*, 1 September 1988.
[116] Ibid.

abandoned. The SDLP held that 'violence is wrong ... and has no contribution to make to the resolution of the conflict in Ireland'.[117] John Hume believed that there was a political alternative: 'The British Government has made clear in an internationally binding agreement that if such agreement on the exercise of self-determination took the form of Irish unity, they would in fact endorse it.'[118] For Sinn Fein, the key question was how to get the British government to recognize Irish national rights. The party sought a 'prior declaration of withdrawal by Britain ... Britain would have to relinquish sovereignty over the North first ...'[119] The *Irish Times* welcomed the breakdown in talks between Hume and Adams: 'it must be true to say that the IRA, Sinn Fein and Gerry Adams benefited from the fact that John Hume was prepared to sit down and talk with them. They gained credibility, stature and possibly a degree of self-confidence.'[120] Bob McCartney in the *News Letter* suggested that 'the talks represented an audacious political gamble by Hume, which had it succeeded, would have concentrated in a pan-nationalist front both the United Ireland policy objectives and a measure of control over the political instrument of terror'.[121]

All thirteen Unionist members of parliament met at the OUP headquarters to demand the recall of parliament and the reintroduction of internment. Mary Holland wrote: 'What everybody in Northern Ireland needs desperately just now is some glimmer of hope that political progress may be possible. At the moment the political parties are paralysed and prevented from talking to each other by the violence.'[122]

The next day hundreds of sub-machine-guns were discovered in a barn in Ballynahinch. It was a Loyalist arms cache. The barn's owners had received a £7,000 grant from the government in 1981 to re-equip and re-tool the 'factory'. In Gibraltar the inquest into the shooting of three IRA members by the SAS began. In Brussels, Scotland Yard officials presented extradition papers requesting the handing over of Patrick Ryan. In London the prime minister, Sir Geoffrey Howe, George Younger, Douglas Hurd, Sir Patrick Mayhew and Tom King held a meeting to discuss the government's Irish policy. In Dublin, Charles Haughey let it be known that at the next Intergovernmental Conference Ireland would be seeking assurances 'that Britain has not adopted a security-only policy in Northern Ireland'.[123]

The worst terror campaign since 1979 was over.

---

[117] *Times*, 6 September 1988.
[118] *Irish Times*, 12 September 1988.
[119] Ibid.
[120] Ibid.
[121] *News Letter*, 9 September 1988.
[122] *Irish Times*, 31 August 1988.
[123] *Times*, 7 September 1988.

8

Languishing in a dispirited state?

By early September 1988, the Anglo-Irish Agreement had three months left to run. Would either partner, or both, decide to abandon a brave but fruitless effort, or would they agree that, since the accord had withstood the strains and stresses of the first three years, it could survive anything?

Advice was not lacking. *The Times* suggested that Mrs Thatcher should consider ways of involving the Unionists and other local politicians in the workings of the Intergovernmental Conference. It also urged the abandonment of administration by Orders in Council and the setting up of a Northern Ireland Grand Committee. The prime minister was encouraged to take the initiative, since *The Times* concluded that the taoiseach was 'not prepared to educate public opinion in Ireland ... [he] was sufficiently ambivalent ... to be undermining the co-operation which the [agreement] has brought about'.[1] Paul Wilkinson, professor of international relations at Aberdeen University, advised the prime minister to take the war to the terrorists. For him security was the priority: 'the defeat of the IRA would be the greatest single achievement of Mrs Thatcher's leadership.'[2] Kevin Boyle and Tom Hadden suggested that Northern Ireland be put in a British, Irish and European context. They accepted that the IRA had succeeded in hijacking the Anglo-Irish agenda, because 'the political objective of the Agreement had not been pursued with sufficient vigour'.[3] The *Spectator* criticized the government for using the 'magic letters SAS as substitute for policy ... keeping the province in a state of suspended political animation'.[4] Brian Walden said that 'we are not merely facing a

---

[1] *Times*, 7 September 1988.
[2] *Times*, 2 September 1988.
[3] *Guardian*, 2 September 1988.
[4] *Spectator*, 3 September 1988.

handful of terrorists, but a community which they, in effect, control . . . the bitter truth is that a sizeable portion of the Northern Ireland community is in complicity with the murderers.'[5]

A strong security initiative was expected. The Ballygawley killings were known to concern the prime minister deeply and she was angry with the security authorities in the province for being so lax as to allow such an atrocity to happen. She was also tired of waiting for the Unionists and the SDLP to sort themselves out. The *Spectator* gave an inkling of her frame of mind when it said that 'the demands of the terrorists are so unlikely to be fulfilled that they are only a pretext and opportunity for self-dramatisation . . . it is naive, as well as cowardly to suppose therefore, that the level of violence can be reduced by the righting of some wrong.'[6]

It was decided at the Downing Street meeting of 6 September 1988 that the Anglo-Irish Agreement was to remain. The policy implications of that decision and of the security review were to become apparent before the third anniversary of the signing of the agreement, on 15 November 1988.

In the Republic the taoiseach was under some pressure from his own party over extradition and from the opposition over his lack of enthusiasm for devolution for Northern Ireland. Opinion polls, however, gave him an eleven-point lead. Haughey met Hume soon after the breakdown of the SDLP–Sinn Fein talks about talks. There was nothing new to report about relations between Dublin and the Unionists. Both initiatives had failed. Molyneaux was being outflanked by Paisley, and Adams was not in total control of the Republican movement. Haughey, who was not in the best of health, was conscious of the need to regain the initiative. Mary Holland encouraged him to think that 'there is a chance here . . . to take the Agreement which had languished in a dispirited state recently and to breathe new life into it. By doing so [Haughey] will make it his own.'[7] *The Times* suggested that the Irish were likely to try and reinstate unemployment, cross-border economic aid, social co-operation and fair employment on the Anglo-Irish agenda. Haughey and Hume resumed their call for a direct exchange of views with leaders of the Unionist community.

In the North, Sir John Hermon warned of the danger of another winter offensive by the IRA. Belfast city centre was surrounded by army road blocks on 9 September 1988, following intelligence that a wave of attacks was planned to coincide with the opening of the Gibraltar inquest. In County Tyrone, a 1,000 lb bomb blew up a police

---

[5] *Sunday Times*, 28 August 1988.
[6] *Spectator*, 20 August 1988.
[7] *Irish Times*, 14 September 1988.

station, injuring twelve people. Colin Abernethy, a leading member of the Ulster Clubs, was assassinated on a commuter train into Belfast. A bomb placed in a taxi exploded near the city centre in Belfast and eight shoppers were injured. In Crawfordsburn, the home of the most senior civil servant in the province was demolished by a bomb. Sir Kenneth Bloomfield, his wife and his teenage son had a 'miraculous' escape. The IRA claimed that Sir Kenneth was the 'key administrator of British colonial policy in the North'.[8] The Republican movement also warned all civil servants to 'resign their posts or face the consequences'.[9] In Derry, the security services discovered 'one of the most deadly arsenals ever found in the city'.[10] In Rossmore, the Garda discovered an IRA training area, recently used for the testing of heavy anti-aircraft machine-guns and Kalashnikov rifles.

A routine Intergovernmental Conference took place in Dublin on Tuesday 13 September. The communiqué gave no clue to the real substance of the discussions, but the following day Lenihan met Home Secretary Hurd in London. They discussed the Guildford Four, the Birmingham Six and internment. The Irish let it be known that 'internment was not on'.[11] Tom King said that he was conscious of a real political will in Dublin to fight terrorism.

In the province itself, the state of the local economy was dominating the political agenda. The Northern Ireland Appropriation debate in late June 1988 indicated the scale of funding for the province. After only six months, £3,618 million of the planned total of £4,564 million for 1988–9 was already committed. This did not include the expenditure on law and order; when that was added, the total for the year reached £5,144 million. The other most substantial budgets were for education (£803 million), housing (£552 million), social security (£825 million), health (£625 million), agriculture (£127 million), industry (£308 million) and roads (£126 million). Unemployment, at 17 per cent, was nearly double the national average. It was the government's decision to extend its privatization plans to the province that provided the first rallying-point in three years for an all-party consensus in Northern Ireland. As Tom King said, most local politicians 'equated privatization with liquidation'.[12] Roy Beggs, MP for East Antrim, saw the plans as 'a phased British economic withdrawal from Northern Ireland'.[13]

Northern Ireland Electricity generated and distributed power in the province. Three of the existing power stations were oil-fired, although

---

[8] *Times*, 13 September 1989.
[9] Ibid.
[10] *Times*, 14 September 1988.
[11] Ibid.
[12] *Hansard*, 28 July 1988, 622.
[13] *Hansard*, 21 July 1988, 1315.

Kilroot 1 was being converted to dual capability. Kilroot 2 was to be completed at a cost of £160 million before privatization in the 1990s. Exciting projects to burn lignite, a source of energy a geological step away from peat, were delayed until after privatization. The privately funded Antrim Power Company had plans and financial backing for a £450 million project to exploit lignite reserves discovered at Crumlin.

The government was known to be concerned at the scale of public subsidies to the Harland and Wolff yard, which totalled £240 million over five years and represented a third of all support given to industry in the province. Peter Viggers, the under-secretary of state for industry at the Northern Ireland Office, declared that 'were there to be an expression of interest in the privatization of the yard, the Government would take any such proposals very seriously'.[14] Short Brothers were also running at a loss. A subsidy of £20 million was provided in 1986–7 and increased to £37 million a year later; an unknown bill awaited the Northern Ireland Office in 1988. Between them, Harland and Wolff and Short Brothers employed about 11,000 workers, mostly Protestants from the Unionist heartland of East Belfast. If both were to be privatized, the government would have to write off accumulated joint losses of near a billion pounds and provide equity of more than £200 million pounds.

In the parliamentary debate, Tom Marshall, deputy opposition spokesman on Northern Ireland, said that 'Shorts and Harland and Wolff are regarded in the Province as symbols of the Government's continued commitment to the economic and industrial infrastructure in the North of Ireland'.[15] Seamus Mallon reflected the cross-party opposition to the privatization plans when he referred to the decision made to 'sacrifice jobs on the altar of Tory ideology'.[16] In August, Harland and Wolff announced that a further 550 jobs were to go, bringing the total workforce at the yard down to 3,250. Short Brothers employed 7,000.

On 28 July 1988 James Molyneaux initiated a debate on the Northern Ireland economy. He said that he and his Unionist colleagues had no particular 'hang-ups in the arguments over the merits of privatization . . . [but] a geographically isolated shipyard and aircraft factory . . . in Belfast . . . provide the main industrial base. The stark fact is that there is no substitute or replacement to be found for either or both in Northern Ireland.'[17] John Hume supported Molyneaux: 'this is one issue on which we are entirely agreed. I therefore ask the

---

[14] *Independent*, 28 May 1988.
[15] *Hansard*, 21 July 1988, 1313.
[16] Ibid., 1317.
[17] *Hansard*, 28 July 1988, 611.

Government to encourage such agreement by rewarding it.'[18] The secretary of state, Tom King, argued against the tone of the debate which he described as 'appallingly depressing'. King recalled his commitment to reduce unemployment in the province: 'unemployment has fallen by 20,000 since its high point in September 1986 . . . people do not moan about the disadvantages they face. They are succeeding and earning a world-wide reputation because of their hard work, determination and skill.'[19]

In West Belfast, a £10 million aid package was announced by Northern Ireland Office minister Richard Needham. This indicated the government's serious intention to help alleviate problems in a socially deprived area of high unemployment. The SDLP called it 'a first step – a small but significant start'.[20] Gerry Adams said it was a 'limited investment programme – clearly insufficient'.[21] Sinn Fein community groups lost out on this new venture, since the Northern Ireland Office looked to the Catholic Church to administer the aid package. The church became the biggest private employer in West Belfast. Additional monies for West Belfast and other deprived areas came from the International Fund for Ireland. By the end of the summer of 1988, a total of £14.2 million in grants and loans had been invested.

Another issue at the heart of the socio-economic debate in the province at this time was the fair employment proposals. A television campaign concentrated on indirect discrimination, following the publication of the White Paper on fair employment. New legislation was promised for the following year. Some commentators doubted the government's commitment to fair employment, given that consultation had started two years earlier in 1986. They compared the rate of change with that of Kenneth Baker's educational reforms, which were completed within three months. The most serious pressure on the government on this particular issue came from the MacBride proposals in the United States. The campaign in Washington was led by the Irish National Council and an increasing number of state legislatures adopted the guidelines suggested by MacBride. The British government opposed what they called the 'reverse discrimination' elements of the proposals, and rejected the idea of setting 'quotas' for the employment of minority groups. The campaign led to the introduction of two far-reaching proposals in Congress. The first, proposed by the Friends of Ireland, sought to impose sanctions on US companies not offering equality of opportunity in Northern Ireland. The second,

---

[18] Ibid., 612.
[19] Ibid., 620.
[20] *News Letter*, 20 July 1988.
[21] *Irish Times*, 20 July 1988.

proposed by Congressman Joe Kennedy, aimed at preventing the US Defence Department from giving contracts to companies in Northern Ireland where inequality of opportunity obtained. Both proposals had serious implications for Short Brothers and Harland and Wolff.

For the Unionist community, the double squeeze of privatization and the US contracts embargo added to their sense of isolation. Talk of independence again surfaced at a DUP conference, where it was agreed to establish an inquiry into constitutional alternatives 'now that Britain was pursuing a policy of political and economic withdrawal'.[22] Paisley called for 'a security and constitutional U-turn by Mrs Thatcher' and urged Haughey to 'back away from the Anglo-Irish deal . . . if they refused to budge . . . Ulster would go it alone . . . independence'.[23] However, the DUP leader kept the door ajar for further dialogue. Paisley had originally advertised his conference address as 'the most important of his political life'; he was expected to slam the door on dialogue with Dublin and London. Under pressure from Molyneaux, he amended the script and kept his options open. In regard to Dublin–Belfast talks, Paisley said: 'Mr Haughey must take the first step . . . give up your aggression, stop claiming what you cannot get, cease giving sanctuary, aid and encouragement or anything else to the IRA.'[24]

This restrained attack reflected a Unionist wish to keep dialogue alive on all fronts. Conor Cruise O'Brien had advised the Unionists to 'cease to make a fuss about the Agreement, [which] will lose much of the charm which it at present possesses in nationalist eyes'.[25] Enoch Powell also supported playing for time, although the arch-integrationist was confident that the Anglo-Irish Agreement would be allowed to wither and die. In the mean time he advised Unionists to 'accept nothing of any kind, no arrangement, no initiative, no agreement'.[26]

Integration – what Powell called 'the ark of your salvation, and the badge of your undying determination'[27] – was taking practical form in the province with the North Down Conservative Association's application for affiliation to the National Union of Conservative Constituency Associations. What Robert McCartney called an 'attempt to bring the people of Northern Ireland into non-sectarian national politics'[28] was not welcomed by Tom King. In a debate on the Northern Ireland Act of 1974 he made his position clear; he supported

---

[22] *News Letter*, 19 September 1988.
[23] *Irish Times*, 19 September 1988.
[24] Ibid.
[25] *News Letter*, 24 June 1988.
[26] *News Letter*, 27 June 1988.
[27] Ibid.
[28] *Times*, 28 May 1988.

devolution, not integration. His reasons for promoting devolution were threefold: 'elected representatives of the province lack adequate opportunity to participate in and take responsibility for discussions about the future of Northern Ireland ... devolution is the form of government most likely to command widespread acceptance and support in the community ... sectarianism must be rooted out of the Province.'[29]

Kevin McNamara, the opposition front-bench spokesman, regretted that, after fourteen years, direct rule remained 'the only type of government which is tolerable for most in both traditions; it is the highest common factor form of government'.[30] The Labour Party also supported devolution.

Sir John Biggs Davison, a leading member of the Friends of the Union, supported integration: 'I am disturbed, dismayed and distressed by the insistence ... on devolved government as distinct from devolved administration ... I wish that Her Majesty's Government would not persist in policies and aims that distance Northern Ireland from the rest of the United Kingdom.'[31] Molyneaux, in a conciliatory speech, noted the 'valuable reassurances' given by McNamara that there would be no political or military withdrawal from Northern Ireland and that the people of Northern Ireland would never be thrust out of the UK against their wishes. He argued that the 'monstrous combination of the Order in Council system and the Anglo-Irish Agreement will continue to strangle all democratic development. Either of these monstrosities makes progress and good government impossible.'[32] Both had contributed to the feeling that Northern Ireland was a place apart, kept separate from the rest of the UK. Molyneaux concluded on a positive note. He and Paisley were 'prepared to assist, to make our contribution to the design of a much wider, more workable and more practical agreement'.[33]

Peter Robinson pressed the government for an indication that it was 'willing to consider an alternative to the Anglo-Irish Agreement'.[34] Seamus Mallon responded to Robinson's invitation to talks, once the Sinn Fein discussions were out of the way, by appealing to Unionists to join with Nationalists to 'show the Government that we have two feet on which to stand, heads on our shoulders with which to think and certain political skills. We do not have to live with the condescension that we

---

[29] *Hansard*, 29 June 1988, 411.
[30] Ibid., 413.
[31] Ibid., 421.
[32] Ibid., 425.
[33] Ibid., 426.
[34] Ibid., 455.

often see in political life.'[35] The tone of the debate was positive and conciliatory.

The next major political development was the publication of the Labour Party policy document on Northern Ireland. The fruit of an intensive review of party policy, it stated that 'no group or party will be allowed to exercise a veto on policies designed to win consent for unification ... we do not believe that it is reasonable or adequate to await passively the dawning of consent ... Labour is committed to working actively to build that consent'.[36] A dual strategy was unveiled, which included a reform of the political, economic and social institutions in the province and a harmonization of institutions, policies and practices between both parts of Ireland. Political reforms would include an immediate review of the government of Northern Ireland, leading to a devolved government and including a power-sharing executive; the incoming Labour administration would enter into talks with the executive, once it had majority support, about possible revisions of the Anglo-Irish Agreement. An effective security policy would remain a necessity for some time to come. There would be a review of the rules governing the permissible use of lethal force by the security services, and plastic bullets would be banned. The Prevention of Terrorism Act and the Northern Ireland Emergency Provisions Act would be repealed and legislation would end supergrass trials and strip-searching and replace the Diplock courts. Consideration would also be given to the creation of an all-Ireland structure for the RUC and the Garda, but without infringing their operational autonomy. Employment targets would be set to reduce, over a five-year period, inequalities between Protestants and Catholics. Additional funding would be provided for the establishment of more integrated schools. A Bill of Rights would be considered. An all-Ireland economic and social policy would be concentrated on energy, transport, social services, agriculture and possibly a common currency. There would be, nevertheless, a commitment to maintain financial support for Ulster for an indefinite period after British withdrawal.

Peter Robinson accused Labour of seeking to 'erode the Britishness of Ulster and push the province towards Dublin rule'.[37] John Hume said 'it was the first time any British Labour Party had set out in detail its strategy for dealing with the problems of Ireland'.[38] Charles Haughey called the document 'timely and constructive'. Dick Spring welcomed the 'commitment to work actively to create consent for

---

[35] Ibid., 458.
[36] *Times*, 22 September 1988.
[37] Ibid.
[38] *News Letter*, 22 September 1988.

unification'.[39] *The Times* called the policy 'a cautious development of Labour policy on Ulster, which repeats calls from the Labour left for speedy British withdrawal'.[40] The *Independent* labelled the document a 'mistake . . . based on a false premise. It describes at length the means by which the objective is to be pursued. It fails, however, to demonstrate that the objective is attainable . . . Informal observers are overwhelmingly of the opinion that Ireland cannot in the foreseeable future be unified by consent. If the Labour party disagrees with that assessment, it must give its reasons.'[41] The *Independent* leader also thought that the new Labour policy gave comfort and encouragement to the IRA, 'which thrives on every indication that Britain would like to leave'.[42] The *Financial Times* concentrated on the importance the document gave to economic, political and social reforms, which would 'eradicate the material and political basis for sectarianism'.[43]

Nearly three years into the life of the Anglo-Irish Agreement, a coherent Labour Party policy was finally available. Kevin McNamara's policies had an unmistakably 'green' tinge. The document was proof that the newly formed opposition team on Northern Ireland was committed to using the Anglo-Irish Agreement as a springboard to Irish unification.

In the June 1988 debate on Northern Ireland, Molyneaux had put considerable emphasis on the Labour Party's commitment not to withdraw from the province and the promise 'that the people of Northern Ireland will never be thrust out of the United Kingdom against their wishes'.[44] By the autumn, this interpretation seemed somewhat optimistic. The Conservatives had called the Unionists' bluff, and the opposition was prepared to capitalize on Unionist weakness and 'engineer' a majority consent for unification. It was not surprising that the Unionists felt under siege.

In Northern Ireland, the Unionists, the SDLP and the Alliance Party all backed devolution. Tom King said that it was now 'urgent for Ulster's constitutional parties to start talking on arrangements for government within the Province'.[45] He added that 'there will be no British withdrawal, political or economic from the Province'.[46] The following day the prime minister visited Northern Ireland. She had a private meeting with Sir Kenneth Bloomfield; the security review

---

[39] *Irish Times*, 22 September 1988.
[40] *Times*, 22 September 1988.
[41] *Independent*, 22 September 1988.
[42] Ibid.
[43] *Financial Times*, 22 September 1988.
[44] *Hansard*, 29 June 1988, 422.
[45] *News Letter*, 27 September 1988.
[46] *Irish News*, 27 September 1988.

following the Ballygawley bombing was nearing its completion and Mrs Thatcher wished to hear the views of the Northern Ireland Office's top civil servant. Sir Kenneth told her of a recent broadcast in which a member of Sinn Fein attempted to explain why the IRA had targeted Bloomfield and his family. Sir Kenneth was reported to be deeply upset at seeing Republican sympathizers attempting to explain away an attempt on his life. A ban on broadcasts by Sinn Fein and other paramilitary groups, considered a 'possible' option in the security review, now become a 'certainty'. Three weeks later the home secretary announced the ban in the House of Commons.

During her visit to Ulster, Mrs Thatcher reiterated her 'determination to rid the province of the cancer of terrorism'.[47] The same day, in Strabane, a home-made bomb, a rocket launcher and two warheads were discovered. A few days earlier a part-time UDR soldier, Stephen McKinney, was shot dead outside his parents' home on the day before he was to leave the province for a university education in England. In West Belfast, Martin Gerard Slone was shot in his home by a UVF hit team. The home secretary, in a speech to the Police Superintendents' Association, announced that legislation would be introduced in the next session of parliament which would make the handling of money for terrorist organizations an offence. The new law would form part of the Prevention of Terrorism Act.

The Northern Ireland director of public prosecutions, Sir Barry Shaw, announced towards the end of September that Private David Holden would not be charged following the death of Aidan McAnespie at a border crossing. Holden had originally been charged with manslaughter, but the DPP ruled that there was no case to answer. McAnespie's family would be entitled to compensation. Shaw also revealed that the parents of the unarmed civilian shot dead by Private Ian Thain in August 1983 had received substantial damages in an out-of-court settlement. Both announcements caused 'surprise and deep concern'[48] in Dublin. The Irish had set up their own inquiry into McAnespie's death and had confirmed the RUC's interpretation of the shooting – that McAnespie had been killed by a ricochet of bullets – but the Dublin government had not expected Holden to be freed to rejoin his unit.

In Gibraltar, the inquest jury into the SAS shooting of the IRA unit of McCann, Farrell and Savage decided by nine votes to two that there was insufficient evidence to support a charge of conspiracy to murder. The killings were lawful. *The Times* commented that the 'inquest has dealt terrorism a blow more subtle but more significant even than the

---

[47] *Times*, 29 September 1988.
[48] *Irish Times*, 27 September 1988.

success of the initial military operation'.[49] The *Irish Times* said 'the families of the three will have little to complain of as regards the proceedings . . . the conduct of the coroner was exemplary'.[50]

The inquest heard that the original intention had been to arrest the three terrorists, but that a police siren had triggered a reaction from them that led to their deaths. Intelligence officers had wrongly assumed that the terrorists would be armed, and that their intention was to detonate a bomb by remote control. The police in Gibraltar had handed over responsibility for the control of the operation to the SAS, and had agreed on a procedure for the arrests using minimum force. Twenty-eight bullet casings were recovered after the three shootings. McCann was shot twice in the head and twice in the back, Farrell had five bullets in her face and neck and three in her back and Savage was shot a total of eighteen times. Professor Alan Watson, a pathologist, called Savage's death 'a frenzied attack'.[51]

Public interest immunity certificates (PIIs) were issued by the minister of defence and the home secretary to restrict cross-examination of the SAS unit to the actual shooting. Questions on security policy were forbidden. The Spanish authorities refused to co-operate with the coroner, because Spain and Britain were in dispute over the sovereignty of Gibraltar. The issue of how much warning the SAS unit had about the movements of the IRA unit before they crossed into the colony was therefore not pursued at the inquest.

After the first week's hearing, indications started emerging in British newspapers of the line of defence likely to be put forward by the SAS men. *The Times* reported that the SAS commander 'will describe how the shooting incident lasted just a few seconds . . . after last week's grim description . . . of the frenzied attacks . . . the SAS version is expected to paint a different picture'.[52]

Patrick McGrary, representing the families of the three dead IRA terrorists, said that unleashing the SAS on the Irish trio was 'like signing their death warrant . . . the unholy high priesthood of violence charged with dangerous and brutal duties in the cause of the state'.[53] Soldier A said in evidence that he thought McCann and Farrell were about to detonate a bomb. Soldier E said Savage was killed because 'he swung around in a crouching stance and put one hand to his hips when challenged'.[54]

On the fourteenth day of the inquest, Ken Asquez retracted a

[49] *Times*, 1 October 1988.
[50] *Irish Times*, 1 October 1988.
[51] *Times*, 9 September 1988.
[52] *Times*, 12 September 1988.
[53] *Times*, 13 September 1988.
[54] *Guardian*, 14 September 1988.

statement he had made to a solicitor soon after the shooting. This evidence, which dealt with the circumstances of Savage's death, had been used in Thames Television's programme *Death on the Rock*. At the inquest Asquez claimed that he had been pressured into giving an untrue account of what he had seen by an intermediary acting for the television team. Thames Television, after discussions with the IBA, decided upon a full inquiry. Asquez's retraction immediately reopened the debate concerning the coverage of the initial shootings in Gibraltar and in particular the programmes *Death on the Rock* and *Spotlight on Gibraltar*.

Charles Moore, in a contribution to the *Spectator* published before the inquest, had encouraged the press to 'go on harassing the Government on the subject. Given the nature of the IRA, it is not, perhaps wrong that British troops should shoot their people in cold blood, but it is shocking that the Government can expect this to be done with no questions asked.'[55] The Asquez retraction led the *Sunday Telegraph* to call on the IBA to revoke Thames Television's franchise; others called for the IBA itself to be abolished. The *Independent* argued that a 'free press is . . . one of the most powerful bulwarks . . . against the arbitrary exercise of power . . . in the fight against terrorism'.[56] The voluntary code of practice that the broadcasting organizations applied to all coverage of Northern Ireland affairs was clearly not stringent enough for the government or for a significant section of the press. A legally enforceable ban now became a distinct possibility.

The new parliamentary session was three weeks away and the party conference season was in full swing. Northern Ireland was not on the agenda of either the Labour or the Conservative conference. The prime minister did however make a forceful speech, during which she thanked those defending democracy against the IRA 'for facing danger while keeping within the law . . . We will not bargain, nor compromise, nor bend the knee to terrorism . . . this Government will never surrender to the IRA. Never.'[57] The prime minister received a nine-minute standing ovation at the end of her conference speech. Security was still the dominant issue of Anglo-Irish affairs. Her Irish partner, Charles Haughey, watched the conference speech from his hospital bed. Despite his illness, he was still firmly in control of the political scene in the Republic. The *Irish Times* – MRBI poll for October 1988 gave him a personal following of 54 per cent, and Fianna Fáil's support was rock steady, with a 24 per cent lead over its nearest rival, Fine Gael.

However, extradition was still a worrying issue. Grass-roots

[55] *Spectator*, 9 July 1988.
[56] *Independent*, 27 September 1988.
[57] *Times*, 15 October 1988.

opposition was hardening, and Haughey had to cope with political realities for which his Hillsborough partner might show little understanding or sympathy. The same *Irish Times* – MRBI poll showed that 44 per cent opposed extradition (up 1 per cent since November 1987) while only 31 per cent approved (down 9 per cent since November 1987).

In the North, attempts at starting all-party discussions on devolution were in trouble following a Radio Ulster interview by Tom King, who had alleged that the Unionists had not made proposals for political development in the North. Molyneaux reacted by calling the secretary of state's comments 'a damn cheek' and promptly refused an offer to discuss devolution with King. The OUP leader's reaction had more to do with the realities of Unionist politics than with indignation at King's words. After the long summer recess, there was no coherent Unionist policy and Molyneaux and Paisley were determined not to be lured into any position that might indicate they were playing a role in the review of the Anglo-Irish Agreement. Having expressed opposition to the accord throughout, they now expected the agreement to be modified, amended or even suspended to accommodate their views. An opinion poll, commissioned by the *Belfast Telegraph* and co-directed by Coopers and Lybrand, indicated that they were not alone in their expectations; of the 1,100 respondents, 37 per cent thought that the agreement would remain unchanged, 26 per cent that it would be wound up and 24 per cent that it would be changed to meet the demands of its opponents. More detailed questions revealed little enthusiasm for the agreement. Seventy per cent of Catholics and 86 per cent of Protestants thought that it had not improved security; 56 per cent of Catholics and 76 per cent of Protestants thought that it had failed to improve the administration of justice; 64 per cent of Catholics thought that it had not improved the position of the minority community. The *Belfast Telegraph* commented: 'clearly there is little encouragement in these figures for anyone to believe that an early accommodation is possible.'[58]

While 67 per cent of all respondents agreed in principle with power-sharing between the constitutional parties, the poll revealed serious differences both between Nationalists and Unionists and within the Unionist pact. Forty-six per cent of all Protestants wanted integration, while 35 per cent of all Catholics supported devolved power-sharing; 22 per cent of all Catholics supported a united Ireland, while only 1 per cent of Protestants did so. Among the Unionists questioned, only 18 per cent supported devolved power-sharing, while 13 per cent were in favour of devolved majority rule. The government's declared political objective had little grass-roots support in the province.

---

[58] *Belfast Telegraph*, 4 October 1988.

The twentieth anniversary of the first civil rights march in Derry on 5 October 1968 was commemorated by parades in the north-west of the province. Gerry Adams and Martin McGuinness walked a route agreed by the RUC. Ian Paisley and Gregory Campbell were stopped from walking the same route; given permission to follow the Adams trail three hours later, they refused the offer, which they interpreted as a ban. Most press comments on the anniversary concluded that the province had moved on a great deal from the days of the first march twenty years earlier: 'the emotions which brought thousands on to the streets have now been tempered by exhaustion ... the principal demands of the civil rights marchers have been met, while the nationalist claim to a united Ireland has not.'[59]

In Belfast, the INLA shot dead Henry McNamee, thought to be an RUC informer. In Derry, a huge arms find in the Creggan estate led to a public row between local SDLP and Sinn Fein councillors regarding the IRA's use of housing estates as arsenals and cover for their activities. RUC officer McCrone was shot dead in Lisburn and Norman McKeowan was killed for working for the security authorities. The UDA put a contract out on one of its former leading gangsters, Jim Craig, who was shot dead by a UVF gang in East Belfast. Victor Rainey also died in the attack. Craig was rumoured to be receiving payments from seventy-two different firms and had been a prime target of the RUC'S anti-racketeering squad. In the same week Colin Hunter's headless corpse was found in a rubbish tip. He had earlier refused to pay protection money.

In Strasburg, Ian Paisley was evicted from the European parliament after shouting at the Pope and unfurling a banner that said, 'John Paul II – Anti-Christ'. The DUP leader said, 'I'd be failing the people who voted for me, if I didn't put forward my views forthrightly and uncompromisingly.'[60] In Letterkenny in County Donegal James Clarke, an escapee from the Maze prison, was ordered to be extradited to Northern Ireland. In Dundalk Patrick McVeigh was detained by the RUC before being released again pending the original appeal on his extradition case. In the West Country, the trial opened of three Irish people accused of conspiring to kill Tom King. At a fringe meeting at the Brighton Conservative Party conference, Enoch Powell said that 'Mrs Thatcher was personally responsible for the nightmare of murder and destruction'[61] and he accused her of a latent but deliberate attempt to disengage from Northern Ireland. At the Conservative conference Peter Brooke, the party chairman, promised to treat seriously an

[59] *Times*, 5 October 1988.
[60] *Times*, 12 October 1988.
[61] *Irish Times*, 13 October 1988.

application for affiliation from the North Down Conservative Association. Integration was slowly but surely making headway.

In the province, integration in education had a major boost with Brian Mawhinney's announcement that the Department of Education in Northern Ireland was to have statutory responsibility for promoting and funding integrated schools. A Coopers and Lybrand poll in April 1988 had indicated widespread support, particularly in Belfast, where three out of every four adults questioned were committed to integrated schools. Lagan College, the first such school in the province, was opened in September 1981, a further secondary school and two primary schools in 1985, a further primary in 1986 and two more in 1987. The *Guardian* called the move 'the most radical reform in educational policies in forty years'.[62] A marriage of Catholic, Gaelic and Nationalist culture with that of a Protestant, British and Unionist tradition had profound implications for curriculum development in the province. It was a revolution in educational circles and was strongly opposed by the Roman Catholic hierarchy, the Presbyterian Church and some elements of the Church of Ireland. The old eleven-plus examination, which had been declared by a High Court ruling earlier in the summer to discriminate unlawfully against girls, was to be replaced. The Irish language was to be given the same status as Welsh had in the schools of Wales. Northern Ireland Office records indicated that about 20,000 school pupils studied Irish, with approximately 2,000 taking O or A levels in the language in 1987. Many thought that the integrated schools initiative was likely to do more in the long run to break down the barrier of cultural segregation than any other single government decision during the first three years of the Anglo-Irish Agreement.

In Downing Street the prime minister, Tom King and Douglas Hurd met to review the progress of the security review intitiated after the Lisburn and Ballygawley attacks. They also decided to send yet another invitation to discussions on devolution to the leaders of the political parties in the province.

Two days later, the home secretary announced that direct statements by representatives of eleven organizations were to be banned on radio and television. The ban applied to the IRA, the INLA, Sinn Fein, the UDA, the UVF, the UFF, the Red Hand Commandos, Cumann Na Mban, Na Fianna Éireann and Saor Éire. Apart from Sinn Fein and the UDA, all these organizations were proscribed and illegal. The new ban did not proscribe Sinn Fein and the UDA but denied them direct access to the airwaves, since, according to the home secretary, their 'appearances have caused widespread offence to viewers and listeners, particularly just after a terrorist outrage . . . the time has come to deny

---

[62] *Guardian*, 6 October 1988.

this easy platform to those who use it to propagate terrorism'.[63] Hurd claimed the ban was not a restriction on reporting terrorist events: 'this is not censorship ... we are putting broadcasters on the same basis as representatives of the written press.'[64] He confirmed that the option had been carefully considered over a period of nearly a year.

Roy Hattersley suggested that the ban was likely to have an adverse reaction abroad, with the government portrayed as the enemy of free expression. Seamus Mallon suggested that government was doing exactly what the gangsters in the UDA and the IRA wanted. Other members of parliament welcomed the ban, one suggesting that the government go one step further and proscribe Sinn Fein, another complaining that such a move should have been made a long time ago. Some MPs blamed the broadcasters, a point developed by Michael Mates, the member for Hampshire East: 'Is it not because the media have collectively declined the opportunity that has been there to put their house in order in this matter that the Government have had to act?'[65] The home secretary defended both the broadcasters and his new ban: 'the broadcasters have had a whole series of individually difficult decisions to take ... it is more clear and straightforward for them to operate under a notice of this sort.'[66]

The BBC's chairman called the ban a 'damaging precedent'[67] and ITN's David Nicholas said the distinction between broadcasters and newspapers was not justified. The NUJ compared the ban to South Africa's press-gagging. The prime minister said that 'to beat off your enemy in a war you have to suspend some of your civil liberties for a time'.[68] This reference to a 'war' echoed the words of Archbishop Eames a week earlier, when he said: 'I think Northern Ireland has to be geared for a war situation ... every possible avenue has to be investigated to gear us for a situation in which we can defeat terrorism.'[69] The archbishop supported the broadcasting ban. A *Reader's Digest* poll of 2,000 of its readers in the United Kingdom revealed that 70 per cent felt that terrorist organizations should not be allowed to express their views on television. Seventy per cent also felt that televised violence affected behaviour, while 66 per cent thought that reporting their activities improved terrorists' status. This was a line of argument long pursued by Conor Cruise O'Brien, who had been one of the Irish ministers responsible for introducing the Section 31 ban on

---

[63] *Hansard*, 19 October 1988, 893.
[64] Ibid., 898.
[65] Ibid., 895.
[66] Ibid., 895.
[67] *Times*, 20 October 1988.
[68] *Times*, 26 October 1988.
[69] *News Letter*, 22 October 1988.

such broadcasts in the Republic: 'the IRA values access to broadcasting, not so much to convey specific propaganda messages ... but for the general purposes of morale, status and perceived legitimacy.'[70] Paul Johnson was another who argued that media references to 'active service units, senior IRA commanders, members of the "general staff" are particularly useful to the IRA in sustaining its self-image as an army fighting a patriotic war, instead of what it is, a criminal organization'.[71]

Other columnists took a different view. Fergus Pyle claimed the 'excuse was politics, but the target was broadcasters'.[72] Hugo Young argued that the principal victims of the ban were the people 'who watch ... in the hope of enlightenment ... nobody has yet managed to dislodge the argument that true reporting is actually the best ally of the free society ... to censor the IRA ... is to exclude from view not the irresistible glamour, but the self-convicting brutality which the terrorist unfailingly conveys'.[73] Roy Hattersley said that 'widespread offence is not an adequate excuse for censorship in a free society'.[74] The president of NBC News said on British television that Britain was now the only western democracy with broadcasting censorship.

The Labour Party divided the House at the end of the debate, indicating yet again a widening of the gulf between government and opposition at Westminster. The broadcasters got on with trying to interpret the Home Office guidelines. Brian Sedgemore called on the broadcasting organizations to force the government ban into the courts, while the BBC's controller in Northern Ireland, Dr Colin Morris, said impartial broadcasting in the province was now illegal, 'since we are now required to discriminate between perfectly constitutional parties and duly elected representatives of the people'.[75] The NUJ cancelled a one-day strike call after consultations with the BBC and ITN, while the broadcasting organizations confirmed that they would alert viewers to the restrictions where they thought it likely that the way a particular news item was reported would be affected. Paul Corrigan, the Sinn Fein leader on Fermanagh Council, refused to be interviewed on Radio Ulster 'because it would not be used',[76] even though the transcript of the interview would be read out on the air. The Unionists welcomed the ban and Stan Gebler Davies, writing from Cork, rejoiced that Gerry Adams would no longer be seen in the Republic.[77]

---

[70] *Times*, 6 April 1988.
[71] *Spectator*, 8 October 1988.
[72] *Irish Times*, 22 October 1988.
[73] *Times*, 3 November 1988.
[74] *Hansard*, 2 November 1988, 1073.
[75] *Independent*, 17 November 1988.
[76] *Guardian*, 11 November 1988.
[77] *Independent*, 23 August 1988.

The day following the broadcasting ban, a suspect's right to silence was withdrawn in Northern Ireland. In a written reply the home secretary said that 'the gross determination and persistent abuse of that right to silence and the training in procedures to avoid it, does pose a challenge to the whole system of justice'.[78] The campaign to amend the seventeenth-century provision which gave suspects the right to remain silent and not offer themselves for cross-examination, thus putting the onus on the prosecution to prove their case, succeeded after pressure from the Association of Chief Constables, the Northern Ireland Police Federation, the lord chief justice, and the prime minister. The home secretary had disclosed on *Panorama* on 10 October 1988 that a 'body of experts from his department was considering the extent to which it would now be proper to allow courts to take into account the fact that someone has been dumb, has not spoken or has spun a yarn'.[79] The accused could still remain silent, but the court could be invited by the prosecution to wonder why. *The Times* commented that 'the Government has seen fit to shift the balance in favour of the rights of society at large'.[80]

Kevin McNamara's comment on the Home Office announcement was to say that 'the province was being used as a laboratory for draconian measures'.[81] The *Independent* regretted that Northern Ireland was being set apart yet again from the rest of the United Kingdom: 'tinkering with the law in Ulster is inconsistent with its policy of keeping Ulster part of the United Kingdom.'[82] The Home Office's moves – both the broadcasting ban and the withdrawal of the right to silence – had in fact brought the province's legal structures into harmony with those of the Republic. In addition, Douglas Hurd's much publicized threat to 'throttle' the IRA's cash supply was based on a detailed study of the Irish Confiscation of Terrorist Funds Act of 1985. Politicians in the Republic could not therefore publicly oppose the British government's new programme of legislation for Northern Ireland.

An estimated 20,000 protesters turned up at Hillsborough Castle gates on Saturday 20 October 1988 to support an anti-agreement rally, twinned with the three-hundredth anniversary of the departure of William of Orange from Holland for England in 1688. One hundred and thirteen districts of the Orange Order were represented and there were a hundred bands. The speeches, however, were low-key; Paisley was absent in the United States, and Molyneaux was at a Friends of the

---

[78] *Times*, 21 October 1988.
[79] *Independent*, 11 October 1988.
[80] *Times*, 21 October 1988.
[81] Ibid.
[82] *Independent*, 25 August 1988.

Union meeting in London. It was the OUP leader's speech at that meeting that was to dominate the political agenda for what remained of the first three years of the Hillsborough accord. Having heard Ian Gow offer an alternative agreement, based on an intergovernmental structure, meetings at ministerial level, a secretariat sited in London or Dublin and a commitment by both parties to guarantee that Northern Ireland would remain British until a majority in the province decided otherwise by means of a border poll, Molyneaux said 'he could live with Eire'.[83] Once the Anglo-Irish Agreement was out of the way and 'the Ulster people are freed from these shackles, Unionists will co-operate to the full in making real the unique relationship between the British and Irish peoples'.[84] When Ivan Foster and Sammy Wilson of the DUP rejected this, Molyneaux recalled the text of the letter he and Paisley had sent to Mrs Thatcher in August 1985: 'In it Mr Paisley and I said that if there was a devolved government at Stormont, we would follow the long established practice whereby Stormont ministers discussed such matters with Eire ministers. In that situation we would be in on the discussions rather than having the two governments going over our heads.'[85] The *News Letter* detected the start of yet another split in the Unionist ranks in the very week that the Hillsborough partners set up their review committee on the Anglo-Irish Agreement. Every political party in the whole of Ireland would be invited to contribute to the review, which it was hoped would be completed early in 1989. It emerged that the Unionists had hoped for a suspension of the Intergovernmental Conference during the review, but the communiqué at the end of the twenty-second meeting indicated that a further meeting of the conference was planned shortly. Ken Maginnis, who confirmed that he had met SDLP representatives for exploratory discussions, claimed that hopes of progress had been 'killed now by duplicitous advisers and careless ministers ... every time Unionists move to a position where progress can be made, another torpedo is launched'.[86] Sammy Wilson said it was the government's 'way of saying it intended to ride roughshod over Unionist feelings and sensitivities'.[87]

The communiqué at the end of the conference in Belfast indicated that the Irish partners were still preoccupied with the administration of justice. A twelve-page document on the legal system in the North was given to Tom King, together with a further submission dealing with harrassment. This last document dealt with a 'search and seal off'

---

[83] *News Letter*, 31 October 1988.
[84] Ibid.
[85] *News Letter*, 1 November 1988.
[86] *News Letter*, 4 November 1988.
[87] *News Letter*, 3 November 1988.

operation by the security forces in the North. Sinn Fein alleged that 'wanton destruction ... [an] orgy of wrecking and the imposition of martial law'[88] followed closely on the broadcasting ban. It was designed, according to Martin McGuinness, to intimidate Catholic neighbourhoods at a time when the media were nervous of quoting Sinn Fein councillors. The RUC announced that sixty-six people had been arrested and charged with terrorist offences; fourteen were charged with murder. A hoard of explosives, ammunition, guns, rocket grenades and mortar-launchers was also captured. A Roman Catholic neighbour-hood group claimed that a thousand Nationalist homes had been 'extensively searched and wrecked'.[89]

In East Belfast, the collapse of government talks with Harland and Wolff led to further fears about the future of the shipyard. Tom King confirmed that the Northern Ireland Office would now pursue privatization plans.

The Conservative Party accepted the application by the North Down Conservative Association for affiliation to the National Union. Peter Brooke wrote that 'it would be the height of folly and irresponsibility for the Conservative party to weaken the forces in favour of maintaining the union'.[90] Within seven months the Conservatives were to win five seats in the local elections in the province, and within a year a parliamentary seat. The Institute for Representative Government in Northern Ireland started a campaign to persuade the Labour Party to stand in elections in the province.

The government's announcement on the withdrawal of the right to silence came a day after the three Irish defendants in the alleged plot to kill Tom King elected not to give evidence. Martina Shanahan, John McCann and Finbarr Cullen were found guilty on a charge of conspiracy to murder. Mr Justice Swinton Thomas said the secretary of state's announcement on the 'right to silence' should have been delayed until the court case was over. Sentencing the three to twenty-five years in gaol, the judge said, 'terrorists who plan murder are not very often caught, and when they are it is incumbent on the courts to reflect the public horror of terrorist crimes of this nature'.[91] The *Irish Times* saw the sentence differently, calling it 'blind justice ... conspiracy is a charge which allows the greatest latitude to the prosecution ... the leap from supposition to certainty beyond reasonable doubt ... was taken by a majority of the jury only after a long deadlock'.[92]

---

[88] *Times*, 15 November 1988.
[89] *News Statesman/Society*, 9 December 1988.
[90] *Times*, 1 November 1988.
[91] *Times*, 28 October 1988.
[92] *Irish Times*, 28 October 1988.

The secretary of state's direct and personal role in the court case and the ill-timed announcement of the withdrawal of a suspect's right to silence made relations between London and Dublin slightly more strained. Haughey, although enjoying huge popularity in the country, was still having to cope with an influential core of anti-extradition TDs in his own parliamentary party. The British and Irish attorney-generals met in early November 1988 to discuss the possibility of taking the heat out of extradition by using the opportunities offered by the Criminal Law Jurisdiction Act of 1976. This Irish Act allowed people wanted in Britain to be tried in the Republic. In the past, Britain had objected to the Act since it feared the rules of evidence were different in the two jurisdictions. Lenihan and Howe discussed the issue and the reform of the Diplock courts when they met in Dublin on 7 November 1988.

The law and new legislation dominated Anglo-Irish political discussions and there was a formality to relations which gave little scope for the exploration of ideas and political options. The trial of Henry Maguire and Alexander Murphy for the murder of Corporals Woods and Howes at Andersonstown was to proceed, the identities of twenty journalists being protected by an agreement reached with Sir Barry Shaw, the Northern Ireland DPP. Brian Hunter, a member of an IRA assassination team, and Davy Payne, caught with the largest haul yet of Loyalist guns and ammunition, received long prison sentences. The UDA gave a warning that those members 'who have been working hand in hand with republican racketeers had been given a week to come clean'.[93] Members of Ulster Resistance raided the guided-missile plant at Short Brothers and escaped with a model of a missile-aiming unit from the high security store. It was recovered a fortnight later in County Armagh, together with red berets with the bronze badge of Ulster Resistance, a rocket launcher with six warheads, a handgun, rifles and some 12,000 rounds of ammunition.

The practical problems of persuading witnesses to appear in court to testify against defendants charged with serious crimes was graphically demonstrated in Judge Chris Milner's court. Dermot Quinn, charged with the attempted murder of two police officers, was discharged when twelve witnesses failed to appear. Four of the twelve turned up when warrants were issued for their arrest. Three of the four came from one family and refused to take the stand following threatening telephone calls. The fourth witness had been warned that his kneecaps would be blown off. Judge Milner recalled that this was the second such case in the last year: 'the province's legal system is breaking down.'[94]

Sir Barry Shaw, the director of public prosecutions for Northern

[93] *Independent*, 2 November 1988.
[94] *Times*, 30 September 1988.

Ireland, announced that there would be no prosecution of the soldiers involved in the shooting of nine members of the IRA at Loughall in May 1987. An inquest would be convened in the New Year. The coroner's court hearing into the shooting of McKerr, Burns and Toman in 1982 started, although public interest immunity certificates issued by Tom King restricted inquiries. The hearing was stopped on its second day following a High Court decision to allow an application for a judicial review of the hearing's proceedings.

It was the eve of the third anniversary of the signing of the Anglo-Irish Agreement. At the lord mayor's banquet in London the prime minister spoke about the struggle against terrorism: 'The Government has been accused by some in the press and media of undermining their freedom to report what they want ... Yes, some of those measures do restrict freedom. But those who choose to live by the bomb and the gun, and those who support them, can't in all circumstances be accorded exactly the same rights as everyone else. We do sometimes have to sacrifice a little of the freedom we cherish in order to defend ourselves from those whose aim is to destroy that freedom altogether, and that is a decision we should not be afraid to take.'[95]

The defeat of terrorism was still the prime minister's priority, the bedrock of her Anglo-Irish policy. During the first three years of the agreement two periods, each about six months in duration, had witnessed serious attempts at developing a political dialogue in the province. The first lasted from the signing at Hillsborough to the one-day strike in March 1984 and the second from the general election of June 1987 to January 1988. The first eighteen months of the agreement were occupied with containing the Unionist rebellion, the last twelve months with defeating the paramilitaries. Anglo-Irish discussions during the Haughey administration were confined to an even shorter timespan, lasting from the election in June 1987 to the extradition crisis in December of that year. Once Haughey had signalled his intention to add a rider to the new Extradition Act, relations with Downing Street were never the same. This was unfortunate, because the Enniskillen bombing marked a noticeable shift in British policy towards Irish affairs, and a clear commitment by the prime minister to involve herself in the issue. If the goodwill which existed between King and Lenihan for most of 1987 could have been developed after Enniskillen, a major breakthrough in Anglo-Irish affairs might have resulted, but

---

[95] *Independent*, 15 November 1988.

Haughey's need to appease his own right-wingers by an amendment to the Extradition Act lost him Thatcher's support and she became positively antagonistic towards him. The taoiseach found himself discarded, like Molyneaux and Paisley. This was why Haughey and the OUP leader flirted with each other for most of 1988. Paisley was isolated from all points of contact.

The Irish played a secondary role in the first three years of the agreement. Dublin would argue that this was from choice, London that it was the result of Mrs Thatcher's tactics. FitzGerald's greatest contribution occurred before the agreement came into existence; Haughey's best period was the run-up to Enniskillen. After that the Irish lost the upper hand and the political agenda was set by London. Haughey may have held the high moral ground during the early months of 1988, but he lost the initiative after the McAnespie inquiry and the difficulties over the extradition of McVeigh. Ireland failed to develop the Anglo-Irish Agreement into a political forum; it remained a security initiative, as the British had intended. The taoiseach co-operated in the security push after the Enniskillen bombing and even more after the debriefing of the *Eksund* crew but party considerations and Irish interests – extradition, the Stalker inquiry, the Gibraltar shootings, the Birmingham Six appeal and the Diplock courts – led to a cooling of the relationship between Dublin and London.

Within Northern Ireland, the Unionists were still opposed to the agreement, but opposition was passive, most of the Unionist community adopting a 'let's wait and see' attitude. That was the initial reaction of SDLP supporters. The Nationalist community was still broadly in support of the agreement, although concerned at the time that had lapsed since its signing, the apparent deadlock over its operation and the tardiness of any visible benefits to the minority community. The Republican movement did feel threatened. The British and Irish security authorities were on the offensive and winning. The legal loopholes that permitted the political wing of the Republican movement a role in the everyday life of the province were slowly being closed. It was uncertain how successful the policy of weaning the Nationalist community away from the Republican paramilitaries had been.

By the end of the first three years of the agreement, 253 further deaths from terrorist activities had to be added to the sad list of victims of the troubles in the province. The Unionist representation at Westminster paid for a press advertisement which claimed that, during those three years, murders had doubled, community conflict had increased and local democracy had died with the closure of the Northern Ireland assembly. Tom King sent an invitation to Molyneaux and Paisley to enter into a new round of talks. A wreath was laid at the foot of Carson's statue outside Stormont and the Ulster Clubs handed in a letter of protest at Maryfield.

In the Republic, there was a major arms find in County Meath. The Irish Ministry of Defence disclosed that border security cost the Republic £180 million a year, 30 per cent of the total Irish expenditure on security. In 1969, it was equivalent to £1 per head per year; in 1988 it was £1 per head per week. In London, the Queen's Speech promised that efforts to eradicate terrorism would continue.

Index

Abernethy, Colin, 232
Adams, Gerry: returned for West Belfast, 14; and relationship of Sinn Fein and IRA, 17; and Anglo-Irish talks, 32; and Anglo-Irish Agreement, 37; and mini-election, 45; and leadership of Republican movement, 103–4, 114, 131; and general election, 140, 141; and Sinn Fein conference, 161; and Enniskillen bombings, 162, 164; and John Hume, 173–5, 203, 213–14, 223, 228–9; and Stalker – Sampson report, 182; and Milltown shootings, 197–8; and Northern Ireland economy, 234; and broadcasting ban, 246; mentioned, 86, 92, 98, 133, 196, 222, 231, 243
Adams, James, 179
Adams, Paddy, 131
Aiken, Thomas, 177
Aitken, Ian, 20, 116, 159
Alderdice, John, 151
Alexander, Andrew, 69–70
Alliance Party, 51, 87–8, 110, 116, 140, 143, 150, 151, 238
Allister, Jim, 85, 137–8, 151
Anderson, Ivan, 142
Anderson, Thomas George, 185
Andersonstown killings, the, 198–203, 205, 209, 218
Anderton, James, 77, 78, 154
Andrews, Sir Robert, 147, 150
Anglo-Irish Agreement, the: terms of, 34–5; initial reaction to, 36–44; passim
Archer, Peter, 138, 139, 147
Armstrong, Fred, 130, 133
Armstrong, Patrick, 155
Armstrong, Sir Robert, 23, 27, 30
Armstrong, Timothy, 177
Asquez, Kenneth, 215, 240–1
Asquith, H. H., 4, 5

Atkins, Humphrey, 13
Attlee, Clement, 7

Baker, Kenneth, 234
Barry, Peter: and Anglo-Irish talks, 16, 23, 25, 29; and Unionists, 40, 59; and mini-election, 45; and Intergovernmental Conference, 47–8; and terrorism, 50; and RUC, 81, 115; and King, 82, 121–2; and Anglo-Irish Agreement, 89, 148; and Haughey, 175; and Prevention of Terrorism Act, 187; and Gibraltar shootings, 194; mentioned, 79, 99, 129, 211
Baxter, John, 218
Beggs, Roy, 143, 164, 232
Bell, Betty, 75–6
Bell, Stuart, 138–9, 181
Benn, Tony, 169, 205
Bergin, Jean, 223
Bergin, William, 223
Biffen, John, 20
Biggs Davison, Sir John, 20, 89, 236
Bingham, John, 98
Birmingham Six, 155, 160, 165–6, 183–4, 187, 204, 207, 252
Bloomfield, Sir Kenneth, 147, 150, 232, 238–9
Boyd, Robert Francis, 38
Boyle, Kevin, 18, 230
Bradford, Hazel, 26, 50, 56
Bradford, Roy, 32–3, 109, 150, 212
Brady, Kevin, 198
Bray, Michael, 114
Breen, Derek, 58
Brennan, Paul, 169
Brittan, Leon, 54
Brooke, Peter, 243–4, 249
Brookeborough, Lord, 8, 73, 115

Brown, Lord Justice, 165
Buller, Roy, 223
Bullock, Stephen, 215
Burke, Ray, (Irish cabinet minister), 185, 190
Burleigh, William, 206
Burns, Sean, 77, 251; *see also* Stalker, Sampson
Burns, Brendan, 52, 191
Burnside, David, 128
Byford, Sir Lawrence, 77

Cairns, Henry, 160
Caithness, Lord, 166
Caldwell, David, 114
Callaghan, Hugh, 165; *see also* Birmingham Six
Callaghan, James, 13
Calvet, David, 118
Campbell, Eddie, 148
Campbell, Gregory, 243
Carlile, Alex, 187
Carron, Owen, (MP), 92
Carroll, 77; *see also* Stalker, Sampson
Carroll, Tommy, 17, 138
Carson, Sir Edward, 5, 47, 107, 116
Carson, John, 84
Carson, Stanley, 154
Carswell, Mr Justice, 48
Carter, Sir Charles, 84, 95–6, 113
Cassidy, Seamus, 49
Catherwood, Sir Frederick, 26
Caulfield, Charles, 164
Celicia, Peti, 194, 195
Chalmers, John, 132
Checkland, Michael, 202, 217
Clancey, Alan, 219
Clarke, Clecky, 200
Clarke, James, 243
Clarke, Tom, 165–6; *see also* Birmingham Six
Cole, John, 20, 24, 133, 200–1, 211
Collins, Gerry, 144, 175, 182, 185, 186
Colville, Lord, 122
Conlan, Gerard, 155
Connolly, Cyril, 24
Conway, John, 202
Cooke, Tom, 132, 133
Cormack, Patrick, 202
Corrigan, Paul, 162, 246
Cooper, Sir Frank, 14
Craig, Jim, 243
Crawford, Ivan, 118
Crotty, Raymond, 129
Culan, Fergus, 131
Cullen, Finbarr, 249
Currie, Austin, 140, 168
Cush, Nathaniel, 145
Cushnahan, John, 42, 60, 151

Dalton, Sean, 228
Daly, Cahal, 51, 98, 130, 200
Daly, Edward, 132, 160
Davidson, Brendan, 223
Davies, Stan Gebler, 90, 101, 246
Davey, Michael, 220
Deery, Patrick, 160
Delaney, Terry, 222
Democratic Unionist Party (DUP): and 1983 election, 14; and New Ireland Forum, 15; and Anglo-Irish talks, 19–29; and Anglo-Irish Agreement, 33, 42, 213; and mini-election, 51–3; and strike, 61–2; and Unionist co-ordinating committee, 72; and RUC, 75; and Loyalist parades, 80; and adjournment policy, 84–6, 104–5, 110–11, 117; and Unionist pact, 87, 90, 124–5; and Northern Ireland Assembly, 89; internal divisions in, 127–8, 137–8, 156; and general election, 143–4
de Valera, Éamon, 90, 157
Dickinson, Robert, 38–9
Diplock courts, 52, 100, 101, 111–13, 144, 158–60, 165, 237, 250, 252
Doherty, Commissioner, 170, 182, 187
Doherty, Gerry, 17
Doherty, Joseph, 220
Doherty, Paddy, 96
Dolan, Peter, 224
Dolan, Sean, 23
Dorr, Noel, 23
Duffy, Francis, 119
Dukes, Alan, 128, 181, 213

Ead, David, 133
Eames, Robert: and Mrs Thatcher, 60, 62; and Unionist leaders, 64, 150; and Anglo-Irish Agreement, 85–6, 142; and RUC, 115, 186; and paramilitaries, 116; and terrorism, 206, 224, 245; and Molyneaux, 211
Early, John, 58
Eksund, 160–1, 165, 169, 170, 175, 176, 205, 252
Emery, Sir Peter, 48–9
Enniskillen bombing, the, 161–5, 168, 204–5, 251, 252
Extradition Act (Irish), 111, 112–13, 144, 158, 165–7, 169, 187, 203, 209, 219, 220, 251

Faulkner, Brian, 10–11
Farrell, Mairead, 193–8, 215, 239–40
Farren, Sean, 168
Feeney, Brian, 219
Fenn, Nicholas, 165, 221
Ferguson, Raymond, 174
Ferguson, Thomas, 162

Ferris, Samuel, 132
Finlay (reserve constable), 154
Finnucane, Dermot, 169
Fitt, Gerry, 13, 14, 43, 73, 140
FitzGerald, Garret: and Anglo-Irish
  discussions, 12–13, 14–17, 20, 25; and
  Mrs Thatcher, 27–8; and Anglo-Irish
  Agreement, 30–2, 34–7, 39–40, 43–4;
  and King, 46–7; and cabinet reshuffle, 54;
  and SDLP, 57; and Reagan, 68; and
  divorce referendum, 90; political difficulties
  of, 100–2; and extradition, 111–13, 155;
  resignation of, 121, 128; and Diplock
  courts, 159–60
Flanagan, Samuel George, 185
Fleming, William, 200
Flynn, Harry, 91
Foreman, Sir Philip, 96
Forsythe, Clifford, 190
Foster, Ivan, 20, 66, 71, 127, 248
Foster, Victor, 52
French, Andrew, 78

Gaddafi, Colonel, 58, 91, 133, 180
Gibraltar shootings, the, 192–7, 203, 205,
  209, 214–18, 220, 222, 231, 239–41, 252
Gibson, Edward, 210
Gibson, Lord Justice, 133–4, 191
Gibson, Mrs, 133–4
Gibson, Norman, 53
Gifford, Lord, 48
Gilmore, Colin James, 180
Gilroy, Eamon, 222
Glencross, David, 214
Glendenning, Pip, 151
Glendenning, Will, 151
Glenholmes, Evelyn, 68–9
Goghlan, Denis, 213
Goodall, David, 23
Goodison, Sir Alan, 23
Gorbachev, Mikhail, 162
Gorst, John, 202
Goulding, Cathal, 10
Gow, Ian, 20, 37, 88, 89, 113, 124, 248
Gracey, Harold, 79–81, 82
Graham, Clive, 203
Graham, William, 133
Green, John Francis, 149
Green, William, 221
Grew, 77; *see also* Stalker, Sampson
Griffiths, Eldon, 74, 198
Guildford Four, 155
Guthrie, Robert, 145
Guy, Jim, 87

Hadden, Tom, 18, 230
Hailsham, Lord, 100, 144, 158
Hamilton, Archie, 226

Hamilton, Nigel, 151
Hamilton, William, 200
Hammell, Patrick, 148
Hammill, Elizabeth, 222
Hanna (family), 223
Hanratty, Gerard, 228
Hanson, David, 37
Harkin, Brendan, 62
Harland and Wolff, 3, 6, 47, 49, 62, 63, 108,
  113, 140–1, 153, 209–10, 233, 235, 249
Harney, Mary, 49
Harris, Martin, 53
Hart, Alan, 119
Harte, Gerard, 227
Hassard, William, 223–4
Hattersley, Roy, 39, 245, 246
Haughey, Charles: and Mrs Thatcher, 12;
  and Anglo-Irish Agreement, 28, 31, 40, 47,
  68, 102–3, 191–2; and Sellafield, 54, 152;
  and extradition, 112, 121, 144, 157–8,
  165, 166–7, 187, 227, 241–2, 250, 251–2;
  and Single European Act, 112; wins
  election, 123, 124; and Reagan, 128–9;
  and Hume, 168, 174, 214; and
  Stalker–Sampson report, 182, 183, 185–7;
  and Birmingham Six, 184; and Prevention
  of Terrorism Act, 187; and Unionists,
  188–9, 207–13, 231, 235; and McAnespie
  incident, 191–2
Havers, Sir Michael, 68
Haviland, Julian, 20
Hayes, Derek, 220
Hayes, Jeremy, 61
Hazlett, James, 75
Heakin, Richard, 224
Heath, Edward, 43, 225
Heffer, Eric, 194
Hendron, Joe, 33
Hermon, Sir John: difficulties of, 18–19; and
  Anglo-Irish Agreement, 30–1, 114; and
  Garda, 45, 142, 163, 182, 187; and strike,
  63–4; and role of RUC, 65–7; and attacks
  on RUC, 71–6, 101; and Stalker inquiry,
  77–81, 188; and funerals policy, 130, 148;
  and security, 134, 176–7, 225, 231; and
  Irish government, 191, 203; announces
  retirement, 222
Heseltine, Michael, 54
Hetherington, Sir Thomas, 154
Hewitt, Thomas, 148
Higgins, Ian, 223
Hill, Paul, 155
Hogarty, Frank, 93
Holden, David Jonathan, 190, 239
Holland, Mary, 19–20, 31–2, 66–7, 100,
  174, 189, 199, 211, 229, 231
Holmes, William, 216
Holroyd, Fred, 149

Hopkins, Adrian, 160, 165, 175
Howard, John, 222
Howe, Sir Geoffrey, 16, 23, 29, 30, 129, 193–4, 208, 214–18, 229, 250
Howes, David, 199, 202, 218, 250
Hughes, Anthony, 136
Hughes, Sean, 91
Hume, John: becomes leader of SDLP, 13; and New Ireland Forum, 14; and Irish government, 23, 25, 168, 231; and Anglo-Irish talks, 32; and Anglo-Irish Agreement, 33, 37, 57; and Sinn Fein, 45, 173–5, 192, 203, 213–14, 223; and hunger strikes, 52; and RUC, 73, 81–2; and Unionists, 86, 101–2, 142, 150, 207; and Northern Ireland Assembly, 88; and Enniskillen bombing, 162; and Stalker–Sampson report, 182; and King, 205, 210; and self-determination, 219; and Northern Ireland economy, 233–4; and Labour Party, 237
Humphreys, Sir Myles, 50, 114
Hunter, Brian, 250
Hunter, Colin, 243
Hunter, Gerry, 165; *see also* Birmingham Six
Hurd, Douglas: and Anglo-Irish talks, 16, 30; becomes home secretary, 23; and Unionists, 49; and extradition, 69; and Birmingham Six, 121; and Labour's Northern Ireland policy, 141, 168; and right to silence, 154; and Criminal Justice Bill, 159; and Prevention of Terrorism Act, 186–7; and paramilitaries, 210, 221, 247; and broadcasting ban, 245
Hutton, Mr Justice, 56, 83, 105, 125

Imbert, Peter, 154
Independent Orange Order, 27, 75
Ingham, Bernard, 133, 217
Inglis, Brian, 53
Irish National Liberation Army (INLA): assassinates Airey Neave, 13; and Kirkpatrick supergrass trial, 31; and Stalker inquiry, 77; and campaign of summer 1986, 92–8; and RUC, 105–6; and Gerry Adams, 114; and killings, 116, 118–19, 225, 243; origins of, 130–1; and feuds, 169–70, 177–8; and threats to DHSS staff, 210; and broadcasting ban, 244
Irish Republican Army (IRA): and Mrs Thatcher, 13, 15; and elective politics, 14, 26; and Anglo-Irish Agreement, 17, 49, 90; and RUC, 46, 58, 75, 105, 176–7; and terrorist incidents, 49–50, 98, 114, 116, 118, 130–6; and security initiatives, 91–4, 169; and Short Brothers, 96; and racketeering, 119; and general election, 142; and UVF, 148–9, 154; and

Enniskillen bombing, 163–4; and Haughey, 166; and extradition, 175; and Gibraltar shootings, 192–3, 196, 241; and Andersonstown killings, 198–200; and SDLP, 214; and attacks on military personnel, 218–19; and offensive of summer 1988, 220–9; and broadcasting ban, 244, 246

Jalloud, Ahmed, 91
Jarvis, Leslie, 132
Jenkins, Peter, 209, 216
Johnson, Paul, 246
Johnston, Gillian, 198
Jones, John, 154
Jones, Michael, 30

Kane, Alan, 75
Kane, Paul Anthony, 169, 219
Kane, William, 177
Kearney, Michael, 119, 131
Keelan, Jim, 148
Kelly, Andrew, 218
Kelly, Anthony, 52
Kelly, Charles, 188, 222
Kelly, Gerard, 52, 91, 103, 114, 139
Kemp, David, 214
Kennedy, Geraldine, 181
Kennedy, Joe, 235
Kennedy, John, 151
Kennedy, Norman, 148
Kielty, Jack, 180
Kilfedder, James, 42, 60, 79–80, 85, 88, 138
Kilroy Silk, Robert, 195
King, Tom: becomes secretary of state, 23–4; and Anglo-Irish talks, 28, 33; and Anglo-Irish Agreement, 38, 41, 43; and RUC, 46, 70–1, 73, 79; and Intergovernmental Conference, 47–8; and extradition, 51; and SDLP, 53, 54–5; and Unionist leaders, 58–60, 62, 151, 173, 207, 210–13, 242; and Northern Ireland Assembly, 88; and Irish government, 100, 152, 191, 203; and Diplock courts, 113; and Northern Ireland referendum, 118; and Maryfield secretariat, 121–2, 125–6; and Northern Ireland (Emergency Provisions) Bill, 129–30; and security, 134, 135, 141, 167, 225–8, 244; and Northern Ireland economy, 153, 234, 249; and right to silence, 154–5; and extradition, 159, 250; and Enniskillen bombings, 161–2; and Stalker–Sampson report, 182, 185, 187–8; and Andersonstown killings, 198–9, 200; and internment, 221, and devolution, 235–6
Kinnock, Neil, 39, 42, 43, 49, 74, 139, 141, 165, 168

Kirkpatrick, Harry, 48, 52, 98, 118, 131; *see also* supergrass trials
Kirkpatrick, Jim, 110
Kyle, John, 93–4

Lambert, Alan, 162
Lane, Lord Justice, 154, 165–6, 183–4, 247
Laverty, Michael, 225
Leach, Joseph, 142
Lemass, Sean, 8
Lenihan, Brian, 28, 129, 148, 152, 155, 159, 184, 191, 203, 232, 250, 251
Leslie, Frank, 56
Levy, Geoffrey, 215–16
Lewis, Sheila, 228
Lillis, Michael, 23
Livingstone, Ken, 139, 149, 168–9, 181, 184, 205
Logue, Gerard, 132
Love, Fred, 223–4
Lowry, Lord Justice, 51, 52, 56, 100
Lynagh, James, 136
Lynch, Seamus, 174
Lyttle, Tommy

McAliskey, Bernadette, 139
McAnespie, Aidan, 189–90, 191, 203, 239, 252
McAtamey, Michael, 152
McAvoy, John, 200
McAvoy, Seamus, 93
McBride, David Leslie, 78
MacBride, Sean, 152–3, 234
MacBride, Tiernan, 184
McBrinn, Liam, 153
McCandlass, James, 50
McCanley, Martin, 77; *see also* Stalker, Sampson
McCann, Brian, 17
McCann, Daniel, 193–8, 215, 239–40
McCann, John, 249
McCarten, Thomas, 118
McCartney, Robert, 85, 124, 128, 137–8, 143, 149, 229, 235
McCelland, Keith, 132
McCluskey, Tony, 119, 131
McCotter, Liam, 221
McCracken, Kevin, 196, 198
McCrea, William, 228
McCrone (RUC), 243
McCullough, James, 177
McCusker, Harold, 39, 43, 50, 56, 64, 117–18, 124, 127, 136, 147, 190, 194
McElwaine, Seamus, 93, 103
McErlean, Thomas, 198
McFarlane, Brendan, 52, 91, 92, 114
McGeever, Jenny, 196
McGeough, Terence, 228

McGill, Paul, 70
McGimpsey, Christopher, 129
McGlinchey, Dominic, 52, 130–1, 166
McGlinchey, Mary, 119
McGrady, Eddie, 33, 143, 205, 206
McGrary, Patrick, 240
McGrillen, Charles, 196, 198
McGuinness, Frank, 32
McGuinness, Martin, 49, 131, 132, 169, 196, 206, 224, 228, 243, 249
McIlwaine, Joe, 145
McKeaveney, Bernard, 119
McKenna, Finbarr, 134
McKenny, Richard, 165; *see also* Birmingham Six
McKeowan, Norman, 243
McKerr, Gervaise, 77, 251; *see also* Stalker, Sampson
McKiernan, Anthony, 177
McKinney, Stephen, 239
McKittrick, David, 36–7, 82, 206
McLaughlin, Patrick, 221
McLean (constable) 142
McLean, David, 220
McLean, Robert, 130, 133
McMichael, John: and UDF, 21–2; and Anglo-Irish Agreement, 50; and Unionist leaders, 56, 76, 127, 156; and strike, 64; and RUC, 66; detained, 71; and Unionist co-ordinating committee, 72; political ambitions of, 93, 108, 120; assassinated, 170
McNamara, Kevin, 139, 147, 168–9, 181, 188, 236, 238, 247
McNamee, Gilbert, 160, 161
McNamee, Henry, 243
Macness, Columbanus, 85
McNichol, Raymond, 223
McQuintan, Alan, 148
McSheffrey, Edward, 160
Mac Stiofáin, Seán, 10, 196
McVeigh, Patrick, 219, 220, 243, 252
Magee, Patrick, 92, 103
Maginnis, Ken, 22, 27, 64, 105, 109, 111, 181, 198, 225, 248
Magrath, William Richard, 148
Maguire, Thomas, 131
Maguire, Henry, 250
Mallaby, Chris, 23
Mallon, Seamus: and SDLP conference, 32; and Anglo-Irish Agreement, 33, 102; elected MP, 53, 54, 103; and Unionist leaders, 52, 168, 213, 236–7; and RUC, 71, 101, 115; and security, 135; and Stalker–Sampson report, 198; and Sinn Fein, 206; and privatization, 233; and broadcasting ban, 245
Malone, Michael, 154

Mann, Mr Justice, 38
Marchant, William, 134
Marlow, Tony, 220
Marshall, Tom, 227, 233
Mates, Michael, 20, 245
Mathews, Michael, 223
Mawhinney, Brian, 20, 54, 152, 244
Mayhew, Sir Patrick, 180–8, 203, 204, 209,
   219, 220, 227, 229, 250
Meese, Edwin, 91, 220
Megrath, Stevan, 154
Miles, Oliver, 175
Millar, Frank, 20, 49, 61–2, 87, 109, 124,
   136, 147, 149, 151
Milligan, Bruce, 104
Milltown shootings, the, 197–8, 203, 205,
   209
Milner, Judge Chris, 250
Mitchell, Bob, 53
Moloney, Ed, 163
Mooney, Raymond, 98
Molyneaux, James: and Anglo-Irish talks,
   20–9; and Anglo-Irish Agreement, 37–8,
   43, 104–8, 135; and protests, 50–1; and
   Downing Street meeting, 58–61; and
   strike, 62–4; and RUC, 65–7, 81–2; and
   Downing Street letter, 69–70; and middle-
   class Unionism, 75–6; and Unionist
   leadership, 84–7, 89–90; and Clontibret
   invasion, 95; government's attitude to,
   99–100; and adjournment protest,
   109–10, 116–18; and dissensions, 124–8,
   167–8; and general election, 142–5; and
   talks about talks, 147; and devolution,
   172–5, 242; and 'living with Eire', 247–8
Moore, Charles, 241
Morley, Brendan, 191
Morley, Laurence, 130
Morris, Colin, 217, 246
Morris, Seamus, 224
Morrison, Danny, 103, 157
Mountbatten, Earl, 13
Moynihan, Daniel, 92
Moyola, Lord, 43, 73
Murphy, Alexander, 250
Murphy, Lennie, 133
Murray, John, 198
Murray, Raymond, 197
Myers, Sir Philip, 77, 78

Nairac, Robert, 149
Nally, Dermot, 23, 27
Naughtie, James, 98
Neave, Airey, 13, 130, 149
Needham, Richard, 110, 234
Nelson, Sarah, 26
Nesbitt, Peter, 131
New Ireland Forum, 14–15, 172

Nicholas, David, 245
Nicholson, Elizabeth, 148
Nicholson, Jim, 52, 53, 148
Nicholson, Mr Justice, 119
Northern Ireland Assembly, 15, 26, 37–8,
   55, 60, 79–80, 87–9
Northern Ireland Constitutional Act (1973),
   13
Northern Ireland (Emergency Provisions) Act
   (1978), 112, 126, 129–30, 202, 237

Ó Brádaigh, Ruairi, 10, 103
O'Brien, Conor Cruise, 36, 40, 50, 53, 68,
   98, 101, 174, 183, 225, 235, 245–6
O'Cleary, Conor, 20
O'Connell, Daniel, 3
O'Connell, Joe, 155
O'Conner, Ian, 133
O'Connor, Dominic Jude, 148
O'Connor, Fionnuala, 63, 212
O'Connor, Lord Justice, 165
O'Dourd, Brendan, 155
Official Unionist Party (OUP): and 1983
   election, 14; and New Ireland Forum, 15;
   and Orange Order, 19; and Anglo-Irish
   Agreement, 37, 42, 61–2; and Unionist
   pact, 49, 87, 90, 99, 106, 124–5, 127, 248;
   and mini-election, 51–4; and strike, 56;
   and Northern Ireland Assembly, 80, 84–5,
   89; and adjournment policy, 104, 110–11;
   and civil disobedience, 117–18; and
   internal dissension, 137–8, 151; and
   general election, 143–4
Ó Fiaich, Cardinal, 68, 85, 114–15, 155,
   174, 190, 200, 206
O'Grady, John, 161
O'Hare, Dessie, 148, 161, 165, 170, 206
Oldman, Jim, 133
O'Leary, Cornelius, 101–2
O'Malley, Desmond, 49, 123
O'Muilleoir, Martin, 221
O'Neill, Terence, 8–9
O'Neil, Tip, 16
Orange Order, 19, 21, 55–6, 61, 74–6,
   80–2, 86, 125, 128, 147–8, 247
O'Reilly, John, 118
O'Toole, Finton, 208
Otley, Fred, 225
Owen, David, 43, 139–40, 195

Paisley, Ian: background of, 8–9; and launch
   of DUP, 10; and Anglo-Irish talks, 20–9;
   and Anglo-Irish Agreement, 33–4, 37–8,
   41, 43, 135; and RUC, 46, 51, 65–7; and
   mini-election, 53–4; and Downing Street
   meeting, 58–61; and strike, 61–2, 64; and
   Downing Street letter, 69; and parades,
   70–1, 80–1; and Northern Ireland

Assembly, 79; and Molyneaux, 99; and adjournment protest, 104; and Unionist leadership, 105–8; and referendum petition, 116–18; and Unionist dissensions, 124–8; and general election, 136–7, 141–4; and talks about talks, 147; and middle-class Unionism, 173; and King, 210–11; and Irish government, 212, 235, 248; and internment, 225

Parker, John, 209

Parnell, C. S., 4

Patten, Chris, 16

Pauley, Mervyn, 29–30

Payne, David, 177, 250

People's Liberation Army, 114

Philips, Sir Cyril, 122

Pimlott, Ben, 164

Pizzarillo, Felix, 220, 222

Powell, Enoch: and Anglo-Irish talks, 20; and Mrs Thatcher, 33, 226, 243; and mini-election, 45, 52, 53; and Westminster, 85, 109, 111; and Northern Ireland Assembly, 88; and Anglo-Irish Agreement, 89, 235; and Paisley, 107; and general election, 140, 143–4

Power, Bill, 165; *see also* Birmingham Six

Power, Michael, 154

Power, Patrick, 165; *see also* Birmingham Six

Powers, Thomas, 118, 131

Prevention of Terrorism Act, 122, 139, 186–7, 202, 237

Prior, James, 13, 15, 64, 87

Proetta, Carmen, 215

Protestant Action Force, 219

Public Order Act, 112, 123, 126–7, 128, 133

Pyle, Fergus, 172, 246

Quinn, Dermot, 250

Quinn, William, 91, 103

Rainey, Cyril, 133

Rainey, Tom, 63, 114

Rainey, Victor, 243

Rampton, Richard, 215

Reagan, Ronald, 16, 28, 68, 69, 91, 128–9, 162

Rees, Merlyn, 24, 47, 61

Reid, Alex, 131, 199

Reid, John, 218

Reynolds, Jerry, 131

Richardson, Carole, 155

Robbins, Michael, 223

Robertson, Andrew, 133

Robertson, George, 194

Robinson, Peter: and Unionist politics, 20–1; and Anglo-Irish Agreement, 26, 38, 39; and Belfast rally, 50–1; and Downing Street meeting, 55; and strike, 61, 63; and

Portadown parade, 70–1, 81; and UDI, 86, 106; and King, 89; and Clontibret invasion, 94–5, 117; and Paisley, 105, 127–8; and Ulster Resistance, 107; and UDA, 108; and council policy, 109; and task force, 124, 136, 147; and resignation, 151, 156; and Enniskillen bombings, 162; and reinstatement, 172–3; and Gibraltar shootings, 198; and SDLP–Sinn Fein talks, 205; and Unionist pact, 207; and SDLP, 212, 236; and Labour Party, 237

Robinson, Mary, 37

Rogers, Sean, 168

Ross, William, 20, 190, 202

Ruane, Jarlath, 220

Runcie, Robert, 174

Russell, Robert, 175, 227

Ryan, Patrick, 91, 92, 180, 195, 223, 229

Sampson, Colin, 77, 82, 134, 180–8, 191, 194, 203, 204, 222

Sands, Bobby, 92

Sapsted, David, 197

Savage, Sean, 193–8, 215, 239–41

Sayer, Eddie, 156

Scarman, Lord, 217

Scott, Nicholas, 16, 22–3, 43, 46, 47, 53–4, 113, 119, 129, 135–6, 144

Seawright, George, 93, 169–70

Sedgemore, Brian, 246

Seymour, Bobby, 220

Shanahan, Martina, 249

Shannon, James, 52

Shaw, Sir Barry, 77, 180–1, 239, 250, 251

Shaw, George, 118

Shaw, George, 133

Shields, Alan, 226

Skinner, Ian, 218

Short Brothers, 47, 48, 52, 63, 96–7, 114, 153, 233, 235, 250

Short, Clare, 139

Sinn Fein: and 1983 election, 14; and SDLP, 17–18, 38, 45, 173–5, 205, 206, 214, 222–3, 228–9; and IRA, 17–18, 26; and Anglo-Irish talks, 30; conference, 32, 161; and Anglo-Irish Agreement, 37, 42; and mini-election, 51–3; and adjournment campaign, 83–4; and Northern Ireland Assembly, 87; electoral policy of, 92; and Irish government, 102–4; and councils, 109, 110, 243; and Irish election, 123; and general election, 140–1, 143; changes in, 151; and Enniskillen bombings, 162–4; and Northern Ireland economy, 234; and broadcasting ban, 239, 244–5, 249

Sloane, Harry, 148–9

Slone, Martin Gerard, 239

Smith, Geoffrey, 183

Smith, Peter, 20
Smyth, Clifford, 173
Smyth, Ethel, 19, 75
Smyth, Martin, 19, 76, 81, 82, 85, 86, 109,
   111, 150, 190
Smyth, William Lawrence, 78
Social Democratic and Labour Party (SDLP):
   split in, 13; and 1983 election, 14; and
   local elections, 17; and Anglo-Irish talks,
   23, 25, 29, 30; conference, 32; and Anglo-
   Irish Agreement, 37, 42, 43, 252; and Sinn
   Fein, 38, 45, 173–5, 205, 206, 214,
   222–3, 228–9; and mini-election, 51–3;
   and devolution, 54–5; and RUC, 57; and
   adjournment campaign, 84; and Northern
   Ireland Assembly, 87; and Irish
   government, 101, 211, 231; and terrorism,
   107; and councils, 109, 110, 243; and
   referendum, 116; and general election,
   140–1, 143; changes in, 151; and
   Unionists, 168, 213, 248; and King, 192,
   205, 210; and devolution, 207, 238; and
   Northern Ireland economy, 234
Spicer, John, 228
Spring, Dick, 29, 121, 123, 181, 213,
   237–8
Stalker, John, 65, 77–9, 82, 101, 115, 134,
   148, 180–8, 191, 194, 203, 204, 222
Stanley, John, 144, 175, 179, 190, 223
Steel, David, 43, 139–40
Steenson, Gerard, 131
Stewart, A. T. Q., 53, 98
Stewart, Ian, 193, 223
Stewart, William, 177
Stone, Michael Anthony, 197–8
Strange, Ken, 222
Strange, Sir Norman, 52
supergrass trials, 48, 52, 98, 115, 118, 131
Sutcliffe, Frank, 224
Swinton Thomas, Mr Justice, 249
Sykes, Sir Richard, 219

Taylor, John, 56, 64, 72, 85, 106, 124, 189
Taylor, Kevin, 77, 78
Taylor, Peter, 25
Tebbitt, Norman, 209
Thain, Ian Richard, 190, 239
Thatcher, Margaret: initial negotiations,
   12–13; and Unionist leaders, 23–6, 30,
   57–61, 69–70, 126; and FitzGerald,
   27–8; and Anglo-Irish Agreement, 34–9,
   42, 49, 90; and Downing Street meeting,
   57–61; and strike, 63; and Downing Street
   letter, 69–70; and Sinn Fein, 92; and legal
   system, 100–1, 158, 159; visits Northern
   Ireland, 115; and Irish election, 124; and
   general election, 136, 140, 143, 144; and
   extradition, 155, 167, 203, 208, 220, 242;
   and Gibraltar shootings, 195, 201, 216;

and internment 221, 225; and terrorism,
   231, 238–9, 241, 251
Thistlethwaite, Eric, 217–18
Thompson, John, 85–6, 123–4
Thomson, Alex, 179
Thomson, Lord, 214, 216, 218
Tibble, Stephen, 91
Tighe, Michael, 77, 180, 185; *see also* Stalker,
   Sampson
Tikko, Ravi, 209
Toman, Eugene, 77, 251; *see also* Stalker,
   Sampson
Toner, Patrick, 17
Toner, Tom, 197
Totten, William, 220
Tracey, John, 148
Turomey, Seamus, 196
Tyrie, Andy, 21, 50, 55–6, 93, 120, 196

Ulster Clubs, 25, 27, 53, 59, 61, 72, 74, 106,
   107–8, 120, 125, 126, 252
Ulster Co-ordinating Committee, 74–5,
   83–5
Ulster Defence Association (UDA): and
   Orange Order, 19; and Belfast rally, 27;
   and Anglo-Irish Agreement, 37, 50, 61;
   and UULF, 55–6; and RUC, 63, 72, 84;
   and racketeering, 93, 119–20, 179, 250;
   and Unionist leaders, 108, 124–5; and
   armaments, 132–3, 177; and Peter
   Robinson, 156; and broadcasting ban,
   244–5
Ulster Freedom Fighters (UFF), 56, 95,
   120–1, 177, 244
Ulster Resistance, 106–7, 110, 120, 135,
   177, 250
United Ulster Loyalist Front (UULF), 21,
   25, 55
Ulster Volunteer Force (UVF), 19, 27, 56,
   98, 132–4, 148–9, 154, 169–70, 177, 185,
   220, 225, 239, 243, 244

Valley, Paul, 63
Viggers, Peter, 233

Wakerley, J. C., 227–8
Walden, Brian, 164, 230–1
Walker, Cecil, 85, 90, 106, 134
Walker, Johnny, 165
Wallace, Colin, 149
Walsh, Dick, 90
Warnock, John 223
Waters, Sir John, 221, 225
Watson, Alan, 240
Watson, Charles, 142
Webb, Roy, 98
Wells, Jim, 70, 110
West, Harley, 151

White, Keith, 71, 74
Whitelaw, William 11, 20, 141
Wilkinson, Paul, 92, 230
Williams, Michael, 50
Wilson, Des, 198
Wilson, Gordon, 163
Wilson, Harold, 24
Wilson, Marie, 163
Wilson, James, 151
Wilson, Samuel (Sammy), 20, 87, 104, 107, 207, 212, 248
Windlesham, Lord, 215

Wood, Seamus, 222–3
Woods, Derek, 199, 202, 218, 250
Workers' Party, 51, 104, 109, 110, 123, 143, 174
Wren, Commissioner, 19, 45–6, 142, 163
Wright, Alan (Northern Ireland Police Federation), 57, 74, 79, 142–3, 221
Wright, Alan (Ulster Clubs), 21–2, 25, 27, 55, 59, 80–1, 82, 93, 107–8, 134, 148, 151

Young, Hugo, 187, 216, 246
Younger, George, 218–19, 229